A Year in Provence

Peter Mayle spent fifteen years in the advertising business, first as a copywriter and then as a reluctant executive, before escaping Madison Avenue in 1975 to write books. His work has been translated into seventeen languages, and he has contributed to the *Sunday Times*, the *Financial Times*, *The Independent*, *Gentlemen's Quarterly* and *Esquire*. He lives in Provence with his wife, three dogs, several builders and numerous guests. He is approaching fifty as slowly as possible.

A
YEAR IN
PROVENCE

PETER MAYLE

ILLUSTRATED BY
LESLIE FORBES

PAN BOOKS
London, Sydney and Auckland

First published 1989 by Hamish Hamilton Ltd, London

This edition published 1993 by Pan Books Ltd,
a division of Pan Macmillan Publishers Limited
Cavaye Place, London SW10 9PG
and Basingstoke

Associated companies throughout the world

ISBN 0 330 33091 8

Copyright © Peter Mayle 1989
Illustrations © Leslie Forbes 1989

The right of Peter Mayle to be identified as the
author of this work has been asserted by him in accordance
with the Copyright, Designs and Patents Act 1988.

All rights reserved. No reproduction, copy or transmission
of this publication may be made without written permission.
No paragraph of this publication may be reproduced, copied or
transmitted save with written permission or in accordance with
the provisions of the Copyright Act 1956 (as amended). Any
person who does any unauthorised act in relation to
this publication may be liable to criminal prosecution
and civil claims for damages.

3 5 7 9 8 6 4

A CIP catalogue record for this book is available from
the British Library

Printed and bound in Great Britain by
Cox & Wyman Ltd, Reading, Berkshire

This book is sold subject to the condition that it shall not,
by way of trade or otherwise, be lent, re-sold, hired out,
or otherwise circulated without the publisher's prior consent
in any form of binding or cover other than that in which
it is published and without a similar condition including this
condition being imposed on the subsequent purchaser

To Jennie,
with love and thanks

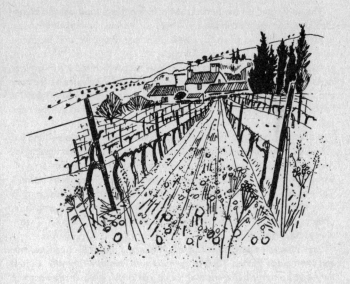

PREFACE TO THE PAPERBACK EDITION

One sad change has taken place since this book was written. Monsieur Soliva, the husband of Tante Yvonne at Lambesc, has died and the restaurant has closed. He was a delightful old man, and we shall miss him.

Otherwise, life in Provence continues much as I have described it — slow, hot and pleasant in the summer; slow, cold and pleasant in the winter. We have lived here for three years now without a day's regret.

I have mixed feelings about the effects that the book has had on our lives. It is always wonderful to receive letters from readers, and the letters have come by the dozen, from places as varied as Beijing and Her Majesty's Prison at Wormwood Scrubs. It is sometimes less wonderful to find the reader on the doorstep, book in hand and tongue hanging out for a glass or two — flattering, but often so unexpected that I have more than once been caught literally with my trousers down. Signing books, dripping from the shower and dressed in a towel, has been a novel experience.

PREFACE TO THE PAPERBACK EDITION

The only cloud on our horizon at the moment is a small one, no bigger than an estate agent's commission. There are hideous rumours of what our local friends call *un boum*. By 1992, they say, Provence will be firmly established as the California of Europe.

I hope they're wrong. It conjures up visions of diet-crazed water drinkers in double-knit pastel jogging ensembles, of cordless telephones by the pool and authentic Provençal-style jacuzzis next to the tennis court. I have a terrible feeling that the French would love it all. It's the refugees who hope that Provence will stay the way they found it.

But at least for today I can look out of the window and see nothing but vines and mountains, and hear no sound except my neighbour cursing his dead tractor. He'll stop at noon and go home for lunch, and then send his wife out to repair the tractor while he goes into the forest with his dog. The summer drought and the forest fires have driven most of the game far away, up towards the Basses Alpes, but hunters are optimists. And if no obliging rabbit or bird should present itself to the gun, *tant pis*. There's always tomorrow.

Christmas is coming, time to place the orders for oysters and *foie gras* and fresh black truffles. Time to promise ourselves that this year we will definitely go to the living *crèche* at the church in Ménerbes. It takes place at midnight, if Monsieur Poncet and his ass have arrived, and providing a suitably tractable baby Jesus has been discovered among the newly born inhabitants of the village. For three years, we have had every intention of going, and for three years we have been ambushed by dinner and the warmth of the wood fire. Full and sleepy, we have poked our noses out into the cold, looked at the Christmas tree of stars in the sky and thought how lucky we are to live here. It will probably be the same again this year.

Peter Mayle
December, 1989

JANUARY

The year began with lunch.

We have always found that New Year's Eve, with its eleventh-hour excesses and doomed resolutions, is a dismal occasion for all the forced jollity and midnight toasts and kisses. And so, when we heard that over in the village of Lacoste, a few miles away, the proprietor of Le Simiane was offering a six-course lunch with pink champagne to his amiable clientele, it seemed like a much more cheerful way to start the next twelve months.

By 12.30 the little stone-walled restaurant was full. There were some serious stomachs to be seen – entire families with the *embonpoint* that comes from spending two or three diligent hours every day at the table, eyes down and conversation postponed in the observance of France's favourite ritual. The proprietor of the restaurant, a man who had somehow perfected the art of hovering despite his considerable size, was dressed for the day in a velvet smoking jacket and bow tie. His moustache, sleek with pomade, quivered with enthusiasm as he rhapsodised over the menu: foie

1

gras, lobster mousse, beef *en croûte*, salads dressed in virgin oil, hand-picked cheeses, desserts of a miraculous lightness, *digestifs*. It was a gastronomic aria which he performed at each table, kissing the tips of his fingers so often that he must have blistered his lips.

The final '*bon appétit*' died away and a companionable near-silence descended on the restaurant as the food received its due attention. While we ate, my wife and I thought of previous New Year's Days, most of them spent under impenetrable cloud in England. It was hard to associate the sunshine and dense blue sky outside with the first of January but, as everyone kept telling us, it was quite normal. After all, we were in Provence.

We had been here often before as tourists, desperate for our annual ration of two or three weeks of true heat and sharp light. Always when we left, with peeling noses and regret, we promised ourselves that one day we would live here. We had talked about it during the long grey winters and the damp green summers, looked with an addict's longing at photographs of village markets and vineyards, dreamed of being woken up by the sun slanting through the bedroom window. And now, somewhat to our surprise, we had done it. We had committed ourselves. We had bought a house, taken French lessons, said our goodbyes, shipped over our two dogs and become foreigners.

In the end, it had happened quickly – almost impulsively – because of the house. We saw it one afternoon and had mentally moved in by dinner.

It was set above the country road that runs between the two mediaeval hill villages of Ménerbes and Bonnieux, at the end of a dirt track through cherry trees and vines. It was a *mas*, or farmhouse, built from local stone which two hundred years of wind and sun had weathered to a colour somewhere between pale honey and pale grey. It had started life in the eighteenth century as one room and, in the haphazard manner of agricultural buildings, had spread to accommodate children, grandmothers, goats and farm implements until it had become an irregular three-storey house. Everything about it was solid. The spiral staircase which rose from the wine *cave* to the top floor was cut from massive slabs of stone. The walls, some of them a metre thick, were built to keep out the winds of the Mistral which, they say, can blow the ears off a

2

donkey. Attached to the back of the house was an enclosed courtyard, and beyond that a bleached white stone swimming pool. There were three wells, there were established shade trees and slim green cypresses, hedges of rosemary, a giant almond tree. In the afternoon sun, with the wooden shutters half-closed like sleepy eyelids, it was irresistible.

It was also immune, as much as any house could be, from the creeping horrors of property development. The French have a weakness for erecting *jolies villas* wherever building regulations permit, and sometimes where they don't, particularly in areas of hitherto unspoiled and beautiful countryside. We had seen them in a ghastly rash around the old market town of Apt, boxes made from that special kind of livid pink cement which remains livid no matter what the weather may throw at it. Very few areas of rural France are safe unless they have been officially protected, and one of the great attractions of this house was that it sat within the boundaries of a National Park, sacred to the French heritage and out of bounds to concrete-mixers.

The Lubéron mountains rise up immediately behind the house to a high point of nearly 3,500 feet and run in deep folds for about forty miles from west to east. Cedars and pines and scrub oak keep them perpetually green and provide cover for boar, rabbits and game birds. Wild flowers, thyme, lavender and mushrooms grow between the rocks and under the trees, and from the summit on a clear day the view is of the Basses-Alpes on one side and the Mediterranean on the other. For most of the year, it is possible to walk for eight or nine hours without seeing a car or a human being. It is a 247,000-acre extension of the back garden, a paradise for the dogs and a permanent barricade against assault from the rear by unforeseen neighbours.

Neighbours, we have found, take on an importance in the country that they don't begin to have in cities. You can live for years in an apartment in London or New York and barely speak to the people who live six inches away from you on the other side of a wall. In the country, separated from the next house though you may be by hundreds of yards, your neighbours are part of your life, and you are part of theirs. If you happen to be foreign and therefore slightly exotic, you are inspected with more than usual interest. And if, in addition, you inherit a long-standing and delicate agricultural arrangement, you are quickly made aware that your attitudes and decisions have a direct effect on another family's well-being.

We had been introduced to our new neighbours by the couple from whom we bought the house, over a five-hour dinner marked by a tremendous goodwill on all sides and an almost total lack of comprehension on our part. The language spoken was French, but it was not the French we had studied in textbooks and heard on cassettes; it was a rich, soupy patois, emanating from somewhere at the back of the throat and passing through a scrambling process in the nasal passages before coming out as speech. Half-familiar sounds could be dimly recognised as words through the swirls and eddies of Provençal: *demain* became *demang*, *vin* became *vang*, *maison* became *mesong*. That by itself would not have been a problem had the words been spoken at normal conversational speed and without further embroidery, but they were delivered like bullets from a machine-gun, often with an extra vowel tacked on to the end for good luck. Thus an offer of more bread – page one stuff in French for beginners – emerged as a single twanging question. *Encoredupango?*

Fortunately for us, the good humour and niceness of our neighbours were apparent even if what they were saying was a mystery. Henriette was a brown, pretty woman with a permanent smile and a sprinter's enthusiasm for reaching the finishing line of each sentence in record time. Her husband Faustin – or Faustang, as we thought his name was spelt for many weeks – was large and gentle, unhurried in his movements and relatively slow with his words. He had been born in the valley, he had spent his life in the valley, and he would die in the valley. His father, Pépé André, who lived next to him, had shot his last boar at the age of eighty and had given up hunting to take up the bicycle. Twice a week he would pedal to the village for his groceries and his gossip. They seemed to be a contented family.

They had, however, a concern about us, not only as neighbours but as prospective partners, and, through the fumes of *marc* and black tobacco and the even thicker fog of the accent, we eventually got to the bottom of it.

Most of the six acres of land we had bought with the house was planted with vines, and these had been looked after for years under the traditional system of *métayage*: the owner of the land pays the capital costs of new vine stock and fertiliser, while the farmer does the work of spraying, cropping and pruning. At the end of the season, the farmer takes two-thirds of the profits and the owner one-third. If the property changes hands, the arrangement comes up for review, and there was Faustin's concern. It was well known that many of the properties in the Lubéron were bought as *résidences secondaires*, used for holidays and amusement, their good agricultural land turned into elaborately planted gardens. There were even cases of the ultimate blasphemy, when vines had been grubbed up to make way for tennis courts. Tennis courts! Faustin shrugged with disbelief, shoulders and eyebrows going up in unison as he contemplated the extraordinary idea of exchanging precious vines for the curious pleasures of chasing a little ball around in the heat.

He needn't have worried. We loved the vines – the ordered regularity of them against the sprawl of the mountain, the way they changed from bright green to darker green to yellow and red as spring and summer turned to autumn, the blue smoke in the pruning season as the clippings were burned, the pruned stumps studding the bare fields in the winter – they were meant to be here. Tennis courts and landscaped gardens weren't. (Nor, for that matter, was our swimming pool, but at least it hadn't replaced any vines.) And, besides, there was the wine. We had the option of taking our profit in cash or in the bottle, and in an average year our share of the crop would be nearly a thousand litres of good ordinary red and pink. As emphatically as we could in our unsteady French, we told Faustin that we would be delighted to continue the existing arrangement. He beamed. He could see that we would all get along very well together. One day, we might even be able to talk to each other.

* * * * *

The proprietor of Le Simiane wished us a happy new year and hovered in the doorway as we stood in the narrow street, blinking into the sun.

'Not bad, eh?' he said, with a flourish of one velvet-clad arm which took in the village, the ruins of the Marquis de Sade's château perched above, the view across to the mountains and the bright, clean sky. It was a casually possessive gesture, as if he was showing us a corner of his personal estate. 'One is fortunate to be in Provence.'

Yes indeed, we thought, one certainly was. If this was winter we wouldn't be needing all the foul-weather paraphernalia – boots and coats and inch-thick sweaters – that we had brought over from England. We drove home, warm and well-fed, making bets on how soon we could take the first swim of the year, and feeling a smug sympathy for those poor souls in harsher climates who had to suffer real winters.

Meanwhile, a thousand miles to the north, the wind that had

started in Siberia was picking up speed for the final part of its journey. We had heard stories about the Mistral. It drove people, and animals, mad. It was an extenuating circumstance in crimes of violence. It blew for fifteen days on end, uprooting trees, overturning cars, smashing windows, tossing old ladies into the gutter, splintering telegraph poles, moaning through houses like a cold and baleful ghost, causing *la grippe*, domestic squabbles, absenteeism from work, toothache, migraine – every problem in Provence that couldn't be blamed on the politicians was the fault of the *sâcré vent* which the Provençaux spoke about with a kind of masochistic pride.

Typical Gallic exaggeration, we thought. If they had to put up with the gales that come off the English Channel and bend the rain so that it hits you in the face almost horizontally, then they might know what a real wind was like. We listened to their stories and, to humour the tellers, pretended to be impressed.

And so we were poorly prepared when the first Mistral of the year came howling down the Rhône valley, turned left and smacked into the west side of the house with enough force to skim roof tiles into the swimming pool and rip a window that had carelessly been left open off its hinges. The temperature dropped 20 degrees in twenty-four hours. It went to zero, then six below. Readings taken in Marseille showed a wind speed of 180 kilometres an hour. My wife was cooking in an overcoat. I was trying to type in gloves. We stopped talking about our first swim and thought wistfully about central heating. And then one morning, with the sound of branches snapping, the pipes burst one after the other under the pressure of water that had frozen in them overnight.

They hung off the wall, swollen and stopped up with ice, and Monsieur Menicucci studied them with his professional plumber's eye.

'*Oh là là,*' he said. '*Oh là là.*' He turned to his young apprentice, whom he invariably addressed as *jeune homme* or *jeune*. 'You see what we have here, *jeune*. Naked pipes. No insulation. Côte d'Azur plumbing. In Cannes, in Nice, it would do, but here . . .'

He made a clucking sound of disapproval and wagged his finger under *jeune*'s nose to underline the difference between the soft winters of the coast and the biting cold in which we were now standing, and pulled his woollen bonnet firmly down over his ears. He was short and compact, built for plumbing, as he would say, because he could squeeze himself into constricted spaces that more ungainly men would find inaccessible. While we waited for *jeune* to set up the blowlamp, Monsieur Menicucci delivered the first of a series of lectures and collected *pensées* which I would listen to with increasing enjoyment throughout the coming year. Today, we had a geophysical dissertation on the increasing severity of Provençal winters.

For three years in a row, winters had been noticeably harder than anyone could remember – cold enough, in fact, to kill ancient olive trees. It was, to use the phrase that comes out in Provence whenever the sun goes in, *pas normale*. But why? Monsieur Menicucci gave me a token two seconds to ponder this phenomenon before warming to his thesis, tapping me with a finger from time to time to make sure I was paying attention.

It was clear, he said, that the winds which brought the cold down from Russia were arriving in Provence with greater velocity than before, taking less time to reach their destination and therefore having less time to warm up en route. And the reason for this – Monsieur Menicucci allowed himself a brief but dramatic pause – was a change in the configuration of the earth's crust. *Mais oui*. Somewhere between Siberia and Ménerbes the curvature of the earth had flattened, enabling the wind to take a more direct route south. It was entirely logical. Unfortunately, part two of the lecture (Why The Earth Is Becoming Flatter) was interrupted by a crack of another burst pipe, and my education was put aside for some virtuoso work with the blow-lamp.

The effect of the weather on the inhabitants of Provence is immediate and obvious. They expect every day to be sunny, and their disposition suffers when it isn't. Rain they take as a personal affront, shaking their heads and commiserating with each other in the cafés, looking with profound suspicion at the sky as though a plague of locusts is about to descend and picking their way with distaste through the puddles on the pavement. If anything worse than a rainy day should come along, such as this sub-zero snap, the result is startling: most of the population disappears.

JANUARY

As the cold began to bite into the middle of January, the towns and villages became quiet. The weekly markets, normally jammed and boisterous, were reduced to a skeleton crew of intrepid stallholders who were prepared to risk frostbite for a living, stamping their feet and nipping from hip flasks. Customers moved briskly, bought and went, barely pausing to count their change. Bars closed their doors and windows tight and conducted their business in a pungent fug. There was none of the usual dawdling on the streets.

Our valley hibernated, and I missed the sounds which marked the passing of each day almost as precisely as a clock: Faustin's rooster having his morning cough; the demented clatter – like nuts and bolts trying to escape from a biscuit tin – of the small Citroën van that every farmer drives home at lunchtime; the hopeful fusillade of a hunter on afternoon patrol in the vines on the opposite hillside; the distant whine of a chainsaw in the forest; the twilight serenade of farm dogs. Now there was silence. For hours on end the valley would be completely still and empty, and we became curious. What was everybody doing?

Faustin, we knew, travelled round the neighbouring farms as a visiting slaughterer, slitting the throats and breaking the necks of rabbits and ducks and pigs and geese so that they could be turned into terrines and hams and *confits*. We thought it an uncharacteristic occupation for a soft-hearted man who spoilt his dogs, but he was evidently skilled and quick and, like any true countryman, he wasn't distracted by sentiment. We might treat a rabbit as a pet or become emotionally attached to a goose, but we had come from cities and supermarkets, where flesh was hygienically distanced from any resemblance to living creatures. A shrink-wrapped pork chop has a sanitised, abstract appearance that has nothing whatever to do with the warm, mucky bulk of a pig. Out here in the country there was no avoiding the direct link between death and dinner, and there would be many occasions in the future when we would be grateful for Faustin's winter work.

But what did everyone else do? The earth was frozen, the vines were clipped and dormant, it was too cold to hunt. Had they all gone on holiday? No, surely not. These were not the kind of gentlemen farmers who spent their winters on the ski slopes or

9

yachting in the Caribbean. Holidays here were taken at home during August, eating too much, enjoying siestas and resting up before the long days of the *vendange*. It was a puzzle, until we realised how many of the local people had their birthdays in September or October, and then a possible but unverifiable answer suggested itself: they were busy indoors making babies. There is a season for everything in Provence, and the first two months of the year must be devoted to procreation. We have never dared ask.

The cold weather brought less private pleasures. Apart from the peace and emptiness of the landscape, there is a special smell about winter in Provence which is accentuated by the wind and the clean, dry air. Walking in the hills, I was often able to smell a house before I could see it, because of the scent of woodsmoke coming from an invisible chimney. It is one of the most primitive smells in life, and consequently extinct in most cities, where fire regulations and interior decorators have combined to turn fire-places into blocked-up holes or self-consciously lit 'architectural features'. The fireplace in Provence is still used – to cook on, to sit round, to warm the toes and please the eye – and fires are laid in the early morning and fed throughout the day with scrub oak from the Lubéron or beech from the foothills of Mont Ventoux. Coming home with the dogs as dusk fell, I always stopped to look from the top of the valley at the long zig-zag of smoke ribbons drifting up from the farms that are scattered along the Bonnieux road. It was a sight that made me think of warm kitchens and well-seasoned stews, and it never failed to make me ravenous.

The well-known food of Provence is summer food – the melons and peaches and asparagus, the courgettes and aubergines, the peppers and tomatoes, the *aioli* and bouillabaisse and monumental salads of olives and anchovies and tuna and hard-boiled eggs and sliced, earthy potatoes on beds of multicoloured lettuce glistening with oil, the fresh goats' cheeses – these had been the memories that came back to torment us every time we looked at the limp and shrivelled selection on offer in English shops. It had never occurred to us that there was a winter menu, totally different but equally delicious.

The cold weather cuisine of Provence is peasant food. It is made to stick to your ribs, keep you warm, give you strength and send you off to bed with a full belly. It is not pretty, in the way that the tiny and artistically garnished portions served in fashionable restaurants are pretty, but on a freezing night with the Mistral coming at you like a razor there is nothing to beat it. And on the night one of our neighbours invited us to dinner it was cold enough to turn the short walk to their house into a short run.

We came through the door and my glasses steamed up in the heat from the fireplace that occupied most of the far wall of the room. As the mist cleared, I saw that the big table, covered in checked oilcloth, was laid for ten; friends and relations were coming to examine us. A television set chattered in the corner, the radio chattered back from the kitchen, and assorted dogs and cats were shooed out of the door as one guest arrived, only to sidle back in with the next. A tray of drinks was brought out, with pastis for the men and chilled, sweet muscat wine for the women, and we were caught in a crossfire of noisy complaints about the weather. Was it as bad as this in England? Only in the summer, I said. For a moment they took me seriously before someone saved me from embarrassment by laughing. With a great deal of jockeying for position – whether to sit next to us or as far away as possible, I wasn't sure – we settled ourselves at the table.

It was a meal that we shall never forget; more accurately, it was several meals that we shall never forget, because it went beyond the gastronomic frontiers of anything we had ever experienced, both in quantity and length.

It started with home-made pizza – not one, but three: anchovy, mushroom and cheese, and it was obligatory to have a slice of each. Plates were then wiped with pieces torn from the two-foot loaves in the middle of the table, and the next course came out. There were pâtés of rabbit, boar and thrush. There was a chunky, pork-based terrine laced with *marc*. There were *saucissons* spotted with peppercorns. There were tiny sweet onions marinated in a fresh tomato sauce. Plates were wiped once more and duck was brought in. The slivers of *magret* that appear, arranged in fan formation and lapped by an elegant smear of sauce on the refined tables of nouvelle cuisine – these were nowhere to be seen. We had entire breasts, entire legs, covered in a dark, savoury gravy and surrounded by wild mushrooms.

We sat back, thankful that we had been able to finish, and watched with something close to panic as plates were wiped yet again and a huge, steaming casserole was placed on the table. This was the speciality of Madame our hostess – a rabbit *civet* of the richest, deepest brown – and our feeble requests for small portions were smilingly ignored. We ate it. We ate the green salad with knuckles of bread fried in garlic and olive oil, we ate the plump round *crottins* of goat's cheese, we ate the almond and cream gâteau that the daughter of the house had prepared. That night, we ate for England.

With the coffee, a number of deformed bottles were produced which contained a selection of locally-made *digestifs*. My heart would have sunk had there been any space left for it to sink to, but there was no denying my host's insistence. I must try one particular concoction, made from an eleventh-century recipe by an alcoholic order of monks in the Basses-Alpes. I was asked to close my

eyes while it was poured, and when I opened them a tumbler of viscous yellow fluid had been put in front of me. I looked in despair round the table. Everyone was watching me; there was no chance of giving whatever it was to the dog or letting it dribble discreetly into one of my shoes. Clutching the table for support with one hand, I took the tumbler with the other, closed my eyes, prayed to the patron saint of indigestion, and threw it back.

Nothing came out. I had been expecting at best a scalded tongue, at worst permanently cauterised taste buds, but I took in nothing but air. It was a trick glass, and for the first time in my adult life I was deeply relieved not to have a drink. As the laughter of the other guests died away, genuine drinks were threatened, but we were saved by the cat. From her headquarters on top of a large *armoire*, she took a flying leap in pursuit of a moth and crash-landed among the coffee cups and bottles on the table. It seemed like an appropriate moment to leave. We walked home pushing our stomachs before us, oblivious to the cold, incapable of speech, and slept like the dead.

Even by Provençal standards, it had not been an everyday meal. The people who work on the land are more likely to eat well at noon and sparingly in the evening, a habit which is healthy and sensible and, for us, quite impossible. We have found that there is nothing like a good lunch to give us an appetite for dinner. It's alarming. It must have something to do with the novelty of living in the middle of such an abundance of good things to eat, and among men and women whose interest in food verges on obsession. Butchers, for instance, are not content merely to sell you meat. They will tell you, at great length, while the queue backs up behind you, how to cook it, how to serve it and what to eat and drink with it.

The first time this happened, we had gone into Apt to buy veal for the Provençal stew called *pebronata*. We were directed towards a butcher in the old part of town who was reputed to have the master's touch and to be altogether *très sérieux*. His shop was small, he and his wife were large, and the four of us constituted a crowd. He listened intently as we explained that we wanted to make this particular dish; perhaps he had heard of it.

He puffed up with indignation, and began to sharpen a large

knife so energetically that we stepped back a pace. Did we realise, he said, that we were looking at an expert, possibly the greatest *pebronata* authority in the Vaucluse? His wife nodded admiringly. Why, he said, brandishing ten inches of sharp steel in our faces, he had written a book about it – a *definitive* book – containing twenty variations of the basic recipe. His wife nodded again. She was playing the rôle of senior nurse to his eminent surgeon, passing him fresh knives to sharpen prior to the operation.

We must have looked suitably impressed, because he then produced a handsome piece of veal and his tone became professorial. He trimmed the meat, cubed it, filled a small bag with chopped herbs, told us where to go to buy the best peppers (four green and one red, the contrast in colour being for aesthetic reasons), went through the recipe twice to make sure we weren't going to commit a *bêtise* and suggested a suitable Côtes du Rhône. It was a fine performance.

Gourmets are thick on the ground in Provence, and pearls of wisdom have sometimes come from the most unlikely sources. We were getting used to the fact that the French are as passionate about food as other nationalities are about sport and politics, but even so it came as a surprise to hear Monsieur Bagnols the floor-cleaner handicapping three-star restaurants. He had come over from Nîmes to sand down a stone floor, and it was apparent from the start that he was not a man who trifled with his stomach. Each day precisely at noon he changed out of his overalls and took himself off to one of the local restaurants for two hours.

He judged it to be not bad, but of course nothing like the Beaumanière at Les Baux. The Beaumanière has three Michelin stars and a 17 out of 20 rating in the Gault-Millau Guide and there, he said, he had eaten a truly exceptional sea bass *en croûte*. Mind you, the Troisgros in Roanne was a superb establishment too, although being opposite the station the setting wasn't as pretty as Les Baux. The Troisgros has three Michelin stars and a 19½ out of 20 rating in the Gault-Millau Guide. And so it went on, as he adjusted his knee pads and scrubbed away at the floor, a personal guide to five or six of the most expensive restaurants in France that Monsieur Bagnols had visited on his annual treats.

He had once been in England, and had eaten roast lamb at a

hotel in Liverpool. It had been grey and tepid and tasteless. But of course, he said, it is well known that the English kill their lamb twice; once when they slaughter it, and once when they cook it. I retreated in the face of such withering contempt for my national cuisine, and left him to get on with the floor and dream of his next visit to Bocuse.

* * * * *

The weather continued hard, with bitter but extravagantly starry nights and spectacular sunrises. One early morning, the sun seemed abnormally low and large, and walking into it everything was either glare or deep shadow. The dogs were running well ahead of me, and I heard them barking long before I could see what they had found.

We had come to a part of the forest where the land fell away to form a deep bowl in which, a hundred years before, some misguided farmer had built a house that was almost permanently in the gloom cast by the surrounding trees. I had passed it many times. The windows were always shuttered, and the only sign of human habitation was smoke drifting up from the chimney. In the yard outside, two large and matted Alsatians and a black mongrel were constantly on the prowl, howling and straining against their chains in their efforts to savage any passers-by. These dogs were known to be vicious; one of them had broken loose and laid open the back of grandfather André's leg. My dogs, full of valour when confronted by timid cats, had wisely decided against passing too close to three sets of hostile jaws, and had developed the habit of making a detour round the house and over a small steep hill. They were at the top now, barking in that speculative, nervous manner that dogs adopt to reassure themselves when they encounter something unexpected in familiar territory.

I reached the top of the hill with the sun full in my eyes, but I could make out the back-lit silhouette of a figure in the trees, a nimbus of smoke around his head, the dogs inspecting him noisily from a safe distance. As I came up to him, he extended a cold, horny hand.

'*Bon jour.*' He unscrewed a cigarette butt from the corner of his mouth and introduced himself. 'Massot, Antoine.'

15

He was dressed for war. A stained camouflage jacket, an army jungle cap, a bandolier of cartridges and a pump-action shotgun. His face was the colour and texture of a hastily cooked steak, with a wedge of nose jutting out above a ragged, nicotine-stained moustache. Pale blue eyes peered through a sprouting tangle of ginger eyebrows, and his decayed smile would have brought despair to the most optimistic dentist. Nevertheless, there was a certain mad amiability about him.

I asked if his hunting had been successful. 'A fox,' he said, 'but too old to eat.' He shrugged, and lit another of his fat Boyards cigarettes, wrapped in yellow maize paper and smelling like a young bonfire in the morning air. 'Anyway,' he said, 'he won't be keeping my dogs awake at night,' and he nodded down towards the house in the hollow.

I said that his dogs seemed fierce, and he grinned. Just playful, he said. But what about the time one of them had escaped and attacked the old man? Ah, that. He shook his head at the painful memory. The trouble is, he said, you should never turn your back on a playful dog, and that had been the old man's mistake. *Une vraie catastrophe.* For a moment, I thought he was regretting the wound inflicted on grandfather André, which had punctured a vein in his leg and required a visit to the hospital for injections and stitches, but I was mistaken. The real sadness was that Massot had been obliged to buy a new chain, and those robbers in Cavaillon had charged him 250 francs. That had bitten deeper than teeth.

To save him further anguish, I changed the subject and asked him if he really ate fox. He seemed surprised at such a stupid question, and looked at me for a moment or two without replying, as though he suspected me of making fun of him.

'One doesn't eat fox in England?' I had visions of the members of the Belvoir Hunt writing to *The Times* and having a collective heart attack at such an unsporting and typically foreign idea.

'No, one doesn't eat fox in England. One dresses up in a red coat and one chases after it on horseback with several dogs, and then one cuts off its tail.'

He cocked his head, astonished. *'Ils sont bizarres, les Anglais.'* And then, with great gusto and some hideously explicit gestures, he described what civilised people did with a fox.

Civet de renard à la façon Massot

Find a young fox, and be careful to shoot it cleanly in the head, which is of no culinary interest. Buckshot in the edible parts of the fox can cause chipped teeth – Massot showed me two of his – and indigestion.

Skin the fox, and cut off its *parties*. Here, Massot made a chopping motion with his hand across his groin, and followed this with some elaborate twists and tugs of the hand to illustrate the gutting process.

Leave the cleaned carcass under cold running water for 24 hours to eliminate the *goût sauvage*. Drain it, bundle it up in a sack and hang it outdoors overnight, preferably when there is frost.

The following morning, place the fox in a casserole of cast iron and cover with a mixture of blood and red wine. Add herbs, onions and heads of garlic, and simmer for a day or two. (Massot apologised for his lack of precision but said that the timing varied according to size and age of fox.)

In the old days, this was eaten with bread and boiled potatoes, but now, thanks to progress and the invention of the deep-fat fryer, one could enjoy it with *pommes frites*.

By now, Massot was in a talkative mood. He lived alone, he told me, and company was scarce in the winter. He had spent his life in the mountains, but maybe it was time to move into the village, where he could be among people. Of course, it would be a tragedy to leave such a beautiful house, so calm, so sheltered from the Mistral, so perfectly situated to escape the heat of the midday sun, a place where he had passed so many happy years. It would break his heart, unless – he looked at me closely, pale eyes watery with sincerity – unless he could render me a service by making it possible for one of my friends to buy his house.

I looked down at the ramshackle building huddled in the shadows, with the three dogs padding endlessly to and fro on their rusting chains, and thought that in the whole of Provence it would be difficult to find a less appealing spot to live. There was no sun, no view, no feeling of space, and almost certainly, a dank and horrid interior. I promised Massot that I would bear it in mind, and he winked at me. 'A million francs,' he said. 'A sacrifice.' And in the meantime, until he left this little corner of paradise, if there was anything I wanted to know about the rural life, he would advise me. He knew every centimetre of the forest, where the mushrooms grew, where the wild boar came to drink, which gun to choose, how to train a hound – there was nothing he didn't know, and this knowledge was mine for the asking. I thanked him. '*C'est normale*,' he said, and stumped off down the hill to his million-franc residence.

* * * * *

When I told a friend in the village that I had met Massot, he smiled.

'Did he tell you how to cook a fox?'

I nodded.

'Did he try to sell his house?'

I nodded.

'The old *blagueur*. He's full of wind.'

I didn't care. I liked him, and I had a feeling that he would be a rich source of fascinating and highly suspect information. With him to initiate me into the joys of rustic pursuits and Monsieur Menicucci in charge of more scientific matters, all I needed now was a navigator to steer me through the murky waters of French bureaucracy, which in its manifold subtleties and inconveniences can transform a molehill of activity into a mountain of frustration.

We should have been warned by the complications attached to the purchase of the house. We wanted to buy, the proprietor wanted to sell, a price was agreed, it was all straightforward. But then we became reluctant participants in the national sport of paper-gathering. Birth certificates were required to prove we existed; passports to prove that we were British; marriage certificates to enable us to buy the house in our joint names; divorce certificates to prove that our marriage certificates were valid; proof that we had an address in England (our driver's licences, plainly addressed, were judged to be insufficient; did we have more formal evidence of where we were living, like an old electricity bill?). Back and forth between France and England the pieces of paper went – every scrap of information except blood type and fingerprints – until the local lawyer had our lives contained in a dossier. The transaction could then proceed.

We made allowances for the system because we were foreigners buying a tiny part of France, and national security clearly had to be safeguarded. Less important business would doubtless be quicker and less demanding of paperwork. We went to buy a car.

It was the standard Citroën *deux chevaux*, a model which has changed very little in the past twenty-five years. Consequently, spare parts are available in every village. Mechanically it is not much more complicated than a sewing machine, and any reasonably competent blacksmith can repair it. It is cheap, and has a comfortingly low top speed. Apart from the fact that the suspension is made of blancmange, which makes it the only car in the world likely to cause sea-sickness, it is a charming and practical vehicle. And the garage had one in stock.

The salesman looked at our driver's licences, valid throughout the countries of the Common Market until well past the year 2000. With an expression of infinite regret, he shook his head and looked up.

'Non.'

'Non?'

'Non.'

We produced our secret weapons: two passports.

'Non.'

We rummaged around in our papers. What could he want? Our marriage certificate? An old English electricity bill? We gave up, and asked him what else, apart from money, was needed to buy a car.

'You have an address in France?'

We gave it to him, and he noted it down on the sales form with great care, checking from time to time to make sure that the third carbon copy was legible.

'You have proof that this is your address? A telephone bill? An electricity bill?'

We explained that we hadn't yet received any bills because we had only just moved in. He explained that an address was necessary for the *carte grise* – the document of car ownership. No address, no *carte grise*. No *carte grise*, no car.

Fortunately, his salesman's instincts overcame his relish for a bureaucratic impasse, and he leaned forward with a solution: if we would provide him with the deed of sale of our house, the whole affair could be brought to a swift and satisfactory conclusion, and we could have the car. The deed of sale was in the lawyer's office, fifteen miles away. We went to get it, and placed it triumphantly on his desk, together with a cheque. Now could we have the car?

'Malheureusement, non.' We must wait until the cheque had been cleared, a delay of four or five days, even though it was drawn on a local bank. Could we go together to the bank and clear it immediately? No, we couldn't. It was lunchtime. The two areas of endeavour in which France leads the world – bureaucracy and gastronomy – had combined to put us in our place.

It made us mildly paranoid, and for weeks we never left home without photocopies of the family archives, waving passports and birth certificates at everyone from the check-out girl at the supermarket to the old man who loaded the wine into the car at the co-operative. The documents were always regarded with interest, because documents are holy things here and deserve respect, but we were often asked why we carried them around. Was this the way one was obliged to live in England? What a strange and tiresome country is must be. The only short answer to that was a shrug. We practised shrugging.

The cold lasted until the final days of January, and then turned perceptibly warmer. We anticipated spring, and I was anxious to hear an expert forecast. I decided to consult the sage of the forest.

Massot tugged reflectively at his moustache. There were signs, he said. Rats can sense the coming of warmer weather before any of those complicated satellites, and the rats in his roof had been unusually active these past few days. In fact, they had kept him awake one night and he had loosed off a couple of shots into the ceiling to quieten them down. *Eh, oui.* Also, the new moon was due, and that often brought a change at this time of year. Based on these two significant portents, he predicted an early, warm spring. I hurried home to see if there were any traces of blossom on the almond tree, and thought about cleaning the swimming pool.

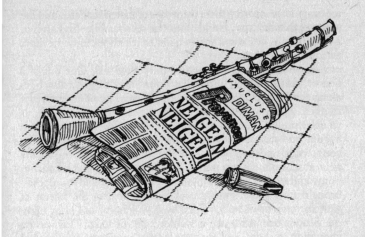

FEBRUARY

The front page of our newspaper, *Le Provençal*, is usually devoted to the fortunes of local football teams, the windy pronouncements of minor politicians, breathless reports of supermarket hold-ups in Cavaillon – '*le Chicago de Provence*' – and the occasional ghoulish account of sudden death on the roads caused by drivers of small Renaults trying to emulate Alain Prost.

This traditional mixture was put aside, one morning in early February, for a lead story which had nothing to do with sport, crime or politics: PROVENCE UNDER BLANKET OF SNOW! shouted the headline with an undercurrent of glee at the promise of the follow-up stories which would undoubtedly result from nature's unseasonable behaviour. There would be mothers and babies miraculously alive after a night in a snowbound car, old men escaping hypothermia by inches thanks to the intervention of public-spirited and alert neighbours, climbers plucked from the side of Mont Ventoux by helicopter, postmen battling against all odds to deliver electricity bills, village elders harking back to

21

previous catastrophes – there were days of material ahead, and the writer of that first story could almost be seen rubbing his hands in anticipation as he paused between sentences to look for some more exclamation marks.

Two photographs accompanied the festive text. One was of a line of white, feathery umbrellas – the snow-draped palm trees along the Promenade des Anglais in Nice. The other showed a muffled figure in Marseille dragging a mobile radiator on its wheels through the snow at the end of a rope, like a man taking an angular and obstinate dog for a walk. There were no pictures of the countryside under snow because the countryside was cut off; the nearest snowplough was north of Lyon, three hundred kilometres away, and to a Provençal motorist – even an intrepid journalist – brought up on the sure grip of baking tarmac, the horror of waltzing on ice was best avoided by staying home or holing up in the nearest bar. After all, it wouldn't be for long. This was an aberration, a short-lived climatic hiccup, an excuse for a second *café crème* and perhaps something a little stronger to get the heart started before venturing outside.

Our valley had been quiet during the cold days of January, but now the snow had added an extra layer of silence, as though the entire area had been soundproofed. We had the Lubéron to ourselves, eerie and beautiful, mile after mile of white icing marked only by occasional squirrel and rabbit tracks crossing the footpaths in straight and purposeful lines. There were no human footprints except ours. The hunters, so evident in warmer weather with their weaponry and their arsenals of salami, baguettes, beer, Gauloises and all the other necessities for a day out braving nature in the raw, had stayed in their burrows. The sounds we mistook for gun shots were branches snapping under the weight of great swags of snow. Otherwise it was so still that, as Massot observed later, you could have heard a mouse fart.

Closer to home, the drive had turned into a miniature mountainscape where wind had drifted the snow into a range of knee-deep mounds, and the only way out was on foot. Buying a loaf of bread became an expedition lasting nearly two hours – into Ménerbes and back without seeing a single moving vehicle, the white humps of parked cars standing as patiently as sheep by the side of the hill leading up to the village. The Christmas-card weather had infected the inhabitants, who were greatly amused by their own efforts to negotiate the steep and treacherous streets, either teetering precariously forward from the waist or leaning even more precariously backward, placing their feet with the awkward deliberation of intoxicated roller-skaters. The municipal cleaning squad, two men with brooms, had cleared the access routes to essential services – butcher, baker, *épicerie* and café – and small knots of villagers stood in the sunshine congratulating each other on their fortitude in the face of calamity. A man on skis appeared from the direction of the Mairie and, with marvellous inevitability, collided with the only other owner of assisted transport, a man on an ancient sled. It was a pity the journalist from *Le Provençal* wasn't there to see it: SNOW CLAIMS VICTIMS IN HEAD-ON COLLISION, he could have written, and he could have watched it all from the steamy comfort of the café.

The dogs adapted to the snow like young bears, plunging into the drifts to emerge with white whiskers and bucking their way across the fields in huge, frothy leaps. And they learned to skate. The pool, that just days before I had been planning to clean and make ready for some early spring swimming, was a block of blue-green ice, and it seemed to fascinate them. On to the ice would go the two front paws, then a tentative third paw, and finally the remaining leg would join the rest of the dog. There would be a moment or two of contemplation at the curiosity of a life in which you can drink something one day and stand on it the next before the tail would start whirring with excitement and a form of progress could be made. I had always thought that dogs were engineered on the principle of four-wheel drive vehicles, with equal propulsion coming from each leg, but the power appears to be concentrated in the back. Thus the front half of the skating dog may have the intention of proceeding in a straight line, but the rear half is wildly out of control, fishtailing from side to side and sometimes threatening to overtake.

The novelty of being marooned in the middle of a picturesque sea was, during the day, a great pleasure. We walked for miles, we chopped wood, we ate enormous lunches and we stayed warm. But at night, even with fires and sweaters and yet more food, the chill came up from the stone floors and out of the stone walls, making the toes numb and the muscles tight with cold. We were often in bed by nine o'clock and often, in the early morning, our breath was visible in small clouds over the breakfast table. If the Menicucci theory was correct and we were living in a flatter world, all future winters were going to be like this. It was time to stop pretending we were in a sub-tropical climate and give in to the temptations of central heating.

I called Monsieur Menicucci, and he asked anxiously about my pipes. I told him they were holding up well. 'That pleases me,' he said, 'because it is minus five degrees, the roads are perilous and I am fifty-eight years old. I am staying at home.' He paused, then added, 'I shall play the clarinet.' This he did every day to keep his fingers nimble and to take his mind off the hurly-burly of plumbing, and it was with some difficulty that I managed to steer the conversation away from his thoughts on the baroque composers and towards the mundane subject of our cold house. Eventually, we agreed that I should pay him a visit as soon as the roads had cleared. He had all kinds of installations at his house, he said – gas, oil, electricity and, his latest acquisition, a revolving solar heating panel. He would show them all to me and I could also meet Madame his wife, who was an accomplished soprano. I was obviously going to have a musical time among the radiators and stopcocks.

The prospect of being warm made us think of summer, and we started to make plans for turning the enclosed courtyard at the back of the house into an open-air living room. There was already a barbecue and a bar at one end, but what it lacked was a large, solid, permanent table. As we stood in six inches of snow, we tried to picture lunchtime in mid-August, and traced on the flagtones a five-foot square, large enough to seat eight bronzed and barefooted people and with plenty of room in the middle for giant bowls of salad, pâtés and cheese, cold roasted peppers, olive bread and chilled bottles of wine. The Mistral gusted through the courtyard and obliterated the shape in the snow, but by then we had decided: the table would be square and the top a single slab of stone.

Like most people who come to the Lubéron, we had been impressed by the variety and versatility of the local stone. It can be *pierre froide* from the quarry at Tavel, a smooth, close-grained pale beige; it can be *pierre chaude* from Lacoste, a rougher, softer off-white, or it can be any one of twenty shades and textures in between. There is a stone for fireplaces, for swimming pools, for staircases, for walls and floors, for garden benches and kitchen sinks. It can be rough or polished, hard-edged or rolled, cut square or in voluptuous curves. It is used where, in Britain or America, a builder might use wood or iron or plastic. Its only disadvantage, as we were finding out, is that it is cold in winter.

What came as a real surprise was the price. Metre for metre, stone was cheaper than linoleum, and we were so delighted by this rather misleading discovery – having conveniently overlooked the cost of laying stone – that we decided to risk the elements and go to the quarry without waiting for spring. Friends had suggested a man called Pierrot at Lacoste, whose work was good and whose prices were correct. He was described to us as *un original*, a character, and a rendezvous was made with him for 8.30 in the morning, while the quarry would still be quiet.

We followed a signpost off the side road out of Lacoste and along a track through the scrub oak towards the open countryside. It didn't look like a light industrial zone, and we were just about to turn back when we nearly fell into it – a huge hole bitten out of the ground, littered with blocks of stone. Some were raw, some worked into tombstones, memorials, giant garden urns, winged angels with intimidating blind stares, small triumphal arches or stocky round columns. Tucked away in a corner was a hut, its windows opaque with years of quarry dust.

We knocked and went in, and there was Pierrot. He was shaggy, with a wild black beard and formidable eyebrows. A piratical man. He made us welcome, beating the top layer of dust from two chairs with a battered trilby hat which he then placed carefully over the telephone on the table.

'English, eh?'

We nodded, and he leant towards us with a confidential air.

'I have an English car, a vintage Aston Martin. *Magnifique.*'

He kissed the tips of his fingers, speckling his beard with white, and poked among the papers on his table, raising puffs from every pile. Somewhere there was a photograph.

The phone started to make gravelly noises. Pierrot rescued it from under his hat and listened with an increasingly serious face before putting the phone down.

'Another tombstone,' he said. 'It's this weather. The old ones can't take the cold.' He looked around for his hat, retrieved it from his head, and covered the phone again, hiding the bad news.

He returned to the business at hand. 'They tell me you want a table.'

I had made a detailed drawing of our table, marking all the measurements carefully in metres and centimetres. For someone with the artistic flair of a five-year-old, it was a masterpiece. Pierrot looked at it briefly, squinting at the figures, and shook his head.

'*Non*. For a piece of stone this size, it needs to be twice as thick. Also, your base would collapse – *pouf!* – in five minutes, because the top will weigh . . .' he scribbled some calculations on my drawing '. . . between three and four hundred kilos.' He turned the paper over, and sketched on the back. 'There. That's what you want.' He pushed the sketch across to us. It was much better than mine, and showed a graceful monolith; simple, square, well-proportioned. 'A thousand francs, including delivery.'

We shook hands on it, and I promised to come back later in the week with a cheque. When I did, it was at the end of a working day, and I found that Pierrot had changed colour. From the top of his trilby down to his boots he was stark white, dusted all over as though he had been rolling in confectioner's sugar, the only man I have ever seen who aged twenty-five years in the course of a working day. According to our friends, whose information I didn't entirely trust, his wife ran the vacuum cleaner over him every night when he came home, and all the furniture in his house, from armchairs to bidets, was made from stone.

At the time, it was easy enough to believe. Deep winter in Provence has a curiously unreal atmosphere, the combination of silence and emptiness creating the feeling that you are separated from the rest of the world, detached from normal life. We could imagine meeting trolls in the forest or seeing two-headed goats by the light of a full moon, and for us it was a strangely enjoyable contrast to the Provence we remembered from summer holidays. For others, winter meant boredom or depression, or worse; the suicide rate in the Vaucluse, so we were told, was the highest in France, and it became more than a statistic when we heard that a man who lived two miles from us had hanged himself one night.

A local death brings sad little announcements, which are posted in the windows of shops and houses. The church bell tolls, and a procession dressed with unfamiliar formality makes its slow way up to the cemetery, which is often one of the most commanding sites in the village. An old man explained why this was so. 'The dead get the best view,' he said, 'because they are there for such a long time.' He cackled so hard at his own joke that he had a coughing fit, and I was worried that his turn had come to join them. When I told him about the cemetery in California where you pay more for a tomb with a view than for more modest accommodation he was not at all surprised. 'There are always fools,' he said, 'dead or alive.'

Days passed with no sign of a thaw, but the roads were now showing strips of black where farmers and their tractors had cleared away the worst of the snow, making a single-lane passage through the drifts either side. This brought out a side of the French motorist that I had never expected to see; he displayed patience, or at least a kind of mulish obstinacy that was far removed from his customary Grand Prix behaviour behind the wheel. I saw it on the roads round the village. One car would be driving cautiously along the clear middle lane and would meet another coming from the opposite direction. They would stop, snout to snout. Neither would give way by reversing. Neither would pull over to the side and risk getting stuck in a drift. Glaring through the windscreens at each other, the drivers would wait in the hope that another car would come up behind them, which would constitute a clear case of *force majeure* and oblige the single car to back down so that superior numbers could proceed.

And so it was with a light foot on the accelerator that I went off to see Monsieur Menicucci and his treasure house of heating appliances. He met me at the entrance to his storeroom, woollen bonnet pulled down to cover his ears, scarf wound up to his chin, gloved, booted, the picture of a man who took the challenge of keeping warm as a scientific exercise in personal insulation. We exchanged politenesses about my pipes and his clarinet and he ushered me inside to view a meticulously arranged selection of

tubes and valves and squat, mysterious machines crouched in corners. Menicucci was a talking catalogue, reeling off heating coefficients and therms which were so far beyond me that all I could do was to nod dumbly at each new revelation.

At last the litany came to an end. '*Et puis voilà*,' said Menicucci, and looked at me expectantly, as though I now had the world of central heating at my fingertips, and could make an intelligent and informed choice. I could think of nothing to say except to ask him how he heated his own house.

'Ah,' he said, tapping his forehead in mock admiration, 'that is not a stupid thing to ask. What kind of meat does the butcher eat?' And, with that mystical question hanging unanswered in the air, we went next door to his house. It was undeniably warm, almost stuffy, and Monsieur Menicucci made a great performance of removing two or three outer layers of clothing, mopping his brow theatrically and adjusting his bonnet to expose his ears to the air.

He walked over to a radiator and patted it on the head. 'Feel that,' he said, 'cast iron, not like the *merde* they use for radiators nowadays. And the boiler – you must see the boiler. But *attention*,' he stopped abruptly and prodded me with his lecturer's finger, 'it is not French. Only the Germans and the Belgians know how to make boilers.' We went into the boiler room, and I dutifully admired the elderly, dial-encrusted machine which was puffing and snorting against the wall. 'This gives twenty-one degrees throughout the house, even when the temperature outside is minus six,' and he threw open the outside door to let in some minus six air on cue. He had the good instructor's gift for illustrating his remarks wherever possible with practical demonstration, as though he was talking to a particularly dense child. (In my case, certainly as far as plumbing and heating were concerned, this was quite justified.)

Having met the boiler, we went back to the house and met Madame, a diminutive woman with a resonant voice. Did I want a *tisane*, some almond biscuits, a glass of Marsala? What I really wanted was to see Monsieur Menicucci in his bonnet playing his clarinet, but that would have to wait until another day. Meanwhile, I had been given much to think about. As I left to go to the car, I looked up at the revolving solar heating apparatus on the roof and saw that it was frozen solid, and I had a sudden longing for a house full of cast iron radiators.

I arrived home to discover that a scale model of Stonehenge had been planted behind the garage. The table had arrived – five feet square, five inches thick, with a massive base in the form of a cross. The distance between where it had been delivered and where we wanted it to be was no more than fifteen yards, but it might as well have been fifty miles. The entrance to the courtyard was too narrow for any mechanical transport, and the high wall and tiled half-roof that made a sheltered area ruled out the use of a crane. Pierrot had told us that the table would weigh between six and eight hundred pounds. It looked heavier.

He called that evening.

'Are you pleased with the table?'

Yes, the table is wonderful, but there is a problem.

'Have you put it up yet?'

No, that's the problem. Did he have any helpful suggestions?

'A few pairs of arms,' he said. 'Think of the Pyramids.'

Of course. All we needed were fifteen thousand Egyptian slaves and it would be done in no time.

'Well, if you get desperate, I know the rugby team in Carcassonne.'

And with that he laughed and hung up.

We went to have another look at the monster, and tried to work out how many people would be needed to manhandle it into the courtyard. Six? Eight? It would have to be balanced on its side to pass through the doorway. We had visions of crushed toes and multiple hernias, and belatedly understood why the previous owner of the house had put a light, folding table in the place we had chosen for our monument. We took the only reasonable course of action open to us, and sought inspiration in front of the fire with a glass of wine. It was unlikely that anyone would steal the table overnight.

As it turned out, a possible source of help was not long in coming. Weeks before, we had decided to rebuild the kitchen, and had spent many enlightening hours with our architect as we were introduced to French building terminology, to *coffres* and *rehausses* and *faux-plafonds* and *vide-ordures*, to *plâtrage* and *dallage* and *poutrelles* and *coins perdus*. Our initial excitement had turned into anti-climax as the plans became more and more dog-eared and, for one reason or another, the kitchen remained untouched. Delays had been caused by the weather, by the plasterer going skiing, by the chief *maçon* breaking his arm playing football on a motor-bike, by the winter torpor of local suppliers. Our architect, an expatriate Parisian, had warned us that building in Provence was very similar to trench warfare, with long periods of boredom interrupted by bursts of violent and noisy activity, and we had so far experienced the first phase for long enough to look forward to the second.

The assault troops finally arrived, with a deafening clatter, while the morning was still hesitating between dawn and daylight. We went outside with bleary eyes to see what had fallen down, and could just make out the shape of a truck, spiked with scaffolding. A cheerful bellow came from the driver's seat.

'Monsieur Mayle?'

I told him he'd found the right house.

'*Ah bon. On va attaquer la cuisine. Allez!*'

The door opened, and a cocker spaniel jumped out, followed by three men. There was an unexpected whiff of aftershave as the chief *maçon* mangled my hand and introduced himself and his team: Didier, the lieutenant Eric and the junior, a massive young man called Claude. The dog, Pénélope, declared the site open by relieving herself copiously in front of the house, and battle commenced.

We had never seen builders work like this, Everything was done on the double: scaffolding was erected and a ramp of planks was built before the sun was fully up, the kitchen window and sink disappeared minutes later, and by ten o'clock we were standing in a fine layer of preliminary rubble as Didier outlined his plans for destruction. He was brisk and tough, with the cropped hair and straight back of a military man; I could see him as a drill instructor in the Foreign Legion, putting young layabouts through their paces until they whimpered for mercy. His speech was percussive, full of the onomatopoeic words like *tok* and *crak* and *boum* that the French like to use when describing any form of collision or breakage – and there was to be plenty of both. The ceiling was coming down, the floor was coming up and all the existing fittings coming out. It was a gutting job, the entire kitchen to be evacuated – *chut*! – through the hole that used to be a window. A wall of polythene sheeting was nailed up to screen the area from the rest of the house, and domestic catering operations were transferred to the barbecue in the courtyard.

It was startling to see and hear the joyful ferocity with which the three masons pulverised everything within sledgehammer range. They thumped and whistled and sang and swore amid the falling masonry and sagging beams, stopping (with some reluctance, it seemed to me) at noon for lunch. This was demolished with the same vigour as a partition wall – not modest packets of sandwiches, but large plastic hampers filled with chickens and sausage and *choucroute* and salads and loaves of bread, with proper crockery and cutlery. None of them drank alcohol, to our relief. A tipsy mason nominally in charge of a forty-pound hammer was a frightening thought. They were dangerous enough sober.

Pandemonium resumed after lunch, and continued until nearly seven o'clock without any break. I asked Didier if he regularly worked a ten- or eleven-hour day. Only in the winter, he said. In the summer it was twelve or thirteen hours, six days a week. He was amused to hear about the English timetable of a late start and an early finish, with multiple tea breaks. '*Une petite journée*' was how he described it, and asked if I knew any English masons who would like to work with him, just for the experience. I couldn't imagine a rush of volunteers.

When the masons had gone for the day, we dressed for a picnic in the Arctic and started to prepare our first dinner in the temporary kitchen. There was a barbecue fireplace and a fridge. A sink and two gas rings were built into the back of the bar. It had all the basic requirements except walls, and with the temperature still below zero walls would have been a comfort. But the fire of vine clippings was burning brightly, the smell of lamb chops and rosemary was in the air, the red wine was doing noble work as a substitute for central heating, and we felt hardy and adventurous. This delusion lasted through dinner until it was time to go outside and wash the dishes.

* * * * *

The first true intimations of spring came not from early blossom or the skittish behaviour of the rats in Massot's roof, but from England. With the gloom of January behind them, people in London were making holiday plans, and it was astonishing how many of those plans included Provence. With increasing regularity, the phone would ring as we were sitting down to dinner – the caller having a cavalier disregard for the hour's time difference between France and England – and the breezy, half-remembered voice of a distant acquaintance would ask if we were swimming yet. We were always non-committal. It seemed unkind to spoil their illusions by telling them that we were sitting in a permafrost zone with the Mistral screaming through the hole in the kitchen wall and threatening to rip open the polythene sheet which was our only protection against the elements.

The call would continue along a course that quickly became predictable. First, we would be asked if we were going to be at home during Easter or May, or whichever period suited the caller. With that established, the sentence which we soon came to dread – 'We were thinking of coming down around then . . .' – would be delivered, and would dangle, hopeful and unfinished, waiting for a faintly hospitable reaction.

It was difficult to feel flattered by this sudden enthusiasm to see us, which had lain dormant during the years we had lived in England, and it was difficult to know how to deal with it. There is nothing quite as thick-skinned as the seeker after sunshine and free lodging; normal social sidesteps don't work. You're booked up that week? Don't worry – we'll come the week after. You have a house full of builders? We don't mind; we'll be out by the pool anyway. You've stocked the pool with barracuda and put a tank trap in the drive? You've become teetotal vegetarians? You suspect the dogs of carrying rabies? It didn't matter what we said; there was a refusal to take it seriously, a bland determination to overcome any feeble obstacle we might invent.

We talked about the threatened invasions to other people who had moved to Provence, and they had all been through it. The first summer, they said, is invariably hell. After that, you learn to say no. If you don't, you will find yourselves running a small and highly unprofitable hotel from Easter until the end of September.

Sound but depressing advice. We waited nervously for the next phone call.

* * * * *

Life had changed, and the masons had changed it. If we got up at 6.30 we could have breakfast in peace. Any later, and the sound effects from the kitchen made conversation impossible. One morning when the drills and hammers were in full song, I could see my wife's lips move, but no words were reaching me. Eventually she passed me a note: Drink your coffee before it gets dirty.

But progress was being made. Having reduced the kitchen to a shell, the masons started, just as noisily, to rebuild, bringing all their materials up the plank ramp and through a window-sized space ten feet above the ground. Their stamina was extraordinary, and Didier – half-man, half fork-lift truck – was somehow able to run up the bouncing ramp pushing a wheelbarrow of wet cement, a cigarette in one side of his mouth and breath enough to whistle out of the other. I shall never know how the three of them were able to work in a confined space, under cold and difficult conditions, and remain so resolutely good-humoured.

Gradually, the structure of the kitchen took shape and the follow-up squad came to inspect it and to coordinate their various contributions. There was Ramon the plasterer, with his plaster-covered radio and basketball boots, Mastorino the painter, Trufelli the tile-layer, Zanchi the carpenter, and the *chef-plombier* himself, with *jeune* two paces behind him on an invisible lead, Monsieur Menicucci. There were often six or seven of them all talking at once among the debris, arguing about dates and availabilities while Christian, the architect, acted as referee.

It occurred to us that, if this energy could be channelled for an hour or so, we had enough bodies and biceps to shift the stone table into the courtyard. When I suggested this, there was instant co-operation. Why not do it now, they said. Why not indeed? We clambered out of the kitchen window and gathered round the table, which was covered with a white puckered skin of frost. Twelve hands grasped the slab and twelve arms strained to lift it. There was not the slightest movement. Teeth were sucked thoughtfully, and everyone walked round the table looking at it until Menicucci put his finger on the problem. The stone is porous, he said. It is filled with water like a sponge. the water has frozen, the stone has frozen, the ground has frozen. *Voilà!* It is immovable. You must wait until it has thawed. There was some desultory talk about blow-lamps and crowbars, but Menicucci put a stop to that, dismissing it as *patati-patata*, which I took to mean nonsense. The group dispersed.

With the house full of noise and dust six days a week, the oasis of Sunday was even more welcome than usual. We could lie in until the luxurious hour of 7.30 before the dogs began agitating for a walk, we could talk to each other without having to go outside, and we could console ourselves with the thought that we were one week closer to the end of the chaos and disruption. What we couldn't do, because of the limited cooking facilities, was to celebrate Sunday as it should always be celebrated in France, with a long and carefully judged lunch. And so, using the temporary kitchen as an excuse, we leapt rather than fell into the habit of eating out on Sunday.

As an appetiser, we would consult the oracular books, and came to depend more and more on the Gault-Millau guide. The Michelin is invaluable, and nobody should travel through France without it, but it is confined to the bare bones of prices and grades and specialities. Gault-Millau gives you the flesh as well. It will tell you about the chef – if he's young, where he was trained; if he's established, whether he's resting on his past success or still trying hard. It will tell you about the chef's wife, whether she is welcoming or *glaciale*. It will give you some indication of the style of the restaurant, and if there's a view or a pretty terrace. It will comment on the service and the clientele, on the prices and the atmosphere. And, often in great detail, on the food and the wine list. It is not infallible, and it is certainly not entirely free from prejudice, but it is amusing and always interesting and, because it is written in colloquial French, good homework for novices in the language like us.

The 1987 guide lists 5,500 restaurants and hotels in a suitably orotund and well-stuffed volume, and picking through it we came across a local entry that sounded irresistible. It was a restaurant at

Lambesc, about half an hour's drive away. The chef was a woman, described as '*l'une des plus fameuses cuisinières de Provence*', her dining room was a converted mill, and her cooking was '*pleine de force et de soleil*'. That would have been enough of a recommendation in itself, but what intrigued us most was the age of the chef. She was eighty.

It was grey and windy when we arrived in Lambesc. We still suffered twinges of guilt if we stayed indoors on a beautiful day, but this Sunday was bleak and miserable, the streets smeared with old snow, the inhabitants hurrying home from the bakery with bread clutched to the chest and shoulders hunched against the cold. It was perfect lunch weather.

We were early, and the huge vaulted dining room was empty. It was furnished with handsome Provençal antiques, heavy and dark and highly polished. The tables were large and so well-spaced that they were almost remote from each other, a luxury usually reserved for grand and formal restaurants. The sound of voices and the clatter of saucepans came from the kitchen, and something smelt delicious, but we had obviously anticipated opening time by a few minutes. We started to tiptoe out to find a drink in a café.

'Who are you?' a voice said.

An old man had emerged from the kitchen and was peering at us, screwing up his eyes against the light coming through the door. We told him we'd made a reservation for lunch.

'Sit down, then. You can't eat standing up.' He waved airily at the empty tables. We sat down obediently, and waited while he came slowly over with two menus. He sat down with us.

'American? German?'

English.

'Good,' he said, 'I was with the English in the war.'

We felt that we had passed the first test. One more correct answer and we might be allowed to see the menus which the old man was keeping to himself. I asked him what he would recommend.

'Everything,' he said. 'My wife cooks everything well.'

He dealt the menus out and left us to greet another couple, and we dithered enjoyably between lamb stuffed with herbs, *daube*, veal with truffles and an unexplained dish called the *fantaisie du chef.* The old man came back and sat down, listened to the order and nodded.

'It's always the same,' he said. 'It's the men who like the *fantaisie.*'

I asked for a half-bottle of white wine to go with the first course, and some red to follow.

'No,' he said, 'you're wrong.' He told us what to drink, and it was a red Côtes du Rhône from Visan. Good wine and good women came from Visan, he said. He got up and fetched a bottle from a vast dark cupboard.

'There. You'll like that.' (Later, we noticed that everybody had the same wine on their table.)

He went off to the kitchen, the oldest head waiter in the world, to pass our order to perhaps the oldest practising chef in France. We thought we heard a third voice from the kitchen, but there were no other waiters, and we wondered how two people with a combined age of over 160 managed to cope with the long hours and hard work. And yet, as the restaurant became busier, there were no delays, no neglected tables. In his unhurried and stately way, the old man made his rounds, sitting down from time to time for a chat with his clients. When an order was ready, Madame would clang a bell in the kitchen and her husband would raise his eyebrows in pretended irritation. If he continued talking, the bell would clang again, more insistently, and off he would go, muttering '*j'arrive, j'arrive*'.

The food was everything the Gault-Millau guide had promised, and the old man had been right about the wine. We did like it. And, by the time he served the tiny rounds of goats' cheese marinated in herbs and olive oil, we had finished it. I asked for another half-bottle, and he looked at me disapprovingly.

'Who's driving?'

'My wife.'

He went again to the dark cupboard. 'There are no half-bottles,' he said, 'you can drink as far as here.' He drew an imaginary line with his finger half way down the new bottle.

The kitchen bell had stopped clanging and Madame came out, smiling and rosy-faced from the heat of the ovens, to ask us if we had eaten well. She looked like a woman of sixty. The two of them stood together, his hand on her shoulder, while she talked about the antique furniture, which had been her dowry, and he interrupted. They were happy with each other and they loved their work, and we left the restaurant feeling that old age might not be so bad after all.

* * * * *

Ramon the plasterer was lying on his back on a precarious platform, an arm's-length below the kitchen ceiling. I passed a beer up to him, and he leant sideways on one elbow to drink it. It looked like an uncomfortable position, either for drinking or working, but he said he was used to it.

'Anyway,' he said, 'you can't stand on the floor and throw stuff up. That one who did the ceiling of the Sistine Chapel – you know, that Italian – he must have been on his back for weeks.'

Ramon finished the beer, his fifth of the day, handed down the empty bottle, belched lightly and returned to his labours. He had a slow, rhythmical style, flicking the plaster on to the ceiling with his trowel and working it into a chunky smoothness with a roll of his wrist. He said that, when it was finished, it would look as though it had been there for a hundred years. He didn't believe in rollers or sprayers or instruments of any sort apart from his trowel and his eye for a line and a curve, which he said was infallible. One evening after he had gone I checked his surfaces with a spirit level. They were all true, and yet they were unmistakably the work of a hand rather than a machine. The man was an artist, and well worth his beer ration.

A breeze was coming through the hole in the kitchen wall, and it felt almost mild. I could hear something dripping. When I went outside I found that the seasons had changed. The stone table was oozing water, and spring had arrived.

* * * * *

MARCH

The almond tree was in tentative blossom. The days were longer, often ending with magnificent evenings of corrugated pink skies. The hunting season was over, with hounds and guns put away for six months. The vineyards were busy again as the well-organised farmers treated their vines and their more lackadaisical neighbours hurried to do the pruning they should have done in November. The people of Provence greeted spring with uncharacteristic briskness, as if nature had given everyone an injection of sap.

The markets changed abruptly. On the stalls, fishing tackle and ammunition belts and waterproof boots and long brushes with steel bristles for amateur chimney-sweeps were replaced by displays of ferocious-looking agricultural implements – machetes and grubbing tools, scythes and hoes with sharp curved prongs, spraying equipment that was guaranteed to bring the rain of death down on any weed or insect foolhardy enough to threaten the grapes. Flowers and plants and tiny new season vegetables were everywhere, and café tables and chairs sprouted on the pavements. There was a feeling of activity and purpose in the air, and one or two optimists were already buying espadrilles from the multi-coloured racks outside the shoe shops.

In contrast to this bustle, work on the house had come to a standstill. Following some primeval springtime urge, the builders had migrated, leaving us with some token sacks of plaster and piles of sand as proof of their intention to come back – one day – and finish what they had so nearly finished. The phenomenon of the vanishing builder is well known throughout the world, but in Provence the problem has its own local refinements and frustrations, and its own clearly defined seasons.

Three times a year, at Easter, August and Christmas, the owners of holiday homes escape from Paris and Zürich and Düsseldorf and London to come down for a few days or weeks of the simple country life. Invariably, before they come, they think of something that is crucial to the success of their holiday: a set of Courrèges bidets, a searchlight in the swimming pool, a re-tiled terrace, a new roof for the servants' quarters. How can they possibly enjoy their rustic interlude without these essentials? In panic, they telephone the local builders and craftsmen. Get it done – it *must* be done – before we arrive. Implicit in these urgent instructions is the understanding that generous payments will be forthcoming if the work is done at once. Speed is of the essence; money isn't.

It is too tempting to ignore. Everyone remembers when Mitterrand first came to power; the rich went into financial paralysis, and sat on their cash. Building work was scarce in Provence then, and who knows when bad times might come again? So the jobs are accepted, and less clamorous clients suddenly find themselves with dormant concrete-mixers and forlorn, uncompleted rooms. Faced with this situation, there are two ways to respond. Neither of them will produce immediate results, but one way will reduce the frustration, and the other will add to it.

We tried both. To begin with, we made a conscious effort to become more philosophical in our attitude to time, to treat days and weeks of delays in the Provençal fashion – that is, to enjoy the sunshine and to stop thinking like city people. This month, next month, what's the difference? Have a pastis and relax. It worked well enough for a week or two, and then we noticed that the building materials at the back of the house were turning green with the first growth of spring weeds. We decided to change our tactics and get some firm dates out of our small and elusive team of workmen. It was an educational experience.

We learned that time in Provence is a very elastic commodity, even when it is described in clear and specific terms. *Un petit quart d'heure* means some time today. *Demain* means some time this week. And, the most elastic time segment of all, *une quinzaine* can mean three weeks, two months or next year, but never, ever does it mean fifteen days. We learned also to interpret the hand language that accompanies any discussion of deadlines. When a Provençal looks you in the eye and tells you that he will be hammering on your door ready to start work next Tuesday for certain, the behaviour of his hands is all-important. If they are still, or patting you reassuringly on the arm, you can expect him on Tuesday. If one hand is held out at waist height, palm downwards, and begins to rock from side to side, adjust the timetable to Wednesday or Thursday. If the rocking develops into an agitated waggle, he's really talking about next week or God knows when, depending on circumstances beyond his control. These unspoken disclaimers, which seem to be instinctive and therefore more revealing than speech, are occasionally reinforced by the magic word *normalement*, a supremely versatile escape clause worthy of an insurance policy. *Normalement* – providing it doesn't rain, providing the truck hasn't broken down, providing the brother-in-law hasn't borrowed the tool box – is the Provençal builder's equivalent of the fine print in a contract, and we came to regard it with infinite suspicion.

But, despite their genial contempt for punctuality and their absolute refusal to use the telephone to say when they were coming or when they weren't, we could never stay irritated with them for long. They were always disarmingly cheerful, they worked long and hard when they were with us, and their work was excellent. In the end, they were worth waiting for. And so, little by little, we reverted to being philosophical, and came to terms with the Provençal clock. From now on, we told ourselves, we would assume that nothing would be done when we expected it to be done; the fact that it happened at all would be enough.

* * * * *

Faustin was behaving curiously. For two or three days he had been clanking up and down on his tractor, towing a contraption of metal intestines which spewed fertiliser to either side as he passed between the rows of vines. He kept stopping to get off the tractor and walk over to a field, now empty and overgrown, which had been planted with melons. He studied the field from one end, remounted his tractor, sprayed some more vines, and returned to study the other end. He paced, he pondered, he scratched his head. When he went home for lunch, I walked down to see what it was he found so fascinating, but to me it looked like any other fallow melon field – a few weeds, some tatters of plastic left over from the strips that had protected last year's crop, half an acre of nothing. I wondered if Faustin suspected it of harbouring buried treasure, because we had already dug up two gold Napoleon coins nearer the house, and he had told us that there were probably more to be found. But peasants don't hide their gold in the middle of cultivated land when it can be squirrelled away more securely under the flagstones or down a well. It was odd.

He came visiting that evening with Henriette, looking unusually spruce and businesslike in his white shoes and orange shirt, and bearing jars of home made rabbit pâté. Half way through his first pastis, he leant forward confidentially. Did we know that the wine produced from our vineyards – Côtes du Lubéron – was about to be given *Appellation Contrôlée* status? He leant back, nodding slowly, and said '*Eh oui*' several times while we absorbed the news. Clearly, said Faustin, the wine would become more expensive and vineyard-owners would make more money. And, clearly, the more vines one has the more money one makes.

There was no arguing with that, so Faustin moved on to a second drink – he drank in an efficient, unobtrusive way, and always reached the bottom of his glass before I expected – and put forward his proposition. It seemed to him that our melon field could be more profitably employed. He inhaled some pastis while Henriette produced a document from her bag. It was a *droit d'implantation*, giving us the right to plant vines, a privilege

42

accorded to us by the government itself. While we looked at the paper, Faustin demolished the nonsensical idea of continuing to grow melons, dismissing them with a wave of his glass as being too demanding in terms of time and water, and always vulnerable to attack by the wild boar who come down from the mountains in the summer. Only last year, Faustin's brother Jacky had lost a third of his melon crop. Eaten by the boars! The profit disappearing into a pig's belly! Faustin shook his head at the painful memory, and had to be revived by a third large pastis.

By chance, he said, he had made some calculations. Our field would accommodate 1,300 new vines in place of the tiresome melons. My wife and I looked at each other. We were equally fond of wine and Faustin, and he obviously had his heart set on progress and expansion. We agreed that the extra vines sounded like a good idea, but thought no more about it after he had left. Faustin is a ruminant among men, not given to hasty action, and in any case, nothing happens quickly in Provence. Perhaps next spring he would get round to it.

At seven o'clock the following morning, a tractor was ploughing up the melon field, and two days later the planting team arrived – five men, two women and four dogs, under the direction of the *chef des vignes* Monsieur Beauchier, a man with forty years' experience of planting vines in the Lubéron. He personally pushed the small plough behind the tractor, making sure that lines were straight and correctly spaced, trudging up and down in his canvas boots, his leathery face rapt in concentration. The lines were staked at each end by bamboo rods and marked by lengths of twine. The field was now stripped and ready to be turned into a vineyard.

The new vines, about the size of my thumb and tipped with red wax, were unloaded from the vans while Monsieur Beauchier inspected his planting equipment. I had assumed that the planting would be done mechanically, but all I could see were a few hollow steel rods and a large triangle made of wood. The planting team gathered round and were assigned their duties, then jostled untidily into formation.

Beauchier led the way with the wooden triangle, which he used like a three-sided wheel, the points making equidistant marks in the earth. Two men followed him with steel rods, plunging them into the marks to make holes for the vines, which were planted and firmed in by the rearguard. The two women, Faustin's wife and daughter, dispensed vines, advice and fashion comments on the assortment of hats worn by the men, particularly Faustin's new and slightly rakish yachting cap. The dogs enjoyed themselves by getting in everyone's way, dodging kicks and tangling themselves in the twine.

As the day wore on, the planters became more widely spaced with Beauchier often two hundred yards in front of the stragglers at the back, but distance was no barrier to conversation. It appears to be part of the ritual that lengthy discussions are always conducted between the two people furthest away from each other, while the intervening members of the team curse the dogs and argue about the straightness of the lines. And so the raucous procession moved up and down the field until mid-afternoon, when Henriette produced two large baskets and work stopped for the Provençal version of a coffee break.

The team sat on a grassy bank above the vines, looking like a scene from Cartier-Bresson's scrapbook, and attacked the contents of the baskets. There were four litres of wine and an enormous pile of the sugared slices of fried bread called *tranches dorées*, dark gold in colour and crisp and delicious to taste. Grandfather André arrived to inspect what had been done, and we saw him poking the earth critically with his stick and then nodding his head. He came over for a glass of wine and sat in the sun, a benign old lizard, scratching a dog's stomach with the end of his muddy stick and asking Henriette what was for dinner. He wanted to eat early so that he could watch *Santa Barbara*, his favourite television soap opera.

The wine had all gone. The men stretched and brushed the crumbs from their mouths and went back to work. By late evening it was finished, and the ragged old melon field was now impeccable, the tiny dots of new vines just visible against the setting sun. The team gathered in our courtyard to unkink their backs and make inroads on the pastis, and I took Faustin to one side to ask him about payment. We'd had the tractor for three days, and dozens of hours of labour. What did we owe them? Faustin was so anxious to explain that he put down his glass. We would pay for the

vines, he said, but the rest was taken care of by the system which operated in the valley, with everyone contributing their time free when major replanting had to be done. It all evened out in the end, he said, and it avoided paperwork and tedious dealings with *les fiscs* about taxes. He smiled and tapped the side of his nose with a finger and then, as though it was a small matter hardly worth mentioning, he asked if we would like 250 asparagus plants put in while we still had the use of the tractor and the men. It was done the next day. So much for our theory that nothing happens fast in Provence.

* * * * *

The Lubéron sounded different in spring. Birds who had been ducking all winter came out of hiding now that the hunters were gone, and their song replaced gunfire. The only jarring noise I could hear as I walked along the path towards the Massot residence was a furious hammering, and I wondered if he had decided to put up a For Sale notice in preparation for the beginning of the tourist season.

I found him on the track beyond his house, contemplating a five-foot stake that he had planted at the edge of a clearing. A rusty piece of tin had been nailed to the top of the stake, with a single angry word daubed in white paint: *PRIVÉ!* Three more stakes and notices were lying on the track, together with a pile of boulders. Massot was obviously intending to barricade the clearing. He grunted good morning and picked up another stake, hammering it into the ground as if it had just insulted his mother.

I asked him what he was doing.

'Keeping out the Germans,' he said, and started to roll boulders into a rough cordon between the stakes.

The piece of land that he was sealing off was some distance from his house, and on the forest side of the track. It couldn't possibly belong to him, and I said I thought it was part of the national park.

'That's right,' he said, 'but I'm French. So it's more mine than the Germans.' He moved another boulder. 'Every summer they come here and put up their tents and make *merde* all over the forest.'

He straightened up and lit a cigarette, tossing the empty packet into the bushes. I asked him if he had thought that maybe one of the Germans might buy his house.

'Germans with tents don't buy anything except bread,' he said with a sniff of disdain. 'You should see their cars – stuffed with German sausage, German beer, tins of sauerkraut. They bring it all with them. Mean? They're real *pisse-vinaigres*.'

Massot, in his new role as protector of the countryside and authority on the economics of tourism, went on to explain the problem of the peasant in Provence. He admitted that tourists – even German tourists – brought money to the area, and that people who bought houses provided work for local builders. But look what they had done to property prices! It was a scandal. No farmer could afford to pay them. We tactfully avoided any discussion of Massot's own attempts at property speculation, and he sighed at the injustice of it all. Then he cheered up, and told me a house-buying story that had ended to his complete satisfaction.

There was a peasant who for years had coveted his neighbour's house; not for the house itself, which was almost a ruin, but for the land that was attached to it. He offered to buy the property, but his neighbour, taking advantage of the sharp rise in house prices, accepted a higher offer from a Parisian.

During the winter, the Parisian spent millions of francs renovating the house and installing a swimming pool. Finally, the work is finished, and the Parisian and his chic friends come down for the long First of May weekend. They are charmed by the house and amused by the quaint old peasant who lives next door, particularly by his habit of going to bed at 8 o'clock.

The Parisian household is awakened at four in the morning by Charlemagne, the peasant's large and noisy cockerel, who crows non-stop for two hours. The Parisian complains to the peasant. The peasant shrugs. It is the country. Cocks must crow. That is normal.

The next morning, and the morning after that, Charlemagne is up and crowing at four o'clock. Tempers are getting frayed, and the guests return to Paris early, to catch up on their sleep. The Parisian complains again to the peasant, and again the peasant shrugs. They part on hostile terms.

In August, the Parisian returns with a house full of guests. Charlemagne wakes them punctually every morning at four. Attempts at afternoon naps are foiled by the peasant, who is doing some work on his house with a jack-hammer and a loud concrete-mixer. The Parisian insists that the peasant silences his cockerel. The peasant refuses. After several heated exchanges, the Parisian takes the peasant to court, seeking an injunction to restrain Charlemagne. The verdict is in favour of the peasant, and the cockerel continues his early morning serenades.

Visits to the house eventually become so intolerable that the Parisian puts it up for sale. The peasant, acting through a friend, manages to buy most of the land.

The Sunday after the purchase goes through, the peasant and his friend celebrate with a huge lunch, the main course of which is Charlemagne, turned into a delicious *coq au vin*.

Massot thought that this was a fine story – defeat for the Parisian, victory and more land for the peasant, a good lunch – it had everything. I asked him if it was true, and he looked at me sideways, sucking on the ragged end of his moustache. 'It doesn't do to cross a peasant' was all he would say, and I thought that if I was a German camper I'd try Spain this summer.

*****

Every day, as the weather stayed mild, there was fresh evidence of growth and greenery, and one of the most verdant patches of all was the swimming pool, which had turned a bilious emerald in the sunshine. It was time to call Bernard the *pisciniste* with his algae-fighting equipment before the plant life started crawling out of the deep end and through the front door.

A job like this is never done in Provence simply on the basis of a phone call and a verbal explanation. There has to be a preliminary visit of inspection – to walk around the problem, to nod knowingly, to have a drink or two and then to make another rendezvous. It is a kind of limbering-up exercise, only to be skipped in cases of real emergency.

On the evening Bernard arrived to look at the pool, I was scrubbing at the garland of green fur that had developed just above the water line, and he watched me for a few moments before squatting down on his haunches and wagging a finger under my nose. Somehow I knew what his first word would be.

'*Non,*' he said, 'you mustn't scrub it. You must treat it. I will bring a product.' We abandoned the green fur and went indoors for a drink, and Bernard explained why he hadn't been able to come earlier. He had been suffering from toothache, but couldn't find a local dentist who was prepared to treat him, because of his strange affliction: he bites dentists. He can't stop himself. It is an incurable reflex. The moment he feels an exploratory finger in his mouth – *tak*!– he bites. He had so far bitten the only dentist in Bonnieux, and four dentists in Cavaillon, and had been obliged to go to Avignon, where he was unknown in dental circles. Fortunately, he had found a dentist who fought back with anaesthetic, knocking Bernard out completely while the repair work was done. The dentist told him afterwards that he had a mouthful of eighteenth-century teeth.

Eighteenth-century or not, they looked very white and healthy against Bernard's black beard as he laughed and talked. He was a man of great charm and, although born and raised in Provence, not at all a country bumpkin. He drank Scotch, the older the better, rather than pastis, and had married a girl from Paris whom we suspected of having a hand in the contents of his wardrobe. Not for him the canvas boots and the old blue trousers and frayed and faded shirts that we were used to seeing; Bernard was dapper, from his soft leather shoes to his large assortment of designer sunglasses. We wondered what kind of ensemble he would wear for the work of chlorinating and barnacle-scraping that was needed before the pool was ready for human occupation.

The day of the spring clean arrived, and Bernard bounded up the steps in sunglasses, grey flannels and blazer, twirling an umbrella in case the rain promised by the weather forecast should come our way. Following him with some difficulty was the secret of his continued elegance, a small, scruffy man weighed down with tubs of chlorine, brushes and a suction pump. This was Gaston, who was actually going to do the job under Bernard's supervision.

Later that morning, I went out to see how they were getting on.

A fine drizzle had set in, and the sodden Gaston was wrestling with the serpentine coils of the suction hose while Bernard, blazer slung nonchalantly round his shoulders, was directing operations from the shelter of his umbrella. There, I thought, is a man who understands how to delegate. If anyone could help us move our stone table into the courtyard, surely it was Bernard. I took him away from his duties at the poolside and we went to study the situation.

The table looked, bigger, heavier and more permanently settled in its garnish of weeds than ever, but Bernard was not discouraged. '*C'est pas méchant,*' he said, 'I know a man who could do it in half an hour.' I imagined a sweating giant heaving the great slabs around as a change from winning tug-of-war contests with teams of horses, but it was more prosaic than that. Bernard's man had just acquired a machine called *un bob*, a scaled-down version of a fork-lift truck, narrow enough to pass through the courtyard doorway. *Voilà!* It sounded easy.

The owner of *le bob* was telephoned and arrived within half an hour, eager to put his new machine into active service. He measured the width of the doorway and assessed the weight of the table. No problem; *bob* could do it. There was a small adjustment to be made here and there, but a mason could take care of that. It was merely a question of removing the lintel over the doorway – just for five minutes – to provide sufficient height for the load to pass through. I looked at the lintel. It was another piece of stone, four feet wide, nine inches thick and deeply embedded in the side of the house. It was major demolition, even to my inexpert eye. The table stayed where it was.

The wretched thing had become a daily frustration. Here we were with hot weather and the outdoor eating season just around the corner – the days we had dreamed about back in England and through the winter – and we had nowhere to put a bowl of olives, let alone a five-course lunch. We seriously considered calling Pierrot at the quarry and asking for an introduction to the Carcassonne rugby team, and then Providence arrived with a screech of brakes and a dusty cocker spaniel.

Didier had been working at a house on the other side of Saint-Rémy, and had been approached by a uniformed *gendarme*.

Would there be any interest, the *gendarme* wondered, in a load of weathered stone, the old, lichen-covered stuff, that could be used to give a new wall instant antiquity? It so happened that one of the jobs on Didier's long list was to build a wall at the front of our house, and he thought of us. The officer of the law wanted to be paid *au noir*, in cash, but stone like that was not easy to find. Would we like it?

We would happily have agreed to half a ton of bird droppings if it meant getting Didier and his entourage back; we had often thought of them as movers of the table before they disappeared, and this seemed like a wink from the gods. Yes, we would have the stone, and could he give us a hand with the table? He looked at it and grinned. 'Seven men,' he said. 'I'll come on Saturday with two when I bring the stone if you can find the rest.' We had a deal, and soon we would have a table. My wife started planning the first outdoor lunch of the year.

We lured three more or less able-bodied young men with the promise of food and drink, and when Didier and his assistants arrived the seven of us took up our positions round the table to go through the ritual of spitting on hands and deciding how best to negotiate the fifteen-yard journey. In circumstances like these, every Frenchman is an expert, and various theories were advanced: the table should be rolled on logs; no, it should be pulled on a wooden pallet; nonsense, it could be pushed most of the way by truck. Didier let everyone finish, and then ordered us to pick it up, two to each side, with him taking one side on his own.

With a reluctant squelch, the slab came out of the ground, and we staggered the first five yards, veins popping with effort while Didier kept up a running commentary of directions. Another five yards, and then we had to stop to turn it so that it could get through the doorway. The weight was brutal, and we were already sweating and aching, and at least one of us thought that he was getting a little old for this kind of work, but the table was now on its side and ready to be inched into the courtyard.

'This,' said Didier, 'is the amusing part.' There was only enough room for two men either side of the slab, and they would have to take the weight while the others pushed and pulled. Two enormous webbing straps were passed under the table, there was more spitting on hands, and my wife disappeared into the house, unable to watch the mashing of feet and four men having simultaneous ruptures. 'Whatever you do,' said Didier, 'don't drop it. *Allez!*' And with curses and skinned knuckles and a chorus of grunts that would have done credit to an elephant in labour, the table slowly crossed the threshold and at long last entered the courtyard.

We compared wounds and sprains before setting up the base – a relatively insignificant structure weighing no more than 300 pounds – and coating its top with cement. One final heave, and the slab went on, but Didier wasn't satisfied; it was a hair's-breadth off centre. Eric the chief assistant was required to kneel under the table on all fours. He supported most of the weight on his back while the top was centred, and I wondered if my insurance covered death on the premises by crushing. To my relief, Eric surfaced without any visible injury, although, as Didier said cheerfully, it's the internal damage that slows a man down in his line of work. I hoped he was joking.

Beers were passed round, and the table was admired. It looked just as we'd imagined on that afternoon in February when we had traced the outline in the snow. It was a good size, and handsome against the stone of the courtyard wall. The perspiration stains and smudges of blood would soon dry off, and then lunch could be served.

In our anticipation of all the pleasures of long outdoor meals there was only one slight regret, because we were coming to the very end of the season for that ugly but delicious fungus which is almost worth its weight in gold, the fresh Vaucluse truffle.

The truffle world is secretive, but strangers can get a glimpse of it by going to one of the villages round Carpentras. There, the cafés do a brisk trade in breakfast jolts of *marc* and Calvados, and an unknown face coming through the door brings muttered conversations to a sudden stop. Outside, men stand in tight, preoccupied groups looking, sniffing and finally weighing wart-encrusted, earth-covered lumps that are handled with reverential care. Money passes, fat, grimy wads of it, in 100, 200 and 500 franc notes, which are double-checked with much licking of thumbs. Attention from outsiders is not welcomed.

This informal market is an early stage in the process which leads to the tables of three-star restaurants and the counters of ruinously expensive Parisian delicatessens like Fauchon and Hédiard. But even here in the middle of nowhere, buying direct from men with dirt under their fingernails and yesterday's garlic on their breath, with dented, wheezing cars, with old baskets or plastic bags instead of smart attaché cases – even here, the prices are, as they like to say, *très sérieux*. Truffles are sold by weight, and the standard unit is the kilo. At 1987 prices, a kilo of truffles bought in the village market cost at least 2,000 francs, payable in cash. Cheques are not accepted, receipts are never given, because the *truffiste* is not anxious to participate in the crackpot government scheme the rest of us call income tax.

So the starting price is 2,000 francs a kilo. With a little massaging along the way from various agents and middlemen, by the time the truffle reaches its spiritual home in the kitchens of Bocuse or Troisgros the price will probably have doubled. At Fauchon, it could easily have reached 5,000 francs a kilo, but at least they accept cheques.

There are two reasons why these absurd prices continue to be paid, and continue to rise – the first, obviously, being that nothing in the world smells or tastes like fresh truffles except fresh truffles. The second is that, despite all the effort and ingenuity that the French have brought to bear on the problem, they haven't been able to cultivate the truffle. They continue to try, and it is not uncommon in the Vaucluse to come across fields that have been planted with truffle-oaks and keep-off notices. But the propagation of truffles seems to be a haphazard affair which is only understood by nature – thus adding to the rarity and the price – and human attempts at truffle breeding haven't come to much. Until they do, there is only one way to enjoy truffles without spending a small fortune, and that is to find them yourself.

We were lucky enough to be given a free course in truffle-hunting techniques by our almost resident expert, Ramon the plasterer. He had tried everything over the years, and admitted to some modest success. He was generous with his advice and, as he smoothed on his plaster and drank his beer, he told us exactly what to do. (He didn't tell us where to go, but then no truffle man would.)

It all depends, he said, on timing, knowledge and patience, and the possession of a pig, a trained hound or a stick. Truffles grow a few centimetres under the ground, on the roots of certain oak or hazel-nut trees. During the season, from November until March, they can be tracked down by nose, providing you have sensitive enough equipment. The supreme truffle detector is the pig, who is born with a fondness for the taste, and whose sense of smell in this case is superior to the dog's. But there is a snag: the pig is not content to wag his tail and point when he has discovered a truffle. He wants to eat it. In fact, he is desperate to eat it. And, as Ramon said, you cannot reason with a pig on the brink of gastronomic ecstasy. He is not easily distracted, nor is he of a size you can fend off with one hand while you rescue the truffle with the other. There he is, as big as a small tractor, rigid with porcine determination and refusing to be budged. Given this fundamental design fault, we weren't surprised when Ramon told us that the lighter and more amenable dog had become increasingly popular.

Unlike pigs, dogs do not instinctively rootle for truffles; they have to be trained, and Ramon favoured the *saucisson* method. You take a slice and rub it with a truffle, or dip it in truffle juice, so that the dog begins to associate the smell of truffles with a taste of heaven. Little by little, or by leaps and bounds if the dog is both intelligent and a gourmet, he will come to share your enthusiasm for truffles, and he will be ready for field trials. If your training has been thorough, if your dog is temperamentally suited to the work, and if you know where to go, you might find yourself with a *chien truffier* who will point the way to the buried treasure. Then, just as he begins to dig for it, you bribe him away with a slice of treated sausage and uncover what you hope will be a lump of black gold.

Ramon himself had eventually settled on another method, the stick technique, which he demonstrated for us, tiptoeing across the kitchen with an imaginary wand held in front of him. Once again, you have to know where to go, but this time you have to wait for the right weather conditions as well. When the sun is shining on the roots of a likely-looking oak, approach cautiously and, with your stick, prod gently around the base of the tree. If a startled fly should rise vertically from the vegetation, mark the spot and dig.

You might have disturbed a member of the fly family whose genetic passion is to lay its eggs on the truffle (doubtless adding a certain *je ne sais quoi* to the flavour). Many peasants in the Vaucluse had adopted this technique because walking around with a stick is less conspicuous than walking around with a pig, and secrecy can be more easily preserved. Truffle hunters like to protect their sources.

The finding of truffles, chancy and unpredictable though it is, began to seem almost straightforward when compared with the skulduggery that goes on in the sales and distribution department. With the relish of an investigative reporter, and frequent winks and nudges, Ramon took us through the most common of the murky practices.

With everything edible in France, certain areas have the reputation for producing the best – the best olives from Nyons, the best mustard from Dijon, the best melons from Cavaillon, the best cream from Normandy. The best truffles, it is generally agreed, come from the Périgord, and naturally one pays more for them. But how do you know that the truffle you buy in Cahors hasn't been dug up several hundred kilometres away in the Vaucluse? Unless you know and trust your supplier, you can't be sure, and Ramon's inside information was that 50 per cent of the truffles sold in the Périgord were born elsewhere and 'naturalised'.

Then there is the uncanny business of the truffle which somehow gains weight between leaving the ground and arriving on the scales. It could be that it has been gift-wrapped in an extra coating of earth. On the other hand, it could be that a heavier substance altogether has found its way inside the truffle itself – invisible until, in mid-slice, your knife lays bare a sliver of metal. *Ils sont vilains, ces types!* Even if you are prepared to sacrifice the flavour of fresh truffles for the protection offered by the canned variety – even then, you can't be sure. One hears rumours. It has been hinted that some French cans with French labels actually contain Italian or Spanish truffles. (Which, if true, must be one of the most profitable and least publicised acts of co-operation ever between Common Market countries.)

Yet, for all the whispers of chicanery and prices which become more ridiculous each year, the French continue to follow their noses and dig into their pockets, and we found ourselves doing the same when we heard that the last truffles of the season were being served at one of our favourite local restaurants.

Chez Michel is the village bar of Cabrières and the headquarters of the *boules* club, and not sufficiently upholstered or pompous to attract too much attention from the Guide Michelin inspectors. Old men play cards in the front; clients of the restaurant eat very well in the back. The owner cooks, Madame his wife takes the orders, members of the family help at table and in the kitchens. It is a comfortable neighbourhood *bistrot* with no apparent intention of joining the culinary merry-go-round which turns talented cooks into brand names and pleasant restaurants into temples of the expense account.

Madame sat us down and gave us a drink, and we asked how the truffles were. She rolled her eyes and an expression close to pain crossed her face. For a moment we thought they had all gone, but it was simply her reaction to one of life's many unfairnesses, which she then explained to us.

Her husband Michel loves to cook with fresh truffles. He has his suppliers, and he pays, as everyone must, in cash, without the benefit of a receipt. For him, this is a substantial and legitimate business cost which cannot be set against the profits because there is no supporting evidence on paper to account for the outlay. Also, he refuses to raise the price of his menus, even when they are studded with truffles, to a level which might offend his regular customers. (In winter, the clientele is local, and careful with its money; the big spenders don't usually come down until Easter.)

This was the problem, and Madame was doing her best to be philosophical about it as she showed us a copper pan containing several thousand francs' worth of non-deductible truffles. We asked her why Michel did it, and she gave a classic shrug – shoulders and eyebrows going upwards in unison, corners of the mouth turning down. '*Pour faire plaisir,*' she said.

We had omelettes. They were moist and fat and fluffy, with a tiny deep black nugget of truffle in every mouthful, a last rich taste of winter. We wiped our plates with bread and tried to guess what a treat like this would cost in London, and came to the conclusion that we had just eaten a bargain. Comparison with London is a sure way of justifying any minor extravagance in Provence.

Michel came out of the kitchen to make his rounds and noticed our bone-clean plates. 'They were good, the truffles?' Better than good, we said. He told us that the dealer who had sold them to him – one of the old rogues in the business – had just been robbed. The thief had taken a cardboard box stuffed with cash, more than 100,000 francs, but the dealer hadn't dared to report the loss for fear that embarrassing questions might be asked about where the money had come from. Now he was pleading poverty. Next year his prices would be higher. *C'est la vie.*

We got home to find the telephone ringing. It is a sound which both of us detest, and there is always a certain amount of manoeuvring to see who can avoid answering it. We have an innate pessimism about telephone calls; they have a habit of coming at the wrong time, and they are too sudden, catapulting you into a conversation you weren't expecting. Letters, on the other hand, are a pleasure to receive, not least because they allow you to consider your reply. But people don't write letters any more. They're too busy, they're in too much of a hurry or, dismissing the service which manages to deliver bills with unfailing reliability, they don't trust the post. We were learning not to trust the telephone, and I picked it up as I would a long-dead fish.

'How's the weather?' asked an unidentified voice.

I said that the weather was good. It must have made all the difference, because the caller then introduced himself as Tony. He wasn't a friend, or even a friend of a friend, but an acquaintance of an acquaintance. 'Looking for a house down there,' he said, in the clipped, time-is-money voice that executives adopt when they talk on their car phones to their wives. 'Thought you could give me a hand. Want to get in before the Easter rush and the frogs put up the prices.'

I offered to give him the names of some property agents. 'Bit of a problem there,' he said. 'Don't speak the language. Order a meal, of course, but that's about it.' I offered to give him the name of a bilingual agent, but that wouldn't do. 'Don't want to get tied up with one firm. Bad move. No leverage.'

We had reached the moment in the conversation when I was

supposed to offer my services, or else say something to terminate this budding relationship before it could bud any further, but the chance was denied me.

'Must go. Can't chat all night. Plenty of time for that when I get down next week.' And then those awful words which put an end to any hopes of hiding: 'Don't worry. I've got your address. I'll find you.'

The line went dead.

* * * * *

APRIL

It was one of those mornings when the early mist hung in wet sheets along the valley under a band of bright blue sky and, by the time we came home from walking, the dogs were sleek with damp, whiskers glittering in the sun. They saw the stranger first, and pranced round him pretending to be fierce.

He stood by the swimming pool, fending off their attentions with a handbag of masculine design and backing ever closer to the deep end. He seemed relieved to see us.

'Dogs all right, are they? Not rabid or anything?' The voice was recognisable as that of our telephone caller, Tony from London, and he and his handbag joined us for breakfast. He was large and prosperously padded round the waistline, with tinted glasses, carefully tousled hair and the pale-coloured casual clothes that English visitors wear in Provence regardless of the weather. He sat down and produced from his bag a bulging Filofax, a gold pen, a packet of duty-free Cartier cigarettes and a gold lighter. His watch was also gold. I was sure that gold medallions nestled in his chest hair. He told us he was in advertising.

He gave us a brief but extremely complimentary account of his business history. He had started his own advertising agency, built it up – 'tough business, bloody competitive' – and had just sold a controlling interest for what he described as heavy money and a five-year contract. Now, he said, he was able to relax, although one would never have guessed from his behaviour that he was a man who had left the cares of office behind. He was in a constant fidget, looking at his watch, arranging and re-arranging his trinkets on the table in front of him, adjusting his glasses and smoking in deep, distracted drags. Suddenly, he stood up.

'Mind if I make a quick call? What's the code for London?'

My wife and I had come to expect this as an inevitable part of welcoming the Englishman abroad into our home. He comes in, he has a drink or a cup of coffee, he makes a 'phone call to check that his business has not collapsed during the first few hours of his absence. The routine never varies, and the substance of the call is as predictable as the routine.

'Hi, it's me. Yes, I'm calling from Provence. Everything OK? Any messages? Oh. None? David didn't call back? Oh shit. Look, I'll be moving around a bit today, but you can reach me on (what's the number here?) Got that? What? Yes, the weather's fine. Call you later.'

Tony put the 'phone down and reassured us about the state of his company, which was managing to stumble along without him. He was now ready to devote his energies, and ours, to the purchase of property.

Buying a house in Provence is not without its complications, and it is easy to understand why busy and efficient people from cities, used to firm decisions and quickly-struck deals, often give up after months of serpentine negotiations that have led nowhere. The first of many surprises, always greeted with alarm and disbelief, is that all property costs more than its advertised price. Most of this is because the French government takes a cut of about eight per cent on all transactions. Then there are the legal fees, which are high. And it is sometimes a condition of the sale that the purchaser pays the agent's commission of three to five per cent. An unlucky buyer could end up paying as much as fifteen per cent on top of the price.

There is, however, a well-established ritual of respectable cheating which has the double attractions, so dear to every French heart, of saving money and screwing the government. This is the two-price purchase, and a typical example would work as follows: Monsieur Rivarel, a businessman in Aix, wishes to sell an old country house that he inherited. He wants a million francs. As it is not his principal residence, he will be liable for tax on the proceeds of the sale, a thought which causes him great distress. He therefore decides that the official, recorded price – the *prix déclaré* – will be 600,000 francs, and he will grit his teeth and pay tax on that. His consolation is that the balance of 400,000 francs will be paid in cash, under the table. This, as he will point out, is an *affaire intéressante* not only for him, but for the buyer, because the official fees and charges will be based on the lower, declared price. V*oilà*! Everyone is happy.

The practical aspects of this arrangement call for a sense of timing and great delicacy on the part of the lawyer, or *notaire*, when the moment comes to sign the act of sale. All the interested parties – the buyer, the seller and the property agent – are gathered in the *notaire*'s office, and the act of sale is read aloud, line by interminable line. The price marked on the contract is 600,000 francs. The 400,000 in cash which the buyer has brought along has to be passed to the seller, but it would be highly improper if this were to happen in front of the *notaire*. Consequently, he feels a pressing need to go to the lavatory, where he stays until the cash has been counted and has changed hands. He can then return, accept the cheque for the declared price, and supervise the signing ceremony without having compromised his legal reputation. It has been said, rather unkindly, that two basic requirements for a rural *notaire* are a blind eye and a diplomatic bladder.

But there can be many obstacles to overcome before the visit to the *notaire*, and one of the most common is the problem of multiple ownership. Under French law, property is normally inherited by the children, with each child having an equal share. All of them must be in agreement before their inheritance is sold, and the more children there are the less likely this becomes, as is the case with an old farmhouse not far from us. It has been passed down from one generation to the next, and ownership is now divided between fourteen cousins, three of whom are of Corsican extraction and thus, according to our French friends, impossible to deal with. Prospective buyers have made their offers, but at any given time nine cousins might accept, two would be undecided, and the Corsicans would say no. The farm remains unsold, and will doubtless pass to the thirty-eight children of the fourteen cousins. Eventually, it will be owned by 175 distant relatives who don't trust each other.

Even if the property should be owned outright by a single acquisitive peasant, such as Massot, there is no guarantee of a straightforward transaction. The peasant may set a price which he thinks is absurdly high, and which will keep him in drink and lottery tickets for the rest of his days. A buyer comes along and agrees the inflated price. The peasant immediately suspects trickery. It's too easy. The price must be too low. He withdraws the house from the market for six months before trying again at a higher figure.

And then there are the trifling inconveniences that are mentioned casually at the last minute: an outbuilding that has been lost to a neighbour in a card game; an ancient right of way which technically permits the passage of herds of goats through the kitchen twice a year; a dispute over well water that has been bitter and unresolved since 1958; the venerable sitting tenant who is bound to die before next spring – there is always something unexpected, and a buyer needs patience and a sense of humour to see the business through.

I tried to prepare Tony for these local oddities as we drove to the office of a property agent whom we knew, but I should have saved my breath. He was, by his own modest admission, a shrewd and resourceful negotiator. He had played hardball with the big boys on Madison Avenue, and it would take more than bureaucracy or a French peasant to get the better of him. I began to doubt the wisdom of introducing him to anyone who didn't have a car 'phone and a personal business manager.

The agent met us at the door of her office, and sat us down with two thick files of property details and photographs. She spoke no English and Tony spoke vestigial French, and since direct communication was impossible he behaved as if she wasn't there. It was a particularly arrogant form of bad manners, made worse by the assumption that even the most derogatory language can be used without the risk of it being understood. And so I passed an embarrassing half hour as Tony flicked through the files, muttering 'Fuck me!' and 'They must be joking' at intervals while I made feeble attempts to translate his comments into some nonsense about his being impressed by the prices.

He had started with the firm intention of finding a village house with no land. He was far too busy to bother with a garden. But as he went through the properties I could see him mentally becoming the Provençal squire with acres of vines and olives. By the time he had finished he was worrying about where he should put his tennis court. To my disappointment, there were three properties which he thought worthy of his attention.

'We'll do those this afternoon,' he announced, making notes in his Filofax and looking at his watch. I thought he was going to commandeer the agent's 'phone for an international call, but he was just reacting to a signal from his stomach. 'Let's hit a restaurant,' he said, 'and we can be back here by two.' The agent smiled and nodded as Tony waved two fingers at her and we left the poor woman to recover.

At lunch, I told Tony that I wouldn't be going with him and the agent that afternoon. He was surprised that I had anything better to do, but ordered a second bottle of wine and told me that money was an international language and he didn't anticipate having any difficulties. Unfortunately, when the bill arrived he discovered that neither his gold American Express card nor the wad of traveller's cheques that he hadn't had time to change were of any interest to the restaurant's proprietor. I paid, and made some remark about the international language. Tony was not amused.

I left him with mixed feelings of relief and guilt. Boors are always unpleasant, but when you're in a foreign country and they are of your own nationality you feel some kind of vague responsibility. The next day, I called the agent to apologise. 'Don't worry,' she said, 'Parisians are often just as bad. At least I couldn't understand what he was saying.'

* * * * *

A final confirmation that warmer weather was here to stay was provided by Monsieur Menicucci's wardrobe. He had come to carry out the preliminary *études* for his summer project, which was our central heating. His woollen bonnet had been replaced by a lightweight cotton model decorated with a slogan advertising sanitary fittings, and instead of his thermal snow shoes he was wearing brown canvas bootees. His assistant, *jeune*, was in a guerilla outfit of army fatigues and jungle cap, and the two of them marched through the house taking measurements as Menicucci delivered himself of assorted *pensées*.

Music was his first subject today. He and his wife had just attended an official artisans and plumbers lunch, followed by ballroom dancing, which was one of his many accomplishments. 'Yes, Monsieur Peter,' he said, 'we danced until six. I had the feet of a young man of eighteen.' I could picture him, nimble and exact, whirling Madame around the floor, and I wondered if he had a special ballroom bonnet for these occasions, because it was impossible to think of him bareheaded. I must have smiled at the thought. 'I know,' he said, 'you're thinking that the waltz is not serious music. For that one must listen to the great composers.'

He then expounded a remarkable theory, which had occurred to him while he was playing the clarinet during one of the power cuts that the French electricity board arranges at regular intervals. Electricity, he said, is a matter of science and logic. Classical music is a matter of art and logic. V*ous voyez?* Already one sees a common factor. And when you listen to the disciplined and logical progression of some of Mozart's work, the conclusion is inescapable: Mozart would have made a formidable electrician.

I was saved from replying by *jeune*, who had finished counting up the number of radiators we would need, and had arrived at a figure of twenty. Menicucci received the news with a wince, shaking his hand as if he'd burned his fingers. '*Oh là là*. This will cost more than *centimes*.' He mentioned several million francs, saw my shocked expression and then divided by a hundred; he had been quoting in old money. Even so, it was a considerable amount. There was the high cost of cast iron, plus the government sales tax, or TVA, of 18·6 per cent. This led him to mention an outrageous fiscal irregularity which typified the villainy of politicians.

'You buy a bidet,' he said, jabbing me with his finger, 'and you pay full TVA. The same for a washer or a screw. But I will tell you something *scandaleux* and altogether wrong. You buy a pot of caviar, and you will pay only 6 per cent TVA, because it is classified as *nourriture*. Now tell me this: who eats caviar?' I pleaded not guilty. 'I will tell you. It is the politicians, the millionaires, the *grosses légumes* in Paris – they are the ones who eat caviar. It's an outrage.' He stumped off, fulminating about caviar orgies in the Elysée Palace, to check *jeune*'s radiator arithmetic.

The thought of Menicucci occupying the premises for five or six weeks, burrowing his way through the thick old walls with a drill that was almost as big as he was and filling the air with dust and running commentaries was not a treat to look forward to. It would be a dirty and tedious process involving almost every room in the house. But one of the joys of Provence, we told ourselves, was that we could live outdoors while this was going on. Even this early in the year, the days were very nearly hot, and we decided to start the outdoor season in earnest one Sunday morning when the sun coming through the bedroom window woke us up at seven o'clock.

All good Sundays include a trip to the market, and we were in Coustellet by eight. The space behind the disused station was lined with elderly trucks and vans, each with a trestle table set up in front. A blackboard showed the day's prices for vegetables. The stallholders, already tanned from the fields, were eating croissants and brioches that were still warm from the bakery across the street. We watched as one old man sliced a baguette lengthways with a wooden-handled pocket knife and spread on fresh goat's cheese in a creamy layer before pouring himself a glass of red wine from the litre bottle that would keep him going until lunchtime.

The Coustellet market is small, compared to the weekly markets in Cavaillon and Apt and Isle-sur-la-Sorgue, and not yet fashionable. Customers carry baskets instead of cameras, and only in July and August are you likely to see the occasional haughty woman down from Paris with her Dior track suit and small, nervous dog.

For the rest of the season, from spring until autumn, it is just the local inhabitants, and the peasants who bring in what they have taken from the earth or the greenhouse a few hours earlier.

We walked slowly along the rows of trestle tables, admiring the merciless French housewife at work. Unlike us, she is not content merely to look at the produce before buying. She gets to grips with it – squeezing aubergines, sniffing tomatoes, snapping the match-stick-thin *haricots verts* between her fingers, poking suspiciously into the damp green hearts of lettuces, tasting cheeses and olives – and, if they don't come up to her private standards, she will glare at the stallholder as if she has been betrayed before taking her custom elsewhere.

At one end of the market, a van from the wine co-operative was surrounded by men rinsing their teeth thoughtfully in the new rosé. Next to them, a woman was selling free-range eggs and live rabbits, and beyond her the tables were piled high with vegetables, small and fragrant bushes of basil, tubs of lavender honey, great green bottles of first pressing olive oil, trays of hothouse peaches, pots of black *tapenade*, flowers and herbs, jams and cheeses – everything looked delicious in the early morning sun.

We bought red peppers to roast and big brown eggs and basil and peaches and goat's cheese and lettuce and pink-streaked onions. And, when the basket could hold no more, we went across the road to buy half a yard of bread – the *gros pain* that makes such a tasty mop for any olive oil or vinaigrette sauce that is left on the plate. The bakery was crowded and noisy, and smelt of warm dough and the almonds that had gone into the morning's cakes. While we waited, we remembered being told that the French spend as much of their income on their stomachs as the English do on their cars and stereo systems, and we could easily believe it.

Everyone seemed to be shopping for a regiment. One round, jolly woman bought six large loaves – three yards of bread – a chocolate brioche the size of a hat, and an entire wheel of apple tart, the thin slices of apple packed in concentric rings, shining under a glaze of apricot sauce. We were aware that we had missed breakfast.

Lunch made up for it: cold roasted peppers, slippery with olive oil and speckled with fresh basil, tiny mussels wrapped in bacon

and barbecued on skewers, salad and cheese. The sun was hot and the wine had made us sleepy. And then we heard the 'phone.

It is a rule of life that, when the 'phone rings between noon and three on a Sunday, the caller is English; a Frenchman wouldn't dream of interrupting the most relaxed meal of the week. I should have let it ring. Tony from advertising was back, and judging by the absence of static on the line he was hideously close.

'Just thought I'd touch base with you.' I could hear him taking a drag on his cigarette, and I made a mental note to buy an answering machine to deal with anyone else who might want to touch base on a Sunday.

'I think I've found a place.' He didn't pause to hear the effect of his announcement, and so missed the sound of my heart sinking. 'Quite a way from you, actually, nearer the coast.' I told him that I was delighted; the nearer the coast he was, the better. 'Needs a lot doing to it, so I'm not going to pay what he's asking. Thought I'd bring my builders over to do the work. They did the office in six weeks, top to bottom. Irish, but bloody good. They could sort this place out in a month.'

I was tempted to encourage him, because the idea of a gang of Irish workmen exposed to the pleasures of a building site in Provence – the sun, cheap wine, endless possibilities for delay and a proprietor too far away to be a daily nuisance – had the makings of a fine comic interlude, and I could see Mr. Murphy and his team stretching the job out until October, maybe getting the family over from Donegal for a holiday during August and generally having a grand time. I told Tony he might be better advised to hire local labour, and to get an architect to hire it for him.

'Don't need an architect,' he said, 'I know exactly what I want.' He would. 'Why should I pay him an arm and a leg for a couple of drawings?' There was no helping him. He knew best. I asked him when he was going back to England. 'This evening,' he said, and then guided me through the next hectic pages of his Filofax: a client meeting on Monday, three days in New York, a sales conference in Milton Keynes. He reeled it off with the mock weariness of the indispensable executive, and he was welcome to every second of it. 'Anyway,' he said, 'I'll keep in touch. I won't finalise on the house for a week or two, but I'll let you know as soon as I've inked it.'

My wife and I sat by the pool and wondered, not for the first time, why we both found it so difficult to get rid of thick-skinned and ungracious people. More of them would be coming down during the summer, baying for food and drink and a bedroom, for days of swimming and lifts to the airport. We didn't think of ourselves as anti-social or reclusive, but our brief experience with the thrustful and dynamic Tony had been enough to remind us that the next few months would require firmness and ingenuity. And an answering machine.

The approach of summer had obviously been on Massot's mind as well, because when I saw him a few days later in the forest he was busy adding a further refinement to his anti-camper defences. Under the signs he had nailed up saying *PRIVÉ!* he was fixing a second series of unwelcoming messages, short but sinister: *Attention! Vipères!* It was the perfect deterrent – full of menace, but without the need for visible proof that is the great drawback of other discouragements such as guard dogs, electrified fences and patrols armed with sub-machine guns. Even the most resolute camper would think twice before tucking himself up in a sleeping bag which might have one of the local residents coiled at the bottom. I asked Massot if there really were vipers in the Lubéron, and he shook his head at yet another example of the ignorance of foreigners.

'*Eh oui,*' he said, 'not big' – he held his hands up, about twelve inches apart – 'but if you're bitten you need to get to a doctor within forty-five minutes, or else . . .' He pulled a dreadful face, head to one side, tongue lolling from the side of his mouth, 'They say that when a viper bites a man, the man dies. But when a viper bites a woman' – he leaned forward and waggled his eyebrows – 'the viper dies.' He snorted with amusement and offered me one of his fat yellow cigarettes. 'Don't ever go walking without a good pair of boots.'

The Lubéron viper, according to Professor Massot, will normally avoid humans, and will attack only if provoked. When this happens, Massot's advice was to run in zig-zags, and preferably uphill, because an enraged viper can sprint – in short, straight bursts on level ground – as fast as a running man. I looked nervously around me, and Massot laughed. 'Of course, you can always try the peasant's trick: catch it behind the head and squeeze until its mouth is wide open. Spit hard into the mouth and *plok*! – he's dead.' He spat in demonstration, hitting one of the dogs on the head. 'But best of all,' said Massot, 'is to take a woman with you. They can't run as fast as men, and the viper will catch them first.' He went home to his breakfast leaving me to pick my way cautiously through the forest and practise my spitting.

* * * * *

Easter weekend arrived, and our cherry trees – about thirty of them – blossomed in unison. From the road, the house looked as if it were floating on a pink and white sea, and motorists were stopping to take photographs or walking tentatively up the drive until barking from the dogs turned them back. One group, more adventurous than the rest, drove up to the house in a car with Swiss plates and parked on the verge. I went to see what they wanted.

'We will picnic here,' the driver told me.

'I'm sorry, it's a private house.'

'No, no,' he said, waving a map at me, 'this is the Lubéron.'

'No, no,' I said, 'that's the Lubéron,' and pointed to the mountains.

'But I can't take my car up *there*.'

Eventually he drove off, puffing with Swiss indignation and leaving deep wheel marks in the grass we were trying to turn into a lawn. The tourist season had begun.

Up in the village on Easter Sunday, the small parking area was full, and not one of the cars had local plates. The visitors explored the narrow streets, looking curiously into people's houses and posing for photographs in front of the church. The young man who spends all day sitting on a doorstep next to the *épicerie* was asking everyone who passed for ten francs to make a 'phone call and taking the proceeds into the café.

The Café du Progrès has made a consistent and successful effort to avoid being picturesque. It is an interior decorator's nightmare, with tables and chairs that wobble and don't match, gloomy paintwork and a lavatory that splutters and gurgles often and noisily next to a shabby ice cream cabinet. The proprietor is gruff, and his dogs are indescribably matted. There is, however, a long and spectacular view from the glassed-in terrace next to the lavatory, and it's a good place to have a beer and watch the play of light on the hills and villages that stretch away towards the Basses-Alpes. A hand-lettered notice warns you not to throw cigarette ends out of the window, following complaints from the clientele of the open-air restaurant below, but if you observe this rule you will be left undisturbed. The regulars stay at the bar; the *terrasse* is for tourists, and on Easter Sunday it was crowded.

There were the Dutch, wholesome in their hiking boots and backpacks; the Germans, armed with Leicas and heavy costume jewellery; the Parisians, disdainful and smart, inspecting their glasses carefully for germs; an Englishman in sandals and an open-necked striped business shirt, working out his holiday finances on a pocket calculator while his wife wrote postcards to neighbours in Surrey. The dogs nosed among the tables looking for sugar lumps, causing the hygiene-conscious Parisians to shrink away. An Yves Montand song on the radio fought a losing battle with the sanitary sound effects, and empty pastis glasses were banged on the bar as the locals started to drift off towards home and lunch.

Outside the café, three cars had converged and were growling at each other. If one of them had reversed ten yards, they could all have passed, but a French driver considers it a moral defeat to give way, just as he feels a moral obligation to park wherever he can cause maximum inconvenience and to overtake on a blind bend. They say that Italians are dangerous drivers, but for truly lethal insanity I would back a Frenchman hurtling down the N100, late and hungry, against all comers.

I drove back from the village and just missed the first accident of the season. An old white Peugeot had gone backwards into a wooden telegraph pole at the bottom of the drive with sufficient force to snap the pole in two. There was no other car to be seen, and the road was dry and dead straight. It was difficult to work out how the back of the car and the pole had contrived to meet with such force. A young man was standing in the middle of the road, scratching his head. He grinned as I pulled up.

I asked him if he was hurt. 'I'm fine,' he said, 'but I think the car is *foutu.*' I looked at the telegraph pole, which was bent over the car, kept from falling by the sagging 'phone line. That also was *foutu.*

'We must hurry,' said the young man. 'Nobody must know.' He put a finger to his lips. 'Can you give me a lift home? It's just up the road. I need the tractor.' He got into the car, and the cause of the accident became clear; he smelt as though he had been marinated in Ricard. He explained that the car had to be removed with speed and secrecy. If the Post Office found that he had attacked one of their poles they would make him pay for it. 'Nobody must know,' he repeated, and hiccupped once or twice for emphasis.

I dropped him off and went home. Half an hour later, I went out to see if the stealthy removal of the car had been accomplished, but it was still there. So was a group of peasants, arguing noisily. Also two other cars and a tractor, which was blocking the road. As I watched, another car arrived and the driver sounded his horn to get the tractor to move. The man on the tractor pointed at the wreck and shrugged. The horn sounded again, this time in a continuous blare that bounced off the mountains and must have been audible in Ménerbes, two kilometres away.

The commotion lasted for another half hour before the Peugeot was finally extracted from the ditch and the secret motorcade disappeared in the direction of the local garage, leaving the telegraph pole creaking ominously in the breeze. The Post Office men came to replace it the following week, and attracted a small crowd. They asked one of the peasants what had happened. He shrugged innocently. 'Who knows?' he said. 'Woodworm?'

* * * * *

Our friend from Paris examined his empty glass with surprise, as if evaporation had taken place while he wasn't looking. I poured some more wine and he settled back in his chair, face tilted up to the sun.

'We still have the heating on in Paris,' he said, and took a sip of the cool, sweet wine from Beaumes de Venise. 'And it's been raining for weeks. I can see why you like it here. Mind you, it wouldn't suit me.'

It seemed to be suiting him well enough, basking in the warmth after a good lunch, but I didn't argue with him.

'You'd hate it,' I said. 'You'd probably get skin cancer from the sun and cirrhosis of the liver from too much plonk, and if you were ever feeling well enough you'd miss the theatre. And anyway, what would you do all day?'

He squinted at me drowsily, and put his sunglasses on. 'Exactly.'

It was part of what had become a familiar litany:

Don't you miss your friends?

No. They come and see us here.

Don't you miss English television?

No.

There must be *something* about England you miss?

Marmalade.

And then would come the real question, delivered half-humorously, half-seriously: what do you *do* all day? Our friend from Paris put it another way.

'Don't you get bored?'

We didn't. We never had time. We found the everyday curiosities of French rural life amusing and interesting. We were enjoying the gradual process of changing the house around so that it suited the way we lived. There was the garden to be designed and planted, a *boules* court to be built, a new language to be learned, villages and vineyards and markets to be discovered – the days went quickly enough without any other distractions, and there were always plenty of those. The previous week, as it happened, had been particularly rich in interruptions.

They started on Monday with a visit from Marcel the Parcel, our postman. He was irritated, barely pausing to shake hands before demanding to know where I had hidden the mail box. He had his rounds to do, it was almost noon, how could I expect him to deliver letters if he had to play *cache-cache* with the mail box? But we hadn't hidden it. So far as I knew, it was down at the end of the drive, firmly planted on a steel post. 'Non,' said the postman, 'it has been moved.' There was nothing for it but to walk down the drive together and spend a fruitless five minutes searching the bushes to see if it had been knocked over. There was no sign that a mail box had ever been there except a small post hole in the ground. 'Voilà,' said the postman, 'it is as I told you.' I found it hard to believe that anyone would steal a mail box, but he knew better. 'It is quite normal,' he said, 'people round here are *mal fini.*' I asked him what that meant. 'Mad.'

Back to the house we went, to restore his good humour with a drink and to discuss the installation of a new mail box that he would be happy to sell me. We agreed that it should be built into the side of an old well, positioned at the regulation height of 70 centimetres above the ground so that he could drop letters in without having to leave his van. Obviously, the well had to be studied and measurements taken, and by then it was time for lunch. Post Office business would be resumed at two o'clock.

A couple of days later, I was summoned from the house by a car horn, and found the dogs circling a new white Mercedes. The driver wasn't prepared to leave the safety of his car, but risked a half-open window. I looked in and saw a small brown couple beaming at me nervously. They complimented me on the ferocity of the dogs and requested permission to get out. They were both dressed for the city, the man in a sharply-cut suit, his wife in hat and cloak and patent leather boots.

How fortunate to find me at home, they said, and what a beautiful house. Had I lived here long? No? Then I would undoubtedly be needing some genuine Oriental carpets. This was indeed my lucky day, because they had just come from an important carpet exhibition in Avignon, and by chance a few choice items remained unsold. Before taking them up to Paris – where people of taste would fight to buy them – the couple had decided to take a drive in the country, and fate had led them to me. To mark the happy occasion, they were prepared to let me choose from their most exquisite treasures at what they described as *very interesting* prices.

While the natty little man had been telling me the good news, his wife had been unloading carpets from the car and arranging them artistically up and down the drive, commenting loudly on the charms of each one: 'Ah, what a beauty!' and 'See the colours in the sun' and 'This one – oh, I shall be sad to see it go'. She trotted back to join us, patent boots twinkling, and she and her husband looked at me expectantly.

The carpet-seller does not enjoy a good reputation in Provence, and to describe a man as a *marchand de tapis* is to imply that he is at best shifty and at worst someone who would steal the corset from your grandmother. I had also been told that travelling carpet-sellers often acted as reconnaissance parties, spying out the land for their burglar associates. And there was always the possibility that the carpets would be fakes, or stolen.

But they didn't look like fakes, and there was one small rug that I thought was very handsome. I made the mistake of saying so, and Madame looked at her husband in well-rehearsed surprise. 'Extraordinary!' she said. 'What an eye Monsieur has. This is indisputably our favourite too. But why not have something a little bigger as well?' Alas, I said, I was penniless, but this was brushed aside as a minor and temporary inconvenience. I could always pay later, with a substantial discount for cash. I looked again at the rug. One of the dogs was lying on it, snoring gently. Madame crooned with delight. 'You see, Monsieur? The *toutou* has chosen it for you.' I gave in. After three minutes of inexpert haggling on my part, the original price was reduced by fifty per cent, and I went to fetch the cheque book. They watched closely while I made out the cheque, telling me to leave the payee's name blank. With a promise to return next year, they drove slowly round our new rug and the sleeping dog, Madame smiling and waving regally from her nest of carpets. Their visit had taken up the entire morning.

The final interruption ended the week on a sour note. A truck had come to deliver gravel and, as I watched it backing towards the spot the driver had chosen to unload, the rear wheels suddenly sunk into the ground. There was a crack, and the truck tilted backwards. A pungent and unmistakable smell filled the air. The driver got out to inspect the damage and said, with unconscious accuracy, the single most appropriate word for the occasion.

'*Merde!*' He had parked in the septic tank.

'So you see,' I said to our friend from Paris, 'one way or another, there's never a dull moment.'

He didn't reply, and I reached over and took off his sunglasses. The sun in his eyes woke him up.

'What?'

* * * * *

MAY

Le premier Mai started well, with a fine sunrise, and as it was a national holiday we thought we should celebrate in correct French fashion by paying homage to the summer sport and taking to our bicycles.

Tougher and more serious cyclists had been training for weeks, muffled against the spring winds in thick black tights and face masks, but now the air was warm enough for delicate amateurs like us to go out in shorts and sweaters. We had bought two lightweight and highly-strung machines from a gentleman in Cavaillon called Edouard Cunty – '*Vélos de Qualité!*' – and we were keen to join the brightly coloured groups from local cycling clubs as they swooped gracefully and without any apparent effort up and down the back country roads. We assumed that our legs, after a winter of hard walking, would be in good enough condition for a gentle ten-mile spin up to Bonnieux and over to Lacoste – an hour of light exercise to limber up, nothing too strenuous.

It was easy enough to begin with, although the narrow, hard saddles made an early impression, and we realised why some cyclists slip a pound of rump steak inside the back of their shorts to cushion the coccyx from the road. But for the first couple of miles there was nothing to do except glide along and enjoy the scenery. The cherries were ripening, the winter skeletons of the vines had disappeared under a cover of bright green leaves, the mountains

76

looked lush and soft. The tyres made a steady thrumming sound, and there were occasional whiffs of rosemary and lavender and wild thyme. This was more exhilarating than walking, quieter and healthier than driving, not too taxing and altogether delightful. Why hadn't we done it before? Why didn't we do it every day?

The euphoria lasted until we began to climb up to Bonnieux. My bicycle suddenly put on weight. I could feel the muscles in my thighs complaining as the gradient became steeper, and my unseasoned backside was aching. I forgot about the beauties of nature and wished I had worn steak in my shorts. By the time we reached the village it hurt to breathe.

The woman who runs the Café Clerici was standing outside with her hands on her ample hips. She looked at the two red-faced, gasping figures bent over their handlebars. '*Mon Dieu*! The Tour de France is early this year.' She brought us beer, and we sat in the comfort of chairs designed for human bottoms. Lacoste now seemed rather far away.

The hill that twists up to the ruins of the Marquis de Sade's château was long and steep and agonising. We were half way up and flagging when we heard a whirr of *dérailleur* gears, and we were overtaken by another cyclist – a wiry, brown man who looked to be in his mid-sixties. '*Bon jour*,' he said brightly, '*bon vélo*', and he continued up the hill and out of sight. We laboured on, heads low, thighs burning, regretting the beer.

The old man came back down the hill, turned, and cruised along next to us. '*Courage*,' he said, not even breathing hard, '*c'est pas loin. Allez!*' And he rode with us into Lacoste, his lean old legs, shaved bare in case of falls and grazes, pumping away with the smoothness of pistons.

We collapsed on the terrace of another café, which overlooked the valley. At least it would be downhill most of the way home, and I gave up the idea of calling an ambulance. The old man had a peppermint *frappé*, and told us that he had done thirty kilometres so far, and would do another twenty before lunch. We congratulated him on his fitness. 'It's not what it was. I had to stop doing the Mont Ventoux ride when I turned sixty. Now I just do these little *promenades*.' Any slight satisfaction we felt at climbing the hill disappeared.

The ride back was easier, but we were still hot and sore when we reached home. We dismounted and walked stiff-legged to the pool, discarding clothes as we went, and dived in. It was like going to heaven. Lying in the sun afterwards with a glass of wine we decided that cycling would be a regular part of our summer lives. It was, however, some time before we could face the saddles without flinching.

* * * * *

The fields around the house were inhabited every day by figures moving slowly and methodically across the landscape, weeding the vineyards, treating the cherry trees, hoeing the sandy earth. Nothing was hurried. Work stopped at noon for lunch in the shade of a tree, and the only sounds for two hours were snatches of distant conversation that carried hundreds of yards on the still air.

Faustin was spending most of his days on our land, arriving just after seven with his dog and his tractor and usually contriving to organise his work so that it ended near the house – close enough to hear the sound of bottles and glasses. One drink to settle the dust and be sociable was his normal ration but, if the visit stretched to two drinks, it meant business – some new step forward in agricultural co-operation which he had been mulling over during his hours among the vines. He never approached a subject directly, but edged towards it, crabwise and cautious.

'Do you like rabbits?'

I knew him well enough to understand that he wasn't talking about the charms of the rabbit as a domestic pet, and he confirmed this by patting his belly and muttering reverently about *civets* and *pâtés*. But the trouble with rabbits, he said, was their appetites. They ate like holes, kilos and kilos. I nodded, but I was at a loss to know where our interests and those of the hungry rabbit coincided.

Faustin stood up and beckoned me to the door of the courtyard. He pointed at two small terraced fields. 'Lucerne,' he said. 'Rabbits love it. You could get three cuts from those fields between now and autumn.' My knowledge of local plant life was far from complete, and I had thought that the fields were covered in some kind of dense Provençal weed which I had been meaning to clear. It was fortunate I hadn't; Faustin's rabbits would never have forgiven me. It was an unexpected triumph for gardening by neglect. In case I had missed the point, Faustin waved his glass at the fields and said again, 'Rabbits love lucerne.' He made nibbling noises. I told him he could have as much as his rabbits could eat, and he stopped nibbling.

'*Bon*. If you're sure you won't need it.' Mission accomplished, he stumped off towards his tractor.

Faustin is slow in many ways, but quick with his gratitude. He was back the following evening with an enormous bouquet of asparagus, neatly tied with red, white and blue ribbon. His wife Henriette was behind him carrying a pickaxe, a ball of string and a tub filled with young lavender plants. They should have been planted long before, she said, but her cousin had only just brought them down from the Basses-Alpes. They must be planted at once.

Labour was divided rather unfairly, it seemed to us. Faustin was in charge of keeping the string straight and drinking pastis; Henriette swung the pickaxe, each planting hole a pick handle's distance from the next. Offers to help were refused. 'She's used to it,' said Faustin proudly, as Henriette swung and measured and planted in the twilight, and she laughed. 'Eight hours of this and you sleep like a baby.' In half an hour it was done – a bed of fifty plants that would be the size of hedgehogs in six months, knee-high in two years, arranged with meticulous symmetry to mark the boundary of the rabbits' lucerne factory.

Whatever had been on the menu for dinner was forgotten, and we prepared the asparagus. There was too much for one meal, more than I could get both hands around, the patriotic tricolour ribbon printed with Faustin's name and address. He told us that it was the law in France for the producer to be identified like this, and we hoped one day to have our own ribbon when our asparagus plants grew up.

The pale shoots were as fat as thumbs, delicately coloured and patterned at the tips. We ate them warm, with melted butter. We ate bread that had been baked that afternoon in the old *boulangerie* at Lumières. We drank the light red wine from the vineyards in the valley. We supported local industry with every mouthful.

Through the open door we could hear the croaking of our resident frog, and the long, sliding song of a nightingale. We took a final glass of wine outside and looked by the light of the moon at the new lavender bed while the dogs rooted for mice in the lucerne fields. The rabbits would eat well this summer and, Faustin had promised, would taste all the better for it in the winter. We realised we were becoming as obsessive about food as the French, and went back indoors to attend to some unfinished business with a goat's cheese.

* * * * *

Bernard the *pisciniste* had brought us a present, and he was assembling it with great enthusiasm. It was a floating armchair for the pool, complete with a drinks compartment. It had come all the way from Miami, Florida, which in Bernard's opinion was the capital of the world for pool accessories. 'The French don't understand these things,' he said disparagingly. 'There are companies making air cushions, but how can you drink on a floating cushion?' He tightened the last wing-nut on the frame and stood back to admire the chair in all its Miami dazzle, a vivid block of styrofoam, plastic and aluminium. 'There. The glass fits here in the arm-rest. You can repose in great comfort. *C'est une merveille.*' He launched the chair into the water, careful not to splash his pink shirt and white trousers. 'You must put it away every night,' he said. 'The gypsies will be here soon for the cherry-picking. They'll steal anything.'

It was a reminder that we had been intending to get some insurance arranged for the house, but with the builders making holes in the walls I couldn't imagine any insurance company taking the risk. Bernard removed his sunglasses in horror. Didn't we know? There was a higher burglary rate in the Vaucluse than anywhere else in France except Paris. He looked at me as if I had committed an act of terminal lunacy. 'You must be protected immediately. I will send a man this afternoon. Stay *en garde* until he comes.'

I thought this was perhaps a little dramatic, but Bernard seemed convinced that robber bands were lurking close by, waiting only for us to go to the village butcher before swooping down in a pantechnicon to pick the house bare. Only last week, he told me, he had found his car jacked up outside his own front door with all four wheels removed. These people were *salauds*.

One reason, apart from idleness, why we had neglected the matter of insurance was that we detested insurance companies, with their weasel words and evasions and extenuating circumstances, and their conditional clauses set in minuscule, illegible type. But Bernard was right. It was stupid to trust to luck. We resigned ourselves to spending the afternoon with a grey man in a suit who would tell us to put a lock on our refrigerator.

It was early evening when the car pulled up in a cloud of dust. The driver had obviously come to the wrong house. He was young and dark and good-looking, resplendent in the costume of a 1950s saxophone player – a wide-shouldered drape jacket shot through with gleaming threads, a lime-green shirt, capacious trousers that narrowed to hug his ankles, shoes of dark blue suede with bulbous crêpe soles, a flash of turquoise socks.

'Fructus, Thierry. *Agent d'assurance.*' He walked into the house with short, jaunty steps. I half expected him to start snapping his fingers and make a few mean moves across the floor. I offered him a beer while I got over my surprise, and he sat down and gave me the benefit of his vibrant socks.

'*Une belle mesong.*' He had a strong Provençal accent which contrasted strangely with the clothes, and which I found reassuring. He was businesslike and serious, and asked if we were living in the house all year round; the high rate of burglaries in the Vaucluse, he said, was partly due to the large number of holiday homes. When houses are left empty for ten months a year, well . . . the shoulders of his jacket escalated in an upholstered shrug. The stories one heard in his profession made you want to live in a safe.

But that needn't concern us. We were permanent. And, furthermore, we had dogs. This was good, and it would be taken into account when he assessed the premium. Were they vicious? If not, perhaps they could be trained. He knew a man who could turn poodles into lethal weapons.

He made some notes in a neat, small hand and finished his beer. We went on a tour of the house. He approved of the heavy wooden shutters and solid old doors, but stopped and sucked his teeth in

front of a small window – a *fenestron* that was less than a foot square. The modern professional burglar, he told us, will often work like Victorian chimney-sweeps used to, sending a child through openings that would be impossible for adults. Since we were in France, there was an official, established size for juvenile burglars; they were all more than 12 centimetres wide, and narrower gaps were therefore childproof. Quite how this had been calculated Monsieur Fructus didn't know, but the little window would have to be barred to make it safe from the depredations of anorexic five-year-olds.

For the second time that day, the itinerant cherry-pickers were held up as a threat to domestic security – Spaniards or Italians, Monsieur Fructus said, working for a pittance of three francs a kilo, here today and gone tomorrow, a grave risk. One cannot be too careful. I promised to stay on the alert and to barricade the window as soon as possible, and to talk to the dogs about being vicious. Reassured, he drove off into the sunset with the sound of Bruce Springsteen bellowing from the car stereo.

The cherry-pickers had started to hold an awful fascination for us. We wanted to see some of these light-fingered scoundrels in the flesh; surely it would be any day now that they would descend on us, because the cherries were certainly ready to pick. We'd tasted them. We now had breakfast on a small terrace which faced the early sun, twenty yards from an old tree bowed down with fruit. While my wife made coffee, I picked cherries. They were cool and juicy, almost black, and they were our first treat of the day.

We knew that organised picking had begun the morning we heard a radio playing somewhere between the house and the road. The dogs went to investigate, bristling and noisy with self-importance, and I followed, expecting to find a gang of swarthy strangers and their larcenous children. The leaves on the trees hid their bodies from the waist upwards. All I could see were various pairs of legs balanced on triangular wooden ladders, and then a great brown moon of a face under a straw trilby poked through the foliage.

'*Sont bonnes, les cerises.*' He offered me a finger, with a pair of cherries dangling from the end. It was Faustin. He and Henriette and assorted relatives had decided to gather the fruit themselves because of the wages demanded by outside labour. Someone had actually asked for five francs a kilo. Imagine! I tried to: an uncomfortable ten-hour working day perched on a ladder and tormented by fruit-flies, nights sleeping rough in a barn or the back of a van – it didn't sound like over-generous pay to me. But Faustin was adamant. It was daylight robbery, *mais enfin*, what could you expect from cherry-pickers? He reckoned to get about two tons of fruit for the jam factory in Apt, and the proceeds would be kept in the family.

The orchards were well-stocked with pickers of all shapes and sizes during the next few days, and I stopped to give two of them a ride into Bonnieux one evening. They were students from Australia, red from the sun and stained with cherry juice. They were exhausted, and complained about the hours and the tedium and the stinginess of the French peasant.

'Well, at least you're seeing a bit of France.'

'France?' said one of them. 'All I've seen is the inside of a flaming cherry tree.'

They were determined to go back to Australia with no good memories of their time in Provence. They didn't like the people. They were suspicious of the food. French beer gave them the runs. Even the scenery was small by Australian standards. They couldn't believe I had chosen to live here. I tried to explain, but we were talking about two different countries. I dropped them off at the café, where they would spend the evening being homesick. They were the only miserable Australians I had ever met, and it was depressing to hear a place that I loved being so thoroughly condemned.

Bernard cheered me up. I had come to his office in Bonnieux with the translation of a letter that he had received from an English client, and he was laughing as he opened the door.

His friend Christian, who was also our architect, had just been asked to re-design a brothel in Cavaillon. There were, *naturellement*, many unusual requirements to be met. The placing of mirrors, for instance, was of crucial importance. Certain fittings not normally found in polite bedrooms would have to be accommodated. The bidets would be working overtime, and they would have to function impeccably. I thought of Monsieur Menicucci and *jeune* trying to adjust their taps and washers while travelling salesmen from Lille chased scantily-clad young ladies through the corridors. I thought of Ramon the plasterer, a man with a definite twinkle in his eye, let loose among the *filles de joie*. He'd stay there for the rest of his life. It was a wonderful prospect.

Unfortunately, said Bernard, although Christian regarded it as an interesting architectural challenge, he was going to turn it down. Madame who ran the enterprise wanted the work finished in an impossibly short time, and she wasn't prepared to close the premises while it was being done, which would place severe demands on the workmen's powers of concentration. Nor was she prepared to pay the TVA, arguing that she didn't charge her clients a sales tax, so why should she have to pay one? In the end, she would hire a couple of renegade masons who would do a fast and clumsy job, and the chance of getting Cavaillon's brothel photographed for the pages of the *Architectural Digest* would be lost. A sad day for posterity.

* * * * *

We were learning what it was like to live more or less permanently with guests. The advance guard had arrived at Easter, and others were booked in until the end of October. Half-forgotten invitations, made in the distant safety of winter were coming home to roost and drink and sunbathe. The girl in the laundry assumed from our sheet count that we were in the hotel business, and we remembered the warnings of more experienced residents.

As it turned out, the early visitors must have taken a course in being ideal guests. They rented a car, so that they weren't dependent on us to ferry them around. They amused themselves during the day, and we had dinner together in the evening. They left when they had said they were going to. If they were all like that, we thought, the summer would pass very pleasantly.

The greatest problem, as we soon came to realise, was that our guests were on holiday. We weren't. We got up at seven. They were often in bed until ten or eleven, sometimes finishing breakfast just in time for a swim before lunch. We worked while they sunbathed. Refreshed by an afternoon nap, they came to life

in the evening, getting into high social gear as we were falling
asleep in the salad. My wife, who has a congenitally hospitable
nature and a horror of seeing people underfed, spent hours in the
kitchen, and we washed dishes far into the night.

Sundays were different. Everybody who came to stay with us
wanted to go to one of the Sunday markets, and they start early.
For once in the week, we and the guests kept the same hours.
Bleary-eyed and unusually quiet, they would doze in the back of
the car during the twenty-minute ride to breakfast in the café
overlooking the river at Isle-sur-la-Sorgue.

We parked by the bridge and woke our friends. They had gone to
bed, reluctant and still boisterous, at two in the morning, and the
bright light was having savage effects on their hangovers. They hid
behind sunglasses and nursed big cups of *café crème*. At the dark
end of the bar, a *gendarme* swallowed a surreptitious pastis. The
man selling lottery tickets promised instant wealth to anyone who
hesitated by his table. Two overnight truck drivers with blue
sandpaper chins attacked their breakfasts of steak and *pommes frites*
and shouted for more wine. The fresh smell of the river came
through the open door, and ducks trod water while they waited for
crumbs to be swept off the terrace.

We set off for the main square, running the gauntlet between
groups of sallow gypsy girls in tight, shiny black skirts selling
lemons and long plaits of garlic, hissing at each other in competition. The stalls were crammed haphazardly along the street – silver
jewellery next to flat wedges of salt cod, wooden barrels of
gleaming olives, hand-woven baskets, cinnamon and saffron and
vanilla, cloudy bunches of gypsophila, a cardboard box full of
mongrel puppies, lurid Johnny Hallyday T-shirts, salmon pink
corsets and brassières of heroic proportions, rough country bread
and dark terrines.

A lanky blue-black Senegalese loped through the turmoil of the
square, festooned with his stock of authentic African tribal
leatherware, made in Spain, and digital watches. There was a roll
of drums. A man in a flat-topped peaked hat, accompanied by a
dog dressed in a red jacket, cleared his throat and adjusted his
portable loudspeaker system to an unbearable whine. Another
drum roll. '*Prix choc*! Lamb from Sisteron! Charcuterie! Tripe! Go

at once to Boucherie Crassard, Rue Carnot. *Prix choc!*' He fiddled again with his loudspeaker and consulted a clip-board. He was the town's mobile broadcasting service, announcing everything from birthday greetings to the local cinema programmes, complete with musical effects. I wanted to introduce him to Tony from advertising; they could have had an interesting time comparing promotional techniques.

Three Algerians with deeply rutted brown faces stood gossiping in the sun, their lunches hanging upside down from their hands. The live chickens they were holding by the legs had a fatalistic air about them, as if they knew that their hours were numbered. Everywhere we looked, people were eating. Stallholders held out free samples – slivers of warm pizza, pink ringlets of ham, sausage dusted with herbs and spiced with green peppercorns, tiny, nutty cubes of nougat. It was a dieter's vision of hell. Our friends started asking about lunch.

We were hours away from lunch, and before that we had to see the non-edible side of the market, the *brocanteurs* with their magpie collections of bits and pieces of domestic history rescued from attics all over Provence. Isle-sur-la-Sorgue has been an antique dealers' town for years; there is a huge warehouse by the station where thirty or forty dealers have permanent pitches, and where you can find almost anything except a bargain. But it was too sunny a morning to spend in the gloom of a warehouse, and we stayed among the outside stalls under the plane trees where the purveyors of what they like to call *haut bric-à-brac* spread their offerings on tables and chairs or on the ground, or hung them from nails in the tree trunks.

Faded sepia postcards and old linen smocks were jumbled up with fistfuls of cutlery, chipped enamel signs advertising purgatives and pomade for unruly moustaches, fire irons and chamber pots, Art Deco brooches and café ashtrays, yellowing books of poetry and the inevitable Louis Quatorze chair, perfect except for a missing leg. As it got closer to noon the prices went down and haggling began in earnest. This was the moment for my wife, who is close to professional standard at haggling, to strike. She had been circling a small plaster bust of Delacroix. The dealer marked it down to seventy-five francs, and she moved in for the kill.

'What's your best price?' she asked the dealer.

'My *best* price, Madame, is a hundred francs. However, this now seems unlikely, and lunch approaches. You can have it for fifty.'

We put Delacroix in the car, where he gazed thoughtfully out of the back window, and we joined the rest of France as the entire country prepared itself for the pleasures of the table.

One of the characteristics which we liked and even admired about the French is their willingness to support good cooking, no matter how remote the kitchen may be. The quality of the food is more important than convenience, and they will happily drive for an hour or more, salivating en route, in order to eat well. This makes it possible for a gifted cook to prosper in what might appear to be the most unpromising of locations, and the restaurant we had chosen was so isolated that on our first visit we'd taken a map.

Buoux is barely large enough to be called a village. Hidden in the hills about ten miles from Bonnieux, it has an ancient Mairie, a modern telephone kiosk, fifteen or twenty scattered houses and the 'Auberge de la Loube', built into the side of the hill with an empty, beautiful valley below it. We had found it with some difficulty in the winter, doubting the map as we went deeper and deeper into the wilderness. We had been the only clients that night, eating in front of a huge log fire while the wind rattled the shutters.

There could hardly have been a greater contrast between that raw night and a hot Sunday in May. As we came round the bend in the road leading to the restaurant we saw that the small parking area was already full, half of it taken up by three horses tethered to the bumper of a decrepit Citroën. The restaurant cat sprawled on the warm roof tiles, looking speculatively at some chickens in the next field. Tables and chairs were arranged along the length of an open-fronted barn, and we could hear the ice buckets being filled in the kitchen.

Maurice the chef came out with four glasses of peach champagne, and took us over to see his latest investment. It was an old open carriage with wooden wheels and cracked leather seats, large enough for half a dozen passengers. Maurice was planning to organise horse-drawn coach excursions through the Lubéron, stopping, *bien sûr*, for a good lunch on the way. Did we think it was an amusing idea? Would we come? Of course we would. He gave us a pleased, shy smile and went back to his ovens.

He had taught himself to cook, but he had no desire to become the Bocuse of Buoux. All he wanted was enough business to allow him to stay in his valley with his horses. The success of his restaurant was based on value for money and good, simple food rather than flights of gastronomic fancy, which he called *cuisine snob*.

There was one menu, at 110 francs. The young girl who serves on Sundays brought out a flat basketwork tray and put it in the middle of the table. We counted fourteen separate hors d'oeuvres – artichoke hearts, tiny sardines fried in batter, perfumed *tabouleh*, creamed salt cod, marinated mushrooms, baby calamari, *tapenade*, small onions in a fresh tomato sauce, celery and chick peas, radishes and cherry tomatoes, cold mussels. Balanced on the top of the loaded tray were thick slices of pâté and gherkins, saucers of olives and cold peppers. The bread had a fine crisp crust. There was white wine in the ice bucket, and a bottle of Châteauneuf-du-Pape left to breathe in the shade.

The other customers were all French, people from the neighbouring villages dressed in their clean, sombre Sunday clothes, and one or two more sophisticated couples looking fashionably out of place in their bright boutique colours. At a big table in the corner, three generations of a family piled their plates high and wished each other *bon appétit*. One of the children, showing remarkable promise for a six-year-old gourmet, said that he preferred this pâté to the one he ate at home, and asked his grandmother for a taste of her wine. The family dog waited patiently by his side, knowing as all dogs do that children drop more food than adults.

The main course arrived – rosy slices of lamb cooked with whole cloves of garlic, young green beans and a golden potato and onion *galette*. The Châteauneuf-du-Pape was poured, dark and heady, 'a wine with shoulders', as Maurice had said. We abandoned plans for an active afternoon, and drew lots to see who would get Bernard's floating armchair.

The cheese was from Banon, moist in its wrapping of vine

leaves, and then came the triple flavours and textures of the dessert: lemon sorbet, chocolate tart and *crème anglaise* all sharing a plate. Coffee. A glass of *marc* from Gigondas. A sigh of contentment. Where else in the world, our friends wondered, could you eat so well in such unfussy and relaxed surroundings? Italy, perhaps, but very few other places. They were used to London, with its over-decorated restaurants, its theme food and its grotesque prices. They told us about a bowl of pasta in Mayfair that cost more than the entire meal each of us had just had. Why was it so difficult to eat well and cheaply in London? Full of easy after-lunch wisdom, we came to the conclusion that the English eat out less often than the French, and when they do they want to be impressed as well as fed; they want bottles of wine in baskets, and finger bowls, and menus the length of a short novel, and bills they can boast about.

Maurice came over and asked if his cooking had pleased us. He sat down while he did some addition on a scrap of paper. '*La douloureuse*,' he said, pushing it over the table. It came to just over 650 francs, or about what two people would pay for a smart lunch in Fulham. One of our friends asked him if he'd ever thought of moving somewhere more accessible, like Avignon or even Ménerbes. He shook his head. 'It's good here. I have everything I want.' He could see himself there and cooking in twenty-five years' time, and we hoped we would still be in a fit state to totter up and enjoy it.

On the way home, we noticed that the combination of food and Sunday has a calming influence on the French motorist. His stomach is full. He is on his weekly holiday. He dawdles along without being tempted by the thrills of overtaking on a blind bend. He stops to take the air and relieve himself in the bushes by the roadside, at one with nature, nodding companionably at passing cars. Tomorrow he will take up the mantle of the kamikaze pilot once again, but today it is Sunday in Provence, and life is to be enjoyed.

JUNE

The local advertising industry was in bloom. Any car parked near a market for longer than five minutes became a target for roving Provençal media executives, who swooped from windscreen to windscreen stuffing small, excitable posters under the wipers. We were constantly returning to our car to find it flapping with messages – breathless news of forthcoming attractions, unmissable opportunities, edible bargains and exotic services.

There was an accordion contest in Cavaillon, with the added delights of 'Les Lovely Girls Adorablement Déshabillées (12 Tableaux)' to entertain us in between numbers. A supermarket was launching Opération Porc, which promised every conceivable part of a pig's anatomy at prices so low that we would rub our eyes in disbelief. There were boules tournaments and bals dansants, bicycle races and dog shows, mobile discothèques complete with disc jokeys, firework displays and organ recitals. There was Madame Florian, claivoyant and alchemist, who was so confident of her supernatural powers that she provided a guarantee of satisfaction with every seance. There were the working girls – from Eve, who described herself as a delicious creature available for saucy rendezvous, to Mademoiselle Roz, who could realise all our fantasies over the telephone, a service that she proudly announced had been banned in Marseille. And there was, one day, a desperate and hastily-written note asking not for our money but for our blood.

The smudged photocopy told the story of a small boy who was waiting to go to America for a major operation, and who needed constant transfusions to keep him alive until the hospital could accept him. '*Venez nombreux et vite,*' said the note. The blood unit would be at the village hall in Gordes at eight the next morning.

When we arrived at 8.30 the hall was already crowded. A dozen beds were arranged along the wall, all occupied, and from the row of upturned feet we could see that a good cross-section of the local population had turned out, easily identified by their footwear: sandals and espadrilles for the shopkeepers, high heels for the young matrons, canvas ankle boots for the peasants and carpet slippers for their wives. The elder women kept a firm grip on their shopping baskets with one hand while they clenched and unclenched the other fist to speed the flow of blood into the plastic bags, and there was considerable debate about whose contribution was the darkest, richest and most nourishing.

We lined up for a blood test behind a thick-set old man with a florid nose, a frayed cap and overalls, who watched with amusement as the nurse made unsuccessful attempts to prick the toughened skin of his thumb.

'Do you want me to fetch the butcher?' he asked. She jabbed once more, harder. '*Merde.*' A swelling drop of blood appeared, and the nurse transferred it neatly into a small tube, added some liquid and shook the mixture vigorously. She looked up from the tube with a disapproving expression.

'How did you come here?' she asked the old man.

He stopped sucking his thumb. 'Bicycle,' he said, 'all the way from Les Imberts.'

The nurse sniffed. 'It astonishes me that you didn't fall off.' She looked at the tube again. 'You're technically drunk.'

'Impossible,' said the old man. 'I may have had a little red wine with breakfast, *comme d'habitude*, but that's nothing. And furthermore,' he said, wagging his bloodstained thumb under her nose, 'a measure of alcohol enriches the corpuscles.'

The nurse was not convinced. She sent the old man away to have a second breakfast, this time with coffee, and told him to come back at the end of the morning. He lumbered off grumbling, holding the wounded thumb before him like a flag of battle.

We were pricked, pronounced sober, and shown to our beds. Our veins were plumbed into the plastic bags. We clenched and unclenched dutifully. The hall was noisy and good-humoured, and people who would normally pass each other on the street without acknowledgement were suddenly friendly, in the way that often happens when strangers are united in their performance of a good deed. Or it might have had something to do with the bar at the end of the room.

In England, the reward for a bagful of blood is a cup of tea and a biscuit. But here, after being disconnected from our tubes, we were shown to a long table manned by volunteer waiters. What would we like? Coffee, chocolate, croissants, brioches, sandwiches of ham or garlic sausage, mugs of red or rosé wine? Eat up! Drink up! Replace those corpuscles! The stomach must be served! A young male nurse was hard at work with a corkscrew, and the supervising doctor in his long white coat wished us all *bon appétit*. If the steadily growing pile of empty bottles behind the bar was anything to go by, the appeal for blood was an undoubted success, both clinically and socially.

Some time later, we received through the post our copy of *Le Globule*, the official magazine for the blood donors. Hundreds of litres had been collected that morning in Gordes, but the other statistic that interested me – the number of litres that had been drunk – was nowhere to be found, a tribute to medical discretion.

* * * * *

Our friend the London lawyer, a man steeped in English reserve, was watching what he called the antics of the frogs from the Fin de Siècle café in Cavaillon. It was market day, and the pavement was a human traffic jam, slow-moving, jostling and chaotic.

'Look over there,' he said, as a car stopped in the middle of the street while the driver got out to embrace an acquaintance, 'they're always mauling each other. See that? *Men kissing*. Damned unhealthy, if you ask me.' He snorted into his beer, his sense of propriety outraged by such deviant behaviour, so alien to the respectable Anglo-Saxon.

It had taken me some months to get used to the Provençal delight in physical contact. Like anyone brought up in England, I had absorbed certain social mannerisms. I had learned to keep my distance, to offer a nod instead of a handshake, to ration kissing to female relatives and to confine any public demonstrations of affection to dogs. To be engulfed by a Provençal welcome, as thorough and searching as being frisked by airport security guards, was, at first, a startling experience. Now I enjoyed it, and I was fascinated by the niceties of the social ritual, and the sign language which is an essential part of any Provençal encounter.

When two unencumbered men meet, the least there will be is the conventional handshake. If the hands are full, you will be offered a little finger to shake. If the hands are wet or dirty, you will be offered a forearm or an elbow. Riding a bicycle or driving a car does not excuse you from the obligation to *toucher les cinq sardines*, and so you will see perilous contortions being performed on busy streets as hands grope through car windows and across handlebars to find each other. And this is only at the first and most restrained level of acquaintance. A closer relationship requires more demonstrative acknowledgement.

As our lawyer friend had noticed, men kiss other men. They squeeze shoulders, slap backs, pummel kidneys, pinch cheeks. When a Provençal man is truly pleased to see you, there is a real possibility of coming away from his clutches with superficial bruising.

The risk of bodily damage is less where women are concerned, but an amateur can easily make a social blunder if he miscalculates the required number of kisses. In my early days of discovery, I would plant a single kiss, only to find that the other cheek was being proffered as I was drawing back. Only snobs kiss once, I was told, or those unfortunates who suffer from congenital *froideur*. I then saw what I assumed to be the correct procedure – the triple kiss, left-right-left, so I tried it on a Parisian friend. Wrong again. She told me that triple-kissing was a low Provençal habit, and that two kisses were enough among civilised people. The next time I saw my neighbour's wife, I kissed her twice. '*Non,*' she said, '*trois fois.*'

I now pay close attention to the movement of the female head. If it stops swivelling after two kisses, I am almost sure I've filled my quota, but I stay poised for a third lunge just in case the head should keep moving.

It's a different but equally tricky problem for my wife, who is on the receiving end and has to estimate the number of times she needs to swivel, or indeed if she needs to swivel at all. One morning she heard a bellow in the street, and turned to see Ramon the plasterer advancing on her. He stopped, and wiped his hands ostentatiously on his trousers. My wife anticipated a handshake, and held out her hand. Ramon brushed it aside and kissed her three times with great gusto. You never can tell.

Once the initial greeting is over, conversation can begin. Shopping baskets and packages are put down, dogs are tied to café tables, bicycles and tools are leaned up against the nearest wall. This is necessary, because for any serious and satisfactory discussion both hands must be free to provide visual punctuation, to terminate dangling sentences, to add emphasis or simply to decorate speech which, as it is merely a matter of moving the mouth, is not on its own sufficiently physical for the Provençal. So the hands and the eternally eloquent shoulders are vital to a quiet exchange of views, and in fact it is often possible to follow the gist of a Provençal conversation from a distance, without hearing the words, just by watching expressions and the movements of bodies and hands.

There is a well-defined silent vocabulary, starting with the hand-waggle which had been introduced to us by our builders. They used it only as a disclaimer whenever talking about time or cost, but it is a gesture of almost infinite flexibility. It can describe the state of your health, how you're getting on with your mother-in-law, the progress of your business, your assessment of a restaurant or your predictions about this year's melon crop. When it is a subject of minor importance, the waggle is perfunctory, and is accompanied by a dismissive raising of the eyebrows. More serious matters – politics, the delicate condition of one's liver, the prospects for a local rider in the Tour de France – are addressed with greater intensity. The waggle is in slow motion, with the upper part of the body swaying slightly as the hand rocks, a frown of concentration on the face.

The instrument of warning and argument is the index finger, in one of its three operational positions. Thrust up, rigid and unmoving, beneath your conversational partner's nose, it signals caution – watch out, *attention*, all is not what it seems. Held just below face level and shaken rapidly from side to side like an agitated metronome, it indicates that the other person is woefully ill-informed and totally wrong in what he has just said. The correct opinion is then delivered, and the finger changes from its sideways motion into a series of jabs and prods, either tapping the chest if the unenlightened one is a man or remaining a few discreet centimetres from the bosom in the case of a woman.

Describing a sudden departure needs two hands: the left, fingers held straight, moves upwards from waist level to smack into the palm of the right hand moving downwards – a restricted version of the popular and extremely vulgar bicep crunch. (Seen at its best during midsummer traffic jams, when disputing drivers will leave their cars to allow themselves the freedom of movement necessary for a left-arm uppercut stopped short by the right hand clamping on the bicep.)

At the end of the conversation, there is the promise to stay in touch. The middle three fingers are folded into the palm and the hand is held up to an ear, with the extended thumb and little finger imitating the shape of a telephone. Finally, there is a parting handshake. Packages, dogs and bicycles are gathered up until the whole process starts all over again fifty yards down the street. It's hardly surprising that aerobics never became popular in Provence. People get quite enough physical exercise in the course of a ten-minute chat.

These and other everyday amusements of life in nearby towns and villages were not doing much for our spirit of exploration and adventure. With so many distractions on our doorstep, we were neglecting the more famous parts of Provence, or so we were told by our friends in London. In the knowledgeable and irritating manner of seasoned armchair travellers, they kept pointing out how conveniently placed we were for Nîmes and Arles and Avignon, for the flamingoes of the Camargue and the *bouillabaisse* of Marseille. They seemed surprised and mildly disapproving when we admitted that we stayed close to home, not believing our excuses that we could never find the time to go anywhere, never felt a compulsion to go church-crawling or monument-spotting, didn't want to be tourists. There was one exception to this rooted existence, and one excursion that we were always happy to make. We both loved Aix.

The corkscrew road we take through the mountains is too narrow for trucks and too serpentine for anyone in a hurry. Apart from a single farm building with its ragged herd of goats, there is nothing to see except steep and empty landscapes of grey rock and green scrub oak, polished into high definition by the extraordinary clarity of the light. The road slopes down through the foothills on the south side of the Lubéron before joining up with the amateur Grand Prix that takes place every day on the RN 7, the *Nationale Sept* that has eliminated more motorists over the years than is comfortable to think about as one waits for a gap in the traffic.

The road leads in to Aix at the end of the most handsome main street in France. The Cours Mirabeau is beautiful at any time of the year, but at its best between spring and autumn, when the plane trees form a pale green tunnel five hundred yards long. The diffused sunlight, the four fountains along the centre of the Cours' length, the perfect proportions which follow da Vinci's rule to 'let the street be as wide as the height of the houses' – the arrangement of space and trees and architecture is so pleasing that you hardly notice the cars.

Over the years, a nice geographical distinction has evolved between work and more frivolous activities. On the shady side of the street, appropriately, are the banks and insurance companies and property agents and lawyers. On the sunny side are the cafés.

I have liked almost every café that I have ever been to in France, even the ratty little ones in tiny villages where the flies are more plentiful than customers, but I have a soft spot for the sprawling cafés of the Cours Mirabeau, and the softest spot of all for the Deux Garçons. Successive generations of proprietors have put their profits under the mattress and resisted all thoughts of redecoration, which in France usually ends in a welter of plastic and awkward lighting, and the interior looks much the same as it must have looked fifty years ago.

The ceiling is high, and toasted to a caramel colour by the smoke from a million cigarettes. The bar is burnished copper, the tables and chairs gleam with the patina bestowed by countless bottoms and elbows, and the waiters have aprons and flat feet, as all proper waiters should. It is dim and cool, a place for reflection and a quiet drink. And then there is the terrace, where the show takes place.

Aix is a university town, and there is clearly something in the curriculum that attracts pretty students. The terrace of the Deux Garçons is always full of them, and it is my theory that they are there for education rather than refreshment. They are taking a degree course in café deportment, with a syllabus divided into four parts.

One: the arrival

One must always arrive as conspicuously as possible, preferably on the back of a crimson Kawasaki 750 motor cycle driven by a young man in head-to-toe black leather and three-day stubble. It is not done to stand on the pavement and wave him goodbye as he booms off down the Cours to visit his hairdresser. That is for *gauche* little girls from the Auvergne. The sophisticated student is too busy for sentiment. She is concentrating on the next stage.

Two: the entrance

Sunglasses must be kept on until an acquaintance is identified at one of the tables, but one must not appear to be looking for company. Instead, the impression should be that one is heading into the café to make a 'phone call to one's titled Italian admirer, when – *quelle surprise!* – one sees a friend. The sunglasses can then be removed and the hair tossed while one is persuaded to sit down.

Three: ritual kissing

Everyone at the table must be kissed at least twice, often three times, and in special cases four times. Those being kissed should remain seated, allowing the new arrival to bend and swoop around the table, tossing her hair, getting in the way of the waiters and generally making her presence felt.

Four: table manners

Once seated, sunglasses should be put back on to permit the discreet study of one's own reflection in the café windows – not for reasons of narcissism, but to check important details of technique: the way one lights a cigarette, or sucks the straw in a Perrier *menthe*, or nibbles daintily on a sugar lump. If these are satisfactory, the glasses can be adjusted downwards so that they rest charmingly on the end of the nose, and attention can be given to the other occupants of the table.

This performance continues from mid-morning until early evening, and never fails to entertain me. I imagine there must be the occasional break for academic work in between these hectic periods of social study, but I have never seen a textbook darken any of the café tables, nor heard any discussion of higher calculus or political science. The students are totally absorbed in showing form, and the Course Mirabeau is all the more decorative as a result.

It would be no hardship to spend most of the day café-hopping, but as our trips to Aix are infrequent we feel a pleasant obligation to squeeze in as much as possible during the morning – to pick up a bottle of *eau-de-vie* from the man in the rue d'Italie and some cheeses from Monsieur Paul in the rue des Marseillais, to see what new nonsense is in the windows of the boutiques which are crammed, chic by jowl, next to older and less transient establishments in the narrow streets behind the Cours, to join the crowds in the flower market, to take another look at the tiny, beautiful place d'Albertas, with its cobbles and its fountain, and to make sure that we arrive in the rue Fréderéric Mistral while there are still seats to be had at Chez Gu.

There are larger, more decorative and more gastronomically distinguished restaurants in Aix, but ever since we ducked into Gu one rainy day we have kept coming back. Gu himself presides over the room – a genial, noisy man with the widest, jauntiest, most luxuriant and ambitious moustache I have ever seen, permanently fighting gravity and the razor in its attempts to make contact with Gu's eyebrows. His son takes the orders and an unseen woman with a redoubtable voice – Madame Gu, perhaps – is audibly in charge of the kitchen. The customers are made up of local businessmen, the girls from Agnes B. round the corner, smart women with their shopping bags and dachshunds and the occasional furtive and transparently illicit couple murmuring intently and ignoring their *aioli*. The wine is served in jugs, a good three-course meal costs 80 francs, and all the tables are taken by 12.30 every day.

As usual, our good intentions to have a quick and restrained lunch disappear with the first jug of wine, and, as usual, we justify our self-indulgence by telling each other that today is a holiday. We don't have businesses to get back to or diaries full of appointments, and our enjoyment is heightened, in a shamefully unworthy way, by the knowledge that the people around us will be back at their desks while we are still sitting over a second cup of coffee and deciding what to do next. There is more of Aix to see, but lunch dulls the appetite for sightseeing, and our bag of cheeses would take a smelly revenge on the way home if they were jostled through the heat of the afternoon. There is a vineyard outside Aix that I have been meaning to visit. Or there is a curiosity that we noticed on the way into town, a kind of mediaeval junk yard, littered with massive relics and wounded garden statuary. There, surely, we will find the old stone garden bench we've been looking for, and they'll probably pay us to take it away.

Matériaux d'Antan takes up a plot the size of an important cemetery by the side of the RN7. Unusually, in a country so determined to safeguard its possessions from robbers that it has the highest padlock population in Europe, the site was completely open to the road: no fences, no threatening notices, no greasy Alsatians on chains and no sign of any proprietor. How trusting, we thought as we parked, to conduct a business without any obvious means of protecting the stock. And then we realised why the owner could afford to be so relaxed about security; nothing on display could have weighed less than five tons. It would have taken ten men and a hydraulic winch to lift anything, and a car transporter to take it away.

If we had been planning to build a replica of Versailles we could have done all our shopping there in one afternoon. A full-size bath, cut from a single slab of marble? Over in the corner, with brambles growing through the plug hole. A staircase for the entrance hall? There were three, of varying lengths, gracefully curved arrangements of worn stone steps, each step as large as a dining table. Great snakes of iron balustrading lay next to them, with or without the finishing touches of giant pineapples. There were entire balconies complete with gargoyles, marble cherubs the size of stout adults, who seemed to be suffering from mumps, terra-cotta amphorae eight feet long, lying in a drunken muddle on their sides, mill wheels, columns, architraves and plinths. Everything one could imagine in stone, except a plain bench.

'Bon jour.' A young man appeared from behind a scaled-up version of the Winged Victory of Samothrace and asked if he could help us. A bench? He hooked his index finger over the bridge of his nose while he thought, then shook his head apologetically. Benches were not his speciality. However, he did have an exquisite eighteenth-century gazebo in wrought iron, or, if we had a sufficiently large garden, there was a fine mock-Roman triumphal arch he could show us, ten metres high and wide enough for two chariots abreast. Such pieces were rare, he said. For a moment, we were tempted by the thought of Faustin driving his tractor through a triumphal arch on his way to the vineyard, a wreath of olive leaves round his straw trilby, but my wife could see the impracticalities of a 250-ton impulse purchase. We left the young man with promises to come back if we ever bought a château.

The answering machine welcomed us home, winking its little red eye to show that people had been talking to it. There were three messages.

A Frenchman whose voice I didn't recognise conducted a suspicious, one-sided conversation, refusing to accept the fact that he was talking to a machine. Our message, asking callers to leave a number where they could be reached, set him off. Why must I give you my number when I am already talking to you? He waited for a reply, breathing heavily. Who is there? Why do you not answer? More heavy breathing. *Allo? Allo? Merde. Allo?* His allotted span on the tape ran out while he was in mid-grumble, and we never heard from him again.

Didier, brisk and businesslike, informed us that he and his team were ready to resume work, and would be attacking two rooms at the bottom of the house. *Normalement*, they would certainly arrive tomorrow, or perhaps the day after. And how many puppies did we want? Pénélope had fallen pregnant to a hairy stranger in Goult.

And then there was an English voice, a man we remembered meeting in London. He had seemed pleasant, but we hardly knew him. This was about to change, because he and his wife were going to drop in. He didn't say when, and he didn't leave a number. Probably, in the way of the itinerant English, they would turn up one day just before lunch. But we'd had a quiet month so far, with few guests and fewer builders, and we were ready for a little company.

They arrived at dusk, as we were sitting down to dinner in the courtyard – Ted and Susan, wreathed in apologies and loud in their enthusiasm for Provence, which they had never seen before, and for our house, our dogs, us, everything. It was all, so they said several times in the first few minutes, super. Their breathless jollity was disarming. They talked in tandem, a seamless dialogue which neither required nor allowed any contribution from us.

'Have we come at a bad time? Typical of us, I'm afraid.'

'Absolutely typical. You must *loathe* people dropping in like this. A glass of wine would be lovely.'

'Darling, look at the pool. Isn't it *pretty*.'

'Did you know the post office in Ménerbes has a little map showing how to find you? *Les Anglais*, they call you, and they fish out this map from under the counter.'

'We'd have been here earlier, except that we bumped into this sweet old man in the village . . .'

'. . . well, his car, actually . . .'

'Yes, his car, but he was sweet about it, darling, wasn't he, and it wasn't really a shunt, more a scrape.'

'So we took him into the café and bought him a drink . . .'

'Quite a few drinks, wasn't it, darling?'

'And some for those funny friends of his.'

'Anyway, we're here now, and I must say it's *absolutely* lovely.'

'And so kind of you to put up with us barging in on you like this.'

They paused to drink some wine and catch their breath, looking around and making small humming noises of approval. My wife, acutely conscious of the slightest symptoms of undernourishment, noticed that Ted was eyeing our dinner, which was still untouched on the table. She asked if they would like to eat with us.

'Only if it's absolutely no trouble – just a crust and a scrap of cheese and maybe *one* more glass of wine.'

Ted and Susan sat down, still chattering, and we brought out sausage, cheeses, salad and some slices of the cold vegetable omelette called *crespaou* with warm, fresh tomato sauce. It was received with such rapture that I wondered how long it had been since their last meal, and what arrangements they had made for their next one.

'Where are you staying while you're down here?'

Ted filled his glass. Well, nothing had actually been booked – 'Typical of us, absolutely typical' – but a little *auberge*, they thought, somewhere clean and simple and not too far away because they'd adore to see the house in the daytime if we could bear it. There must be half a dozen small hotels we could recommend.

There were, but it was past ten, getting close to bedtime in Provence, and not the moment to be banging on shuttered windows and locked doors and dodging the attentions of hotel guard dogs. Ted and Susan had better stay the night and find somewhere in the morning. They looked at each other, and began a duet of gratitude that lasted until their bags had been taken upstairs. They cooed a final good night from the guest room window, and we could still hear them chirruping as we went off to bed. They were like two excited children, and we thought it would be fun to have them stay for a few days.

The barking of the dogs woke us just after three. They were

intrigued by noises coming from the guest room, heads cocked at the sound of someone being comprehensively sick, interspersed with groans and the splash of running water.

I always find it difficult to know how best to respond to other people's ailments. I prefer to be left alone when I'm ill, remembering what an uncle had told me long ago. 'Puke in private, dear boy,' he had said. 'Nobody else is interested in seeing what you ate.' But there are other sufferers who are comforted by the sympathy of an audience.

The noises persisted, and I called upstairs to ask if there was anything we could do. Ted's worried face appeared round the door. Susan had eaten something. Poor old thing had a delicate stomach. All this excitement. There was nothing to be done except to let nature take its course, which it then loudly did again. We retreated to bed.

The thunder of falling masonry started shortly after seven. Didier had arrived as promised, and was limbering up with a sawn-off sledgehammer and an iron spike while his assistants tossed sacks of cement around and bullied the concrete-mixer into life. Our invalid felt her way slowly down the stairs, clutching her brow against the din and the bright sunlight, but insisting that she was well enough for breakfast. She was wrong, and had to leave the table hurriedly to return to the bathroom. It was a perfect morning with no wind, no clouds and a sky of true blue. We spent it finding a doctor who would come to the house, and then went shopping for suppositories in the pharmacy.

Over the next four or five days, we came to know the chemist well. The unlucky Susan and her stomach were at war. Garlic made her bilious. The local milk, admittedly rather curious stuff, put her bowels in an uproar. The oil, the butter, the water, the wine – nothing agreed with her, and twenty minutes in the sun turned her into a walking blister. She was allergic to the South.

It's not uncommon. Provence is such a shock to the Northern system; everything is full-blooded. Temperatures are extreme, ranging from over a hundred degrees down to minus twenty. Rain, when it comes, falls with such abandon that it washes roads away and closes the autoroute. The Mistral is a brutal, exhausting wind, bitter in winter and harsh and dry in summer. The food is full of strong, earthy flavours that can overwhelm a digestion used to a less assertive diet. The wine is young and deceptive, easy to drink but sometimes higher in alcoholic content than older wines that are treated with more caution. The combined effects of the food and climate, so different from England, take time to get used to. There is nothing bland about Provence, and it can poleaxe people as it had poleaxed Susan. She and Ted left us to convalesce in more temperate surroundings.

Their visit made us realise how fortunate we were to have the constitutions of goats and skins that accepted the sun. The routine of our days had changed, and we were living outdoors. Getting dressed took thirty seconds. There were fresh figs and melons for breakfast, and errands were done early, before the warmth of the sun turned to heat in mid-morning. The flagstones round the pool were hot to the touch, the water still cool enough to bring us up from the first dive with a gasp. We slipped into the habit of that sensible Mediterranean indulgence, the siesta.

The wearing of socks was a distant memory. My watch stayed in a drawer, and I found that I could more or less tell the time by the position of the shadows in the courtyard, although I seldom knew what the date was. It didn't seem important. I was turning into a contented vegetable, maintaining sporadic contact with real life through telephone conversations with people in faraway offices. They always asked wistfully what the weather was like, and were not pleased with the answer. They consoled themselves by warning me about skin cancer and the addling effect of sun on the brain. I didn't argue with them; they were probably right. But, addled, wrinkled and potentially cancerous as I might have been, I had never felt better.

The masons were working stripped to the waist, enjoying the weather as much as we were. Their main concession to the heat was a slightly extended lunch break, which was monitored to the minute by our dogs. At the first sound of hampers being opened and plates and cutlery coming out, they would cross the courtyard at a dead run and take their places by the table, something they never did with us. Patient and unblinking, they would watch every mouthful with underprivileged expressions. Invariably, it worked. At the end of lunch they would skulk back to their lairs under the rosemary hedge, their cheeks bulging guiltily with Camembert or *cous-cous*. Didier claimed that it fell off the table.

Work on the house was going according to schedule – that is, each room was taking three months from the day the masons moved in to the day that we could move in. And we had the prospect of Menicucci and his radiators to look forward to in August. In another place, in less perfect weather, it would have been depressing, but not here. The sun was a great tranquilliser, and time passed in a haze of well-being; long, slow, almost torpid days when it was so enjoyable to be alive that nothing else mattered. We had been told that the weather often continued like this until the end of October. We had also been told that July and August were the two months when sensible residents left Provence for somewhere quieter and less crowded, like Paris. Not us.

JULY

My friend had rented a house in Ramatuelle, a few kilometres from Saint-Tropez. We wanted to see each other, despite a mutual reluctance to brave the bad-tempered congestion of high summer traffic. I lost the toss, and said I'd be there by lunchtime.

After driving for half an hour I found myself in a different country, inhabited mostly by caravans. They were wallowing towards the sea in monstrous shoals, decked out with curtains of orange and brown and window stickers commemorating past migrations. Groups of them rested in the parking areas by the side of the autoroute, shimmering with heat. Their owners, ignoring the open countryside behind them, set up picnic tables and chairs with a close and uninterrupted view of the passing trucks, and within easy breathing distance of the diesel fumes. As I turned off the autoroute to go down to Sainte-Maxime, I could see more caravans stretching ahead in a bulbous, swaying convoy, and I gave up any thoughts of an early lunch. The final five kilometres of the journey took an hour and a half. Welcome to the Côte d'Azur.

It used to be beautiful, and rare and expensive pockets of it still are. But compared with the peace and relative emptiness of the

Lubéron it seemed like a madhouse, disfigured by overbuilding, overcrowding and overselling: villa developments, *steack pommes frites*, inflatable rubber boats, genuine Provençal souvenirs made from olive wood, pizzas, water-skiing lessons, night clubs, go-kart tracks – the posters were everywhere, offering everything.

The people whose business it is to make a living from the Côte d'Azur have a limited season, and their eagerness to take your money before autumn comes and the demand for inflatable rubber boats stops is palpable and unpleasant. Waiters are impatient for their tips, shopkeepers snap at your heels so that you won't take too long to make up your mind, and then refuse to accept 200-franc notes because there are so many forgeries. A hostile cupidity hangs in the air, as noticeable as the smell of Ambre Solaire and garlic. Strangers are automatically classified as tourists and treated like nuisances, inspected with unfriendly eyes and tolerated for cash. According to the map, this was still Provence. It wasn't the Provence I knew.

My friend's house was in the pine forests outside Ramatuelle, at the end of a long private track, completely detached from the lunacy three kilometres away on the coast. He was not surprised to hear that a two-hour drive had taken more than four hours. He told me that to be sure of a parking spot for dinner in Saint-Tropez it was best to be there by 7.30 in the morning, that going down to the beach was an exercise in frustration and that the only guaranteed way to get to Nice airport in time to catch a plane was by helicopter.

As I drove back home in the evening against the caravan tide, I wondered what it was about the Côte d'Azur that continued to attract such hordes every summer. From Marseille to Monte Carlo, the roads were a nightmare and the sea shore was covered in a living carpet of bodies broiling in the sun, flank to oily flank for mile after mile. Selfishly, I was glad they wanted to spend their holidays there rather than in the open spaces of the Lubéron, among more agreeable natives.

Some natives, of course, were less agreeable than others, and I met one the next morning. Massot was *en colère*, kicking at the undergrowth in the small clearing near his house and chewing at his moustache in vexation.

'You see this?' he said. 'Those *salauds*. They come like thieves in the night and leave early in the morning. *Saloperie* everywhere.' He showed me two empty sardine cans and a wine bottle which proved beyond any reasonable doubt that his arch-enemies the German campers had been trespassing in his private section of the national park. That in itself was bad enough, but the campers had treated his elaborate defence system with contempt, rolling back boulders to make a gap in the barricade and – *sales voleurs*! – stealing the notices that warned of the presence of vipers.

Massot took off his jungle cap and rubbed the bald spot on the back of his head as he considered the enormity of the crime. He looked in the direction of his house, standing on tiptoe first on one side of the path, then on the other. He grunted.

'It might work,' he said, 'but I'd have to cut down the trees.'

If he removed the small forest that stood between his house and the clearing, he would be able to see the headlights of any car coming down the track and loose off a couple of warning shots from his bedroom window. But, then again, those trees were extremely valuable, and added to the general desirability of the house he was trying to sell. No buyer had yet been found, but it was only a matter of time before somebody recognised it for the bargain it was. The trees had better stay. Massot thought again, and suddenly brightened up. Maybe the answer was *pièges à feu*. Yes, he liked that.

I had heard about *pièges à feu*, and they sounded horrendous – concealed snares that exploded when they were disturbed, like miniature mines. The thought of fragments of German camper flying through the air was alarming to me, but clearly very amusing to Massot, who was pacing round the clearing saying *boum*! every three or four yards as he planned his minefield.

Surely he wasn't serious, I said, and in any case I thought that *pièges à feu* were illegal. Massot stopped his explosions and tapped the side of his nose, sly and conspiratorial.

'That may be true,' he said, 'but there's no law against notices.' He grinned, and raised both arms above his head. '*Boum!*'

Where were you twenty years ago, I thought, when they needed you on the Côte d'Azur?

Perhaps Massot's anti-social instincts were being intensified by the heat. It was often in the nineties by mid-morning, and the sky turned from blue to a burnt white by noon. Without consciously thinking about it, we adjusted to the temperature by getting up earlier and using the cool part of the day to do anything energetic. Any sudden or industrious activity between midday and early evening was out of the question; like the dogs, we sought out the shade instead of the sun. Cracks appeared in the earth, and the grass gave up trying to grow. For long periods during the day the only sounds were those made by the *cigales* round the house, the bees in the lavender and bodies toppling into the pool.

I walked the dogs each morning between six and seven, and they discovered a new sport, more rewarding than chasing rabbits and squirrels. It had started when they came across what they thought was a large animal made of bright blue nylon. Circling it at a safe distance, they barked until it stirred and finally woke. A rumpled face appeared from one end, followed a few moments later by a hand offering a biscuit. From then on, the sight of a sleeping bag among the trees meant food. For the campers, it must have been disquieting to wake up and see two whiskery faces only inches away, but they were amiable enough about it once they had recovered from the shock.

Strangely enough, Massot was half right. They were mostly Germans, but not the indiscriminate rubbish-tippers that he complained about. These Germans left no trace; everything was bundled into giant backpacks before they shuffled off like two-legged snails into the heat of the day. In my short experience of litter in the Lubéron, the French themselves were the most likely offenders, but no Frenchman would accept that. At any time of the year, but particularly in the summer, it was well known that foreigners of one stripe or another were responsible for causing most of the problems in life.

The Belgians, so it was said, were to blame for the majority of accidents because of their habit of driving in the middle of the road, forcing the famously prudent French driver into ditches to avoid being *écrasé*. The Swiss and the non-camping section of the German population were guilty of monopolising hotels and restaurants and pushing up property prices. And the English – ah, the English. They were renowned for the frailty of their digestive systems and their preoccupation with drains and plumbing. 'They have a talent for diarrhoea,' a French friend observed. 'If an Englishman hasn't got it, he is looking for somewhere to have it.'

There is just enough of a hint of truth in these national insults to sustain their currency, and I was witness to an interlude in one of Cavaillon's busiest cafés which must have confirmed the French in their opinion of English sensitivities.

A couple with their small son were having coffee, and the boy indicated his need to go to the lavatory. The father looked up from his two-day-old copy of the *Daily Telegraph*.

'You'd better make sure it's all right,' he said to the boy's mother. 'Remember what happened in Calais?'

The mother sighed, and made her way dutifully into the gloom at the rear of the café. When she reappeared it was at high speed, and she looked as if she had just eaten a lemon.

'It's *disgusting*. Roger is not to go in there.'

Roger became immediately interested in exploring a forbidden lavatory.

'I've got to go,' he said, and played his trump card. 'It's number two. I've got to go.'

'There isn't even a seat. It's just a *hole*.'

'I don't care. I've got to go.'

'You'll have to take him,' said the mother. 'I'm not going in there again.'

The father folded his newspaper and stood up, with young Roger tugging at his hand.

'You'd better take the newspaper,' said the mother.

'I'll finish it when I get back.'

'*There's no paper*,' she hissed.

'Ah. Well, I'll try to save the crossword.'

The minutes passed, and I was wondering if I could ask the mother exactly what had happened in Calais, when there was a loud exclamation from the back of the café.

'*Poo!*'

It was the emerging Roger, followed by his ashen-faced father holding the remnants of his newspaper. Conversation in the café stopped as Roger gave an account of the expedition at the top of his voice. The *patron* looked at his wife and shrugged. Trust the

English to make a spectacle out of a simple visit to the *wa-wa*.

The equipment that had caused such consternation to Roger and his parents was a *toilette à la Turque*, which is a shallow porcelain tray with a hole in the middle and foot-rests at each side. It was designed, presumably by a Turkish sanitary engineer, for maximum inconvenience, but the French had added a refinement of their own – a high-pressure flushing device of such velocity that unwary users can find themselves soaked from the shins down. There are two ways of avoiding sodden feet: the first is to operate the flushing lever from the safety of dry land in the doorway, but since this requires long arms and the balance of an acrobat, the second option – not to flush at all – is unfortunately much more prevalent. To add to the problem, some establishments install an energy-saving device which is peculiar to the French. The light switch, always located on the outside of the lavatory door, is fitted with an automatic timer that plunges the occupant into darkness after thirty-eight seconds, thus saving precious electricity and discouraging loiterers.

Amazingly enough, *à la Turque* lavatories are still being manufactured, and the most modern café is quite likely to have a chamber of horrors in the back. But, when I mentioned this to Monsieur Menicucci, he leapt to the defence of French sanitary ware, insisting that at the other end of the scale were lavatories of such sophistication and ergonometric perfection that *even an American* would be impressed. He suggested a meeting to discuss two lavatories we needed for the house. He had some marvels to show us, he said, and we would be ravished by the choice.

He arrived with a valise full of catalogues, and unloaded them on to the table in the courtyard as he made some mystifying remarks about vertical or horizontal evacuation. As he had said, there was a wide choice, but they were all aggressively modern in design and colour – squat, sculptural objects in deep burgundy or burnt apricot. We were looking for something simple and white.

'*C'est pas facile*,' he said. People nowadays wanted new forms and colours. It was all part of the French sanitary revolution. The traditional white was not favoured by the designers. There was, however, one model he had seen recently which might be exactly what we wanted. He rummaged through his catalogues and – yes, he was sure of it – this was the one for us.

'*Voilà! La W.C. haute couture!*' He pushed the catalogue over to us and there, lit and photographed like an Etruscan vase, was the Pierre Cardin lavatory.

'You see?' said Menicucci. 'It is even signed by Cardin.' And so it was, up on the top and well out of harm's way. Apart from the signature it was perfect, a handsome design that looked like a lavatory and not like a giant goldfish bowl. We ordered two.

It was a saddened Menicucci who telephoned a week later to tell us that the House of Cardin no longer made our lavatories. *Une catastrophe* but he would continue his researches.

A further ten days passed before he reappeared, now in triumph, coming up the steps to the house waving another catalogue above his head.

'*Toujours couture!*' he said. '*Toujours couture!*'

Cardin may have left the bathroom, but his place had been taken by the gallant Courrèges, whose design was very similar and who had exercised remarkable restraint in the matter of the signature, leaving it off altogether. We congratulated Menicucci, and he allowed himself a celebratory Coca-Cola. He raised his glass.

'Today the lavatories, tomorrow the central heating,' he said, and we sat for a while in the 90-degrees sunshine while he told us how warm we were going to be and went through his plan of attack. Walls were to be broken, dust would be everywhere, the noise of the jackhammer would take over from the bees and the crickets. There was only one bright spot about it, said Menicucci. It would keep the guests away for a few weeks. *Eh, oui.*

But before this period of enforced and ear-splitting seclusion we were expecting one last guest, a man so maladroit and disaster-prone, so absent-minded and undomesticated, so consistently involved in household accidents that we had specifically asked him to come on the eve of demolition so that the debris of his visit could be buried under the rubble of August. It was Bennett, a close friend for fifteen years who cheerfully admitted to being the World's Worst Guest. We loved him, but with apprehension.

He called from the airport, several hours after he was due to arrive. Could I come down and pick him up? There had been a slight problem with the car hire company, and he was stranded.

I found him in the upstairs bar at Marignane, comfortably installed with a bottle of champagne and a copy of the French edition of *Playboy*. He was in his late forties, slim and extremely good-looking, dressed in an elegant suit of off-white linen with badly scorched trousers. 'Sorry to drag you out,' he said, 'but they've run out of cars. Have some champagne.'

He told me what had happened and, as usual with Bennett, it was all so unlikely that it had to be true. The plane had arrived on time, and the car he had reserved, a convertible, was waiting for him. The top was down, it was a glorious afternoon and Bennett, in an expansive mood, had lit a cigar before heading towards the autoroute. It had burned quickly, as cigars do when fanned by a strong breeze, and Bennett had tossed it away after twenty minutes. He became aware that passing motorists were waving at him, so in return he waved to them; how friendly the French have become, he thought. He was some miles up the autoroute before he realised that the back of the car was burning, set on fire by the discarded cigar butt that had lodged in the upholstery. With what he thought was tremendous presence of mind, he pulled on to the hard shoulder, stood up on the front seat and urinated into the flames. And that was when the police had found him.

'They were terribly nice,' he said, 'but they thought it would be best if I brought the car back to the airport, and then the car rental people had a fit and wouldn't give me another one.'

He finished his champagne and gave me the bill. What with all the excitement, he said, he hadn't managed to change his traveller's cheques. It was good to see him again, still the same as ever, charming, terminally clumsy, beautifully dressed, permanently short of funds. My wife and I had once pretended to be his maid and manservant at a dinner party when we were all so broke that we shared out the tip afterwards. We always had fun with Bennett, and dinner that night lasted into the early hours of the morning.

The week passed as uneventfully as could be expected, given that our guest was a man who could, and often did, spill his drink over himself while looking at his watch, and whose immaculate white trousers never survived the first course of dinner unsoiled.

There were one or two breakages, the odd drowned towel in the swimming pool, a sudden panic when he realised that he had sent his passport to the dry cleaners, some worrying moments when he thought he had eaten a wasp, but no true calamities. We were sad to see him go, and hoped he would come back soon to finish the four half empty glasses of Calvados we found under his bed, and to pick up the underpants that he had left hanging decoratively from the hat rack.

* * * * *

It was Bernard who had told us about the old station café in Bonnieux. Solid and serious was how he described it, a family restaurant of the kind that used to exist all over France before food became fashionable and *bistrots* started serving slivers of duckling instead of *daube* and tripe. Go soon, Bernard said, because *la patronne* talks about retiring, and take a big appetite with you. She likes to see clean plates.

The station at Bonnieux has been closed for more than forty years, and the path that leads to it is potholed and neglected. From the road there is nothing to see – no signs, no menus. We had passed by dozens of times, assuming that the building was unoccupied, not knowing that a crowded car park was hidden behind the trees.

We found a space between the local ambulance and a mason's scarred truck, and stood for a moment listening to the clatter of dishes and the murmur of conversation that came through the open windows. The restaurant was fifty yards from the station, foursquare and unpretentious, with faded lettering just legible in hand-painted capitals: Café de la Gare.

A small Renault van pulled into the car park, and two men in overalls got out. They washed their hands at the old sink against the outside wall, using the yellow banana of soap that was mounted over the taps on its bracket, and elbowed the door open, hands still wet. They were regulars, and went straight to the towel which hung from a hook at the end of the bar. By the time they had dried their hands two glasses of pastis and a jug of water were waiting for them.

It was a big, airy room, dark at the front and sunny at the back, where windows looked over fields and vineyards towards the hazy bulk of the Lubéron. There must have been forty people, all men, already eating. It was only a few minutes past noon, but the Provençal has a clock in his stomach, and lunch is his sole concession to punctuality. *On mange à midi*, and not a moment later.

Each table had its white paper cover and two unlabelled bottles of wine, a red and a pink, from the Bonnieux co-operative two hundred yards away on the other side of the road. There was no written menu. Madame cooked five meals a week, lunch from Monday to Friday, and customers ate what she decided they would eat. Her daughter brought us a basket of good, chewy bread, and asked us if we wanted water. No? Then we must tell her when we wanted more wine.

Most of the other customers seemed to know each other, and there were some spirited and insulting exchanges between the tables. An enormous man was accused of slimming. He looked up from his plate and stopped eating long enough to growl. We saw our electrician and Bruno who lays the stone floors eating together in a corner, and recognised two or three other faces that we hadn't seen since work had stopped on the house. The men were sunburned, looking fit and relaxed as if they had been on holiday. One of them called across to us.

'*C'est tranquille chez vous*? Peaceful without us?'

We said we hoped they would be coming back when work started again in August.

'*Normalement, oui.*' The hand waggled. We knew what that meant.

Madame's daughter returned with the first course, and explained that it was a light meal today because of the heat. She put down an oval dish covered with slices of *saucisson* and cured ham, with tiny gherkins, some black olives and grated carrots in a sharp marinade. A thick slice of white butter to dab on the *saucisson*. More bread.

Two men in jackets came in with a dog and took the last empty table. There was a rumour, so Madame's daughter said, that the older of the two men had been the French Ambassador to a

117

country in the Middle East. *Un homme distingué*. He sat there among the masons and plumbers and truck drivers, feeding his dog small pieces of sausage.

Salad arrived in glass bowls, the lettuce slick with dressing, and with it another oval dish. Noodles in a tomato sauce and slices of roast loin of pork, juicy in a dark onion gravy. We tried to imagine what Madame would serve up in the winter, when she wasn't toying with these light meals, and we hoped that she would have second thoughts about retiring. She had taken up her position behind the bar, a short, comfortably proportioned woman, her hair still dark and thick. She looked as though she could go on for ever.

Her daughter cleared away, emptied the last of the red wine into our glasses and, unasked, brought another bottle with the cheese. The early customers were starting to leave to go back to work, wiping their moustaches and asking Madame what she proposed to give them tomorrow. Something good, she said.

I had to stop after the cheese. My wife, who has never yet been defeated by a menu, had a slice of *tarte au citron*. The room began to smell of coffee and Gitanes, and the sun coming through the window turned the smoke blue as it drifted above the heads of the three men sitting over thimble-sized glasses of *marc*. We ordered coffee and asked for a bill, but bills were not part of the routine. Customers settled up at the bar on the way out.

Madame told us what we owed. Fifty francs each for the food, and four francs for the coffee. The wine was included in the price. No wonder the place was full every day.

Was it really true she was going to retire?

She stopped polishing the bar. 'When I was a little girl,' she said, 'I had to choose whether to work in the fields or in the kitchen. Even in those days I hated the land. It's hard, dirty work.' She looked down at her hands, which were well-kept and surprisingly young-looking. 'So I chose the kitchen, and when I married we moved here. I've been cooking for thirty-eight years. It's enough.'

We said how sorry we were, and she shrugged.

'One becomes tired.' She was going to live in Orange, she said, in an apartment with a balcony, and sit in the sun.

It was two o'clock, and the room was empty except for an old man with white stubble on his leather cheeks, dipping a sugar lump into his Calvados. We thanked Madame for a fine lunch.

'*C'est normale,*' she said.

The heat outside was like a blow on the skull and the road back to the house was a long mirage, liquid and rippling in the glare, the leaves on the vines drooping, the farm dogs silent, the countryside stunned and deserted. It was an afternoon for the pool and the hammock and an undemanding book, a rare afternoon without builders or guests, and it seemed to pass in slow motion.

By the evening, our skins prickling from the sun, we were sufficiently recovered from lunch to prepare for the sporting event of the week. We had accepted a challenge from some friends who, like us, had become addicted to one of the most pleasant games ever invented, and we were going to try to uphold the honour of Ménerbes on the *boules* court.

Long before, during a holiday, we had bought our first set of *boules* after watching the old men in Roussillon spend an enjoyably argumentative afternoon on the village court below the post office. We had taken our *boules* back to England, but it is not a game that suits the damp, and they gathered cobwebs in a barn. They had been almost the first things we unpacked when we came to live in Provence. Smooth and tactile, they fitted into the palm of the hand, heavy, dense, gleaming spheres of steel that made a satisfying *chock* when tapped together.

We studied the techniques of the professionals who played every day next to the church at Bonnieux – men who could drop a *boule* on your toe from twenty feet away – and came home to practise what we had seen. The true aces, we noticed, bent their knees in a crouch and held the *boule* with the fingers curled round and the palm facing downwards, so that when the *boule* was thrown, friction from the fingers provided backspin. And there were the lesser elements of style – the grunts and encouragements that helped every throw on its way, and the shrugs and muttered oaths when it landed short or long. We soon became experts in everything except accuracy.

There were two basic types of delivery: the low, rolling throw that skittered along the ground, or the high-trajectory drop shot, aimed to knock the opponent's *boule* off the court. The precision of some of the players we watched was remarkable, and for all our crouching and grunting it would take years of applied effort before we would be welcomed to a serious court like the one in Bonnieux.

Boules is an essentially simple game, which a beginner can enjoy from the first throw. A small wooden ball, the *cochonnet*, is tossed up the court. Each player has three *boules*, identified by different patterns etched into the steel, and at the end of the round the closest to the *cochonnet* is the winner. There are different systems of scoring, and all kinds of local bye-laws and variations. These, if carefully planned, can be of great advantage to the home team.

We were playing on our own court that evening, and the game was therefore subject to Lubéron Rules:

1. Anyone playing without a drink is disqualified.
2. Incentive cheating is permitted.
3. Disputes concerning the distance from the *cochonnet* are mandatory. Nobody's word is final.
4. Play stops when darkness falls unless there is no clear winner, in which case blind man's *boules* are played until there is a torchlight decision or the *cochonnet* is lost.

We had gone to some trouble to construct a court with deceptive slopes and shallow hollows to baffle visitors, and had roughened the playing surface so that our luck would have a sporting chance against superior skill. We were quietly confident, and I had the added advantage of being in charge of the pastis; any signs of consistent accuracy from the visiting team would be countered by bigger drinks, and I knew from personal experience what big drinks did to one's aim.

Our opponents included a girl of sixteen who had never played before, but the other three had at least six weeks of practice between them, and were not to be treated lightly. As we inspected the playing surface, they made disparaging comments about its lack of regularity, complained about the angle of the setting sun and made a formal request for dogs to be banned from the court. The old stone roller was trundled up and down to humour them. Moistened fingers were held in the air to gauge the strength of the breeze, and play commenced.

There is a distinct, if slow, rhythm to the game. A throw is made, and play stops while the next to throw strolls up for a closer look and tries to decide whether to bomb or whether to attempt a low, creeping delivery that will sidle round the other *boules* to kiss the *cochonnet*. A contemplative sip of pastis is taken, the knees are flexed, the *boule* loops through the air, thuds to earth and rolls with a soft crunching sound to its resting place. There are no hurried movements and almost no sporting injuries. (One exception being Bennett, who had scored a broken roof tile and self-inflicted concussion of the toe during his first and last game.)

Intrigue and gamesmanship make up for the lack of athletic drama, and the players that evening behaved abominably. *Boules* were moved by stealth, with accidental nudges of the foot. Players poised to throw were distracted by comments on their stance, offers of more pastis, accusations of stepping over the throwing line, warnings of dogs crossing the court, sightings of imaginary grass snakes and conflicting bad advice from every side. There were no clear winners at half-time, when we stopped to watch the sunset.

To the west of the house, the sun was centred in the vee made by two mountain peaks in a spectacular display of natural symmetry. Within five minutes it was over, and we played on in the *crépuscule*, the French word that makes twilight sound like a skin complaint. Measuring distances from the *cochonnet* became more difficult and more contentious, and we were about to agree on a dishonourable draw when the young girl whose first game it was put three *boules* in a nine-inch group. Foul play and alcohol had been defeated by youth and fruit juice.

We ate out in the courtyard, the flagstones sun-warm under our bare feet, the candlelight flickering on red wine and brown faces. Our friends had rented their house to an English family for August, and they were going to spend the month in Paris on the proceeds. According to them, all the Parisians would be down in Provence, together with untold thousands of English, Germans, Swiss and Belgians. Roads would be jammed; markets and restaurants impossibly full. Quiet villages would become noisy and everyone without exception would be in a filthy humour. We had been warned.

We had indeed. We had heard it all before. But July had been far less terrible than predicted, and we were sure that August could be dealt with very easily. We would unplug the 'phone, lie dow by the pool and listen, whether we liked it or not, to the concerto for jackhammer and blowtorch, conducted by Maestro Menicucci.

AUGUST

'There is a strong rumour,' said Menicucci, 'that Brigitte Bardot has bought a house in Roussillon.' He put his spanner down on the wall and moved closer so that there was no chance of *jeune* overhearing any more of Miss Bardot's personal plans.

'She intends to leave Saint-Tropez.' Menicucci's finger was poised to tap me on the chest. 'And I don't blame her. Do you know' – tap, tap, tap went the finger – 'that at any given moment during any day in the month of August there are five thousand people making *pipi* in the sea?'

He shook his head at the unsanitary horror of it all. 'Who would be a fish?'

We stood in the sun sympathising with the plight of any marine life unfortunate enough to be resident in Saint-Tropez while *jeune* toiled up the steps carrying a cast-iron radiator, a garland of copper piping slung round his shoulders, his Yale University T-shirt dark with sweat. Menicucci had made a significant sartorial concession to the heat, and had discarded his usual heavy corduroy trousers in favour of a pair of brown shorts that matched his canvas boots.

It was the opening day of *les grands travaux*, and the area in front of the house resembled a scrapyard. Piled around an oily workbench of great antiquity were some of the elements of our central heating system – boxes of brass joints, valves, soldering guns, gas canisters, hacksaws, radiators, drilling bits, washers and spanners and cans of what looked like black treacle. This was only the first delivery; the water tank, the fuel tank, the boiler and the burner were still to come.

Menicucci took me on a guided tour of the components, emphasising their quality. *'C'est pas de la merde, ça.'* He then pointed out which walls he was going to burrow through, and full realisation of the weeks of dust and chaos ahead sunk in. I almost wished I could spend August in Saint-Tropez with the half-million incontinent holidaymakers already there.

They and millions more had come down from the north in the course of a single massively constipated weekend. Twenty-mile traffic jams had been reported on the autoroute at Beaune, and anyone getting through the tunnel at Lyon in less than an hour was considered lucky. Cars and tempers became overheated. The breakdown trucks had their best weekend of the year. Fatigue and impatience were followed by accidents and death. It was a traditionally awful start to the month, and the ordeal would be repeated four weeks later in the opposite direction during the exodus weekend.

Most of the invaders passed us by on their way to the coast, but there were thousands who made their way into the Lubéron, changing the character of markets and villages and giving the local inhabitants something new to philosophise about over their pastis. Café regulars found their usual places taken by foreigners, and stood by the bar grizzling over the inconveniences of the holiday season – the bakery running out of bread, the car parked outside one's front door, the strange late hours that visitors kept. It was admitted, with much nodding and sighing, that tourists brought money into the region. Nevertheless, it was generally agreed that they were a funny bunch, these natives of August.

It was impossible to miss them. They had clean shoes and indoor skins, bright new shopping baskets and spotless cars. They drifted through the streets of Lacoste and Ménerbes and Bonnieux in a sightseer's trance, looking at the people of the village as if they too were quaint rustic monuments. The beauties of nature were loudly praised every evening on the ramparts of Ménerbes, and I particularly liked the comments of an elderly English couple as they stood looking out over the valley.

'What a marvellous sunset,' she said.

'Yes,' replied her husband. 'Most impressive for such a small village.'

Even Faustin was in fine holiday humour. His work on the vines was finished for the time being, and there was nothing he could do but wait for the grapes to ripen and try out his repertoire of English jokes on us. 'What is it,' he asked me one morning, 'that changes from the colour of a dead rat to the colour of a dead lobster in three hours?' His shoulders started to shake as he tried to suppress his laughter at the unbearably funny answer. '*Les Anglais en vacances,*' he said, '*vous comprenez?*' In case I hadn't fully grasped the richness of the joke, he then explained very carefully that the English complexion was known to be so fair that the slightest exposure would turn it bright red. '*Même sous un rayon de lune,*' he said, shuddering with mirth, 'even a moonbeam makes them pink.'

Faustin in waggish mood early in the morning was transformed into Faustin the sombre by the evening. He had heard news from the Côte d'Azur, which he told to us with a terrible relish. There had been a forest fire near Grasse, and the Canadair planes had been called out. These operated like pelicans, flying out to sea and scooping up a cargo of water to drop on the flames inland. According to Faustin, one of the planes had scooped up a swimmer and dropped him into the fire, where he had been *carbonisé*.

Curiously, there was no mention of the tragedy in *Le Provençal*, and we asked a friend if he had heard anything about it. He looked at us and shook his head. 'It's the old August story,' he said. 'Every time there's a fire someone starts a rumour like that. Last year they said a water-skier had been picked up. Next year it could be a doorman at the Negresco in Nice. Faustin was pulling your leg.'

It was difficult to know what to believe. Odd things were possible in August, and so we were not at all surprised when some friends who were staying in a nearby hotel told us that they had seen an eagle at midnight in their bedroom. Well, perhaps not the eagle itself, but the unmistakable and huge *shadow* of an eagle. They called the man on night duty at the desk, and he came up to their room to investigate.

Did the eagle seem to come from the wardrobe in the corner of the room? Yes, said our friends. *Ah bon*, said the man, the mystery is solved. He is not an eagle. He is a bat. He has been seen leaving that wardrobe before. He is harmless. Harmless he may be, said our friends, but we would prefer not to sleep with a bat, and we would like another room. *Non*, said the man. The hotel is full. The three of them stood in the bedroom and discussed bat-catching techniques. The man from the hotel had an idea. Stay there, he said. I shall return with the solution. He reappeared a few minutes later, gave them a large aerosol can of fly-killer and wished them good night.

* * * * *

The party was being held in a house outside Gordes, and we had been asked to join a few friends of the hostess for dinner before the other guests arrived. It was an evening that we anticipated with mixed feelings – pleased to be invited, but far from confident about our ability to stay afloat in a torrent of dinner party French. As far as we knew, we were going to be the only English-speakers there, and we hoped we wouldn't be separated from each other by too many breakneck Provençal conversations. We had been asked to arrive at what for us was the highly sophisticated hour of nine o'clock, and we drove up the hill towards Gordes with stomachs rumbling at being kept waiting so late. The parking area behind the house was full. Cars lined the road outside for fifty yards, and every other car seemed to have a Parisian 75 number plate. Our fellow guests were not going to be a few friends from the village. We began to feel we should have worn less casual clothes.

We walked inside and found ourselves in magazine country, decorated by *House and Garden* and dressed by *Vogue*. Candlelit tables were arranged on the lawn and the terrace. Fifty or sixty people, cool and languid and wearing white, held glasses of champagne in jewelled fingers. The sound of Vivaldi came through the open doorway of a floodlit barn. My wife wanted to go home and change. I was conscious of my dusty shoes. We had blundered into a *soirée*.

127

Our hostess saw us before we could escape. She at least was reassuringly dressed in her usual outfit of shirt and trousers.

'You found somewhere to park?' She didn't wait for an answer. 'It's a little difficult in the road because of that ditch.'

We said it didn't seem at all like Provence, and she shrugged. 'It's August.' She gave us a drink and left us to mingle with the beautiful people.

We could have been in Paris. There were no brown, weathered faces. The women were fashionably pallid, the men carefully barbered and sleek. Nobody was drinking pastis. Conversation was, by Provençal standards, whisper-quiet. Our perceptions had definitely changed. At one time, this would have seemed normal. Now it seemed subdued and smart and vaguely uncomfortable. There was no doubt about it; we had turned into bumpkins.

We gravitated towards the least chic couple we could see, who were standing detached from the crowd with their dog. All three were friendly, and we sat down together at one of the tables on the terrace. The husband, a small man with a sharp, Norman face, told us that he had bought a house in the village twenty years before for 3,000 francs, and had been coming down every summer since then, changing houses every five or six years. He had just heard that his original house was back on the market, over-restored and decorated to death and priced at a million francs. 'It's madness,' he said, 'but people like *le tout Paris*' – he nodded towards the other guests – 'they want to be with their friends in August. When one buys, they all buy. And they pay Parisian prices.'

They had begun to take their places at the tables, carrying bottles of wine and plates of food from the buffet. The women's high heels sank into the gravel of the terrace, and there were some refined squeals of appreciation at the deliciously primitive setting – *un vrai dîner sauvage* – even though it was only marginally more primitive than a garden in Beverly Hills or Kensington.

The Mistral started, suddenly and most inconveniently, while there was still plenty of uneaten shrimp salad on the tables. Lettuce leaves and scraps of bread became airborne, plucked from plates and blown among the snowy bosoms and silk trousers, scoring the occasional direct hit on a shirt front. Table cloths snapped and billowed like sails, tipping over candles and wine glasses. Carefully arranged coiffures and composures were ruffled. This was a little too *sauvage*. There was a hasty retreat, and dinner was resumed under shelter.

More people arrived. The sound of Vivaldi from the barn was replaced by a few seconds of electronic hissing, followed by the shrieks of a man undergoing heart surgery without anaesthetic: Little Richard was inviting us to get down and boogie.

We were curious to see what effect the music would have on such an elegant gathering. I could imagine them nodding their heads in time to a civilised tune, or dancing in that intimate crouch the French adopt whenever they hear Charles Aznavour, but *this* – this was a great sweating squawk from the jungle. AWOPBOPALOOWOPAWOPBAMBOOM! We climbed the steps to the barn to see what they would make of it.

Coloured strobe lighting was flashing and blinking, synchronised with the drumbeat and bouncing off the mirrors propped against the walls. A young man, shoulders hunched and eyes half-closed against the smoke of his cigarette, stood behind the twin turntables, his fingers coaxing ever more bass and volume from the knobs on the console.

GOOD GOLLY MISS MOLLY! screamed Little Richard. The young man went into a spasm of delight, and squeezed out an extra decibel. *YOU SURE LOVE TO BALL*! The barn vibrated, and *le tout Paris* vibrated with it, arms and legs and buttocks and breasts jiggling and shaking and grinding and flailing around, teeth bared, eyes rolling, fists pumping the air, jewellery out of control, buttons bursting under the strain, elegant façades gone to hell as everyone writhed and jerked and twitched and *got down*.

Most of them didn't bother with partners. They danced with their own reflections, keeping one eye, even in the midst of ecstasy, fixed on the mirrors. The air was filled with the smell of warm and scented flesh, and the barn turned into one huge throb, seething and frenzied and difficult to cross without being spiked by elbows or lashed by a whirling necklace.

Were these the same people who had been behaving so decorously earlier in the evening, looking as though their idea of a wild time might be a second glass of champagne? They were bouncing away like amphetamine-stuffed teenagers, and they seemed set for the night. We dodged and sidestepped through the squirming mass and left them to it. We had to be up early in the morning. We had a goat race to go to.

We had first seen the poster a week before, taped to the window of a *tabac*. There was to be a *Grande Course de Chèvres* through the streets of Bonnieux, starting from the Café César. The ten runners and their drivers were listed by name. There were numerous prizes, bets could be placed and, said the poster, animation would be assured by a grand orchestra. It was clearly going to be a sporting event of some magnitude, Bonnieux's answer to the Cheltenham Gold Cup or the Kentucky Derby. We arrived well before the race to be sure of a good position.

By nine o'clock it was already too hot to wear a watch, and the terrace in front of the Café César was spilling over with customers having their breakfast of *tartines* and cold beer. Against the wall of the steps leading down to the rue Voltaire, a large woman had established herself at a table, shaded by a parasol that advertised *Véritable Jus de Fruit*. She beamed at us, riffling a book of tickets and rattling a cash box. She was the official bookmaker, although there was a man taking off-track bets in the back of the café, and she invited us to try our luck. 'Look before you bet,' she said. 'The runners are down there.'

We knew they weren't far away; we could smell them and their droppings, aromatic as they cooked in the sun. We looked over the wall, and the contestants looked back at us with their mad, pale eyes, masticating slowly on some pre-race treat, their chins fringed with wispy beards. They would have looked like dignified mandarins had it not been for the blue and white jockey caps that each of them was wearing, and their racing waistcoats, numbered to correspond with the list of runners. We were able to identify Bichou and Tisane and all the rest of them by name, but it was not enough to bet on. We needed inside information, or at least some help in assessing the speed and staying power of the runners. We asked the old man who was leaning on the wall next to us, confident in the knowledge that he, like every Frenchman, would be an expert.

'It's a matter of their *crottins*,' he said. 'The goats who make the most droppings before the race are likely to do well. An empty goat is faster than a full goat. *C'est logique.'* We studied form for a few minutes, and No. 6, Totoche, obliged with a generous effort. *'Voilà,'* said our tipster, 'now you must examine the drivers. Look for a strong one.'

Most of the drivers were refreshing themselves in the café. Like the goats, they were numbered and wore jockey caps, and we were able to pick out the driver of No. 6, a brawny, likely-looking man who seemed to be pacing himself sensibly with the beer. He and the recently emptied Totoche had the makings of a winning team. We went to place our bet.

'Non.' Madame the bookmaker explained that we had to get first, second and third in order to collect, which ruined our calculations. How could we know what the dropping rate had been while we were away looking at the drivers? A certainty had dwindled into a long shot, but we went for No. 6 to win, the only female driver in the race to come second and a goat called Nénette, whose trim fetlocks indicated a certain fleetness of hoof, to come in third. Business done, we joined the sporting gentry in the little *place* outside the café.

The grand orchestra promised by the poster – a van from Apt with a sound system in the back – was broadcasting Sonny and Cher singing 'I've Got You, Babe'. A thin, high-chic Parisienne we recognised from the night before started to tap one dainty white-shod foot, and an unshaven man with a glass of pastis and a heavy paunch asked her to dance, swivelling his substantial hips as an inducement. The Parisienne gave him a look that could have turned butter rancid, and became suddenly interested in the contents of her Vuitton bag. Aretha Franklin took over from Sonny and Cher, and children played hopscotch among the goat droppings. The *place* was packed. We wedged ourselves between a German with a video camera and the man with the paunch to watch as the finishing line was prepared.

A rope was strung across the *place*, about eight feet above the ground. Large balloons, numbered from one to ten, were filled with water and tied at regular intervals along the length of the rope. Our neighbour with the paunch explained the rules: each of the drivers was to be issued with a sharp stick, which had two functions. The first was to provide a measure of encouragement for any goats reluctant to run; the second was to burst their balloons at the end of the race to qualify as finishers. *Evidemment*, he said, the drivers would get soaked, which would be droll.

The drivers had now emerged from the café, and were swaggering through the crowd to collect their goats. Our favourite driver, No. 6, had his pocket knife out, and was putting a fine point on each end of his stick, which I took to be a good sign. One of the other drivers immediately lodged a complaint with the organisers, but the dispute was cut short by the arrival of a car which had somehow managed to creep down through one of the narrow streets. A young woman got out. She was holding a map. She looked extremely puzzled. She asked the way to the autoroute.

The way to the autoroute, unfortunately, was blocked by ten goats, two hundred spectators and a musical van. Nevertheless, said the young woman, that is where I am going. She got back in the car and started inching forward.

Consternation and uproar. The organisers and some of the drivers surrounded the car, banging on the roof, brandishing sticks, rescuing goats and children from certain death beneath the barely moving wheels. Spectators surged forward to see what was going on. The car, embedded in humanity, was forced to stop, and the young woman sat looking straight ahead, tight-lipped with exasperation. *Reculez!* shouted the organisers, pointing back in the direction the car had come from, and waving at the crowd to make way. With a vicious crunch of gears, the car reversed, whining angrily up the street to the sound of applause.

The contestants were called to the starting line, and drivers checked the fastening of the cords around the goats' necks. The goats themselves were unaffected by the drama of the occasion. No. 6 was trying to eat the waistcoat worn by No. 7. No. 9, our outsider, Nénette, insisted on facing backwards. The driver picked her up by her horns and turned her round, jamming her between his knees to keep her pointing in the right direction. Her jockey cap had been knocked over one eye, giving her a rakish and demented air, and we wondered about the wisdom of our bet. We were counting on her to take third place, but with impaired vision and no sense of geography this seemed unlikely.

They were under starter's orders. Weeks, maybe months, of training had prepared them for this moment. Horn to horn, waistcoat to waistcoat, they waited for the starting signal. One of the drivers belched loudly, and they were off.

Within fifty yards, it became apparent that these goats were not instinctive athletes, or else they had misunderstood the purpose of the event. Two of them applied their brakes firmly after a few yards, and had to be dragged along. Another remembered what it should have done half an hour before, and paused at the first bend to answer a call of nature. Nénette, possibly because she was half-blinkered by her cap, overshot the turn and pulled her driver into the crowd. The other runners straggled up the hill, stimulated by various methods of persuasion.

'Kick them up the arse!' shouted our friend with the paunch. The Parisienne, who was hemmed in next to us, winced. This encouraged him to give her the benefit of his local knowledge. 'Did you know,' he said, 'that the last one to finish gets eaten? Roasted on a spit. *C'est vrai.*' The Parisienne pulled her sunglasses from their nest in her hair and put them on. She didn't look well.

The course followed a circuit around the high part of the village, looping back down to the old fountain which had been transformed into a water obstacle with a plastic sheet stretched between some hay bales. This had to be waded or swum just before the final sprint to the line of balloons outside the café – a brutal test of co-ordination and stamina.

Progress reports were being shouted down by spectators at the half-way mark, and news reached us that No. 1 and No. 6 were fighting it out in the lead. Only nine goats had been counted going past; the tenth had *disparu*. 'Probably having its throat cut,' said the man with the paunch to the Parisienne. She made a determined effort, and pushed through the crowd to find less offensive company near the finishing line.

There was a splash from the fountain, and the sound of a woman's voice raised to scold. The water obstacle had claimed its first victim – a little girl who had miscalculated the depth, and who stood waist-deep in the water, bedraggled and bawling with surprise.

'*Elles viennent, les chèvres!*'

The girl's mother, in desperation at the thought of her child being trampled to a pulp by the contestants, hitched up her skirt and plunged into the water. 'What thighs!' said the man with the paunch, kissing the tips of his fingers.

With a clatter of hoofs, the leading runners approached the fountain and skidded into the hay bales, showing very little enthusiasm for getting wet. Their drivers grunted and cursed and tugged and finally manhandled their goats into the water and out the other side to the finishing straight, their sodden espadrilles squelching on the tarmac, their sticks poised like lances. The positions at half-way mark had been maintained, and it was still No. 1 and No. 6, Titine and Totoche, skittering up to the line of balloons.

No. 1, with an enormous backhand swipe, exploded his balloon first, showering the Parisienne, who stepped smartly backwards into a pile of droppings. No. 6, for all his stick-sharpening before the race, had more difficulty, just managing to burst his balloon before the next runners reached the line. One by one, or in dripping groups, they staggered in until all that remained was a single swollen balloon banging from the line. No. 9, the wayward Nénette, had not completed the course. 'The butcher's got her,' said the man with the paunch.

We saw her as we walked back to the car. She had broken her cord and escaped from her driver, and was perched high above the street in a tiny walled garden, her cap hanging from one horn, eating geraniums.

* * * * *

'Bonjour, maçon.'

'Bonjour, plombier.'

The team had arrived for another loud, hot day, and were exchanging greetings and handshakes with the formality of people who had never met before, addressing each other by *métier* rather than by name. Christian the architect, who had worked with them for years, never referred to them by their first names, but always by a rather grand and complicated hyphenation which combined surname with profession; thus Francis, Didier and Bruno became

Menicucci-Plombier, Andreis-Maçon and Trufelli-Carreleur. This occasionally achieved the length and solemnity of an obscure aristocratic title, as with Jean-Pierre the carpet layer, who was officially known as Gaillard-Poseur de Moquette.

They were gathered around one of many holes that Menicucci had made to accommodate his central heating pipes, and were discussing dates and schedules in the serious manner of men whose lives were governed by punctuality. There was a strict sequence to be followed: Menicucci had to complete laying his pipes; the masons were then to move in and repair the damage, followed by the electrician, the plasterer, the tile-layer, the carpenter and the painter. Since they were all good Provençaux, there was no chance at all that dates would be observed, but it provided the opportunity for some entertaining speculation.

Menicucci was enjoying his position of eminence as the key figure, the man whose progress would dictate the timetable of everyone else.

'You will see,' he said, 'that I have been obliged to make a Gorgonzola of the walls, but what is that, *maçon*? Half a day to repair?'

'Maybe a day,' said Didier. 'But when?'

'Don't try to rush me,' said Menicucci. 'Forty years as a plumber have taught me that you cannot hurry central heating. It is *très, très délicat*.'

'Christmas?' suggested Didier.

Menicucci looked at him, shaking his head. 'You joke about it, but think of the winter.' He demonstrated winter for us, wrapping an imaginary overcoat around his shoulders. 'It is minus ten degrees.' He shivered, pulling his bonnet over his ears. 'All of a sudden, the pipes start to leak! And why? Because they have been placed too quickly and without proper attention.' He looked at his audience, letting them appreciate the full drama of a cold and leaking winter. 'Who will be laughing then? Eh? Who will be making jokes about the plumber?'

It certainly wouldn't be me. The central heating experience so far had been a nightmare, made bearable only by the fact that we could stay outside during the day. Previous construction work had at least been confined to one part of the house, but this was everywhere. Menicucci and his copper tentacles were unavoidable. Dust and rubble and tortured fragments of piping marked his daily passage like the spoor of an iron-jawed termite. And, perhaps worst of all, there was no privacy. We were just as likely to find *jeune* in the bathroom with a blowlamp as to come across Menicucci's rear end sticking out of a hole in the living room wall. The pool was the only refuge, and even there it was best to be completely submerged so that the water muffled the relentless noise of drills and hammers. We sometimes thought that our friends were right, and that we should have gone away for August, or hidden in the deep freeze.

The evenings were such a relief that we usually stayed at home, convalescing after the din of the day, and so we missed most of the social and cultural events that had been organised for the benefit of summer visitors to the Lubéron. Apart from a bottom-numbing evening in the Abbey of Senanque, listening to Gregorian chants as we sat on benches of appropriately monastic discomfort, and a concert held in a floodlit ruin above Oppède, we didn't move from the courtyard. It was enough just to be alone and to be quiet.

Hunger eventually forced us out one night when we discovered that what we had planned to have for dinner had acquired a thick coating of grit from the day's drilling. We decided to go to a simple restaurant in Goult, a small village with an invisible population and no tourist attractions of any kind. It would be like eating at home, but cleaner. We beat a layer of dust from our clothes and left the dogs to guard the holes in the walls.

It had been a still, oppressively hot day, and the village smelt of heat, of baked tarmac and dried-out rosemary and warm gravel. And people. We had chosen the night of the annual fête.

We should have known, because every village celebrated August in one way or another – with a *boules* tournament or a donkey race or a barbecue or a fair, with coloured lights strung in the plane trees and dance floors made from wooden planks laid across scaffolding, with gypsies and accordion players and souvenir sellers and rock groups from as far away as Avignon. They were noisy, enjoyable occasions unless, like us, you were suffering from the mild concussion brought on by spending the day in a construction site. But we were there and we wanted the dinner that we had already mentally ordered. What were a few extra people compared to the delights of a salad made with warm mussels and bacon, chicken tickled with ginger and the chef's clinging and delicious chocolate cake?

At any other time of the year, the sight of more than a dozen people in the village streets would indicate an event of unusual interest – a funeral, perhaps, or a price-cutting war between the two butchers who had adjacent shops a few yards from the café. But this was an exceptional night; Goult was playing host to the world, and the world was obviously as hungry as we were. The restaurant was full. The terrace outside the restaurant was full. Hopeful couples lurked in the shadows under the trees, waiting for a free table. The waiters looked harassed. The proprietor, Patrick, looked tired but satisfied, a man with a temporary gold mine. 'You should have called,' he said. 'Come back at ten and I'll see what I can do.'

Even the café, which was large enough to hold the entire population of Goult, could offer standing room only. We took our drinks across the road, where stalls had been set up in a hollow square around the monument honouring the men of the village who had fought and died in the wars, fallen for the glory of France. Like most war memorials we had seen, it was respectfully well kept, with a cluster of three new *tricolore* flags sharp and clean against the grey stone.

The windows in the houses round the square were open and the occupants leant out, their flickering television sets forgotten behind them as they watched the slow-moving confusion below. It was more of a market than anything else, local artisans with their carved wood and pottery, wine-growers and honey-makers, a few antique dealers and artists. The heat of the day could be felt in the stone walls and seen in the way that the lazy, drifting crowd was walking, weight back on the heels, stomachs out, shoulders relaxed in a holiday slouch.

Most of the stands were trestle tables, with artefacts displayed on print tablecloths, often with a notice propped up saying that the owner could be found in the café if there was any risk of a sale. One stand, larger and more elaborate than the others, looked like an outdoor sitting room, furnished with tables and chairs and chaises longues and decorated with potted palms. A dark, stocky man in shorts and sandals sat at one of the tables with a bottle of wine and an order book. It was Monsieur Aude, the artist *ferronnier* of Saint-Pantaléon, who had done some work on the house. He beckoned us to sit down with him.

The *ferronnier* is a man who works with iron and steel, and in rural France he is kept busy making bars and gates and shutters and grilles to keep out the burglars who are assumed to be behind every bush. Monsieur Aude had progressed beyond these simple security devices, and had discovered that there was a market for replicas of classical eighteenth- and nineteenth-century steel furniture. He had a book of photographs and designs, and if you wanted a park bench or a baker's grill or a folding campaign bed such as Napoleon might have used, he would make it for you, then season it, being a superb judge of rust, to the required state of antiquity. He worked with his brother-in-law and a small beagle bitch and he could be relied upon to quote a delivery time of two weeks for anything, and to arrive with it three months later. We asked him if business was good.

He tapped his order book. 'I could open a factory – Germans, Parisians, Belgians. This year they all want the big round tables and these garden chairs.' He moved the chair next to him so that we could see the graceful arch of the legs. 'The problem is that they think I can make everything in a couple of days, and as you know . . .' he left the sentence unfinished, and chewed reflectively on a mouthful of wine. A couple who had been circling the stand came up and asked about a campaign bed. Monsieur Aude opened his book and licked the point of his pencil, then looked up at them. 'I have to tell you,' he said with a completely straight face, 'that it might take two weeks.'

It was almost eleven by the time we started to eat, and well past midnight when we got home. The air was warm and heavy and abnormally still. It was a night for the pool, and we slipped into the water to float on our backs and look at the stars – the perfect end to a sweltering day. A long way off, from the direction of the Côte d'Azur, there was a mutter of thunder and the brief flicker of lightning, distant and ornamental, somebody else's storm.

It reached Ménerbes in the dark and early hours of the morning, waking us with a clap that shook the windows and startled the dogs into a chorus of barking. For an hour or more it seemed to stay directly above the house, rolling and exploding and floodlighting the vineyard. And then it rained with the intensity of a burst dam, crashing on the roof and in the courtyard, dripping down the chimney and seeping under the front door. It stopped just after dawn and, as if nothing had happened, the sun came up as usual.

We had no electricity. A little later, when we tried to call the Electricité de France office, we found we had no 'phone line. When we walked round the house to see what the storm had destroyed we saw that half the drive had been washed into the road, leaving ruts as wide as tractor wheels and deep enough to be dangerous to any normal car. But there were two silver linings: it was a beautiful morning, and there were no workmen. They were undoubtedly too busy with their own leaks to worry about our central heating. We went for a walk in the forest, to see what the storm had done there.

It was dramatic, not because of any uprooted trees, but because of the effects of the deluge on earth that had been baked for weeks. Wraiths of steam rose among the trees, and with them a continuous hissing sound as the heat of the new day started to dry the undergrowth. We came back for a late breakfast filled with the optimism that sunshine and blue sky can inspire, and we were rewarded by a working 'phone, with Monsieur Fructus on the end of it. He had called to see if his insurance policy had suffered any damage.

We told him that the only casualty had been the drive.

'C'est bieng,' he said, 'I have a client who has fifty centimetres of water in his kitchen. It sometimes happens. August is bizarre.'

He was right. It had been a strange month, and we were glad it was over so that life could return to the way it had been before, with empty roads and uncrowded restaurants and Menicucci back in long trousers.

SEPTEMBER

Overnight, the population of the Lubéron dwindled. The *résidences secondaires* – some fine old houses among them – were locked and shuttered, their gateposts manacled with rusting lengths of chain. The houses would stay empty now until Christmas, so obviously, visibly empty that it was easy to understand why housebreaking in the Vaucluse had achieved the importance of a minor industry. Even the most poorly equipped and slow-moving of burglars could count on several undisturbed months in which to do his work, and in past years there had been some highly original thefts. Entire kitchens had been dismantled and taken away, old Roman roof tiles, an antique front door, a mature olive tree – it was as if a discerning burglar was setting up house with the choicest items he could find, selected with a connoisseur's eye from a variety of properties. Maybe he was the villain who had taken our mail box.

We began to see our local friends again as they emerged from the summer siege. Most of them were recovering from a surfeit of guests, and there was a certain awful similarity in the stories they told. Plumbing and money were the main topics, and it was astonishing how often the same phrases were used by mystified,

141

apologetic or tight-fisted visitors. Unwittingly, they had compiled between them The Sayings of August.

'What do you mean, they don't take credit cards? Everyone takes credit cards.'

'You've run out of vodka.'

'There's a very peculiar smell in the bathroom.'

'Do you think you could take care of this? I've only got a 500-franc note.'

'Don't worry. I'll send you a replacement as soon as I get back to London.'

'I didn't realise you had to be so careful with a septic tank.'

'Don't forget to let me know how much those calls to Los Angeles were.'

'I feel terrible watching you slave away like that.'

'You've run out of whisky.'

As we listened to the tales of blocked drains and guzzled brandy, of broken wine glasses in the swimming pool, of sealed wallets and prodigious appetites, we felt that we had been very kindly treated during August. Our house had suffered considerable damage, but from the sound of it our friends' houses had suffered too. At least we hadn't had to provide food and lodging for Menicucci while he was wreaking havoc.

In many ways, the early part of September felt like a second spring. The days were dry and hot, the nights cool, the air wonderfully clear after the muggy haze of August. The inhabitants of the valley had shaken off their torpor and were getting down to the main business of the year, patrolling their vineyards every morning to examine the grapes that hung for mile after mile in juicy and orderly lines.

Faustin was out there with the rest of them, cupping the bunches in his hand and looking up at the sky, sucking his teeth in contemplation as he tried to second guess the weather. I asked him when he thought he was going to pick.

'They should cook some more,' he said. 'But the weather in September is not to be trusted.'

He had made the same gloomy comment about the weather every month of the year so far, in the resigned and plaintive tones used by farmers all over the world when they tell you how hard it is to scratch a living from the land. Conditions are never right. The rain, the wind, the sunshine, the weeds, the insects, the government – there is always at least one fly in their ointment, and they take a perverse pleasure in their pessimism.

'You can do everything right for eleven months a year,' said Faustin, 'and then – *pouf* – a storm comes and the crop is hardly fit for grape juice.' *Jus de raiseng* – he said it with such scorn that I could imagine him leaving a spoilt crop to rot on the vines rather than waste his time picking grapes that couldn't even aspire to become *vin ordinaire*.

As if his life were not already filled with grief, nature had put a further difficulty in his way: the grapes on our land would have to be picked at two separate times, because about five hundred of our vines produced table grapes which would be ready before the *raisins de cuve*. This was *un emmerdement*, made tolerable only because of the good price that table grapes fetched. Even so, it meant that there were two possible occasións when disappointment and disaster could strike and, if Faustin knew anything about it, strike they undoubtedly would. I left him shaking his head and grumbling to God.

To make up for the mournful predictions of Faustin, we received a daily ration of joyful news from Menicucci, now coming to the end of his labours on the central heating system and almost beside himself with anticipation as the day of firing up the boiler approached. Three times he reminded me to order the oil, and then insisted on supervising the filling of the tank to make sure that the delivery was free from foreign bodies.

'*Il faut faire très attention*,' he explained to the man who brought the oil. 'The smallest piece of *cochonnerie* in your fuel will affect my burner and clog the electrodes. I think it would be prudent to filter it as you pump it into the tank.'

The fuel man drew himself up in outrage, parrying Menicucci's wagging finger with his own, oily and black-rimmed at the tip. 'My fuel is already triple-filtered. *C'est impeccable.*' He made as if to kiss his fingertips and then thought better of it.

'We shall see,' said Menicucci. 'We shall see.' He looked with suspicion at the nozzle before it was placed inside the tank, and the fuel man wiped it ostentatiously on a filthy rag. The filling ceremony was accompanied by a detailed technical discourse on the inner workings of the burner and the boiler which the fuel man listened to with scant interest, grunting or saying *Ah bon?* whenever his participation was required. Menicucci turned to me as the last few litres were pumped in. 'This afternoon we will have the first test.' He had an anxious moment as a dreadful possibility occurred to him. 'You're not going out? You and Madame will be here?' It would have been an act of supreme unkindness to deprive him of his audience. We promised to be ready and waiting at two o'clock.

We gathered in what had once been a dormitory for donkeys, now transformed by Menicucci into the nerve centre of his heating complex. Boiler, burner and water tank were arranged side by side, joined together by umbilical cords of copper, and an impressive array of painted pipes – red for hot water, blue for cold, *très logique* – fanned out from the boiler and disappeared into the ceiling. Valves and dials and switches, bright and incongruous against the rough stone of the walls, awaited the master's touch. It looked extremely complicated, and I made the mistake of saying so.

Menicucci took it as a personal criticism, and spent ten minutes demonstrating its astonishing simplicity, flicking switches, opening and closing valves, twiddling dials and gauges and making me thoroughly bewildered. '*Voilà!*' he said after a final flourish on the switches. 'Now that you understand the apparatus, we will start the test. *Jeune!* Pay attention.'

The beast awoke with a series of clicks and snuffles. '*Le brûleur,*' said Menicucci, dancing round the boiler to adjust the controls for the fifth time. There was a thump of air, and then a muffled roar. 'We have combustion!' He made it sound as dramatic as the launch of a space shuttle. 'Within five minutes, every radiator will be hot. Come!'

He scuttled round the house, insisting that we touch each radiator. 'You see? You will be able to pass the entire winter *en chemise.*' By this time, we were all sweating profusely. It was eighty degrees outside, and the indoor temperature with the heating full on was insufferable. I asked if we could turn it off before we dehydrated.

'*Ah non.* You must leave it on for twenty-four hours so that we can verify all the joins and make sure there are no leaks. Touch nothing until I return tomorrow. It is most important that everything remains at maximum.' He left us to wilt, and to enjoy the smell of cooked dust and hot iron.

* * * * *

There is one September weekend when the countryside sounds as though rehearsals are being held for World War Three. It is the official start of the hunting season, and every red-blooded Frenchman takes his gun, his dog and his murderous inclinations into the hills in search of sport. The first sign that this was about to happen came through the post – a terrifying document from a gunsmith in Vaison-la-Romaine, offering a complete range of artillery at pre-season prices. There were sixty or seventy models to choose from, and my hunting instincts, which had been dormant since birth, were aroused by the thought of owning a Verney Carron Grand Bécassier, or a Ruger ·44 Magnum with an electronic sight. My wife, who has a well-founded lack of confidence in my ability to handle any kind of dangerous equipment, pointed out that I hardly needed an electronic sight to shoot myself in the foot.

We had both been surprised at the French fondness for guns. Twice we had visited the homes of outwardly mild and unwarlike men, and twice we had been shown the family arsenal; one man had five rifles of various calibres, the other had eight, oiled and polished and displayed in a rack on the dining room wall like a lethal piece of art. How could anyone need eight guns? How would you know which one to take with you? or did you take them all, like a bag of golf clubs, selecting the ·44 Magnum for leopard or moose and the Baby Bretton for rabbit?

After a while, we came to realise that the gun mania was only part of a national fascination with outfits and accoutrements, a passion for looking like an expert. When a Frenchman takes up cycling or tennis or skiing, the last thing he wants is for the world to mistake him for the novice that he is, and so he accessorises himself up to professional standard. It's instant. A few thousand francs and there you are, indistinguishable from any other seasoned ace competing in the Tour de France or Wimbledon or the Winter Olympics. In the case of *la chasse*, the accessories are almost limitless, and they have the added attraction of being deeply masculine and dangerous in their appearance.

We were treated to a preview of hunting fashions in Cavaillon market. The stalls had stocked up for the season, and looked like small paramilitary depots: there were cartridge bandoliers and plaited leather rifle slings; jerkins with myriad zippered pockets and game pouches that were washable and therefore *très pratique*, because bloodstains could be easily removed; there were wilderness boots of the kind used by mercenaries parachuting into the Congo; fearsome knives with nine-inch blades and compasses set into the handle; lightweight aluminium water bottles which would probably see more pastis than water; webbing belts with D-rings and a special sling to hold a bayonet, presumably in case the ammunition ran out and game had to be attacked with cold steel; forage caps and commando trousers, survival rations and tiny collapsible field stoves. There was everything a man might need for his confrontation with the untamed beasts of the forest except that indispensable accessory with four legs and a nose like radar, the hunting dog.

Chiens de chasse are too specialised to be bought and sold across a counter, and we were told that no serious hunter would consider buying a pup without first meeting both parents. Judging by some of the hunting dogs we had seen, we could imagine that finding the father might have been difficult, but among all the hybrid curiosities there were three more or less identifiable types – the liver-coloured approximation of a large spaniel, the stretched beagle, and the tall, rail-thin hound with the wrinkled, lugubrious face.

Every hunter considers his dog to be uniquely gifted, and he will have at least one implausible story of stamina and prowess to tell you. To hear the owners talk, you would think that these dogs were supernaturally intelligent creatures, trained to a hair and faithful unto death. We looked forward with interest to seeing them perform on the opening weekend of the season. Perhaps their example would inspire our dogs to do something more useful than stalk lizards and attack old tennis balls.

Hunting in our part of the valley started shortly after seven o'clock one Sunday morning, with salvoes coming from either side of the house and from the mountains behind. It sounded as though anything that moved would be at risk, and when I went out for a walk with the dogs I took the biggest white handkerchief I could find in case I needed to surrender. With infinite caution, we set off along the footpath that runs behind the house towards the village, assuming that any hunter worth his gun licence would have moved well away from the beaten track and into the tangled undergrowth further up the mountain.

There was a noticeable absence of birdsong; all sensible or experienced birds had left at the sound of the first shot for somewhere safer, like North Africa or central Avignon. In the bad old days, hunters used to hang caged birds in the trees to lure other birds close enough for a point-blank shot, but that had been made illegal, and the modern hunter now had to rely on woodcraft and stealth.

I didn't see much evidence of that, but I did see enough hunters and dogs and weaponry to wipe out the entire thrush and rabbit population of southern France. They hadn't gone up into the forest; in fact, they had barely left the footpath. Knots of them were gathered in the clearings – laughing, smoking, taking nips from their khaki-painted flasks and cutting slices of *saucisson*, but of active hunting – man versus thrush in a battle of wits – there was no sign. They must have used up their ration of shells during the early morning fusillade.

Their dogs, however, were anxious to get to work. After months of confinement in kennels, they were delirious with liberty and the scents of the forest, tracking back and forth, noses close to the ground and twitching with excitement. Each dog wore a thick collar with a small brass bell – the *clochette* – hanging from it. We were told that this had a double purpose. It signalled the dog's whereabouts so that the hunter could position himself for the game that was being driven towards him, but it was also a precaution against shooting at something in the bushes that sounded like a rabbit or a boar and finding that you had shot your own dog. No responsible hunter, *naturellement*, would ever shoot at anything he couldn't see – or so I was told. But I had my doubts. After a morning with the pastis or the *marc*, a rustle in the bushes might be too much to resist, and the cause of the rustle might be human. In fact, it might be me. I thought about wearing a bell, just to be on the safe side.

Another benefit of the *clochette* became apparent at the end of the morning: it was to help the hunter avoid the humiliating experience of losing his dog at the end of the hunt. Far from the disciplined and faithful animals I had imagined them to be, hunting dogs are wanderers, led on by their noses and oblivious to the passage of time. They have not grasped the idea that hunting stops for lunch. The bell doesn't necessarily mean that the dog will come when called, but at least the hunter can tell roughly where he is.

Just before noon, camouflage-clad figures started to make their way to the vans parked at the side of the road. A few had dogs with them. The rest were whistling and shouting with increasing irritation, making a bad-tempered hissing noise – '*Vieng ici!*' *Vieng ici!*' – in the direction of the symphony of bells that could be heard coming from the forest.

Response was patchy. The shouts became more bad-tempered, degenerating into bellows and curses. After a few minutes the hunters gave up and went home, most of them dogless.

We were joined a little later for lunch by three abandoned hounds who came down to drink the swimming pool. They were greatly admired by our two bitches for their devil-may-care manner and exotic aroma, and we penned them all in the courtyard while we wondered how we could get them back to their owners. We consulted Faustin.

'Don't bother,' he said. 'Let them go. The hunters will be back in the evening. If they don't find their dogs, they'll leave a *coussin*.'

It always worked, so Faustin said. If the dog was in the forest, one simply left something with the scent of the kennel on it – a cushion or, more likely, a scrap of sacking – near the spot where the dog had last been seen. Sooner or later, the dog would come back to its own scent and wait to be picked up.

We let the three hounds out, and they loped off, baying with excitement. It was an extraordinary, doleful sound, not a bark or a howl but a lament, like an oboe in pain. Faustin shook his head. 'They'll be gone for days.' He himself didn't hunt, and regarded hunters and their dogs as intruders who had no right to be nosing around his precious vines.

He had decided, he told us, that the moment had come to pick the table grapes. They would start as soon as Henriette had finished servicing the *camion*. She was the mechanically minded member of the family, and every September she had the job of coaxing another few kilometres out of the grape truck. It was at least thirty years old – maybe more, Faustin couldn't remember exactly – blunt-nosed and rickety, with open sides and bald tyres. It had ceased to be roadworthy years ago, but there was no question of buying a new truck. And why waste good money having it serviced at a garage when you had a mechanic for a wife? It was only used for a few weeks a year, and Faustin was careful to take it on the back roads to avoid meeting any of those officious little *flics* from the police station at Les Baumettes, with their absurd regulations about brakes and valid insurance.

Henriette's ministrations were successful, and the old truck gasped up the drive early one morning, loaded with shallow wooden grape trays, just deep enough for a single layer of bunches. Stacks of trays were placed along each line of vines, and the three of them – Faustin, Henriette and their daughter – took their scissors and set to work.

It was a slow and physically uncomfortable business. Because the appearance of table grapes is almost as important as their taste, every bunch had to be examined, every bruised or wrinkled grape snipped off. The bunches grew low, sometimes touching the earth and hidden by leaves, and the pickers' progress was in yards per hour – squatting down, cutting, standing up, inspecting, snipping, packing. The heat was fierce, coming up from the ground as well as beating down on the necks and shoulders. No shade, no breeze, no relief in the course of a ten-hour day except the break for lunch. Never again would I look at a bunch of grapes in a bowl without thinking of backache and sunstroke. It was past seven when they came in for a drink, exhausted and radiating heat, but satisfied. The grapes were good and three or four days would see them all picked. I said to Faustin that he must be pleased with the weather. He pushed back his hat and I could see the line sharp across his forehead where the burnt brown skin turned white.

'It's too good,' he said. 'It won't last.' He took a long pull at his pastis as he considered the spectrum of misfortunes that could occur. If not storms, there might be a freak frost, a plague of locusts, a forest fire, a nuclear attack. Something was bound to go wrong before the second batch of grapes was picked. And, if it didn't, he could console himself with the fact that his doctor had put him on a diet to reduce his cholesterol level. Yes, that was certainly a grave problem. Reassured at having remembered that fate had recently dealt him a black card, he had another drink.

* * * * *

It had taken me some time to get used to having a separate, purpose-built room devoted exclusively to wine – not a glorified cupboard or a cramped cavity under the stairs, but a genuine *cave*. It was buried in the bottom of the house, with permanently cool stone walls and a floor of gravel, and there was space for three or four hundred bottles. I loved it. I was determined to fill it up. Our friends were equally determined to empty it. This gave me the excuse to make regular visits – errands of social mercy – to the vineyards so that guests should never go thirsty.

In the interests of research and hospitality, I went to Gigondas and Beaumes-de-Venise and Châteauneuf-du-Pape, none of them bigger than a large village, all of them single-minded in their dedication to the grape. Everywhere I looked, there were signs advertising the *caves* that seemed to be at fifty-yard intervals. *Dégustez nos vins!* Never has a invitation been accepted with more enthusiasm. I had *dégustations* in a garage in Gigondas and a château above Beaumes-de-Venise. I found a powerful and velvety Châteauneuf-du-Pape for 30 francs a litre, squirted into plastic containers with a marvellous lack of ceremony from what looked like a garage pump. In a more expensive and more pretentious establishment, I asked to try the *marc*. A small cut-glass bottle was produced, and a drop was dabbed on the back of my hand, whether to sniff or to suck I wasn't quite sure.

After a while, I bypassed the villages and started to follow the signs, often half hidden by vegetation, that pointed deep into the countryside where the wines baked in the sun, and where I could buy direct from the men who made the wine. They were, without exception, hospitable and proud of their work and, to me at least, their sales pitch was irresistible.

It was early afternoon when I turned off the main road leading out of Vacqueyras and followed the narrow, stony track through the vines. I had been told that it would lead me to the maker of the wine I had liked at lunchtime, a white Côtes-du-Rhône. A case or two would fill the void in the *cave* that had been made by the last raiding party we had entertained. A quick stop, no more than ten minutes, and then I would get back home.

The track led to a sprawl of buildings, arranged in a square U around a courtyard of beaten earth, shaded by a giant plane tree and guarded by a drowsy Alsatian who welcomed me with a half-hearted bark, doing his duty as a substitute for a doorbell. A man in overalls, holding an oily collection of spark plugs, came over from his tractor. He gave me his forearm to shake.

I wanted some white wine? Of course. He himself was busy nursing his tractor, but his uncle would take care of me. '*Edouard! Tu peux servir ce monsieur?*'

The curtain of wooden beads hanging across the front door parted, and Uncle Edward came blinking into the sunshine. He was wearing a sleeveless vest, cotton *bleu de travail* trousers and carpet slippers. His girth was impressive, comparable with with trunk of the plane tree, but even that was overshadowed by his nose. I had never seen a nose quite like it – wide, fleshy and seasoned to a colour somewhere between rosé and claret, with fine purple lines spreading out across his cheeks. Here was a man who clearly enjoyed every mouthful of his work.

He beamed, the lines on his cheeks looking like purple whiskers. '*Bon. Une petite dégustation.*' He led me across the courtyard and slid back the double doors of a long, windowless building, telling me to stay just inside the door while he went to switch on the light. After the glare outside, I could see nothing, but there was a reassuring smell, musty and unmistakable, the air itself tasting of fermented grapes.

Uncle Edward turned on the light and closed the doors against the heat. A long trestle table and half a dozen chairs were placed under the single light bulb with its flat tin shade. In a dark corner, I could make out a flight of stairs and a concrete ramp leading down into the cellar. Crates of wine were stacked on wooden pallets around the walls, and an old refrigerator hummed quietly next to a cracked sink.

Uncle Edward was polishing glasses, holding each one up to the light before placing it on the table. He made a neat line of seven glasses, and began to arrange a variety of bottles behind them. Each bottle was accorded a few admiring comments: 'The white monsieur knows, yes? A very agreeable young wine. The rosé, not at all like those thin rosés one finds on the Côte d'Azur. Thirteen degrees of alcohol, a proper wine. There's a light red – one could drink a bottle of that before a game of tennis. That one, *par contre*, is for the winter, and he will keep for ten years or more. And then . . .'

I tried to stop him. I told him that all I wanted were two cases of the white, but he wouldn't hear of it. Monsieur had taken the trouble to come personally, and it would be unthinkable not to taste a selection. Why, said Uncle Edward, he himself would join me in a progress through the vintages. He clapped a heavy hand on my shoulder and sat me down.

It was fascinating. He told me the precise part of the vineyard that each of the wines had come from, and why certain slopes produced lighter or heavier wines. Each wine we tasted was accompanied by an imaginary menu, described with much lip-smacking and raising of the eyes to gastronomic heaven. We mentally consumed *écrevisses*, salmon cooked with sorrel, rosemary-flavoured chicken from Bresse, roasted baby lamb with a creamy garlic sauce, an *estouffade* of beef and olives, a *daube*, loin of pork spiked with slivers of truffle. The wines tasted progressively better and became progressively more expensive; I was being traded up by an expert, and there was nothing to be done except sit back and enjoy it.

'There is one more you should try,' said Uncle Edward, 'although it is not to everybody's taste.' He picked up a bottle and poured a careful half glass. It was deep red, almost black. 'A wine of great character,' he said. 'Wait. It needs *une bonne bouche*.' He left me surrounded by glasses and bottles, feeling the first twinges of an afternoon hangover.

'Voilà.' He put a plate in front of me – two small round goats' cheeses, speckled with herbs and shiny with oil – and gave me a knife with a worn wooden handle. He watched as I cut off a piece of cheese and ate it. It was ferociously strong. My palate, or what was left of it, had been perfectly primed and the wine tasted like nectar.

Uncle Edward helped me load the cases into the car. Had I really ordered all this? I must have done. We had been sitting in the convivial murk for nearly two hours, and one can make all kinds of expansive decisions in two hours. I left with a throbbing head and an invitation to come back next month for the *vendange*.

Our own *vendange*, the agricultural highlight of the year, took place during the last week of September. Faustin would have liked it to be a few day later, but he had some private information about the weather which convinced him that it would be a wet October.

The original party of three that had picked the table grapes was reinforced by Cousin Raoul and Faustin's father. His contribution was to walk slowly behind the pickers, prodding among the vines with his stick until he found a bunch of grapes that had been overlooked and then shouting – he had a good, carrying bellow for a man of eighty-four – for someone to come back and do the job properly. In contrast to the others in their shorts and vests, he was dressed for a brisk November day in a sweater, a cap and a suit of heavy cotton. When my wife appeared with a camera, he took off his cap, smoothed his hair, put his cap back on and struck a pose, waist-deep in vines. Like all our neighbours, he loved having his portrait taken.

Slowly and noisily, the rows were picked clean, the grapes piled into plastic crates and stacked in the back of the truck. Every evening now, the roads were busy with vans and tractors towing their purple mountains to the wine co-operative at Maubec, where they were weighed and tested for alcoholic content.

To Faustin's surprise, the crop was gathered without incident, and to celebrate he invited us to go with him to the co-operative when he made the last delivery. 'Tonight we will see the final figures,' he said, 'and then you will know how much you can drink next year.'

We followed the truck as it swayed off into the sunset at twenty

miles an hour, keeping to narrow roads that were stained with fallen, squashed grapes. There was a queue waiting to unload. Burly men with roasted faces sat on their tractors until it was their turn to back up to the platform and tip their loads down the chute – the first stage of their journey to the bottle.

Faustin finished unloading, and we went with him into the building to see our grapes going into the huge stainless steel vats. 'Watch that dial,' he said. 'It shows the degrees of alcohol.' The needle swung up, quivered and settled at 12·32 per cent. Faustin grunted. He would have liked 12·50 and an extra few days in the sun might have done it, but anything above 12 was reasonable. He took us over to the man who kept the tallies of each delivery and peered at a line of figures on a clipboard, matching them with a handful of slips of paper he pulled from his pocket. He nodded. It was all correct.

'You won't go thirsty.' He made the Provençal drinking gesture, fist clenched and thumb pointing towards his mouth. 'Just over one thousand two hundred litres.'

It sounded like a good year to us, and we told Faustin we were pleased. 'Well,' he said, 'at least it didn't rain.'

* * * * *

OCTOBER

The man stood peering into the moss and light undergrowth around the roots of an old scrub oak tree. His right leg was encased up to the thigh in a green rubber fishing wader; on the other foot was a running shoe. He held a long stick in front of him and carried a blue plastic shopping basket.

He turned sideways on to the tree, advanced the rubber-clad leg and plunged his stick nervously into the vegetation, in the manner of a fencer expecting a sudden and violent riposte. And again, with the rubber leg pushed forward: on guard, thrust, withdraw, thrust. He was so absorbed by his duel that he had no idea that I was watching, equally absorbed, from the path. One of the dogs went up behind him and gave his rear leg an exploratory sniff.

He jumped – *merde*! – and then saw the dog, and me, and looked embarrassed. I apologised for startling him.

'For a moment,' he said, 'I thought I was being attacked.'

I couldn't imagine who he thought was going to sniff his leg before attacking him, and I asked what he was looking for. In reply, he held up his shopping basket. '*Les champignons.*'

This was a new and worrying aspect of the Lubéron. It was, as I already knew, a region full of strange things and even stranger people. But surely mushrooms, even wild mushrooms, didn't

156

attack fully grown men. I asked him if the mushrooms were dangerous.

'Some can kill you,' he said.

That I could believe, but it didn't explain the rubber boot or the extraordinary performance with the stick. At the risk of being made to feel like the most ignorant of city-reared dunces, I pointed at his right leg.

'The boot is for protection?'

'*Mais oui.*'

'But against what?'

He slapped the rubber with his wooden sword and swaggered down towards me, D'Artagnan with a shopping basket. He delivered a backhand cut at a clump of thyme and came closer.

'*Les serpents.*' He said it with just the trace of a hiss. 'They are preparing for winter. If you disturb them – sssst! – they attack. It can be very grave.'

He showed me the contents of his shopping basket, snatched from the forest at the risk of life and limb. To me, they looked highly poisonous, varying in colour from blue-black to rust to violent orange, not at all like the civilised white mushrooms sold in the markets. He held the basket under my nose, and I breathed in what he called the essence of the mountains. To my surprise, it was good – earthy, rich, slightly nutty – and I looked at the mushrooms more closely. I had seen them in the forest, in evil-looking clusters under the trees, and had assumed that they were instant death. My booted friend assured me that they were not only safe, but delicious.

'But,' he said, 'you must know the deadly species. There are two or three. If you're not sure, take them to the pharmacy.'

It had never occurred to me that a mushroom could be clinically tested before being permitted to enter an omelette but, since the stomach is by far the most influential organ in France, it made perfect sense. The next time I went into Cavaillon, I toured the pharmacies. Sure enough, they had been converted into mushroom guidance centres. The window displays, normally devoted to surgical trusses and pictures of young women reducing the cellulite on their slim bronzed thighs, now featured large mushroom identification charts. Some pharmacies went even further, and filled their windows with piles of reference books which described and illustrated every species of edible fungus known to man.

I saw people going into the pharmacies with grubby bags which they presented at the counter rather anxiously, as though they were undergoing tests for a rare disease. The small, muddy objects in the bags were solemnly inspected by the resident white-coated expert, and a verdict was pronounced. I suppose it made an interesting change from the usual daily round of suppositories and liver tonics. I found it so distracting that I almost forgot why I had come to Cavaillon – not to loiter around pharmacies but to shop for bread at the local shrine of baking.

Living in France had turned us into bakery addicts, and the business of choosing and buying our daily bread was a recurring pleasure. The village bakery in Ménerbes, with its erratic opening hours – 'Madame will re-open when she has finished making her *toilette*,' I was told one day – had first encouraged us to visit other bakeries in other villages. It was a revelation. After years of taking bread for granted, more or less as a standard commodity, it was like discovering a new food.

We tried the dense, chewy loaves from Lumières, fatter and flatter than the ordinary *baguette*, and the dark-crusted *boules*, as big as squashed footballs, from Cabrières. We learned which breads would keep for a day, and which would be stale in three hours; the best bread for making *croûtons* or for spreading with *rouille* to launch into a sea of fish soup. We became used to the delightful but initially surprising sight of bottles of champagne offered for sale next to the tarts and tiny individual pastries that were made fresh every morning and gone by noon.

Most of the bakeries had their own touches which distinguished their loaves from mass-produced supermarket bread: slight variations from conventional shapes, an extra whorl of crusty decoration, an elaborate pattern, the artist baker signing his work. It was as if the sliced, wrapped, machine-made loaf had never been invented.

In Cavaillon, there are seventeen bakers listed in the *Pages Jaunes*, but we had been told that one establishment was ahead of all the rest in terms of choice and excellence, a veritable *palais de pain*. At Chez Auzet, so they said, the baking and eating of breads

and pastries had been elevated to the status of a minor religion.

When the weather is warm, tables and chairs are placed on the pavement outside the bakery so that the matrons of Cavaillon can sit with their hot chocolate and almond biscuits or strawberry tarts while they give proper, leisurely consideration to the bread they will buy for lunch and dinner. To help them, Auzet has printed a comprehensive bread menu, the *Carte des Pains*. I took a copy from the counter, ordered coffee, sat in the sun and started to read.

It was another step in my French education. Not only did it introduce me to breads I had never heard of before, it told me with great firmness and precision what I should be eating with them. With my *apéritif*, I could choose between the tiny squares called *toasts*, a *pain surprise* which might be flavoured with finely chopped bacon, or the savoury *feuillets salés*, That was simple. The decisions became more complicated when the meal itself was being chosen. Supposing, for example, I wanted to start with *crudités*. There were four possible accompaniments: onion bread, garlic bread, olive bread or roquefort bread. Too difficult? In that case, I could have seafood, because the gospel according the Auzet authorised only one bread to eat with seafood, and that was thinly-sliced rye.

And so it went on, listing with uncompromising brevity what I should eat with *charcuterie*, foie gras, soup, red and white meat, game with feathers and game with fur, smoked meats, mixed salads (not to be confused with the separately listed green salads) and three different consistencies of cheese. I counted eighteen varieties of bread, from thyme to pepper, from nuts to bran. In a fog of indecision, I went inside the shop and consulted Madame. What would she recommend with calves' liver?

She set off on a short tour of the shelves, and then selected a stubby brown *banette*. While she was counting out my change, she told me about a restaurant where the chef serves a different bread with each of the five courses on his menu. There's a man who understands bread, she said. Not like some.

I was beginning to understand it, just as I was beginning to understand mushrooms. It had been an instructive morning.

* * * * *

Massot was in lyrical mood. He had just left his house to go into the forest and kill something when I met him on a hill overlooking a long stretch of vineyards. With his gun under his arm and one of his yellow cigarettes screwed into the corner of his mouth, he stood contemplating the valley.

'Look at those vines,' he said. 'Nature is wearing her prettiest clothes.'

The effect of this unexpectedly poetic observation was slightly spoiled when Massot cleared his throat noisily and spat, but he was right; the vines were spectacular, field after field of russet and yellow and scarlet leaves, motionless in the sunlight. Now that the grapes had all been picked there were no tractors or human figures to interfere with our appreciation of the view. Work on the vines wouldn't start again until the leaves had fallen and the pruning began. It was a space between seasons, still hot, but not quite summer and not yet autumn.

I asked Massot if there had been any progress in the sale of his property, maybe a nice German couple who had fallen in love with the house while camping nearby.

He bristled at the mention of campers. 'They couldn't afford a house like mine. In any case, I have taken it off the market until 1992. You'll see. When the frontiers are abolished, they'll all be looking for houses down here – English, Belgians . . .' He waved his hand airily to include the other Common Market nationalities. 'Prices will become much more important. Houses in the Lubéron will be *très recherchées*. Even your little place might fetch a million or two.'

It was not the first time that 1992 had been mentioned as the year when the whole of Provence would be showered with foreign money, because in 1992 the Common Market would come into its own. Nationalities would be forgotten as we all became one big happy family of Europeans. Financial restrictions would be lifted – and what would the Spaniards and Italians and the rest of them do? What else but hurry down to Provence waving their cheque books and looking for houses.

It was a popular thought, but I couldn't see why it should happen. Provence already had a considerable foreign population; they had found no problem buying houses. And, for all the talk of

European integration, a date on a piece of paper wasn't going to stop the bickering and bureaucracy and jockeying for special preference which all the member countries – notably France – used when it suited them. Fifty years might see a difference; 1992 almost certainly would not.

But Massot was convinced. In 1992, he was going to sell up and retire, or possibly buy a little *bar-tabac* in Cavaillon. I asked him what he'd do with his three dangerous dogs, and for a moment I thought he was going to burst into tears.

'They wouldn't be happy in a town,' he said. 'I'd have to shoot them.'

He walked along with me for a few minutes, and cheered himself up by muttering about the profits that were certain to come his way, and about time too. A lifetime of hard work should be rewarded. A man should spend his old age in comfort, not breaking his back on the land. As it happened, his land was exceptional in the valley for its ill-kempt appearance, but he always spoke of it as though it were a cross between the gardens at Villandry and the manicured vineyards of Château Lafite. He turned off the path to go into the forest and terrorise some birds, a brutal, greedy and mendacious old scoundrel. I was becoming quite fond of him.

The way home was littered with spent shotgun cartridges fired by the men whom Massot dismissed as *chasseurs du sentier*, or footpath hunters – miserable namby-pambies who didn't want to get their boots dirty in the forest, and who hoped that birds would somehow fly into their buckshot. Among the scattered shell cases were crushed cigarette packets and empty sardine cans and bottles, souvenirs left by the same nature lovers who complained that the beauty of the Lubéron was being ruined by tourists. Their concern for conservation didn't extend to removing their own rubbish. A messy breed, the Provençal hunter.

I arrived at the house to find a small conference taking place around the electricity meter which was hidden behind some trees in the back garden. The man from Electricité de France had opened the meter to read it, and had discovered that a colony of ants had made a nest. The figures were obscured. It was impossible to establish our consumption of electricity. The ants must be removed. My wife and the man from the EDF had been joined by Menicucci, whom we now suspected of living in the boiler room, and who liked nothing better than to advise us on any domestic problem that might arise.

'*Oh là là.*' A pause while Menicucci bent down for a closer look at the meter. '*Ils sont nombreux, les fourmis.*' For once, he had made an understatement. The ants were so numerous that they appeared as one solid black block, completely filling the metal box that housed the meter.

'I'm not touching them,' said the EDF man. 'They get into your clothes and bite you. The last time I tried to brush away an ants' nest I had them with me all afternoon.'

He stood looking at the squirming mass, tapping his screwdriver againt his teeth. He turned to Menicucci. 'Do you have a blowlamp?'

'I'm a plumber. Of course I have a blowlamp.'

'*Bon.* Then we can burn them off.'

Menicucci was aghast. He took a step backwards and crossed himself. He smote his forehead. He raised his index finger to the position that indicated either extreme disagreement, or the start of a lecture, or both.

'I cannot believe what I have just heard. A blowlamp? Do you realise how much current passes through here?'

The EDF man looked offended. 'Of course I know. I'm an electrician.'

Menicucci affected to be surprised. '*Ah bon?* Then you will know what happens when you burn a live cable.'

'I would be very prudent with the flame.'

'Prudent! Prudent! *Mon Dieu,* we could all perish with the ants.'

The EDF man sheathed his screwdriver and crossed his arms. 'Very well. I will not occupy myself with the ants. You remove them.'

Menicucci thought for a moment and then, like a magician setting up a particularly astonishing trick, he turned to my wife. 'If Madame could possibly bring me some fresh lemons – two or three will be enough – and a knife?'

Madame the magician's assistant came back with the knife and lemons, and Menicucci cut each into four quarters. 'This is an *astuce* that I was taught by a very old man,' he said, and muttered something impolite about the stupidity of using a blowlamp – '*putain de chalumeau*' – while the EDF man sulked under a tree.

When the lemons were all quartered, Menicucci advanced on the nest and started to squeeze lemon juice back and forth over the ants, pausing between squeezes to observe the effect that the downpour of citric acid was having.

The ants surrendered, evacuating the meter box in panic-stricken clumps, climbing over each other in their haste to escape. Menicucci enjoyed his moment of triumph. '*Voilà, jeune homme*,' he said to the EDF man, 'ants cannot support the juice of fresh lemons. That is something you have learned today. If you leave slices of lemon in your meters you will never have another infestation.'

The EDF man took it with a marked lack of graciousness, complaining that he was not a lemon-supplier and that the juice had made the meter sticky. 'Better sticky than burnt to a cinder,' was Menicucci's parting shot as he returned to his boiler. '*Beh oui*. Better sticky than burnt.'

* * * * *

The days were warm enough for swimming, the nights cool enough for fires, Indian summer weather. It finally ended in the excessive style that was typical of the Provençal climate. We went to bed in one season and woke up in another.

The rain had come in the night, and continued for most of the following day; not the fat, warm drops of summer, but grey sheets that fell in a vertical torrent, sluicing through the vineyards, flattening shrubs, turning flower beds into mud and mud into brown rivers. It stopped in the late afternoon, and we went to look at the drive – or, rather, where the drive had been the previous day.

It had already suffered in the big storm of August, but the ruts made then were scratches compared to what we now saw: a succession of craters led down to the road, where most of the drive had been deposited in sodden piles. The rest of it was in the melon field opposite the house. Some of the gravel and stones had

travelled more than a hundred yards. A recently detonated minefield could hardly have looked worse, and nobody except a man
who hated his car would have attempted to drive to the house from
the road. We needed a bulldozer just to tidy up the mess, and
several tons of gravel to replace what the rain had washed away.

I called Monsieur Menicucci. Over the months, he had
established himself as a human version of the Yellow Pages, and,
since he had a regard verging on the proprietorial for our house, his
recommendations had been made, so he told us, as though it were
his own money at stake. He listened as I told him of the lost drive,
making interjections – *quelle catastrophe* was mentioned more
than once – to show that he appreciated the extent of the problem.

I finished talking, and I could hear Menicucci making a verbal
list of our requirements: '*Un bulldozer, bien sûr, un camion, une
montagne de gravier, un compacteur . . .*' There were a few
moments of humming, probably a snatch of Mozart to assist the
mental processes, and then he made up his mind. '*Bon.* There is a
young man, the son of a neighbour, who is an artist with the
bulldozer, and his prices are correct. He's called Sanchez. I will
ask him to come tomorrow.'

I reminded Menicucci that the drive was not possible for an
ordinary car.

'He's used to that,' said Menicucci. 'He will come on his *moto*
with special tyres. He can pass anywhere.'

I watched him negotiate the drive the next morning, doing
slalom turns to avoid the craters and standing up on his footrests as
he drove over the mounds of earth. He cut the engine and looked
back at the drive, a study in colour co-ordinated *moto chic.* His hair
was black, his leather jacket was black, his bike was black. He wore
aviator sunglasses with impenetrable reflective lenses. I wondered
if he knew our insurance agent, the formidably hip Monsieur
Fructus. They would have made a good pair.

Within half an hour, he had made a tour of the minefield on
foot, estimated a price, telephoned to order the gravel and given us
a firm date, two days away, for his return with the bulldozer. We
had our doubts that he was real and, when Menicucci called that
evening in his capacity as supervisor of catastrophes, I said that
Monsieur Sanchez had surprised us with his efficiency.

'It runs in the family,' Menicucci said. 'His father is a melon millionaire. The son will be a bulldozer millionaire. They are very serious, despite being Spanish.' He explained that Sanchez *père* had come to France as a young man to find work, and had developed a method of producing earlier and more succulent melons than anyone else in Provence. He was now, said Menicucci, so rich that he worked for only two months a year and lived during the winter in Alicante.

Sanchez *fils* arrived as promised, and spent the day re-arranging the landscape with his bulldozer. He had a delicacy of touch that was fascinating to watch, redistributing tons of earth as accurately as if he were using a trowel. When the drive was level, he smoothed the surface with a giant comb, and invited us to see what he had done. It looked too immaculate to walk on, and he had given it a slight camber so that any future downpours would run off into the vines.

'*C'est bon?*'

As good as the autoroute to Paris, we said.

'*Bieng. Je revieng demaing.*' He climbed into the control tower of his bulldozer and drove off at a stately fifteen miles an hour. Tomorrow the gravel would be laid.

The first vehicle to disturb the combed perfection of the drive's surface crawled up to the house the next morning and stopped with a shudder of relief in the parking area. It was a truck that looked to be even more venerable than Faustin's grape wagon, sagging so low on its suspension that the rusty exhaust pipe nearly touched the ground. A man and a woman, both round and weatherbeaten, were standing by the truck and looking with interest at the house, obviously itinerant field workers hoping for one last job before heading further south for the winter.

They seemed a nice old couple, and I felt sorry for them.

'I'm afraid the grapes have all been picked,' I said.

The man grinned and nodded. 'That's good. You were lucky to get them in before the rain.' He pointed up to the forest behind the house. 'Plenty of mushrooms there, I should think.'

Yes, I said, plenty.

They showed no sign of going. I said they were welcome to leave their truck outside the house and pick some mushrooms.

'No, no,' said the man. 'We're working today. My son is on his way with the gravel.'

The melon millionaire opened the back doors of the truck and took out a long-handled mason's shovel and a wide-toothed wooden rake. 'I'll leave the rest for him to unload,' he said. 'I don't want to squash my feet.'

I looked inside. Packed tight up against the back of the seats and stretching the length of the truck was a miniature steam roller, the *compacteur*.

While we waited for his son, Monsieur Sanchez talked about life and the pursuit of happiness. Even after all these years, he said, he still enjoyed the occasional day of manual labour. His work with the melons was finished by July, and he got bored with nothing to do. It was very agreeable to be rich, but one needed something else, and, as he liked working with his hands, why not help his son?

I had never employed a millionaire before. I don't have much time for them as a rule, but this one put in a good long day. Load after load of gravel was delivered and tipped on to the drive by the son. The father shovelled and spread, and Madame Sanchez followed behind with the wooden rake, pushing and smoothing. Then the *compacteur* was unloaded; it was like a massive baby carriage with handlebars, and it was wheeled ceremoniously up and down the drive with Sanchez the son at the controls, shouting instructions at his parents – another shovelful here, more raking there, mind your feet, don't tread on the vines.

It was a true family effort, and by the end of the afternoon we had a pristine ribbon of crushed, putty-coloured gravel worthy of being entered for the Concours d'Elégance sponsored by *Bulldozer Magazine*. The *compacteur* was inserted into the back of the truck; the parents into the front. Young Sanchez said that the price would be less than his estimate, but he would work it out exactly and his father would come round to deliver the bill.

The next morning when I got up, there was an unfamiliar van parked outside the house. I looked for a driver, but there was nobody in the vines or in the outbuildings. It was probably an idle hunter who couldn't be bothered to walk up from the road.

We were finishing breakfast when there was a tap on the window and we saw the round brown face of Monsieur Sanchez. He wouldn't come into the house, because he said his boots were too dirty. He had been in the forest since six o'clock, and he had a present for us. From behind his back he produced his old checked cap, bulging with wild mushrooms. He gave us his favourite recipe – oil, butter, garlic and chopped parsley – and told us a dreadful story about three men who had died after an ill-chosen mushroom supper. A neighbour had found them still at the table with wide, staring eyes – Monsieur Sanchez gave us a demonstration, rolling his eyes back in his head – completely paralysed by malignant fungus. But we were not to worry, he said. He would stake his life on the mushrooms in his cap. *Bon appétit*!

My wife and I ate them that evening, studying each other between mouthfuls for signs of paralysis and eye-rolling. They tasted so much better than ordinary mushrooms that we decided to invest in a guide book and to share a pair of anti-snake boots.

* * * * *

There comes a time in the restoration of an old house when the desire to see it finished threatens all those noble aesthetic intentions to see it finished properly. The temptation to settle for the short cut nags away as the delays add up and the excuses multiply: the carpenter has severed a fingertip, the mason's truck has been stolen, the painter has *la grippe*, fittings ordered in May and promised for June don't arrive until September, and all the time the concrete-mixer and the rubble and the shovels and pickaxes become more and more like permanent fixtures. During the hot months of summer, tranquillised by the sun, it had been possible to look with a patient eye at the uncompleted jobs throughout the house. Now that we were spending more time indoors with them, patience had been replaced by irritation.

With Christian the architect, we went through the rooms to establish who had to do what, and how long it would take.

'*Normalement*,' said Christian, a man of great charm and implacable optimism, 'there is only six or seven days of work. A little masonry, some plastering, two days of painting, *et puis voilà. Terminé*.'

We were encouraged. As we said to Christian, there had been dark moments recently when we imagined waking up on Christmas morning still surrounded by the debris of a building site.

He threw up everything in horror – hands, eyebrows and shoulders. What a thought. It was inconceivable that these mere finishing touches should be delayed any longer. He would telephone the various members of the *équipe* immediately to organise a week of intensive activity. Progress would be made. No, more than progress; a conclusion.

One by one, they came at odd times to the house: Didier and his dog at seven in the morning. The electrician at lunchtime, Ramon the plasterer for an evening drink. They came, not to work, but to look at the work that had to be done. They were all astonished that it had taken so long, as though people other than themselves had been responsible. Each of them told us, confidentially, that the problem was always that one had to wait for the other fellow to finish before one could start. But, when we mentioned Christmas, they roared with laughter. Christmas was *months* away; they could almost build a complete house by Christmas. There was, however, a common reluctance to name a day.

When can you come? we asked.

Soon, soon, they said.

We would have to be content with that. We went out to the front of the house, where the concrete-mixer stood guard over the steps to the front door, and imagined a cypress tree standing in its place.

Soon, soon.

NOVEMBER

The French peasant is an inventive man, and he hates waste. He is reluctant to discard anything, because he knows that one day the bald tractor tyre, the chipped scythe, the broken hoe and the gearbox salvaged from the 1949 Renault van will serve him well and save him from disturbing the contents of that deep, dark pocket where he keeps his money.

The contraption that I found at the edge of the vineyard was a rusty monument to his ingenuity. A 100-litre oil drum had been sliced in half lengthways and mounted on a framework of narrow-gauge iron piping. An old wheel, more oval than round, had been bolted on to the front. Two handles of unequal length protruded from the back. It was, so Faustin told me, a *brouette de vigneron* – a wheelbarrow, purpose-built at minimal expense for the pruning season.

All the vines had now been stripped of their leaves by the autumn winds, and the tangled shoots looked like coiled clumps of brown barbed wire. Some time before the sap started to rise next spring they would have to be cut back to the main stem. The clippings, or *sarments*, were of no agricultural use, too fibrous to rot into the ground during the winter, and too numerous to leave piled in the corridors between the vines where the tractors would pass. They would have to be gathered up and burnt; hence the *brouette de vigneron*.

It was the simplest kind of mobile incinerator. A fire was lit in the bottom of the oil drum, the *sarments* were clipped and thrown on the fire, and the barrow was pushed along to the next vine. When the drum was full, the pale grey ash was scattered on the ground and the process began again. It was, in its primitive way, a model of efficiency.

Walking back to the house just before dusk, I saw a slim plume of blue smoke rising from the corner of the field where Faustin was pruning and burning. He straightened up and rubbed his back, and his hand felt cold and stiff when I shook it. He pointed along the rows of clipped vines, twisted claws black against the sandy soil.

'Nice and clean, eh? I like to see them nice and clean.' I asked him to leave some *sarments* for me to gather up to use on the barbecue next summer, and I remembered seeing them once in a shop which called itself a food boutique in New York – Genuine Vine Clippings, they were labelled, and they were guaranteed to impart That Authentic Barbecue Flavor. They had been trimmed to a standard length and neatly trussed with straw twine, and they cost two dollars for a small bunch. Faustin couldn't believe it.

'People buy them?'

He looked at the vines again, estimating how many hundreds of dollars he had burned in the course of the day, and shook his head. Another cruel blow. He shrugged.

'*C'est curieux.*'

* * * * *

Our friend, who lived deep in Côtes du Rhône country north of Vaison-la-Romaine, was to be honoured by the winegrowers of his village and admitted to the Confrérie Saint-Vincent, the local equivalent of the Chevaliers du Tastevin. The investiture was to take place in the village hall, followed by dinner, followed by dancing. The wines would be strong and plentiful and the winegrowers and their wives would be out in force. Ties were to be worn. It was that kind of occasion.

Years before, we had been to another Chevaliers' dinner, in Burgundy. Two hundred people in full evening dress, rigid with decorum at the start of the meal, had turned into a friendly mob singing Burgundian drinking songs by the time the main course was served. We had blurred but happy memories of watching the sozzled Chevaliers after dinner, trying to find and then to unlock their cars, with the amiable assistance of the Clos Vougeot police force. It had been our first experience of an evening formally dedicated to mass intoxication, and we had enjoyed it enormously. Any friend of the grape was a friend of ours.

The village hall was officially called the *Salle des Fêtes*. It was a fairly recent construction, designed with a complete disregard for its mediaeval surroundings by the anonymous and overworked French architect whose mission in life is to give every village its own eyesore. This was a classic of the contemporary blockhouse school – a box of raw brick and aluminium-trimmed glass set in a garden of tarmac, devoid of charm but rich in neon light fittings.

We were greeted at the door by two substantial, rosy-faced men in white shirts, black trousers and wide scarlet sashes. We told them we were guests of the new Confrère.

'*Bieng, bieng. Allez-y.*' Meaty hands patted us on the back and into the big room.

At one end was a raised platform, furnished with a long table and a microphone. Smaller tables, set for dinner, were placed down either side of the room and across the far end, leaving a large space in the middle which was packed with wine-growers and their friends.

The level of conversation was deafening; men and women who are used to talking to each other across a vineyard find it difficult to adjust their volume, and the room echoed and boomed with voices that had been developed to compete with the Mistral. But, if the voices had come straight in from the fields, the clothes were definitely from the Sunday-best *armoire*: dark suits and shirts whose collars looked uncomfortably tight round weatherbeaten necks for the men; vividly coloured and elaborate dresses for the women. One couple, more couture-conscious than the rest, had outfits of startling splendour. The woman shimmered in a dress of grey bugle beads, and small matching grey feathers were sewn to the back of her stockings so that her legs appeared to flutter when she walked. Her husband wore a white jacket trimmed with black piping, a frilled shirt with more black piping and black evening trousers. Either his nerve or his resources had run out at that point, because his shoes were sensible, thick-soled and brown. Nevertheless, we felt sure that they were the couple to watch when the dancing started.

We found our friend and his family. He was glancing round the room, looking puzzled and almost ill-at-ease, and we thought that the solemnity of the occasion had brought on an attack of Confrère's nerves. The problem, however, was altogether more serious.

'I can't see a bar anywhere,' he said. 'Can you?'

There were barrels of wine against one of the walls. There were bottles of wine on the tables. We were in a village which would float on a sea of Côtes du Rhône if all the *caves* were emptied, but there was no bar. And, now that we studied our fellow revellers, we made another worrying discovery. Nobody was holding a glass.

We were prevented from making an indiscreet grab at a bottle on the nearest table by a fanfare on the loudspeaker system, and the Confrères filed in and took up their position behind the table on the dais – a dozen or more figures in cloaks and wide-brimmed hats, some holding parchment scrolls, one with an imposingly fat book. Any moment now, we thought, the *vin d'honneur* would be served to signal the start of the ceremony.

The Mayor embraced the microphone and delivered the opening speech. The senior Confrère gave a speech. His assistant, the keeper of the fat book, gave a speech. One by one the three new Confrères were summoned to the dais and eulogised at length for their love of wine and good fellowship. One by one, they replied with speeches accepting the honours bestowed upon them. I detected a certain huskiness in the voice of our friend which others may have mistaken for emotion. I knew it to be thirst.

As a finale, we were asked to join in the singing of a song written in the Provençal language by Frédéric Mistral.

'*Coupo santo e versanto,*' we sang in praise of the sainted and overflowing goblet, '*A-de-reng beguen en troupo lou vin pur de nostre plant*' – let us all drink together the pure wine of our growth, and about time too. The investiture had taken just over an hour, and not a drop had passed anyone's lips.

There was a noticeable eagerness to be seated, and at last the sainted goblets were filled, emptied and refilled. An air of relief spread throughout the tables, and we were able to relax and consider the menu.

Quail in aspic came first; the heads, which we were told cost two francs each, were detachable and could be used again at a future banquet. Then there was sea bass. These were mere preliminaries, the chef's limbering-up exercises before attacking the sirloin of Charolais beef *en croûte*. But, before that, there was a small and deadly item described as a *Trou Provençal* – a sorbet made with the minimum of water and the maximum of *marc*. Its purpose, so we were told, was to clear the palate; in fact it was sufficiently powerful to anaesthetize not only the palate, but the sinus passages and the front portion of the skull as well. But the chef knew what he was doing. After the initial jolt of frozen alcohol wore off, I could feel a hollowness in the stomach – the *trou* – and I could face the rest of the long meal with some hope of being able to finish it.

The beef made its entrance to the strains of a second fanfare, and was paraded around the tables by the waiters and waitresses before being served. The white wine gave way to the pride of the local wine-growers, a formidably heavy red, and the courses kept coming until, after the serving of soufflés and champagne, it was time to rise up and dance.

The band was of the old school, clearly not interested in performing for people who simply like to hop up and down; they wanted to see *dancing*. There were waltzes and quicksteps and several numbers which might have been gavottes, but for me the highlight of the evening was the tango interlude. I don't think it is given to many of us to witness fifty or sixty couples in the advanced stages of inebriation attempting the swoops and turns and heel-stamping flourishes of the true tango artist, and it was a sight I shall never forget. Elbows were cocked, heads flicked from side to side, desperate and off-balance charges were made with twinkling feet from one end of the room to the other, potential collision and disaster was everywhere. One diminutive man danced blind, his head sunk into the *décolletage* of his taller partner. The couple in bugle beads and frilled shirt, moulded together at the groin with their backs arching outwards, lunged and dipped through the crowd with a dexterity unknown outside the tango palaces of Buenos Aires.

Miraculously, nobody was injured. When we left, some time after one o'clock, the music was still playing and the dancers, stuffed with food and awash with wine, were still dancing. Not for the first time, we marvelled at the Provençal constitution.

We arrived back at the house the following day to find that its appearance had changed; there was an unfamiliar tidiness in front of the steps which led up to the door. The cement-mixer, which had for months been an integral part of the façade of the house, was no longer there.

It was an ominous sign. As much as we disliked having its hulk parked outside, it was at least a guarantee that Didier and his masons would return. Now they had crept in and taken it – *our* cement-mixer – probably to use on a six-month job somewhere the other side of Carpentras. Our hopes of having a finished house by Christmas suddenly seemed like a bad attack of misplaced optimism.

Christian, as usual, was sympathetic and reassuring.

'They had to go to Mazan . . . an emergency job . . . the roof of an old widow's house . . .'

I felt guilty. What were our problems compared to the plight of a poor old widow exposed to the elements?

'Don't worry,' Christian said. 'Two days, maybe three, and then they'll be back to finish off. There's plenty of time before Christmas. It's weeks away.'

Not many weeks away, we thought. My wife suggested kidnapping Didier's cocker spaniel, closer to his heart even than the cement-mixer, and keeping it as a hostage. It was a fine, bold scheme, except that the dog never left Didier's side. Well, if not his dog, maybe his wife. We were prepared to consider almost anything.

The unfinished jobs – temporary windows and chinks in the masonry in particular – were made more apparent by the first sustained Mistral of winter. It blew for three days, bending the cypress tree in the courtyard into a green C, tearing at the tatters of plastic in the melon fields, worrying away at loose tiles and shutters, moaning through the night. It was malevolent and inescapable, a wind to lower the spirits as it threw itself endlessly against the house, trying to get in.

'Good weather for suicide,' Massot said to me one morning as the wind flattened his moustache against his cheeks. *'Beh oui.* If this continues, we'll see a funeral or two.'

Of course, he said, this was nothing like the Mistrals of his boyhood. In those days, the wind blew for weeks on end, doing strange and horrible things to the brain. He told me the story of Arnaud, a friend of his father's.

Arnaud's horse was old and tired and no longer strong enough for farm work. He decided to sell it and buy a fresh young horse, and walked the fifteen kilometres to Apt market one windy morning leading the old nag behind him. A buyer was found, the price was agreed, but the young horses for sale that day were poor, thin specimens. Arnaud walked home alone. He would return next week in the hope that better animals would be on sale.

The Mistral continued all that week, and was still blowing when Arnaud walked again to Apt market. This time he was lucky, and bought a big dark horse. It cost him almost double what he had made on the sale of the old horse, but, as the dealer said, he was paying for youth. The new horse had years of work in him.

Arnaud was only two or three kilometres from his farm when the horse broke free from its leading rein and bolted. Arnaud ran after it until he could run no more. He searched in the scrub and in the vineyards, shouting into the wind, cursing the Mistral that had unsettled the horse, cursing his bad luck, cursing his lost money. When it became too dark to search any longer, he made his way home, angry and despairing. Without a horse, he couldn't work the land; he would be ruined.

His wife met him at the door. An extraordinary thing had happened: a horse, a big dark horse, had come running up the track and had gone into one of the outbuildings. She had given it water and pulled a cart across the opening to block its escape.

Arnaud took a lantern and went to look at the horse. A broken lead rein hung from its head. He touched its neck, and his fingers came away stained. In the light of the lantern, he could see the sweat running down its flanks, and pale patches where the dye had worn off. He had bought back his old horse. In rage and shame he went up into the forest behind his farm and hanged himself.

Massot lit a cigarette, hunching his shoulders and cupping his hands against the wind.

'At the inquest,' he said, 'someone had a sense of humour. The cause of death was recorded as suicide while the balance of the mind was disturbed by a horse.'

Massot grinned and nodded. All his stories, it seemed, ended brutally.

'But he was a fool,' Massot said. 'He should have gone back and shot the dealer who sold him the horse – *paf*! – and blamed it on the Mistral. That's what I'd have done.' His reflections on the nature of justice were interrupted by the whine of an engine in low gear, and a Toyota four-wheel-drive truck, as wide as the footpath, slowed down briefly to give us time to jump out of the way. It was Monsieur Dufour, the village grocer and scourge of the Lubéron's *sanglier* population.

We had seen the heads of *sangliers* mounted on the walls of butchers' shops, and had paid no more attention to them than to any other of the strange rustic decorations that we saw from time to time. But once or twice during the summer the *sangliers* had come down from the dry upper slopes of the mountain to drink from the swimming pool and steal melons, and we could never look a stuffed head in the eye again after seeing the living animals. They were black and stout and longer in the leg than a conventional pig, with worried, whiskery faces. We loved our rare glimpses of them, and wished that the hunters would leave them alone. Unfortunately, *sangliers* taste like venison, and are consequently chased from one end of the Lubéron to the other.

Monsieur Dufour was the acknowledged champion hunter, a modern and mechanised Nimrod. Dressed in his combat uniform, his truck bristling with high-powered armaments, he could drive up the rocky trails and reach the *sanglier*-infested upper slopes while less well-equipped hunters were still coughing their way up on foot. On the flat bed of his truck was a large wooden chest containing six hounds, trained to track for days on end. The poor old pigs didn't stand much of a chance.

I said to Massot that I thought it was a shame the *sangliers* were hunted quite so relentlessly by so many hunters.

'But they taste delicious,' he said. 'Specially the young ones, the *marcassins*. And besides, it's natural. The English are too sentimental about animals, except those men who chase foxes, and they are mad.'

The wind was strengthening and getting colder, and I asked Massot how long he thought it would last.

'A day, a week. Who knows?' He leered at me. 'Not feeling like suicide, are you?'

I said I was sorry to disappoint him, but I was well and cheerful, looking forward to the winter and Christmas.

'Usually a lot of murders after Christmas.' He said it as though he was looking forward to a favourite television programme, a bloody sequel to the Mistral suicides.

I heard gunfire as I walked home, and I hoped Dufour had missed. No matter how long I lived here, I would never make a true countryman. And, as long as I preferred to see a wild boar on the hoof instead of on the plate, I'd never make an adopted Frenchman. Let him worship his stomach; I would maintain a civilised detachment from the bloodlust that surrounded me.

This noble smugness lasted until dinner. Henriette had given us a wild rabbit, which my wife had roasted with herbs and mustard. I had two helpings. The gravy, thickened with blood, was wonderful.

* * * * *

Madame Soliva, the eighty-year-old chef whose *nom de cuisine* was Tante Yvonne, had first told us about an olive oil that she said was the finest in Provence. She had better credentials than anyone we knew. Apart from being a magnificent cook, she was olive oil's answer to a Master of Wine. She had tried them all, from Alziari in Nice to the United Producers of Nyons, and in her expert and considered view the oil produced in the valley of Les Baux was the best. One could buy it, she told us, from the little mill in Maussane-les-Alpilles.

When we lived in England, olive oil had been a luxury, to be saved for the making of fresh mayonnaise and the dressing of salads. In Provence, it was an abundant daily treat which we

bought in five-litre *bidons* and used for cooking, for marinating goats' cheeses and red peppers, and for storing truffles. We dipped our bread in it, bathed our lettuce in it and even used it as a hangover preventative. (One tablespoon of oil, taken neat before drinking, was supposed to coat the stomach and protect it against the effects of too much young pink wine.) We soaked up olive oil like sponges, and gradually learned to distinguish between different grades and flavours. We became fussy and no doubt insufferable about our oil, never buying it from shops or supermarkets, but always from a mill or a producer, and I looked forward to oil-buying expeditions almost as much as trips to the vineyards.

An essential part of a day out is lunch, and before going anywhere new we always studied the Gault-Millau guide as well as the map. We discovered that Maussane was perilously close to the Baumanière at Les Baux, where the bills are as memorable as the cooking, but we were saved from temptation by Madame Soliva. 'Go to Le Paradou,' she told us, 'and have lunch at the café. And make sure you're there by noon.'

It was a cold, bright day, good eating weather, and we walked into the Bistro du Paradou a few minutes before midday with appetites sharpened by the smell of garlic and woodsmoke that greeted us. An enormous fire, a long room filled with old marble-topped tables, a plain tiled bar, a busy clatter coming from the kitchen – it had everything. Except, as the *patron* explained, somewhere for us to sit.

The room was still empty, but he said it would be full within fifteen minutes. He shrugged in apology. He looked at my wife, so near and yet so far from a good lunch, her face a study in tragic deprivation. At the sight of a woman so clearly in distress, he relented, sat us at a table facing the fire, and put a thick glass carafe of red wine between us.

The regulars started coming through the door in noisy groups, going straight to the places they occupied every day. By 12.30 every seat was taken and the *patron*, who was also the only waiter, was a plate-laden blur.

The restaurant worked on the simple formula of removing the burden of decision from its customers. As in the station café at

Bonnieux, you ate and drank what you were given. We had a crisp, oily salad and slices of pink country sausage, an *aioli* of snails and cod and hard-boiled eggs with garlic mayonnaise, creamy cheese from Fontvieille and a home-made tart. It was the kind of meal that the French take for granted and tourists remember for years. For us, being somewhere between the two, it was another happy discovery to add to our list, somewhere to come back to on a cold day with an empty stomach in the certain knowledge that we would leave warm and full.

We arrived at the olive oil mill in Maussane two months early. The new crop of olives wouldn't be gathered until January, and that was the time to buy oil at its most fresh. Luckily, said the manager of the mill, last year's crop had been plentiful and there was still some oil left. If we would like to have a look around, he would pack a dozen litres for us to take away.

The official name of the establishment – Coopérative Oléicole de la Vallée des Baux – was almost too long to fit on the front of the modest building that was tucked away at the side of a small road. Inside, every surface seemed to have been rubbed with a fine coating of oil; floors and walls were slick to the touch, the stairs that led up to the sorting platform were slippery underfoot. A group of men sat at a table sticking the Coopérative's ornate gold labels on to bottles and flasks filled with the greenish-yellow oil – pure and natural, as the notice on the wall said, extracted by a single cold pressing.

We went into the office to pick up the squat, two-litre jugs that the manager had packed in a carton for us, and he presented each of us with bars of olive oil soap.

'There is nothing better for the skin,' he said, and he patted his cheeks with dainty fingertips. 'And, as for the oil, it is a masterpiece. You'll see.'

Before dinner that night, we tested it, dripping it on to slices of bread that had been rubbed with the flesh of tomatoes. It was like eating sunshine.

* * * * *

The guests continued to come, dressed for high summer and hoping for swimming weather, convinced that Provence enjoyed a Mediterranean climate and dismayed to find us in sweaters, lighting fires in the evening, drinking winter wines and eating winter food.

Is it always as cold as this in November? Isn't it hot all the year round? They would look dejected when we told them about snowdrifts and sub-zero nights and bitter winds, as though we had lured them to the North Pole under false tropical pretences.

Provence has been accurately described as a cold country with a high rate of sunshine, and the last days of November were as bright and as blue as May, clean and exhilarating and, as far as Faustin was concerned, profoundly ominous. He was predicting a savage winter, with temperatures so low that olive trees would die of cold as they had done in 1976. He speculated with grim enjoyment about chickens being frozen stiff and old people turning blue in their beds. He said there would undoubtedly be extended power cuts, and warned me to have the chimney swept.

'You'll be burning wood night and day,' he said, 'and that's when chimneys catch fire. And when the *pompiers* come to put out the fire they'll charge you a fortune unless you have a certificate from the chimneysweep.'

And it could be much worse than that. If the house burnt down as the result of a chimney fire, the insurance company wouldn't pay out unless one could produce a certificate. Faustin looked at me, nodding gravely as I absorbed the thoughts of being cold, homeless and bankrupt, and all because of an unswept chimney.

But what would happen, I asked him, if the certificate had been burnt with the house? He hadn't thought of that, and I think he was grateful to me for suggesting another disastrous possibility. A connoisseur of woe needs fresh worries from time to time, or he will become complacent.

I arranged for Cavaillon's premier chimneysweep, Monsieur Beltramo, to come up to the house with his brushes and suction cleaners. A tall man with a courtly manner and an aquiline, sooty profile, he had been a chimney sweep for twenty years. Not once, he told me, had a chimney cleaned by him ever caught fire. When he was finished, he made out the *certificat de ramonage*, complete with smudged fingermarks, and wished me a pleasant winter. 'It won't be a cold one this year,' he said. 'We've had three cold winters in a row. The fourth is always mild.'

I asked him if he was going to clean Faustin's chimney, and exchange weather forecasts.

'No. I never go there. His wife sweeps the chimney.'

DECEMBER

The postman drove at high speed up to the parking area behind the
house and reversed with great élan into the garage wall, crushing a
set of rear lights. He didn't appear to have noticed the damage as he
came into the courtyard, smiling broadly and waving a large
envelope. He went straight to the bar, planted his elbow and
looked expectant.

'*Bonjour, jeune homme!*'

I hadn't been called young man for years, and it wasn't the
postman's normal habit to bring the mail into the house. Slightly
puzzled, I offered him the drink that he was waiting for.

He winked. 'A little pastis,' he said. 'Why not?'

Was it his birthday? Was he retiring? Had he won the big prize
in the Loterie Nationale? I waited for him to explain the reason for
his high spirits, but he was too busy telling me about the *sanglier*
that his friend had shot the previous weekend. Did I know how to
prepare these creatures for the pot? He took me through the whole

gory process, from disembowelment to hanging, quartering and cooking. The pastis disappeared – it wasn't, I realised, his first of the morning – and a refill accepted. Then he got down to business.

'I have brought you the official Post Office calendar,' said the postman. 'It shows all the Saints' Days, and there are some agreeable pictures of young ladies.'

He took the calendar from its envelope and leafed through the pages until he found a photograph of a girl wearing a pair of coconut shells.

'*Voilà!*'

I told him that he was most kind to think of us, and thanked him.

'It's free,' he said. 'Or you can buy it if you want to.'

He winked again, and I finally understood the purpose of the visit. He was collecting his Christmas tip, but since it would be undignified simply to arrive at the front door with an outstretched hand, we had to observe the ritual of the calendar.

He took his money and finished his drink and roared off to his next call, leaving the remnants of his rear light on the drive.

My wife was looking at the calendar when I came back into the house.

'Do you realise,' she said, 'that it's only three weeks until Christmas, and there's still no sign of the builders?'

And then she had an idea that only a woman could have had. It was obvious, she thought, that the birthday of Jesus Christ was not a sufficiently important deadline for the completion of work on the house. Somehow or other, Christmas would come and go and it would be February by the time everyone recovered from their New Year hangovers and holidays. What we should do was to invite the builders to a party to celebrate the end of the job. But not just the builders; their wives must come too.

The intuitive cunning of this suggestion was based on two assumptions. First, that the wives, who never saw the work that their husbands did in other people's houses, would be so curious that they would find the invitation irresistible. And second, that no wife would want her husband to be the one not to have finished his part of the work. This would cause loss of face among the other wives and public embarrassment, followed by some ugly recriminations in the car on the way home.

It was an inspiration. We fixed a date for the last Sunday before Christmas and sent out the invitations: champagne from 11 o'clock onwards.

Within two days, the cement-mixer was back in front of the house. Didier and his assistants, cheerful and noisy, resumed where they had left off as though there had never been a three-month hiatus. No excuses were made, and no direct explanation given for the sudden return to work. The closest Didier came to it was when he mentioned casually that he wanted to have everything finished before he went skiing. He and his wife, he said, would be delighted to accept our invitation.

We had worked out that if everyone came there would be twenty-two people, all with good Provençal appetites. And, as it was so close to Christmas, they would be looking for something a little more festive than a bowlful of olives and a few slices of *saucisson*. My wife started making lists of provisions, and terse footnotes and reminders were scattered throughout the house: Rabbit terrine! *Gambas* and mayonnaise! Individual pizzas! Mushroom tart! Olive bread! How many quiches? – the scraps of paper were everywhere, making my one-word list – champagne – look sparse and inadequate.

The gastronomic highlight was delivered one cold morning by a friend who had relatives in Périgord. It was an entire foie gras – raw, and therefore a fraction of the price of the prepared product. All we had to do was cook it and add some slivers of black truffle.

We unwrapped it. The previous owner must have been a bird the size of a small aircraft, because the liver was enormous – a rich, dark yellow mass that filled both my hands when I lifted it on to the chopping board. Following our friend's instructions, I cut it up and compressed it into glass preserving jars, inserting pieces of truffle with nervous fingers. This was like cooking money.

The jars were sealed, and placed in a huge saucepan of boiling water for precisely ninety minutes. After cooling off, they were refrigerated, then laid to rest in the *cave*. My wife crossed foie gras off her list.

It felt strange to be coming to the end of the year under blue skies, and without the frenzy that characterises the weeks before an English Christmas. The only hint of festive preparations in our valley was the strange noise coming from the house of Monsieur Poncet, about a mile away from us. On two successive mornings as I walked past, I heard terrible squawks – not cries of fear or pain, but of outrage. I didn't think they were human, but I wasn't sure. I asked Faustin if he had noticed them.

'Oh, that,' he said. 'Poncet is grooming his ass.'

On Christmas Eve, there was to be a living *crèche* in the church in Ménerbes, and the ass of Monsieur Poncet had an important supporting role. Naturally, he had to look his best, but he had an aversion to being brushed and combed, and he was not the kind of ass to suffer grooming quietly. Doubtless he would be presentable on the night, said Faustin, but one would be wise to stay well away from his hind legs, as he was reputed to have an impressive kick.

Up in the village, casting was in progress for the Infant Jesus. Babies of a suitable age and disposition were required to present themselves, and temperament – the ability to rise to the big occasion – would be all-important, as the proceedings did not start until midnight.

Apart from that, and the cards that the postman stuffed in the mailbox, Christmas might have been months away. We did not have a television, and so we were spared the sight of those stupefyingly jolly commercials. There were no carol singers, no office parties, no strident countdowns of the remaining shopping days. I loved it. My wife was not so sure; something was missing. Where was my Christmas spirit? Where was the mistletoe? Where was the Christmas tree? We decided to go into Cavaillon to find them.

We were rewarded at once by the sight of Santa Claus. Dressed in baggy red *bouclé* trousers, a Rolling Stones T-shirt, red fur-trimmed pixie hat and false beard, he came weaving towards us as we walked down the Cours Gambetta. It looked from a distance as though his beard was on fire, but as he came closer we saw the stub of a Gauloise among the whiskers. He lurched past in a cloud of Calvados fumes, attracting considerable attention from a group of small children. Their mothers would have some explaining to do.

The streets were strung with lights. Music came through the

open doorways of bars and shops. Christmas trees were stacked in clumps on the pavement. A man with a throat microphone was selling bedlinen from a stall in an alley. 'Take a look at that, Madame. Pure Dralon! I'll give you five thousand francs if you can find a fault in it!' An old peasant woman began a millimetre by millimetre inspection, and the man snatched it away.

We turned the corner and nearly collided with the carcass of a deer, hanging outside the door of a butcher's shop, gazing blindly at the carcass of a *sanglier* hanging next to it. In the window, a line of tiny nude birds, their necks broken and their heads neatly arranged on their breastbones, were offered as a special pre-Christmas promotion, seven for the price of six. The butcher had closed their beaks and set them in a garnish of evergreen leaves and red ribbon. We shuddered, and moved on.

There was no doubt about the most important ingredient in a Provençal Christmas. Judging by the window displays, the queues and the money changing hands, clothes and toys and stereo equipment and baubles were of incidental importance; the main event of Christmas was food. Oysters and crayfish and pheasant and hare, pâtés and cheeses, hams and capons, gâteaux and pink champagne – after a morning spent looking at it all we were suffering from visual indigestion. With our tree and our mistletoe and our dose of Christmas spirit, we came home.

Two uniformed men were waiting for us, parked outside the house in an unmarked car. The sight of them made me feel guilty, of what, I didn't know, but uniformed men have that effect on me. I tried to think what crimes I had committed recently against the Fifth Republic, and then the two men got out of the car and saluted. I relaxed. Even in France, where bureaucratic formality approaches the level of art, they don't salute before they arrest you.

In fact, they weren't policemen, but firemen, *pompiers* from Cavaillon. They asked if they could come into the house, and I wondered where we had put our chimneysweep's certificate. This was obviously a spot check designed to catch any householder with a soiled flue.

We sat round the dining room table. One of the men opened an attaché case. 'We have brought the official calendar of the Pompiers de Vaucluse.' He laid it on the table.

'As you will see, it shows all the Saints' Days.'

And so it did, just like our Post Office calendar. But, instead of photographs of girls wearing coconut shell brassières, this calendar was illustrated with pictures of firemen scaling tall buildings, administering first aid to accident victims, rescuing mountaineers in distress and manning loaded firehoses. The *pompiers* in rural France provide an overall emergency service, and they will retrieve your dog from a pothole in the mountains or take you to hospital, as well as fight your fires. They are in every way an admirable and deserving body of men.

I asked if a contribution would be acceptable.

'*Bien sûr.*'

We were given a receipt which also entitled us to call ourselves Friends of the Cavaillon Fire Department. After more salutes, the two *pompiers* left to try their luck further up the valley, and we hoped that their training had prepared them for attacks by vicious dogs. Getting a contribution out of Massot would be only marginally less hazardous than putting out a fire. I could imagine him, squinting out from behind his curtains, shotgun at the ready, watching his Alsatians hurl themselves at the intruders. I had once seen the dogs attack the front wheel of a car for want of anything human, ripping away at the tyre as though it were a hunk of raw beef, slavering and spitting out shreds of rubber while the terrified driver endeavoured to reverse out of range, and Massot looked on, smoking and smiling.

We were now a two-calendar family, and as the days before Christmas slipped by we anticipated the delivery of a third, which would be worth a substantial contribution. Every Tuesday, Thursday and Saturday for the past twelve months, the heroes of the sanitation department had stopped at the end of our drive to pick up shamefully large piles of empty bottles, the evil-smelling remains of *bouillabaisse* suppers, dog-food cans, broken glasses, sacks of rubble, chicken bones and domestic fall-out of every size and description. Nothing defeated them. No heap, however huge and ripe, was too much for the man who clung to the back of the truck, dropping off at each stop to toss the garbage into an open, greasy hold. In the summer, he must have come close to asphyxiation and, in the winter, close to tears with the cold.

190

He and his partner eventually turned up in a Peugeot which looked as if it was enjoying its final outing before going to the scrapyard – two cheerful, scruffy men with hard handshakes and pastis breath. On the back seat, I could see a brace of rabbits and some bottles of champagne, and I said that it was good to see them picking up some full bottles for a change.

'It's not the empty bottles we mind,' said one of them. 'But you should see what some people leave for us.' He wrinkled his face and held his nose, little finger extended elegantly in the air. '*Dégueulasse.*'

They were pleased with their tip. We hoped they would go out and have a glorious, messy meal, and let someone else clear up.

* * * * *

Didier was squatting on his haunches with a dustpan and brush, sweeping crumbs of cement out of a corner. It was heartening to see this human machine of destruction engaged in such delicate chores; it meant that his work was over.

He stood up and emptied the dustpan into a paper sack and lit a cigarette. 'That's it,' he said. '*Normalement*, the painter will come tomorrow.' We walked outside, where Eric was loading the shovels and buckets and toolboxes on to the back of the truck. Didier grinned. 'It doesn't bother you if we take the cement-mixer?'

I said I thought we could manage without it, and the two of them pushed it up a plank ramp and roped it tight against the back of the driver's cabin. Didier's spaniel watched the progress of the cement-mixer with her head cocked, and then jumped into the truck and lay along the dashboard.

'*Allez!*' Didier held out his hand. It felt like cracked leather. 'See you on Sunday.'

The painter came the next day, and painted, and left. Jean-Pierre the carpet-layer arrived. The wives had obviously decided that everything should be ready for their state visit.

By Friday night, the carpet was laid except for the last couple of metres.

'I'll come in tomorrow morning,' said Jean-Pierre, 'and you'll be able to move the furniture in the afternoon.'

By midday, all that remained to do was to fit the carpet under a wooden batten at the threshold of the room. It was while Jean-Pierre was drilling the holes to screw in the batten that he went through the hot water pipe which ran under the floor, and a jet of water rose in a small and picturesque fountain, framed by the doorway.

We cut off the water supply, rolled back the sodden carpet, and called Monsieur Menicucci. After a year of alarms and emergencies, I knew his number off by heart, and I knew what his first words would be.

'*Oh là là.*' He meditated in silence for a moment. 'The floor will have to be broken so that I can solder the pipe. You had better warn Madame. There will be a little dust.'

Madame was out buying food. She was expecting to return to a bedroom, bathroom and dressing room that were dry, clean and carpeted. She would be surprised. I advised Jean-Pierre to go home for medical reasons. She would probably want to kill him.

'What's that noise?' she said when I met her as she was parking the car.

'It's Menicucci's jackhammer.'

'Ah yes. Of course.' She was unnaturally, dangerously calm. I was glad Jean-Pierre had left.

Menicucci, in his search for the leak, had drilled out a trench in the floor, and we were able to see the hot water pipe with its neat hole.

'*Bon,*' he said. 'Now we must make sure there's no blockage in the pipe before I solder. You stay there and watch. I will blow through the tap in the bathroom.'

I watched. Menicucci blew. I received a gout of dusty water in the face.

'What do you see?' he shouted from the bathroom.

'Water,' I said.

'*Formidable.* The pipe must be clear.'

He made his repairs, and went home to watch the rugby on television.

We started mopping up, telling each other that it really wasn't too bad. The carpet would dry out. There was barely enough rubble to fill a bucket. The scorch marks from the blowlamp could be painted over. All in all, as long as one disregarded the jagged, gaping trench, it was possible to look at the rooms and consider them finished. In any case, we had no choice. Sunday was only hours away.

We weren't expecting anyone before 11.30, but we had under-estimated the magnetic appeal that champagne has for the French, and the first knock on the door came shortly after half past ten. Within an hour, everyone except Didier and his wife had arrived. They lined the walls of the living room, awkward with politeness and dressed in their best, darting away from the sanctuary of the walls from time to time to swoop on the food.

As the waiter in charge of keeping glasses filled, I became aware of yet another fundamental difference between the French and the English. When the English come for drinks, the glass is screwed firmly into the hand while talking, smoking or eating. It is set aside with reluctance to deal with calls of nature that require both hands – blowing the nose or visiting the lavatory – but it is never far away or out of sight.

It is different with the French. They are no sooner given a glass before they put it down, presumably because they find conversation difficult with only one hand free. So the glasses gather in groups, and after five minutes identification becomes impossible. The guests, unwilling to take another person's glass but unable to pick out their own, look with longing at the champagne bottle. Fresh glasses are distributed, and the process repeats itself.

I was wondering how long it would be before our supply of glasses ran out and we had to resort to tea cups when there was the familiar sound of a diesel engine in labour, and Didier's truck pulled up behind the house, and he and his wife came in through the back door. It was strange. I knew that Didier had a car, and his wife was dressed from head to toe in fine brown suède which must have sat very uneasily on the gritty seat of the truck.

Christian came across the room and took me aside.

'I think we might have a little problem,' he said. 'You'd better come outside.'

I followed him. Didier took my wife's arm and followed me. As we walked round the house, I looked back and saw that everyone was coming.

'*Voilà!*' said Christian, and pointed at Didier's truck.

On the back, in the space usually reserved for the cement-mixer, was a bulbous shape, three feet high and four feet across. It was wrapped in brilliant green crêpe paper, and dotted with bows of white and red and blue.

'It's for you from all of us,' said Christian. '*Allez.* Unwrap it.'

Didier made a stirrup with his hands, and with effortless gallantry, his cigarette between his teeth, plucked my wife from the ground and lifted her to shoulder height so that she could step on to the back of the truck. I climbed up after her, and we peeled off the green wrapping.

The last strips of paper came away to applause and some piercing whistles from Ramon the plasterer, and we stood in the sunshine on the back of the truck, looking at the upturned faces that surrounded us, and our present.

It was an antique jardinière, a massive circular tub that had been cut by hand from a single block of stone long before the days of cutting machines. It was thick-sided, slightly irregular, a pale, weathered grey. It had been filled with earth and planted with primulas.

We didn't know what to say or how to say it. Surprised, touched and floundering in our inadequate French, we did the best we could. Mercifully, Ramon cut us short.

'*Merde!* I'm thirsty. That's enough speeches. Let's have a drink.'

The formality of the first hour disappeared. Jackets came off and the champagne was attacked in earnest. The men took their wives round the house, showing off their work, pointing out the English bathroom taps marked 'hot' and 'cold', trying the drawers to check that the carpenter had finished the interiors smoothly, touching everything in the manner of curious children.

Christian organised a team to unload the great stone tub from the truck, and eight tipsy men in their Sunday clothes somehow managed to avoid being maimed as the lethal mass was manoeuvred down two sagging planks and on to the ground. Madame Ramon supervised. '*Ah, les braves hommes,*' she said. 'Mind you don't get your fingernails dirty.'

The Menicuccis were the first to leave. Having acquitted themselves with honour among the pâtés and cheeses and flans and champagne, they were off to a late lunch, but not before observing the niceties. They made a ceremonial tour of the other guests, shaking hands, kissing cheeks, exchanging *bons appétits*. Their farewell lasted fifteen minutes.

The others looked as though they were settled for the remainder of the day, eating and drinking their way steadily through everything within reach. Ramon appointed himself the official comedian, and told a series of jokes which became progressively coarser and funnier. He stopped for a drink after explaining how to determine the sex of pigeons by putting them in the refrigerator.

'What made a nice woman like your wife ever marry a terrible old *mec* like you?' asked Didier.

With great deliberation, Ramon put down his champagne and held his hands out in front of him like a fisherman describing the one that got away. Fortunately, he was prevented from going into further revelations by a large piece of pizza which his wife delivered firmly into his mouth. She had heard the routine before.

As the sun moved across the courtyard and left it in afternoon shadow, the guests began to make their tours of departure, with more hand-shaking and kissing and pauses for one final glass.

'Come and have lunch,' said Ramon. 'Or dinner. What's the time?'

It was three o'clock. After four hours of eating and drinking, we were in no state for the *cous-cous* that Ramon was promoting.

'Ah well,' he said, 'if you're on a diet, *tant pis.*'

He gave his wife the car keys and leaned back in the passenger seat, hands clasped across his stomach, beaming at the thought of a solid meal. He had persuaded the other couples to join him. We waved them off and went back to the empty house, the empty plates and the empty glasses. It had been a good party.

We looked through the window at the old stone tub, bright with flowers. It would take at least four men to move it away from the garage and into the garden, and organising four men in Provence was, as we knew, not something that could be arranged overnight. There would be visits of inspection, drinks, heated arguments. Dates would be fixed, and then forgotten. Shoulders would be shrugged and time would pass by. Perhaps by next spring we would see the tub in its proper place. We were learning to think in seasons instead of days or weeks. Provence wasn't going to change its tempo for us.

Meanwhile, there was enough foie gras left over to have in warm, thin slices with salad, and one surviving bottle of champagne cooling in the shallow end of the swimming pool. We put some more logs on the fire and thought about the imminent prospect of our first Provençal Christmas.

It was ironic. Having had guests throughout the year, who often had to endure great inconvenience and primitive conditions because of the building work, we now had the house, clean and finished, to ourselves. The last guests had left the previous week, and the next were arriving to help us see in the New Year. But on Christmas Day we would be alone.

We woke up to sunshine and a quiet, empty valley, and a kitchen with no electricity. The gigot of lamb that was ready to go into the oven had a reprieve, and we faced the terrible possibility of bread and cheese for Christmas lunch. All the local restaurants would have been booked up for weeks.

It is at times like this, when crisis threatens the stomach, that the French display the most sympathetic side of their nature. Tell them stories of physical injury or financial ruin and they will either laugh or commiserate politely. But tell them you are facing gastronomic hardship, and they will move heaven and earth and even restaurant tables to help you.

We telephoned Maurice, the chef at the Auberge de la Loube in Buoux, and asked him if there had been any cancellations. No. Every seat was taken. We explained the problem. There was a horrified silence, and then: 'You may have to eat in the kitchen, but come anyway. Something will be arranged.'

He sat us at a tiny table between the kitchen door and the open fire, next to a large and festive family.

'I have gigot if you like it,' he said. We told him we had thought of bringing our own and asking him to cook it, and he smiled. 'It's not the day to be without an oven.'

We ate long and well and talked about the months that had gone as quickly as weeks. There was so much we hadn't seen and done:

our French was still an ungainly mixture of bad grammar and builders' slang; we had managed somehow to miss the entire Avignon festival, the donkey races at Goult, the accordion competition, Faustin's family outing to the Basses-Alpes in August, the wine festival in Gigondas, the Ménerbes dog show and a good deal of what had been going on in the outside world. It had been a self-absorbed year, confined mostly to the house and the valley, fascinating to us in its daily detail, sometimes frustrating, often uncomfortable, but never dull or disappointing. And, above all, we felt at home.

Maurice brought glasses of *marc* and pulled up a chair.

"Appy Christmas,' he said, and then his English deserted him. '*Bonne Année.*'

* * * * *

Peter Mayle
Toujours Provence £5.99

The days pass slowly but the weeks rush by. We now measure the year in ways that have little to do with diaries and dates, *Merci Provence* . . .

A Year in Provence has passed . . . yet the dream lives on.

And Peter Mayle, now known throughout the Lubéron as 'The English *Écrevisse*', slowly begins to turn native in the old stone farmhouse at the foot of the mountains between Avignon and Aix.

Toujours Provence finds him skulking through British Customs with a suitcase full of truffles, tracking down a man whose ambition is to make toads sing the "Marseillaise', taking *pastis* lessons and looking nervously over his shoulder at forest fires.

From vantage points as varied as the Cannes Film Festival, the *caves* at Châteauneuf-du-Pape and the Ménerbes Dog Show, Peter Mayle hilariously and memorably recounts the pleasures and pitfalls of the Provençal paradise – for today and for ever.

'Splendidly amusing . . . filled with things which will help you to understand, at least in part, the glory of this wonderful place'
Dirk Bogarde, Weekend Telegraph

'Peter Mayle has achieved every Briton's dream . . . a delightful sequel'
Daily Express

'Peter Mayle's first book was about losing his virginity in southern France; his second is a frank confession of the joys of intimacy with it. This collection of anecdotes and anniversary waltzes is a chatty adieu in which smugness is kept at bay by likeable enthusiasm'
Frederic Raphael, The Sunday Times

Peter Mayle
Expensive Habits £5.99

A guide to most things your accountant would never recommend

'Most of us are born with a latent tendency towards extravagance . . .'

Despite writing the phenomenally successful *A Year in Provence* and its sequel, *Toujours Provence*, Peter Mayle still claims to be anything but a rich man.

He is, however, perennially fascinated by the spending habits of those who are.

Now, after years of diligent and costly research, comes *Expensive Habits* – an eye-opening account of *most* of the best things in life. Peter Mayle has stopped at nothing to prove that they are definitely not free.

From Havana cigars and hand-made shoes, to hundred-dollar haircuts, from truffles, vintage champagne and stretch limousines to caviare and cashmere, here is every delightful excess you can imagine (and plenty more that you probably can't).

W9-BKW-643

"Lady Jayne, I have given my word I will not say anything about tonight. And I would never go back on my word. But you must see that I cannot just let the matter rest. You have said yourself you are not behaving as you ought."

She looked mutinous as she said, "And just what do you mean to do about it?"

He only wished he knew. For now, the best thing would be to make a strategic withdrawal so that he could regroup.

"I shall call upon you this afternoon, to take you for a drive in Hyde Park. That is when I shall tell you what action I plan to take." Once he'd decided what it would be.

"I shall be ready," she said, lifting her chin in a fashion that told him she was preparing to fight him every inch of the way. "This is it," she said, waving her hand at the frontage of an imposing mansion.

Having shown him where she lived, she ducked down a passage that led to the mews at the back. Then she turned around and stood quite still, staring up at him for a minute, with her head on one side as though trying to work him out.

"You have surprised me," she said at last. "I would never have imagined you could be so…decent."

* * *

An Escapade and an Engagement
Harlequin® Historical #1096—July 2012

Author Note

The Earl of Caxton has two granddaughters.

You may have read about Miss Aimée Peters in *Captain Corcoran's Hoyden Bride*. Having grown up in exile, Aimée was desperate to find security and put down roots. To that end, she travelled to Yorkshire to become a governess—only to find that her employer was not what she'd expected....

In *An Escapade and an Engagement* you will meet her cousin, Lady Jayne Chilcott. People think she is her grandfather's pampered darling. But she feels suffocated by the propriety of her lifestyle and longs for the kind of adventure she is sure Aimée must have had. The product of a bitterly unhappy arranged marriage, Lady Jayne vows she will only marry for love. But where is she ever going to find a man who will inspire anything more than mild contempt when her grandfather guards her so zealously that she never meets anyone new, let alone exciting?

That is until she clashes with the grim-faced Lord Ledbury, an ex-soldier who has come to London to find a suitable woman to become his bride. Lady Jayne has the right pedigree. But does he really want to get tangled up with a girl who is never happier than when up to her neck in mischief?

ANNIE BURROWS

An
Escapade
and an
Engagement

HARLEQUIN®
entertain, enrich, inspire™

If you purchased this book without a cover you should be aware that this book is stolen property. It was reported as "unsold and destroyed" to the publisher, and neither the author nor the publisher has received any payment for this "stripped book."

Recycling programs
for this product may
not exist in your area.

ISBN-13: 978-0-373-29696-5

AN ESCAPADE AND AN ENGAGEMENT

Copyright © 2012 by Annie Burrows

All rights reserved. Except for use in any review, the reproduction or utilization of this work in whole or in part in any form by any electronic, mechanical or other means, now known or hereafter invented, including xerography, photocopying and recording, or in any information storage or retrieval system, is forbidden without the written permission of the publisher, Harlequin Enterprises Limited, 225 Duncan Mill Road, Don Mills, Ontario, Canada M3B 3K9.

This is a work of fiction. Names, characters, places and incidents are either the product of the author's imagination or are used fictitiously, and any resemblance to actual persons, living or dead, business establishments, events or locales is entirely coincidental.

This edition published by arrangement with Harlequin Books S.A.

For questions and comments about the quality of this book please contact us at Customer_eCare@Harlequin.ca.

® and TM are trademarks of Harlequin Enterprises Limited or its corporate affiliates. Trademarks indicated with ® are registered in the United States Patent and Trademark Office, the Canadian Trade Marks Office and in other countries.

www.Harlequin.com

Printed in U.S.A.

Available from Harlequin® Historical and
ANNIE BURROWS

One Candlelit Christmas #919
"The Rake's Secret Son"
The Earl's Untouched Bride #933
*The Viscount and the Virgin #1012
A Countess by Christmas #1021
Giftwrapped Governess #1063
"Governess to Christmas Bride"
An Escapade and an Engagement #1096
Captain Corcoran's Hoyden Bride #330

*Silk & Scandal

Also available from Historical *Undone!*

Notorious Lord, Compromised Miss

**Did you know that these novels are also
available as ebooks? Visit www.Harlequin.com.**

To Carol Townend, author of the "Wessex Weddings"—
whose hospitality is legendary, and whose insightful
and experienced advice has been of enormous help to me
in the completion of this book.

Chapter One

Lord Ledbury glared up at the ruched silk canopy of the bed he'd inherited from his brother, wide awake now, when not an hour since he'd felt so drained he was sure he could have slept for a week.

He hated this bed. He hated its soft feather mattress and the mounds of bedding that felt as though they were suffocating him. He hated the valet whom…no, that was going too far. He could not hate Jenkins for doing a job to the best of his limited ability. It was just that he was not Fred.

He could have talked to Fred as he'd undressed and prepared to go to bed. Probably managed to laugh off the more ludicrous aspects of the evening's sortie behind what felt like enemy lines—as they'd done time without number during the preceding six years of active service. No matter what deprivations they'd had to endure because of the damn fool orders some pompous ass higher up the chain of command had issued.

But he'd been obliged to leave Fred behind when he'd taken up residence in Lavenham House. And though he'd never experienced such luxury, never had so many servants in his life since coming to live here, he'd never felt so alone or so ill at ease. A spy must feel like this, he reflected bitterly, kicking off his covers and turning onto his side to glare at the fire glowing smugly in its ornate marble fireplace. Without benefit of his uniform to vouch for his identity. Cut off from his regiment, his comrades. Entrusted with orders that he alone could carry out.

Dammit, he was more likely to get some sleep outside on a park bench wrapped up in his old army greatcoat than he was in here, suffocated by all the trappings deemed necessary to coddle a lord. When he thought of all the times he'd slept out of doors, with conditions so harsh he would wake in the morning with his blanket frozen to the ground...

He sat bolt upright. At the end of this street there was a small park, with benches dotted about in it. And in spite of Jenkins' ill-concealed disgust, his army greatcoat still hung in the armoire....

He just had to get out of Mortimer's house for a while, and away from Mortimer's servants, even if there was no escaping the obligations Mortimer's sudden and unexpected death had foisted upon him.

Muttering imprecations under his breath, he got out of bed and pulled on a random selection of clothing by guesswork in the flickering shadows cast by the fire, making sure only of his army greatcoat. He sighed as he shrugged himself into it, feeling as though he was being taken into the arms of a friend. As though there was a part of him that was still Major Cathcart, even though everyone was suddenly calling him Lord Ledbury now.

He rubbed his hand briskly over the crown of his head to tidy his bed-rumpled light brown hair in the way that had become second nature to him on campaign as he left the bedroom, wishing it was as easy to smooth down his ragged temper.

His mouth flattened into a grim line as he limped down the stairs. He had not quite recovered from the interview with the Earl of Lavenham, that was half the trouble. He'd been braced to hear something unpleasant. Nothing less than a dire emergency would have induced his grandfather to summon him to Courtlands. And what he'd learned about his younger brother during that interview had certainly been a shock. But what still left him with a nasty taste in his mouth had been the confirmation that if only Charlie had been the sort who could have concealed his preference for men *he* might have returned to his regiment, been killed or maimed, and nobody would have given a damn.

The night porter leaped to his feet as he saw his master approach. He opened his mouth, as though about to say something, but one look was all it took to have the man hand him his cane, open the door for him and scuttle back to his chair without uttering whatever objection he had been about to raise.

Lord Ledbury heaved a sigh of relief as he stepped outside. He'd done all his grandfather had asked of him. Made all the sacrifices demanded. He'd resigned his commission, moved out of his lodgings and into Lavenham House. Bought the clothes, and begun to play the part, but…

He breathed in deeply as he made for the square. The night air was redolent of…soot, actually. And damp. With a hint of something indefinably green about it that could not be mistaken for anything other than the smell of springtime in England. It took him less time than he

would have thought before he was pushing open the
gate, considering the state of his leg. For which small
mercy he was truly thankful. He might be able to find
a measure of peace if he could only stretch out on one
of the benches and look up at the night sky through a
tracery of leaves.

Thanks to Mortimer's ignominious demise, he'd become a lord. And, as the last hope of the Cathcarts, he
was going to have to find a bride. A bride worthy of
becoming the next Countess of Lavenham. To that end,
tonight he'd attended his first ball since he'd become
Lord Ledbury.

He gave an involuntary shudder as his mind flashed
back to the glittering ballroom, the eager faces of the
matchmaking mamas who'd clustered round him, the
horrible feeling of being under siege...

And, goddammit—but wouldn't you know it with
the way his evening had been going—when he finally
reached the bench on which he'd set his heart he found
it already occupied.

By a strapping redcoat and a somewhat-reluctant female, to judge by the way she was beating at his broad
shoulders with her clenched fists while he carried on
kissing her.

He acted without thinking.

'Take your hands off her!' His voice, honed through
years of bellowing orders across parade grounds, made
them both jump.

The soldier turned to scowl at Lord Ledbury over
his shoulder.

'This is none of your business,' he snarled.

'I am making it my business,' he retorted. 'This sort
of behaviour is completely unacc—'

He broke off, stunned to silence when he caught sight of the female who was still struggling to disentangle herself from the redcoat's determined grasp. It was Lady Jayne Chilcott. He'd seen her earlier, at the ball he'd attended, and immediately asked his host who she was. For she was, without a doubt, the prettiest creature he'd ever clapped eyes on.

Berry, the former schoolfriend whose sister's come-out ball it was, had pulled a face.

'That,' he'd said scathingly, 'is Lady Jayne Chilcott—otherwise known as Chilblain Jayne. Lucy is in raptures to have her attend tonight, since she normally only goes to the most select gatherings. Her grandfather is the Earl of Caxton. Pretty high in the instep himself—and you will only have to observe her behaviour for half an hour to see why she's earned the soubriquet.'

He'd promptly changed his mind about asking for an introduction, taken a seat and Berry's advice. He'd watched her. It had not taken quite half an hour to agree that she *did* look as though she was regretting coming to a place that was frequented by people so far beneath her in station.

At least that was what he had assumed then. But now, as he studied the insignia that proclaimed the lowly rank of the soldier who'd been kissing her so passionately, he revised his opinion. He had thought, from her refusal to dance with any of the men who'd been falling over themselves to break through her icy reserve, that she was as cold and proud as Berry had warned him she was.

But she did not look proud now. She looked like a rather young girl torn between fright and embarrassment at the compromising nature of the situation he'd just interrupted.

It was in stark contrast to the anger blazing from her would-be seducer's eyes.

'I repeat,' said Lord Ledbury firmly, 'take your hands off Lady Jayne this instant.'

It was more than just his innate sense of chivalry that made him so determined to rescue Lady Jayne. In spite of what Berry had said, and the derisive way he'd said it, he hadn't been able to prevent that initial interest steadily growing into a sense of something resembling comradeship as the awful evening had dragged on.

As she had doggedly rebuffed all overtures with chilling finality, he'd found some comfort in knowing he wasn't the only person there battling under siege conditions. After a while he'd even begun to derive a perverse sort of amusement from the way her courtiers grovelled at her feet on one side of the dance floor, while he sat in state on the other, repelling all invaders with equal determination. Though at least the men who flocked around her had some excuse. He knew the matchmaking mamas who clamoured round *him* were interested only in his newly acquired wealth and title.

'The state of your face won't matter,' his grandfather had predicted, running his eyes over the furrow on his forehad that a stray bullet had ploughed across when he'd been only a lieutenant. 'Not now that you are such a catch. Wealthy in your own right and heir to an earldom. All you will have to do is turn up and sit on the sidelines and they will come to you. You mark my words.'

The mere thought of having to fend off flocks of avaricious harpies had made entering that ballroom one of the hardest things he'd ever done. Particularly with his grandfather's words still ringing in his ears. Knowing that none of them would have given him a second glance before Mortimer had died and catapulted him into the peerage tied him up into knots inside. Yes, he'd gone there to start looking for a wife. But did they have to make it so obvious they all wanted his rank, his position?

And not him?

But Lady Jayne would have attracted as many suitors were she a penniless nobody as she was so stunningly beautiful. He could not remember ever having seen a more perfect face. She had a flawless complexion, a little rosebud of a mouth and a profusion of golden ringlets that tumbled round her gently rounded shoulders. He had not been able to discern what colour her eyes were, but in a perfect world they would be cornflower-blue.

She'd shot him one cool, assessing look when he'd first come in and sat down. Later, when they'd both been surrounded by a crowd of toadeaters, their eyes had actually met, and for one instant he'd felt sure she was telling him she hated the attention, the flattery, the insincerity of it all, just as much as he did.

Not long after that, she'd risen to her feet and stalked from the room.

Once she'd gone, and he'd been the only prize catch left in the ballroom, he'd felt as though he had a target painted in the middle of his chest. Whilst she, too, had been repulsing unwelcome advances, he'd felt—no matter how erroneously—as if he had at least one ally in the place.

Once she'd gone, all the reasons why he didn't want to be there had become so overwhelming he had no longer been able to bear it. The heat of that stuffy room had made his head feel muzzy. The tension that hadn't left him since he'd taken the decision to do his duty by his family had become too great for a body so weakened by prolonged illness. He'd ached all over. He'd scarce known how to keep a civil tongue in his head. He'd had to leave, to get out of there and head home.

Only it hadn't been his home he had gone back to. It was still Mortimer's house. Another jarring reminder that he wasn't living his own life any more.

It would do him good, he suddenly realized, to knock somebody down. He had been spoiling for a fight ever since he'd walked away from his grandfather, bristling with the determination to prove once and for all that he was a better man than Mortimer and Charlie put together.

'Get up,' he snarled, advancing on the redcoat, who still had his arms round Lady Jayne. Mortimer and Charlie were both beyond his reach, one being dead and the other in Paris. And a man could not come to blows with his own grandfather, no matter what the provocation.

But this redcoat was just about his own height. And though he was younger, and probably fitter, the lad had not been tempered into fighting steel in the heat of battle.

The man got to his feet. Slowly.

'You are a disgrace to your uniform,' he said, angered still further by his slovenly posture when anyone under *his* command would have known to snap to full attention when he'd used that particular tone of voice. 'I would derive great personal satisfaction in seeing you brought up on a charge for this night's work. No officer should force his attentions upon an unwilling female.

If you were under my command you would be lucky to escape with a flogging.'

But before he had a chance to add that he would give the man a chance to settle the matter between them with their fists, Lady Jayne leaped to her feet and interposed her own body between him and the soldier, crying out, 'Oh, no! You could not be so cruel!'

'Cruel?' He was stunned by her reaction. 'You think it is cruel to rescue you from a situation that is plainly causing you distress?'

He steadfastly ignored the little voice that reminded him that he had been spoiling for a fight for ages. That this redcoat was just in the way when he happened to be in need of someone upon whom to vent his frustration. That if he had come across a young officer in the throes of a passionate clinch with a female as pretty as this one in Portugal he would have winked at the man, wished him luck and been on his way.

Ah, but this was no sloe-eyed señorita, nor the willing wife of a local grandee, he argued back. This was a young English lady, and she had not appeared willing. On the contrary, she'd been struggling with the lout. She'd looked frightened.

'I admit, I was a little taken aback by Harry's ardour,' said Lady Jayne. 'For he has never really kissed me like that before. But mostly I was afraid somebody might come by and discover us.'

'Do you really expect me to believe you were only trying to fight him off because you feared discovery?'

Though now he came to think of it she must have come here of her own free will, even if she *had* taken fright at the last minute.

'Yes!' she cried, lifting her chin to glare at him defiantly. 'Not that I expect a man like *you* to understand,' she said with contempt. 'But since my grandfather has forbidden Harry to approach me we *can* only meet in secret.'

He had not thought he could get any angrier. But her words were so inflammatory. What did she mean, *a man like you?* Why could she not just express her gratitude that he was here to rescue her? And, most of all, why wouldn't she get out of the way so he could just lay into this sneaking, slovenly excuse for a soldier?

'Did it never occur to you that your grandfather might have your best interests at heart? That it would be better to stay away from him?'

Lady Jayne was a great heiress. Her grandfather, so Berry had informed him, had no direct male heir, and it was common knowledge that he intended to bequeath to her the bulk of his fortune. Some penniless nobody was obviously not a suitable partner for a girl who would inherit so much. All this Harry had to recommend him, by the looks of it, was a handsome face, a pair of broad shoulders—and a ruthless streak.

'So you mean to betray us?' she said frostily.

Harry moved to stand beside her. He took her hand in his and raised it to his chest, where he pressed it to his heart.

'This is not the end. I shall not let it be. I swore that I would not let anything part us and I meant it. I still mean it.'

'Oh, Harry,' she said, turning to him with a woebegone face. 'I shall never forgive myself if he has you flogged.' She shot a glance of loathing in Lord Ledbury's direction. 'I knew I should never have agreed to this meeting.'

And as they stood there, gazing soulfully into each other's eyes, Lord Ledbury felt his irrational spurt of anger drain away.

If she was in love with this man, no matter what his own opinion of him was, no wonder she had behaved the way she had done in that ballroom earlier. Lord, he knew just how she must have felt. Had not his own grandfather ripped him from all that he knew, all that he loved, and set his feet on another path—one that he would never willingly have trod?

'Oh, for heaven's sake!' he snapped, annoyed that he was now obliged to continue in the role of upholder of propriety or he was going to look a complete fool. Even though half of him wished he could walk away and leave them to it. 'Stop acting like some heroine out of a bad melodrama and call your maid over. It is time you went home.'

She made no such move—only hung her head, looking shamefaced.

'Oh, Lord. Never say you came out without her?'

She could not even raise her eyes to meet his when she nodded.

This was getting worse and worse. He could not in all conscience leave her alone with a man who had no scruples about enticing a trusting young woman to meet him in secret, at dawn, without even the benefit of a maid to keep things within spitting distance of propriety.

'I suppose I shall be obliged to escort you home, then,' he snapped. 'And we'll have to hope nobody catches the pair of us—else *we* shall be the ones embroiled in scandal.' Which would completely ruin his plans.

He'd decided that since marrying was his inescap-

able destiny he would jolly well find a wife who would
be such a superlative countess that generations to come
would speak of her in awe. He wasn't necessarily going
to find her in Almack's. He'd made a point of launching his campaign in the house of a man of little wealth,
but sterling character, to demonstrate that attaching a
woman of high rank was not his primary objective. He
wanted the woman he married to have a certain...*something* that everyone would recognise.

Even him, when he came across it.

There was no way he was going to live down to his
family's low expectations by tumbling into a match
with a girl he scarcely knew in a way that reeked of
suppressed scandal.

'Well, what are you waiting for, man?' He turned
the full force of his frustration on the hapless young
soldier. 'Get back to your barracks before I think better of covering for the pair of you. And pray that your
absence has not been discovered.'

They both turned to him, faces alight with hope.

'You mean you have changed your mind?'

'I can still change it back if you don't remove yourself from the vicinity, double-quick,' he growled at the
soldier. 'But first your name and rank.'

'Thank you, sir,' he said. 'Lieutenant Kendell, sir.'
Then, pausing only to press one last kiss upon Lady
Jayne's hand, Harry made a run for it.

Chapter Two

Lady Jayne gazed up at him, a perplexed frown creasing her brow.

'Why did you let him go?'

He looked steadily back at her, wondering why she wasn't asking a more pertinent question. Such as, how could Harry have just abandoned her without so much as asking his name? He could have been one of the most notorious seducers of womankind for all he knew.

'I can always report him later, if you like,' he replied scathingly. It was what he ought to do. He eyed the object of Lady Jayne's affection with disdain as he scuttled away into the shadows. It was hard to believe a man could behave so dishonourably towards a woman with whom he was genuinely in love.

'No, no! Please don't!' She seized his arm. 'It is all my fault. I know it was very wrong of us to meet in secret, but he loves me so very much…' Her little fingers kneaded at his sleeve as she plunged on. 'And I know I should not have come here without bringing my maid. But you see the doors are all locked tight at night, and

I could hardly expect Josie to climb out of a window, could I?'

'You climbed out of a window?' A sudden foreboding gripped him. 'How do you plan to get back in?' If he was going to have to knock upon her front door to return her to her guardians at this hour in the morning, the fat would be in the fire and no mistake.

'Oh, the same way, of course. But never mind that. It is Josie that I am worried about. She did try to talk me out of coming. I promise you she did. But she is only a servant, after all. She has to do what I tell her.'

'And you took ruthless advantage of the fact?'

'I...I suppose I did, yes.' She caught her lower lip between her teeth. 'And now, if you tell anyone I was out here without her, when she is under such strict orders never to let me out of her sight, they will turn her off without a character. Which would be grossly unfair. Oh, no...' Her eyes shimmered. 'I could not bear it if she was to lose her job and Harry was to be cashiered out of the regiment just because I have not behaved as I ought.'

To his astonishment, one single, enormous tear rolled down her cheek. And it struck him that everything about her behaviour at the ball earlier had been an act. And that Berry would never have said what he had about her if he'd seen this side of her. She might have appeared cold and haughty on the outside but inside she must have been counting the minutes until she could escape. It put him in mind of the way he'd been at that age, at stuffy dinners put on by the regiment to persuade local dignitaries they had nothing to fear from having them quartered nearby. All the junior officers had been under strict orders to be on their best behaviour. And later they'd made up for it by running out into the backstreets and behaving completely disgracefully as an antidote to all those hours of hypocritical posturing.

Lady Jayne might have come out here without a thought for anyone but herself, but now that he'd made her see that her misdemeanour could wreak havoc on the lives of others she was genuinely contrite. Just as sorry as *he'd* been the day after that banquet when the locals hadn't seen the funny side of finding that ugly statue in the middle of the river, bedecked in pondweed, but had regarded the desecration of their patron saint as an act of sacrilege.

'Never mind all that for the moment,' he said brusquely, to mask the fact that he was sorely tempted to promise her he would never breathe a word to anyone. And that wasn't just because of her contrition. Even if she hadn't cared a rap for the repercussions, he didn't have any right to castigate anyone for climbing out of a window to escape the crushing sense of family expectation. Not when he had done more or less the same thing himself. The only difference between them was that he'd had the liberty to walk out of his own front door when he'd felt the walls of his own personal prison closing in on him.

'What we have to do now is get you home without your escapade becoming common knowledge. Where do you live?'

'Oh, then you mean to help us?'

Her whole face lit up. She gave him such a dazzling smile that, in spite of that tear on her cheek, or perhaps because of it, he suddenly saw why her Harry had been unable to resist her. Any man with red blood flowing through his veins would risk the wrath of his commanding officer for a chance to hold such a divine creature in his arms. And for a kiss... What would he not risk for one kiss? The mere thought of bending to sip at that little rosebud of a mouth sent blood flowing hotly through his veins.

He inhaled slowly, savouring the feeling of being a healthy male responding to the possibilities inherent in being alone in a dark, secluded place with a pretty female in an entirely natural way.

To say that it was a relief was putting it mildly. He had assured his grandfather that medically there was nothing to prevent him from siring the next generation of Cathcarts. But the truth was he had not felt any interest in sex since he'd had his leg smashed at Orthez. All his energy had been spent on surviving—first the field hospital and then the foul transport back to England. And then one fever after another. And even though he'd been mobile enough to think about returning to active service some weeks ago, until his grandfather's shocking revelation had put a stop to it, he'd had no inclination to resume any kind of sex life. No matter how temptingly the offers he'd received had been presented.

He couldn't resist reaching out and gently, with one thumb, wiping away the tear that had reached the point of her chin. And as he felt the warmth of her skin against his own his body reacted as if he'd received a jolt of electricity.

Her own breath hitched, as though the current of lust that had seared through him had arced across to her, too.

It had been so long since he'd held a woman in his arms, so long since he'd wanted to, that for a moment he was tempted to tell her that if he might only kiss her...

He cleared his throat and forced his eyes away from

her mouth. What he ought to do was act the gentleman and take her straight home.

At once.

But the temptation to prolong this unexpectedly erotic encounter was too great to resist. He found himself saying the first thing—well, the first polite thing—that came into his head.

'Perhaps if you could explain exactly how such a great heiress comes to be tangled up with a man of his station...'

'You sound just like my grandfather!'

Her scorn doused his ardour as effectively as a bucket of cold water. Did he really look so much older than her that she bracketed him with her grandfather? No wonder she'd flinched when he touched her. It was just as well he had not voiced his crazy idea that she could purchase his silence on the whole matter with a kiss. She probably already thought he was a brute for merely breaking up her *tête-à-tête*.

'That is all he can think about,' she grumbled, impervious to the errant thoughts skirmishing through his brain. 'Rank and fortune. He never lets me meet anyone interesting or new! He was furious when he found out I had formed an attachment to Harry. As soon as he got wind of our friendship and learned that he has no title, no prospects at all, he forbade me to so much as speak to him. And banished me to London.'

'That sounds like an eminently sensible measure,' he said, loath though he was to take the side of anyone's grandfather in the suppression of youthful desires. 'You are far too trusting for your own good. A girl with more sense would know it really is not safe to meet men in the park, on her own, at daybreak.'

Particularly not when that lush mouth of hers could have such a startling effect on a man's libido.

'It certainly is not!' She looked furious. 'Because who knows *what* kind of person one might come across...prowling around the place, spying on people...?'

'I was not spying!'

'Then what were you doing? Something underhanded, I have no doubt.'

'Not a bit of it. I simply could not sleep, that's all.' At her look of scorn, he added, 'My leg hurt like the very devil, and the damn London servants will insist on banking up the fire and keeping all the windows shut. I had to get outside and get some fresh air. Though why the d...deuce I'm telling you all this I cannot think.'

She'd slipped under his guard, somehow. Taken him by surprise with her line of questioning.

Nettled, he snapped, 'That is all beside the point. I have no need to justify my actions...'

'No. You are a man,' she said bitterly. 'Men can do whatever they want, no matter who they hurt in the process, and nobody ever calls them to account.'

'You could not be more wrong. A man with any pride at all puts duty before his natural inclination. Duty to the Crown. Duty to his family...' He pulled himself up.

She'd done it again. Got him speaking his mind instead of saying what was appropriate to the occasion. Though God only knew *what* was appropriate to say on an occasion such as this. He would swear no etiquette book contained a chapter upon proper conversation in which to engage whilst escorting a woman home from a clandestine meeting with an ineligible suitor.

He eyed her with misgiving.

She clearly thought she was in love with her handsome young officer. But she could not really know much about him if they had only managed snatched moments together, like this. He wouldn't be a bit surprised to find her feelings had more to do with the uniform than the man inside it. He'd learned from experience that a scarlet jacket could have a powerful effect upon a susceptible female.

'And speaking of family,' he said, ruthlessly returning to the most pressing issue, 'your grandfather probably thought you would get over what he hoped was just a girlish infatuation if he offered you other distractions.'

Lady Jayne glowered at him before tossing her head and setting off briskly along a path that led in the opposite direction from the one he had used to enter the square. As he caught up with her, she said, 'It was more than that. I overheard him giving Lady Penrose strict instructions to get me safely married off before the end of the Season.' She laughed bitterly. 'Though how he expects her to accomplish that when he won't allow her to take me anywhere but *ton* parties, where I mix with people I have known all my life, I have no idea. *Ooh.*' She clenched her fists. 'You cannot begin to imagine what my time in Town has been like. Boring, boring, boring! I was beginning to think I knew just what a canary bird feels like, shut up in a gilded cage, by the time Harry arrived in Town. That first note he sent me, begging me to meet him…' Her fists uncurled as she trailed off.

'He kept on sending notes to me through Josie. To let me know which events he could gain entry to. And we began to meet in the gardens, or in a quiet room of the house, while the balls were going on downstairs, with Lady Penrose never suspecting a thing!'

He frowned down at her as they crossed the road and set off down Mount Street. He wished he had not already given his word not to tell anyone about this night's assignation. The more he learned about Harry, the more untrustworthy he sounded. And if anything happened to Lady Jayne because he'd kept quiet about this night's work he would feel responsible.

Although warning her guardians of what was going on would probably not do much good anyway. From what Lady Jayne had just said, her chaperone was clearly not up to the task of guarding such a highly spirited charge.

He rubbed his hand over the crown of his head. He couldn't report her to those who ought to protect her. Should he just warn her, then, of his mounting suspicions regarding Harry's motives? No. Given her reactions to him so far, she would probably assume he was yet another overbearing male attempting to oppress her. And he rather thought she would derive as much pleasure from flouting him as she did from outwitting her grandfather and chaperone.

But she really needed somebody who knew about Harry, and the lengths she would go to in order to get her own way, to watch over her. Somebody who wouldn't be fooled by the haughty, unapproachable facade she'd employed at the ball.

'Lady Jayne, I have given my word I will not say anything about tonight. And I would never go back on my word. But you must see that I cannot just let the matter rest. You have said yourself you are not behaving as you ought.'

She looked mutinous as she said, 'And just what do you mean to do about it?'

He only wished he knew. For now, the best thing would be to make a strategic withdrawal so that he could regroup.

'I shall call upon you this afternoon, to take you for a drive in Hyde Park. That is when I shall tell you what action I plan to take.' Once he'd decided what it would be.

'I shall be ready,' she said, lifting her chin in a fashion that told him she was preparing to fight him every inch of the way. 'This is it,' she said, waving her hand at the frontage of an imposing mansion.

Having shown him where she lived, she ducked down a passage that led to the mews at the back.

Then she turned round and stood quite still, staring up at him for a minute, with her head on one side as though trying to work him out.

'You have surprised me,' she said at last. 'I would never have imagined you could be so...decent,' she finished on a shrug.

'What did you think I would be like, then?' It shouldn't have made such an impact to hear that she'd had any expectations of him at all, considering they had only glanced at each other across a ballroom.

'Oh, I don't know... At the ball you looked so...hard. All those women who threw themselves at your feet had about as much impact on you as waves dashing themselves up against a cliff. And then, when you spoke of flogging Harry, I really thought for a minute that...'

She looked abashed. 'But you are really not cruel at all, are you?'

'I have sent men to their death without giving it a sec-

ond thought,' he retaliated, lest she think his leniency
with her on this one occasion meant he was a soft touch.

'Ah, but you don't take delight in it. That makes all
the difference.'

He was about to defend himself from the charge of
not being cruel when she stole all the breath from his
lungs by hitching up her skirts and tucking them into
a belt at her waist.

He knew he ought not to look. But how could he do
her the disservice of not appreciating such a shapely
pair of legs, covered in what looked like a junior footman's breeches, especially when not a day ago the sight
would not have interested him in the slightest?

He was still swallowing too hard to ask if she needed
any assistance in getting back into the house undetected
when she scampered over to the horse trough and clambered up onto its rim. From there she swung herself up
onto the stable roof.

Darting him an impish grin as she reached for the
lower branches of a gnarled old apple tree, she said, 'I
don't think you are such a cross old stick as you look.'

Having fired that Parthian shot, she clambered from
one bough to another with the agility of a monkey, giving him one tantalizing glimpse of a perfectly formed
bottom as she leaned over to push up a sash window
which had been left open an inch, before vanishing
into the house.

For some minutes all he could do was stand there,
rock hard and breathing heavily, feeling as though he'd
been hit by some kind of energising force.

He'd begun the night seething with resentment and
frustration. But now he was savouring the delicious
sensation of knowing everything was in working order.

And it had not been achieved through the determined wiles of some doxy. No, in spite of everything, it had been a natural response to a society female. He chuckled. It was good to know that there was one, at least, amongst them that it would be no hardship to take to bed. He eyed the window, half wondering what would happen if he were to climb up after her and...

The window slammed shut. He took a step back into the deeper shadows close to the stable. He'd come to London to contract a respectable alliance, not get embroiled in a scandal. It was no use standing here gazing up at the window through which she'd disappeared, wondering if the branches of that apple tree would bear his weight.

But the fact that he was thinking along those lines at all was immensely cheering.

He turned and walked away with a grin on his face. Lady Jayne was what was termed a handful. Continuing an association with her was going to bring him no end of trouble. He could feel it. And yet he was not dreading their next encounter. Not by a long shot.

In fact, he couldn't remember when he'd last felt so alive.

'Lor, miss, I been that worried about you,' exclaimed Josie, leaping to her feet, dashing across the room and hauling Lady Jayne in over the windowsill. 'Thank heavens you're back safe and sound and no harm done.'

'I am sorry you have been so worried,' said Lady Jayne. 'And I promise you,' she said vehemently, turning to shut the sash firmly behind her, 'that I shall never do anything so thoughtless and reckless and selfish ever again.'

Josie, who had been with her since she was twelve years old, and therefore knew her moods well, looked at her sharply.

'What happened? Something, I can tell. Have you fallen out with your young man?'

Lady Jayne shook her head. 'No, nothing like that.'

Although, in a way, she supposed she had. Even before Lord Ledbury had come along and put an end to their encounter she had wondered if it had been a mistake to leave the house to meet Harry. The darkened windows of the houses she'd snuck past had seemed to glare at her menacingly, so that she had already been feeling uneasy by the time she'd entered the square. It was not like sneaking out at dawn for an unsupervised ride or walk around Darvill Park, her grandfather's estate in Kent. She might run into *anyone* in a public park.

'We'd best get you into your night rail and into bed before that maid of Lady Penrose's comes in with your breakfast,' said Josie, turning her round and briskly unhooking the back of her gown while she undid her breeches.

She'd already been feeling distinctly uneasy when she'd found Harry. And then, instead of just taking her hand and murmuring the sort of endearments he generally employed during their snatched meetings, he had pulled her down onto the bench next to him and hauled her into his arms.

'I cannot bear to go on like this, my darling,' he'd said in accents of despair. 'There is nothing for it. We shall have to elope.'

Before she'd had a chance to say she would never do anything of the sort, he had kissed her full on the mouth. His moustache had scoured her upper lip in a most unpleasant way, and some of the bristles had gone up her nostrils. And what with his arms crushing her ribcage, half his moustache up her nose, and his mouth clamped over hers, she had felt as though she was suffocating. It had all been a far cry from what she had expected her first kiss to be like. When eventually she permitted some man to kiss her... And that was another thing, she reflected with resentment as she stepped out of her gown and breeches. She had not given him permission. He had just pounced. And he had been so very strong and unyielding that for a moment or two she had panicked.

It was not easy, even now, to keep perfectly still while Josie untied her stay laces and she relived those horrible moments in Harry's determined embrace. How relieved she had been when Lord Ledbury had come upon the scene, looking so ferocious. Not that she would ever admit *that* to a living soul. She ducked her head guiltily so that Josie could throw her night rail over her head.

She had not felt grateful for long, though. The way he'd looked at Harry, as though he wanted to tear him limb from limb, had caused her fear to come rushing back—although its focus had no longer been upon herself.

But then he'd dismissed Harry, wiped away the one tear she had not been able to hold back, and taken her home as though there was nothing the least bit untoward about walking through the streets at daybreak with a person he'd just caught in a compromising position.

She went to the dressing-table stool and sat down heavily.

Until the viscount had talked about getting Harry

brought up on a charge it had never occurred to her
that others might have to pay any penalty for her misdemeanours. She had cheerfully flouted the rules, safe
in the knowledge that any punishment meted out to
her would be relatively mild. Lady Penrose might have
forbidden her to attend any balls for a few nights, or
curtailed her shopping expeditions. Which would have
been no punishment at all.

At the very worst she had thought she might get
sent home to Kent. Which would have felt like a victory, of sorts.

It had taken the grim-faced viscount to make her see
that there would inevitably be repercussions for others
tangled up in her affairs, too. To wake her up to the
fact that she would never have forgiven herself if Josie
had lost her job, or Harry had been cashiered out of his
regiment, on her account. Thankfully he had listened
to her pleas for leniency for Harry and Josie, and had
given his word not to speak of what he knew about her
activities tonight.

She reached up and patted Josie on the hand as her
faithful maid began to brush out her hair, separating it
into strands so that she could put it in the plaits she always wore to bed. How could she not have considered
that others might have to pay for her misdemeanours?
How could she have been so selfish?

She raised her head and regarded her reflection in
the mirror with distaste.

People were always telling her how very much she
resembled her father. They were beginning to whisper
that she was as cold and heartless as him, too, because
of the wooden expression she had taken so many years
to perfect.

But you couldn't tell what a person was really like from just looking at their face. Only think of how wrong she'd been about Lord Ledbury. Earlier tonight, when she'd noticed him at Lucy Beresford's come-out ball, she'd thought him one of the most disagreeable men she'd ever seen. He had not smiled once, though people had been falling over themselves to try and amuse him.

She'd really disliked the way he'd behaved, as though he was doing Lucy's brother an immense favour by making his first public appearance as Lord Ledbury in his home. She'd thought Lucy a complete ninny for going into raptures about him for being some kind of war hero. He looked just the sort of man to *enjoy* hacking people to bits, and there was nothing heroic about such behaviour.

But he wasn't cruel at all. He could have ruined her reputation, and Harry's career, and left Josie destitute if he was the kind of man who revelled in inflicting pain on others. But he had chosen not to.

She looked at her cool expression again and felt a little comforted. She might look like her father, but she wasn't like him—not inside, where it mattered. Was she?

She gave an involuntary shiver.

'Not long now, miss. Then we'll get you all snug and warm in your bed,' said Josie, misinterpreting the reaction.

Lady Jayne did not bother to correct her mistake. She had no intention of adding to her maid's worries by telling her what had happened. Or confiding in anybody that Lord Ledbury's very forbearance, when she knew she deserved his contempt, had made her feel as though she had behaved in as selfish a fashion as her father had ever done.

She couldn't bear to look at herself any longer. Had she really encouraged Harry to fall so hopelessly in love with her that he'd acted recklessly enough to jeopardise his whole career? In just such a way had her womanising father destroyed the women who'd been foolish enough to fall for his handsome face and surface charm.

Not that Lord Ledbury would let that happen. Not now. He was bound to prevent her from seeing Harry again. He had made it clear he disapproved of a woman of her rank having a relationship with a man who had no fortune of his own. Or at the very least a title.

At last Josie had finished her hair, and she could get into bed and pull the coverlets up comfortingly to her chin as she wriggled down into the pillows.

Though she couldn't get comfortable. How likely was it that Lord Ledbury would be able to deter Harry from contacting her again? Not even her grandfather had managed that.

She chewed on her thumbnail. She did like Harry. Quite a lot. And she had been quite cut up when her grandfather had sent her to London to put an end to the association that had started when his regiment was stationed in Kent for training. And she had been pleased to see him again.

Until he had told her that the separation had almost broken his heart.

Oh, how she hoped Lord Ledbury could persuade him to abandon his pursuit of her! Because if he couldn't she was going to have to tell him herself that she had never really loved him. She had not seen it before tonight. But now that she was looking at her behaviour through Lord Ledbury's censorious eyes she had to face the fact that a very large part of Harry's attraction had derived from the satisfaction gained in knowing that to see him was to defy her grandfather.

Oh, heavens. Lord Ledbury would be quite entitled to write her off as a shallow, thoughtless, selfish creature.

She shut her eyes and turned onto her side as Josie slid from the room and shut the door softly behind her. Her stomach flipped over. She did not want to be the kind of girl who could casually break a man's heart in a spirit of defiance. Though she had never dreamed Harry's feelings were so deeply engaged. She tried to excuse herself. She had not done it deliberately! She had thought… She frowned, looking back on her behaviour with critical eyes. She had not thought at all, she realized on a spurt of shame that seared through her so sharply she had to draw up her legs to counteract it. Harry had just turned up when she was so frustrated with her life in Town that she'd been silently screaming at the weight of the restrictions imposed on her.

Though they were not all entirely the fault of her chaperone. She herself had made a stupid vow not to dance with anyone this Season, lest they take it as a sign she might welcome their suit.

Though, she comforted herself, even before Lord Ledbury had caught them she had begun to see that, in all conscience, she could not continue to encourage Harry. It had only been a moment before he'd come upon them. The moment when Harry had urged her to elope and she'd known she could never do anything of the sort. Even before he had kissed her, and it had become so very unpleasant, she had known she would have to break it off.

That was the moment when she'd known she was not in love with Harry. Not in that deep, all-consuming way which might induce a woman to give up everything—as her aunt Aurora, so her mother had told her, had done when she had eloped with an impecunious local boy.

'Oh, Harry.' She sighed. She hoped he would get over her quickly. He should, for she was not worth the risks he had taken. Anyway, he was certainly going to have more important things to think about than her in the near future. The newspapers were full of Bonaparte's escape from Elba. Every available regiment was being posted overseas in an attempt to halt his triumphal progress through France. And what with all the excitement of travelling to foreign climes and engaging in battles, he would soon, she hoped, be able to put her out of his mind altogether.

Though she would feel guilty for toying with a man's feelings for a considerable time to come.

Shutting her eyes, she uttered a swift prayer for him to meet a nice girl of his own class, who would love him back the way he deserved to be loved.

Chapter Three

'Lord Ledbury is coming to take you for a drive today? Are you quite sure?'

Lady Penrose regarded her over the top of her lorgnettes, which she was using to peruse the pile of correspondence that had arrived that morning.

'Yes,' said Lady Jayne, crossing her fingers behind her back. 'Did I not mention it last night?'

Lady Penrose looked pensive. 'I was aware he was at the Beresfords' last night, of course. But not that you had been formally introduced. Nor that an invitation had been given. Or accepted. In fact you should not have accepted at all.' She laid her glasses down with evident irritation. 'You know it was quite wrong of you to do such a thing. The young man ought to have applied to me for the permission which I alone am in a position to give.'

Though Lady Jayne hung her head, her spirits leaped at the possibility that Lord Ledbury was not going to have it all his own way after all. In any confrontation between the hard-faced viscount and her stern duenna regarding a breach of form she would lay odds on Lady

Penrose emerging victorious. Lady Penrose was such a stickler for etiquette. It was why her grandfather had appointed this distant relative to oversee her Season.

'She won't stand any nonsense from you,' he had warned her. 'And she is astute enough to spot a fortune-hunter a mile off. Yes, Lady Penrose will get you safely married before the Season's out...'

Lady Jayne felt the sting of his rejection afresh. He had been so keen to get her off his hands. His attitude had made her even more determined to take up with Harry when he had shown up. At least Harry *liked* her.

'Although,' mused Lady Penrose, 'since he is exactly the sort of man your grandfather would wish to encourage, I am inclined to permit the outing to go ahead.'

When Lady Jayne's eyes widened in shock, her duenna explained, 'I dare say he slid into bad habits during his years on active service. I have seen this kind of thing before with younger sons who never expected to inherit. It will take him a while to adjust to polite society, no doubt. We will have to make allowances for him.'

'Will we?'

'Of course,' said Lady Penrose, looking at her as though she was an imbecile. 'He is now a most eligible *parti*. It would be foolish beyond measure to make a to-do simply because he seems to have forgotten the way things ought to be done. I shall rearrange your engagements for today accordingly.'

Lady Jayne practically gaped at Lady Penrose. Up till now she had been scornful of just about all the young men who had attempted to fix their interest with her. Not that she'd had any objection to Lady Penrose frostily sending those men about their business. For she had no intention of marrying anyone—not this Season! If her grandfather thought he could marry her off just like that then he had another think coming.

She stayed angry for the rest of the day. By the time Lord Ledbury arrived to take her for the drive he had coerced her into taking with him she was almost ready to tell him to do his worst. Except for the fact that he might know Harry's commanding officer. It would only take one word in the right quarters to ensure he paid dearly for last night's foolishness. Which reflection only made her crosser than ever. It was so unfair that *he* could get away with behaving as badly as he wished and even a high stickler like Lady Penrose would forgive him because of his rank.

And then he had the gall to turn up at her front door in a *barouche*. If she had to be seen out and about with him, could it not at least have been in something a bit more dashing—like a phaeton? Did he not know that this was the very first time Lady Penrose had permitted her to go out driving with a man in the park?

No, she fumed, climbing in, he did not know. Or care. For he was not really her suitor.

At least there was some consolation in that. She twitched her furs up to her chin and glared at the groom's back as Lord Ledbury sat down next to her. She felt him giving her a hard look, but he said nothing. And continued to say nothing all the way to the park.

As they bowled along the streets she conceded that she supposed she could see why he had chosen such a stuffy, staid form of transport. With a groom to drive there was nothing to distract him from the lecture he looked as though he was itching to give her. He'd probably only held back last night because of that single tear remorse had wrung from her. Yes—she would warrant he'd feared she would cry in earnest if he shouted at her the way he'd shouted at Harry. That pensive expression as he'd wiped that teardrop from her chin had probably been due to him imagining how dreadful it would be to have to escort a weeping female home through the darkened streets.

It also accounted for the way he was darting her assessing glances now, as though she was an unexploded bomb that might go off in any direction should he make an unwise move.

Not that he would have succeeded in making her cry if he *had* shouted at her. She had learned almost from the cradle the knack of keeping her emotions well controlled. It had started with her determination never to let her father reduce her to tears. She'd refused to give him the satisfaction!

By the time they drove through the gates of the park she had managed to compose her features into the carefully blank mask behind which she always sheltered when on the receiving end of a dressing-down.

Though there was nothing Lord Ledbury could say to her that she had not heard a thousand times before—from someone whose opinion actually mattered to her.

'You are angry with me, Lady Jayne,' he observed dispassionately. 'It appears that since we parted you have decided to regard me as your enemy.'

'How can I be anything other than angry,' she retorted, 'when you *think* you have me at your mercy?'

He sighed. Her emphasis on that word *think* confirmed his belief that she was no docile creature to meekly reform after a stern talking-to.

'Even those who have been at war a long time can become allies against a common foe. Or act within agreed limits under a flag of truce.'

'I…I don't understand.' But she was intrigued. What could he possibly be thinking to make a remark like that?

'Perhaps we have more in common than you might think. For example, you told me that you were sent to London to contract a marriage, in spite of your preferences. Well, I too have been set upon a path I would rather not have trod. And before you rehash that argument about men only ever doing what they want, no matter who they tread down in the process,' he put in quickly, when she drew a breath to give him the benefit of her opinion, 'I would advise you not to judge us all by the conduct of the males to whom you are closely related. For I assume it is their conduct which has formed your opinion of my sex?'

'I… Well, um, yes.'

It had started with her father. He had made no secret of the fact that he resented her for being the only child of his to survive past infancy, when what he wanted from his wife was an heir. If she ever inadvertently crossed his path, the way he would look at her—his eyes so icy, his lips flattening in displeasure—would chill her to the marrow. It meant that she had spent most of her childhood roaming wild about their estate in an effort to keep well out of his way. There had been one groom who had taken it upon himself to teach her to ride, but apart from him she had never met a man who'd shown her the slightest bit of concern.

Until she'd gone to live with her grandfather. And his horror on discovering that she could barely read or write, let alone know the first thing about mixing in polite society, had resulted in him going to the other extreme. He had hired a succession of tutors and governesses who invariably gave up on her, telling him that she was impossible.

The real problem was that no matter how hard she had tried to absorb all the information they'd attempted to cram into her brain, there had always been more. So that no matter how hard she'd worked, she had never managed to measure up. It had felt as though not a single day passed without her being sent to her grandfather's study to hear how far she fell short of the standards he expected from a young lady living beneath his roof.

The set of her lips as she went into a brown study put him in mind of exactly the way he felt about his own brothers. Mortimer, his father's pride and joy, had gambled and whored his way through life, only to end up breaking his neck by falling from his horse dead drunk. And Charlie, his mother's precious baby, had been packed off to France, where he was living exactly as he pleased—no doubt at enormous expense—because the laws over there were far more lenient towards men of his stamp.

'I, too,' he said with a curl to his lip, 'have male relatives who care for nothing but their own pleasure. And they have left me with the unenviable task of cleaning up the mess they've created. Though it is far from being what I would wish to do at this juncture in my life, now that I have become a viscount I have had to resign my commission and embark on a hunt for a wife.'

'That's silly. I mean, there's absolutely no need to resign your commission just because your family is putting pressure on you to marry. Plenty of officers with titles marry, and even take their wives on campaign with them. And I should have thought that our country is in particular need of every experienced officer it can get if we are to keep Bonaparte from rampaging all over Europe again.'

'That was exactly what I said to my grandfather when he insisted I sold out!'

It was extraordinary to hear her voice his own objections with almost the same vehemence as he'd felt when his grandfather had banged his fist on the desk, his face turning purple with rage as he'd bawled, 'I want you married and setting up your nursery without delay. I let your father persuade me that Mortimer needed time to make his own choice. *Hah!* See where that got me! Chased every skirt in the neighbourhood and told me to my face he was enjoying himself too much to settle down. Well, I shan't make the same mistake with you! Either get yourself to Town and pick a bride, or I shall pick one for you.'

He shot Lady Jayne a wry smile. 'But after a lengthy…discussion…' the details of which he would never reveal to a living soul '…I realized that even though, as you correctly state, England does need experienced officers, Wellington himself would agree that the preservation of an old and distinguished family is of at least equal importance as trouncing the Corsican tyrant.'

He paused, gripping the handle of his cane so hard she wondered he did not snap the head clean off.

'My grandfather is old,' he said eventually, 'and, though he won't admit it, not in the best of health. Over the last year he has suffered a series of nasty shocks.

You probably know that both my father and then my older brother suffered fatal accidents within months of each other. He has become seriously concerned about the continuation of our family line. And, as he so pithily put it, anyone can lead troops into battle, but I am the last hope of the Cathcart family.'

His stomach swooped into the same knot as it had done that day, when he'd seen his entire life's achievements brushed aside as being of no consequence. For a moment the demons that had plagued his childhood had come swarming back. The demons that had insisted he was of no intrinsic worth. How could he be, when even his own parents did their best to ignore his very existence, whilst pampering and coddling his brothers?

But then he'd remembered that, in spite of what his grandfather had said about *anyone* being able to lead troops into battle, there was a damned sight more to being an officer than he knew. Earning the men's respect, for one thing, was no sinecure. The majority of them came from the gutters, and had a natural distrust of anyone who represented authority. But they'd learned to trust him with their lives. Depended on decisions he'd made for their very survival. And, more than that, he'd maintained their morale—even when times were at their toughest.

The demons had fled, whimpering, as he'd drawn on all the self-confidence he'd acquired during the eleven years he'd served in the army. Eleven years during which he'd grown from a diffident boy into a seasoned veteran.

His grandfather had implied that his only function in life was to father the next generation. But, by God, he was going to do more than that. If he could organize a regiment, then he could damn well learn to manage the estates that were now his responsibility.

And, what was more, he would make a better job of it than either of his self-indulgent brothers could have done.

'So... You are saying that you sympathise with my plight because you know what it feels like to be pushed into marrying when you don't really want to?'

'Something like that,' he said with a hard smile, continuing, 'I certainly admire the fact that you have not allowed your head to be turned by all the flattering attention you attract. From what I observed last night, one would expect you to be hanging out for a duke, or at the very least a marquess.' That was probably what Berry had assumed when she made it obvious she was not interested in any of the men who'd tried to get her to dance. 'You have half the male population of London at your feet, and yet you have set your heart on a man with no rank and few prospects.'

She was not cold and proud at all, or she couldn't have rushed headlong into such an inappropriate relationship.

He turned towards her to make his next point, to find her looking up at him, wide-eyed, and his breath caught in his throat. Cornflower-blue. The exact shade to round off the perfection of her features.

Damnation.

He'd half hoped that he would be able to detect some flaw upon seeing her in broad daylight. She had, after all, been on the far side of the ballroom the night before. And everyone knew candlelight was particularly flattering. And then in the park it had been so dark he might well have imagined her beauty was far beyond that which really existed. But here they were, their faces mere inches away, and her utter perfection had just literally taken his breath away.

'Your Harry…Lieutenant Kendell…must be so dazzled by you,' he eventually managed to grate, 'that he has completely lost his head.'

And perhaps that really *was* the truth. Perhaps he was no fortune-hunter at all. With those big blue eyes, that glorious mane of golden curls and that utterly kissable little mouth, she was capable of ensnaring just about any man she set her sights on. If she had given the lowly lieutenant the least bit of encouragement, she might easily have enslaved him.

But she wasn't going to enslave *him*. He whipped his gaze away from her mouth to glare at a hapless matron whose own barouche happened to be passing theirs. He was not going to allow this attraction, no matter how strong, to deflect him from his primary objective. Which was to marry a paragon of some kind.

He was not only going to learn how to manage his estates to the admiration of his peers, he was going to marry a woman who would excite envy and admiration. Not a girl whose very nature meant she was bound to teeter permanently on the brink of one scandal or another.

'Um… Actually…' She faltered on the verge of confessing the truth. He had just said he admired the way she was not hanging out for a man with a grand title. It was so rarely she heard any praise for anything she did that she was loath to admit she didn't deserve even that.

Not that she *did* think people should attempt to marry for social advancement.

'I believe that people should only marry for love,' she declared.

'I might have guessed,' he said, so scathingly her temper flared up all over again.

Her own family had been quite needlessly torn apart when her aunt Aurora had eloped with a man the Earl of Caxton had decided was beneath her, socially. Her grandfather would still not permit anyone to mention her name. Which had, according to Josie, wounded her mother deeply. Yet the man with whom she had eloped had been the son of a gentleman. There had been no need to banish them both and forbid any communication between the sisters, surely?

There had always been a sort of gaping hole in the family where Aunt Aurora and her husband ought to have been round which they all had to tiptoe. And she had long since come to the conclusion that her grandfather had behaved in a perfectly ridiculous fashion. Just because his daughter had fallen in love with a man of whom he did not approve.

'If two people love each other—really love each other—then nothing should be allowed to stand in their way,' she said vehemently.

His heart sank. For he'd hoped that in the light of day she'd somehow wake up and see that Harry was not worth the risks she was taking. And then he could forget about this detour and return his full attention to the important business of scouring London Society for his bride.

But the tone of her voice revealed a determination that no amount of arguing was going to be able to shake. She left him with no alternative. He was going to have to employ a little subterfuge so that he could limit her exposure to potential danger, whilst keeping close enough to protect her should it become necessary.

'Then who am I to stand in the way of true love?' he said, with such sarcasm she just knew she wasn't going to like whatever he was going to say next. 'Not that I condone your behaviour, young lady. Nor his. Especially not his.'

Ah, that was more like it. She knew how to deal with a man who spoke to her with just that tone of disapproval in his voice.

She lifted her chin and looked him straight in the eye.

'You have no right to criticise my behaviour.'

He quite liked it when she squared up to him, he realized, leaning back against the squabs to study her mutinous expression. When she dropped the frigid mask she employed to deceive the rest of Society and revealed her true self. It made him feel privileged to get a glimpse of a facet of her nature she permitted nobody else to see.

He'd felt like this last night, too, when she'd been pleading with him to spare her maid. She'd completely forgotten all about acting as though she didn't care about anything. Her eyes had glowed with a similar fervour, and those petal-soft lips had trembled with emotion....

It was only with a great effort that he tore his eyes from those tantalizingly tempting lips. It made his voice quite gruff when he said, 'Catching you in the arms of your lover last night gives me *every* right to speak my mind. I know what you are capable of. I know what you are really like.'

He raised one gloved hand to silence her when she drew breath to object.

'And I cannot, in all conscience, just allow you to

carry on as you have been doing. Dammit, if anyone else had caught the pair of you together there would have been hell to pay. I have no confidence that if I do not, personally, put a curb on your behaviour you will not carry on sneaking out to meet him in secret. And it must stop. Do you hear me?'

She nodded, her lips pressed hard together on the reflection that there was nothing so infuriating as being ordered to do something she had already decided on doing.

'Now, it will not be as bad as all that. If you do me one favour I am willing to arrange for you to see your young man, in circumstances which will compromise neither him nor you.'

'You will do *what?*' How could the man be so exasperating? She had been relying on him insisting she give Harry up completely.

'I will arrange for you two to meet. But only when I, myself, will be your chaperon.' He half turned towards her again. 'Now, look. Everyone knows I have only very recently sold out. What could be more natural than for me to be seen about with other military men? Lieutenant Kendell will be accepted into certain situations if he is with me. And I seem to be exactly the sort of man your family would encourage you to mix with. The fact that we are here, riding out together, with only my own servants to chaperon us, is proof of that. It will be quite easy for me to ensure that you may see each other whenever his duties permit. In a properly managed, decorous fashion. Not in this sneaking way in which you have so far engaged.'

She felt ready to explode. The last thing she could do was tell him he had got completely the wrong idea about her and Harry. He had already made her feel stupid and selfish. If she admitted that she had fallen into the relationship in a fit of pique with her grandfather, and was now quite keen to wriggle out of it again, she would never live it down!

She was going to have to appear to agree to his terms. Oh, Lord, and that meant that she would have to meet Harry again and tell him to his face that she did not love him. Could never marry him.

It would be painful. Very painful. But in a way would it not be a fitting punishment for the way she had led Harry on these past months?

Though she still could not understand why on earth Lord Ledbury was so keen to act as a go-between. Just when she had been relying on him to put an end to what was becoming an increasingly untenable situation, he was coming to their aid—as though he had every sympathy for what he assumed was a pair of star-crossed lovers.

'Why are you doing this?'

He took a deep breath. 'I am going to ask you to do something for me that means I shall have to take you into my confidence. I am going to trust you to keep what I am about to tell you to yourself. Just as you are trusting me to keep my mouth shut about your continuing relationship with Lieutenant Kendell.'

He was going to trust her with a secret? A great deal of her irritation with him ebbed away. Even if his words did contain that thinly veiled threat about *him* keeping quiet so long as *she* kept quiet, nobody had ever reposed any confidence in her upon any matter whatsoever. On the contrary—all her life her male relatives had been drumming it into her that she was completely useless.

'I want you to help a...a friend of mine.' He frowned. 'Perhaps it is best I go back to the beginning. You know I was wounded at Orthez last February?'

'No.' But hadn't he said something about not being able to sleep because his leg troubled him? She looked down at it. Then her eyes flicked to the cane she recalled he'd made use of when he'd limped into Lucy's ballroom the previous night.

She caught her lower lip between her teeth, feeling really ashamed of all the nasty things she'd thought about him just because he'd looked so grim-faced.

'Stupidest thing, really,' he admitted, looking a bit uncomfortable. 'My horse got shot out from under me, and instead of jumping clear I let the damn thing roll on me. Clumsy. I was pretty well out of it for a while. And then I came to in the field hospital, with Milly defending me like a tigress from surgeons whose sole idea of a cure is to amputate anything that looks the least bit untidy. So, you see, she saved my leg.'

He held up one finger as though keeping score.

'Then, eventually, I got sent back to England on a transport, while the rest of my regiment pushed across the border into France. Milly's father, who was the regimental quartermaster, gave his permission for her to come with me as my nurse, thank God, else the fever I contracted would most probably have carried me off.'

He held up another finger.

'I was weak as a kitten all through last summer. And desperately hard up. But thanks to Milly's ingenuity and Fred's skill at foraging—perhaps I should mention Fred is, or was, my batman—I slowly began to recover. And then winter came, and I took an inflammation of the lungs. It looked as though I was done for, but they both stuck with me even though by this time I could not even pay their wages...'

'But you are a wealthy man!'

'I am a wealthy man *now,*' he corrected her. 'Before Mortimer died I had to live on my pay. And what with doctors' bills and so forth...'

'But surely if you had applied to your family, they would have...?'

'I have already told you that you are not alone in being disappointed in your male relatives, Lady Jayne. I wrote on several occasions, but never received any reply.'

'How can that be? Did they not receive your letters? Do you suppose they went astray?'

'Oh, no,' he said, looking particularly grim. 'The minute my brother died the family's man of business came to inform me that I was now Viscount Ledbury— proving that they had known exactly where I was, and how I was circumstanced, all along.'

And they'd left him? Hovering between life and death? Oh, how could they?

'Would it surprise you to learn that my first reaction on hearing of my older brother's death was gratitude— for at last I had the means to reward the only two people who had shown any loyalty towards me?'

'Not one bit.'

She was only surprised that he was so determined to do his duty by a family that had neglected him so woefully. A family that, by the sound of it, cared as little for him as hers did for her. She found herself wanting to lay her hand upon his sleeve and tell him she understood all about that particular kind of pain. But that would be the very last thing he would want. She knew that for certain because the last thing *she* wanted was for anyone to discover that she was constantly repressing a keening wail of her own. *Why does nobody love me? Or even like me?*

'When I learned that I would have to move into Lavenham House and actively start looking for a wife, I set Milly up in a snug little house in Bedford Place and gave her a generous allowance. I told Fred to stay with her, though I would have preferred to have kept him on as my valet. But, you see, she has no acquaintance in London. I could not just abandon her, after all she has done for me. It is no exaggeration to say I owe her my life. And, no matter how bleak things looked, she always looked on the bright side. She kept our spirits up. It could not have been easy for her, coming to what was to her a foreign country and having to adapt to its ways. And its climate.'

And then there was the fact that when he'd told her he was going to have to leave the army, get married and take up his position in Society, she had burst into tears and told him she was in love with him. Not that he was altogether sure he believed her, but still… He hated the thought that everything he did now must be hurting the only person who had ever said they loved him.

'I worry about her,' he admitted. 'Only last week I went round to see them both and she came running down to the kitchen dressed in an outfit that made her look…tawdry. When she told me how much she'd laid out for the gown I could not believe she'd spent so much and ended up looking so cheap. To be frank, she desperately needs guidance. From a woman of good taste.'

His eyes skimmed her outfit. She was wearing a carriage dress of deep blue, a jaunty little bonnet that

framed the natural beauty of her face and chinchilla
furs about her shoulders to shield her from the breeze,
which was quite brisk that day.

'I know it will involve a great personal sacrifice for
you to spend time with a woman of Milly's class, but
I cannot think of anyone else I would rather she emulate. I cannot imagine you ever choosing anything that
did not become you.'

He thought she was a woman of good taste? That
was two compliments he had paid her within the space
of a few minutes. Two more than she'd ever had in her
life, apart from on her looks—which did not count since
she hated the fact she resembled her father so closely.

'I promised her father I would take good care of her,
but I find it is not enough to just give her a house and
an allowance. I am afraid if I do not find some way to
restrain her she will end up becoming…easy prey to
men who have no scruples. It was while my valet was
shaving me this morning that I thought of you.'

It had suddenly struck him that setting Lady Jayne
a task would make her feel as though he was making
her pay for allowing her to see Harry—rather than let
her suspect he felt compelled to keep an eye on her. Or,
more specifically, Kendell.

And she had complained of feeling bored. She would
enjoy the sensation of having a little adventure. And
this time he could ensure the adventure was harmless.

'I realized that you would be the perfect person to
teach Milly a little about genteel behaviour and style.
For you are not so high in the instep that you would
look down your nose at Milly and make her feel uncomfortable.'

She'd given her heart to a low-ranking, impoverished

soldier, hadn't she? And she had no qualms about engaging in a spot of deception when it suited her purposes.

'And I cannot do the thing myself, much as I would wish it, because—well, you must see how it is. Were I still just Major Cathcart nobody would pay any attention. But now I am Lord Ledbury. If I were to escort her to a modiste everyone would think she is my mistress.'

Worst of all, if he relaxed the stance he had taken towards her Milly herself might start to think she was making some headway with him. And he could not encourage her to think she meant any more to him than— well, than Fred did. They had all become very close, living as they had done this past year. They'd become more like friends than master and servants. But you couldn't be just friends with a woman. Not, at any rate, a woman who said she was in love with you.

'She...she isn't your mistress?'

'If she was, I would be the one to take her shopping, wouldn't I?'

'Oh,' she replied, a little perplexed. It sounded so very odd for a man to go to such lengths to see to a woman's welfare. Not to let anyone think she *was* his mistress, which was the natural conclusion to draw. Unless... Suddenly his reference to them having more in common than she might guess, his interrogation of her opinion of marriages between persons of unequal rank, and the way he'd sung Milly's praises all began to make sense.

Lord Ledbury was in love! With a girl of lowly station. No wonder he had looked so kindly on her own situation. No wonder he had jumped to all the wrong conclusions, too. His head must be so full of doomed love affairs between persons of different ranks that he could see them everywhere.

'Say no more,' she said, gently laying her hand upon his arm. Her heart went out to him. No wonder he looked rather cross most of the time. He was the living image of all the tortured, romantic heroes she had ever read about in the books Josie had smuggled in to her.

'Not surprising you can't take to reading,' she had said, 'if all you have is that rubbishy stuff meant for little children. This is what young ladies of your age enjoy.'

'Life can be so unfair,' Lady Jayne said to Lord Ledbury softly, completely forgiving him for every harsh word he had uttered, every criticism he had levelled at her. When a man was in the throes of a painful, thwarted love affair, it was bound to make him a little short-tempered.

'Of course you do not want anyone to say unpleasant things about your…friend. I shall be only too pleased to meet her, and help her in any way I can.'

In fact it would be quite wonderful to be the one giving advice to someone else, instead of constantly being on the receiving end of it. Even if it was only on matters of fashion and etiquette.

'Somehow,' he said with a smile, 'I never doubted it.'

Was that a third compliment? She positively glowed with pleasure.

But then his expression turned hard and businesslike once more.

'I have already told you that I am in Town primarily to find a bride,' he said. 'And, since our families would definitely approve of a match between *us,* I propose to make it seem as though I am trying to fix my interest with you. And you would do well to make it appear as though you reciprocate that interest,' he said quite sternly, 'if you want to continue seeing Lieutenant Kendell. Though I warn you, I will not allow this covert operation to interfere with my primary objective. Which is to find a woman who is worthy of holding the title of Countess of Lavenham. Is that clear?'

She turned to look out of the carriage as though somebody she knew had caught her eye. As though Lord Ledbury had not just cut her to the quick with one throwaway remark. After all those compliments, genuine compliments, she had begun to think that he quite liked her. But now he'd made it plain that he would rather not have to spend any time with her at all.

'Abundantly,' she replied coldly. 'Though,' she observed after a moment or two, 'I cannot help but remark that I think you are carrying your sense of duty too far.'

'By which I assume you mean you think I ought to marry for love.'

Yes! If he was in love with Milly then he ought to marry her, and that was that. Why, earls married widows with shady reputations, or even actresses upon occasion. It caused a bit of a scandal—but when had what others thought ever stopped a man of rank from doing just as he pleased?

'It is the *only* reason one should marry...'

'Well, there we will have to agree to differ.'

Oh, the man was impossible. But there was no point in trying to make him see how foolish he was being. Apart from the fact he was a man, and men always thought they knew best, they were only—as he'd put it—working together under a flag of truce.

And yet she couldn't help feeling rather sorry for

him. The poor man must be in hell, being in love with
one woman whilst feeling duty-bound to marry another.
True, she had been packed off to London to be married
off, but at least her affections had not really been engaged elsewhere. He could not even elope, as her aunt
had done—not when he had so many responsibilities.
He was not that kind of man. She had only met him the
night before, but already she could tell he was determined always to do the right thing. No matter what the
personal cost. Why, he wouldn't even take Milly shopping in case it gave rise to the suspicion that the woman
he loved was his mistress. Even though most men of
his class would have made her his mistress in reality,
without batting an eyelid.

Well, she would not say any more upon that topic.
Not only would it be like prodding at a decaying tooth,
but they did not know each other well enough to share
those kind of confidences.

Though she would do whatever she could to help his
lady-friend. Apart from any other consideration, she rel-
ished the chance to be really, truly useful to someone
for the very first time in her life.

'Oh!' she said, clapping her hands in glee. 'I have just
had a brilliant idea. I shall be in Conduit Street tomorrow. I have to purchase some new gloves. If you could
arrange for Milly to loiter outside the front of Madame
Pichot's at about ten o'clock I could pretend to recognise
her, and introduce her to Lady Penrose as an old friend.'

He looked at her with approval, making her swell
with pleasure when he said, 'Yes, I think that could
work.'

Not for long. She sighed. The first thing Lady Penrose would do, upon her introducing a new friend,

would be to write to her grandfather and enquire if Milly was proper company for her to keep. And as soon as he wrote back, disclaiming all knowledge of any such person amongst her acquaintance, the game would be up. But there was no saying how long it might take for a letter to reach him if he were not at Darvill Park for any reason. So they might have a few days before their ruse was discovered.

And in that time she would do all she could to help the pair who, for reasons of stupid custom—because he was all bound up with doing his duty rather than following his heart—could not be together even though they plainly should be.

'Tell me how I might recognise her,' she said. 'What does she look like?'

'Milly? Oh, she is…' He looked at her, a puzzled frown on his brow. 'She is quite a bit taller than you. Dark hair and eyes. Strong. Plain of face,' he said, his eyes wandering over her features individually and softening. 'Nothing much to look at at all, really.'

And yet he loved her. She was plain, and poor, and yet the eyes that could look as hard as chips of granite turned all soft and smoky when he thought about her.

Because they had shared all those hardships and she'd come through them all with flying colours.

Jayne knew she would never have been able to nurse a man through such a difficult time. She had no skills, no experience. And would never be allowed anywhere near a sick room in any case.

She turned her head away abruptly while she grappled with a fierce stab of jealousy for the girl who, despite all her disadvantages, had managed to capture the heart of a man like this. A man unlike anyone she'd ever met before. Now that she wasn't quite so cross with him she could admit that she found his rough-hewn face ruggedly attractive. Even that terrible scar, which at first sight had made him look a bit scary, now only served as a reminder that he was a battle-hardened soldier, a man to be admired for his bravery.

She heaved a deep sigh. If any man in London deserved to find happiness with the woman he loved, then it was this man.

It was such a pity he couldn't see it for himself.

Chapter Four

The next evening, Lady Jayne had barely arrived at the Cardingtons' before Lord Ledbury came over.

He bowed to Lady Penrose. 'May I claim the hand of Lady Jayne during the next waltz? Not to dance, but to take the air on the terrace?'

'Oh, may I, Lady Penrose?' Lady Jayne put in hastily, before Lady Penrose could object. 'Lord Ledbury was terribly wounded at Orthez. He does not dance.'

She hoped that putting those two statements together might make Lady Penrose soften towards him. Not that she believed he *could* not dance if he wanted to. After all, he was fit enough to go prowling around public parks at dawn. But he clearly wanted to talk to her—and not many men, she had noted, were capable of carrying on sensible conversations while executing the complex figures of any dance, let alone the waltz.

'It is rather warm in here,' said Lady Penrose, after a visible struggle with herself. Having been given the information that Lord Ledbury did not dance, she had little choice but to relax her rigid rules just a little, or risk losing the first suitor in whom her charge had shown any interest. 'Perhaps you might go and sit on that bench, just there.' She indicated a spot just through the open doors, which would be clearly visible from where she sat. 'It is a little unorthodox, but in *your* case,' she said with a slight smile, 'I think there would be no harm in it. I shall have a footman send you out some lemonade.'

Lady Jayne could barely stifle a giggle at the implication that nobody could get up to anything improper whilst drinking lemonade.

'Phew!' she said as they made their way to the open doors. 'It is a good thing you are such a catch, or you would never have got away with that.'

Lord Ledbury flinched. It was just typical that the first woman to rouse his interest should dismiss him so airily. But what else could he expect? She was determined to marry for love. And he'd learned from the cradle that there was nothing in him to inspire affection. His own parents, who'd had no trouble at all doting on his other brothers, had seemed barely able to recall they had a third son. True, his father had only had time for Mortimer, while his mother had practically smothered Charlie, but that had done nothing to soothe the sting of their joint rejection of him. Or to lessen the impact of Lady Jayne's indifference to him now.

He took himself to task as he took his place next to her on the designated bench. He had rank and wealth to offer a woman now. And there were plenty who would be perfectly satisfied with that. He only had to recall how they'd flocked round him at Lucy Beresford's ball.

He had no need of love—not in the kind of marriage he intended to contract.

Particularly not from a flighty little piece like this.

'You are looking very pleased with yourself this evening,' he observed dryly. 'I suppose I should have expected it. You are never happier than when you are up to your neck in mischief, are you?'

She turned to stare at him, wide-eyed, at the unfairness of that remark, and saw that he looked as though he was really annoyed with her about something. Though, cudgel her brains as she might, she could not think what.

That morning she had driven up to the front of Madame Pichot's at the prearranged hour, in Lady Penrose's town carriage, and, seeing a tall, dark-haired girl loitering on the pavement, gazing wistfully at the window display, had sat forward and said artlessly, 'My goodness. Can that be Milly? Whatever can she be doing in Town?'

And then she had leaped out nimbly and darted up to the girl to make sure she was the right person. By the time Lady Penrose had exited the carriage with rather more decorum she'd thought enough time had passed for her to have extracted the news from her supposed friend that she had recently come into some money, quite unexpectedly, and had come up to Town to purchase a fashionable wardrobe.

Having imparted that information to Lady Penrose, she had then swept Milly into the shop, chattering about the newest fashions in that month's *La Belle Assemblée,* and naturally the modiste, seeing the two on such good terms, had assumed Milly must be a somebody, and treated her accordingly.

'Now you are looking at me,' Lord Ledbury was saying, 'as though you expect me to congratulate you for this morning's work. Did you come here expecting me to thank you?'

'Well, yes,' she replied, growing more mystified at his ill humour by the minute.

Milly had certainly been thrilled at the way the morning had turned out. She had admitted that she would never have dared set foot in an establishment like Madame Pichot's. But now she would be able to return whenever she wanted, after an introduction like that. Even if Lady Jayne was not able to go with her, Madame Pichot would never let one of her customers leave her shop looking anything less than elegant. Which was surely what Lord Ledbury wanted?

'Well, I cannot thank you for issuing her with a false name. Milly informs me that she is now to be known as Miss Amelia Brigstock!'

Oh, so that was it. 'That is entirely your fault,' she retorted, stung by his determination to find fault with her in spite of all she had achieved on his behalf. 'You omitted to tell me her full name.' And she had not criticised him for his lack of foresight, had she? She had just plugged up the leak as best she could, to make sure the whole campaign did not sink before it even got underway. 'Since she was supposed to be a long-lost friend, newly come to Town, I could hardly ask her what it was, could I? When Lady Penrose asked me to introduce her I had to come up with something.'

His hands tightened on the head of his cane. A muscle twitched in his jaw.

She reminded herself that he was not in the best of health, and that being in pain could make anyone short-tempered.

Whilst arranging her skirts into decorous folds, making sure the train was well out of the way of his feet, she resolutely stifled the pang of hurt his lack of gratitude had inflicted. Only when she was confident she could do so in a calm, even tone, did she point out, 'And I assumed Milly must be short for something. Amelia is a good, safe kind of name for a girl who is supposed to be completely respectable, though not from the top drawer. And the name Brigstock just popped into my head.'

'Her name is Milly,' he grated. 'Just Milly. And there is nothing wrong with that.'

'There is if I am to invite her to go about with me and pretend that we are bosom friends.'

He looked aghast. 'I have not asked you to do that! Surely you only need to take her shopping a few times to teach her the difference between taste and tawdriness?'

She mellowed a little. How could she not, when he was demonstrating such faith in her fashion sense?

But still... 'You have not thought this through at all, have you? I have not gone shopping with a *friend* once since coming to Town. If I am to suddenly wish to do so with Milly, then Lady Penrose has got to believe she is someone exceptional. A special friend. Or she will become suspicious.'

Lady Jayne never went shopping with friends? He'd thought that was how all fashionable young ladies spent their days.

They were both obliged to suspend any effort at conversation when a footman approached with the drinks that had given them the excuse to go out onto the terrace. But once Lady Jayne had taken just one sip, she pointed out rather tartly, 'You wished me to exercise some influence on her. Which I have promised to do. But you did not give me enough information to see me through any social awkwardness which presenting her to Lady Penrose would entail. I did my best to smooth over that awkwardness. I thought it was what you military types called thinking on your feet.'

He eyed her with misgiving. All he'd wanted was some pretext for making her think they were doing each other a favour—something to distract her from questioning his real motives behind monitoring her and Lieutenant Kendell's meetings so closely.

He could never have guessed just how little freedom she had—not even to go shopping. He'd assumed she'd been exaggerating when she'd said she felt caged, but now he understood what she had meant. It must be intolerable. No wonder she resorted to telling lies and climbing out of windows. Though he couldn't very well encourage her propensity for getting into mischief by admitting that. So, instead, he observed, 'All you have done is make everything twice as complicated as it need be by adding yet another layer to the deception you are practising upon Lady Penrose.'

Guilt made her stomach twinge. She did not want to practise any deception upon Lady Penrose at all. After living under her aegis for only a few weeks she had discovered that, though reserved and inclined to be strict, basically she was a kind woman. So kind, in fact, that after observing the two girls together in the shop she had invited Milly back to Mount Street. Immediately catching on to what a marvellous opportunity this would be to spend some time together in private and concoct a suitable background story, Milly had accepted the invitation with alacrity.

'I am sure you wish to catch up with each other,' Lady Penrose had said once they arrived, and then had retired to her own room leaving them entirely unsupervised.

Lady Jayne did not think she had ever laughed so much since… No, she had *never* laughed so much as she had done that afternoon, closeted in her room with Milly and her lively sense of humour. She had wondered if this was what it would be like to have a close female friend. She had no idea. She had never had *any* friends she had chosen for herself. Her grandfather vetted everyone she came into contact with so closely that by the time they measured up to his impossibly high standards she had lost interest in them.

Milly was like a breath of fresh air. Even though Jayne had been a little jealous of the esteem in which Lord Ledbury held her to begin with, once they had retired to the privacy of Lady Jayne's room and got talking—well! Milly had seen so much, had had so many exciting adventures growing up in the tail of the army, and recounted them so amusingly that Lady Jayne forgot to be anything but completely enthralled. How she wished she might have had but a tithe of Milly's experiences. Once her parents had died, and she had gone to live with her grandfather, Lady Jayne had not set foot outside Kent. While there, she had scarcely been allowed off the estate except for church on Sunday, or to visit the few neighbouring families of whom her grandfather approved. She felt so green and naive and ignorant beside Milly.

After she had gone, Lady Penrose had summoned her to her room.

'That girl appears to have acted upon you like a tonic,' she'd said, the moment Lady Jayne had taken a seat. 'I had thought just at first she looked a little…common…' Lady Penrose had arched an enquiring brow.

'That is one thing I hope to help her with while she

is in Town,' she had said, seizing her opportunity. 'I had hoped, if I might supervise her purchase of a new wardrobe and just give her a nudge—you know, about what is truly stylish...'

Lady Penrose had continued to look at her in silence, that eyebrow raised, until Lady Jayne had admitted, 'Well, no, she is not from a terribly good family. But I do like her.' And by that time it had been the truth.

'There is nothing wrong with having a few friends from lower levels of Society, provided one does not let them become too encroaching,' Lady Penrose had said with a pointed look.

Lady Jayne had nodded her understanding. Any friendship with a person of Milly's class would be allowed to go so far, but no further.

'I have not been able to help noticing,' she had then said, with a troubled air, 'that you have not been very happy while you have been staying with me. It was one of the reasons why I decided we should accept Miss Beresford's invitation to attend her come-out, even though she is not from one of the families your grandfather approved. I had wondered, when you expressed an interest in attending, if you and *she* had struck up a friendship?'

Lady Jayne had only gone to that wretched ball because Harry had let her know he could be there, and they had arranged an assignation in the library, but she couldn't very well admit that.

When Lady Penrose saw that she had no intention of making any response to her tentative enquiry, she continued, 'I have rarely seen you smile, and certainly never heard you laugh, until Miss Brigstock came upon the scene.' She smiled. 'For that alone I am inclined to like her.'

'I hate having to deceive Lady Penrose,' Lady Jayne said now to Lord Ledbury with feeling. 'I wish it was not necessary.'

'Yet Milly tells me you have invited her to go shopping again tomorrow?'

'And then to Gunter's for ices.' Her face brightened considerably. 'She will enjoy that, will she not?'

'She will,' he said, wondering what was making her look so cheerful. He would not have thought that a sheltered Society beauty like her could have anything in common with an army brat. Was she really so lonely that she could look forward to going shopping and having ices with a girl like Milly? If what she said about disliking deceiving Lady Penrose was true, then he could only believe she was so lonely that even Milly's company seemed appealing, or...

Hang it. How could he have forgotten the reason she'd agreed to meet Milly in the first place? Lieutenant Kendell. He'd promised that if she took Milly shopping he would reward her with a sight of her lovelorn lieutenant.

His mood, which had not been all that good to begin with, plummeted still further as he saw that, in spite of knowing Lady Jayne was not at all the kind of girl he could ever seriously consider marrying, it was still galling to know her face would never light up at the prospect of spending time with him.

Even if she hadn't already been in love with someone else, she'd already let him know, in no uncertain terms, that he held no appeal for her whatsoever. That he was, in short, a *cross old stick*.

He turned from her abruptly, using the excuse of placing his empty glass down on the stone coping to conceal any of the feelings that, heaven forbid, might be revealed in his expression. Nor did he particularly want to watch her light up when he told her what steps he had already taken in accordance with the promise he'd made her.

'I have taken a box at Drury Lane. I shall be inviting you to join a party I shall get up next Tuesday. Be sure to attend.'

Lady Jayne glowered at him. The ingrate! After all she had done, the lengths she was prepared to go to be of help to him and Milly, all he could do was bark further orders at her.

He got to his feet.

'The waltz has finished and we must make our way back to Lady Penrose,' he said.

It was so insulting for him to attempt to escape her presence the moment the last strains of music died away that she remained right where she was. And it struck her that this was another reason why she'd always agreed to see Harry. He actually *wanted* to be with her. She wasn't a responsibility who'd been thrust on him. And whenever the time came for them to part he always pleaded for just a few more moments.

'Have you not forgotten something?'

'No.'

'Well, then, may I make a suggestion that if the need should arise,' she said, getting to her feet in her own good time, 'you may send a note via Josie, my maid. You can rely on her discretion.'

'Smuggled letters?' He looked at her, aghast. 'I am

beginning to feel as if I have walked into some kind of badly written play.'

The entire situation was getting out of hand. He'd correctly deduced that Lady Jayne could be a bit of a handful, but she was far more than that. She was like a force of nature. He had only asked her to give Milly a few hints about what a truly elegant lady would wear, and all of a sudden they were best friends—going out and buying ices at Gunters, and now this!

'Not such a great strategist, are you, if even *I* can see that we might need to contact one another before Tuesday? I can foresee any number of circumstances arising which might require *me* to contact *you*. And there will be no way for me to do so openly. Lady Penrose would never let me have private communication with a young man.' She shot his scarred face one scathing glance. 'A relatively young man,' she corrected herself, 'without close supervision. Do not be deceived by the fact she allowed us to sit outdoors for the duration of this dance. Normally she guards me far more closely.'

'I am not a bit surprised,' he snapped, stung by the way she'd once again pointed out that he was far too old and battered for a fresh young beauty like her to give him a second glance. 'If I were in charge of you I would post guards on your door at night.'

'It would not do you a bit of good if you did,' she replied waspishly, 'since I always go out by the window when I do not wish anyone to know where I am going.'

She could not believe he had goaded her into saying that when it was completely untrue. She had only crept out that way once since coming to London, and the outcome had been so appalling she had vowed never to do so again. She could not believe, either, the power he

had to wound her when she scarcely knew him. Or that
he could make her so cross that she could not stop herself from lashing out in a completely irrational manner.

His shocked gasp did, at least, give her a moment's
satisfaction. But only until she took her seat beside Lady
Penrose and watched him walk stiffly away—when she
realized she would have much rather heard him praise
her for her resourcefulness and thank her for being so
helpful.

And how likely was that?

Lady Jayne had never looked forward to a trip to the
theatre so much. She couldn't wait to see Lord Ledbury's face when he saw she'd prevailed upon Lady
Penrose to take Milly along as one of their party. Lady
Penrose had not minded in the least. It was not as if
she'd begged to have Milly admitted to a *ton* event.
Why, anyone could go to the theatre.

And one morning in Milly's company had convinced
her that Lord Ledbury was being as ridiculous as her
own grandfather had been. There was no sensible reason why he should not marry Milly. She was just as
bright and far more pleasant than any well-born lady
he was ever likely to meet.

Besides, the way he'd criticised her at the Cardingtons' still rankled. She was determined to show him
that not only could she teach Milly how to dress well,
but she could turn her into the kind of woman he could
take anywhere.

Lord Ledbury was waiting for them in the doorway
to the box he'd acquired. He greeted Lady Penrose before turning to her.

'This is Miss Amelia Brigstock,' she said, the second

he noticed who was standing beside her. 'I do hope you don't mind me bringing her along? Only she is such a very good friend of mine.'

The smile of welcome stayed on his lips, but to her surprise it died from his eyes and the muscles in his jaw twitched as though he was grinding his teeth.

She watched in mounting bewilderment at the total lack of any perceptible sign of softening from Lord Ledbury as Milly curtsied, and offered her hand, and blushed prettily, exactly as any young lady just presented to such an imposing aristocrat might have done.

Having been as short with Milly as politeness would allow, he then turned his attention back to her.

'Permit me to introduce you to the other members of my party,' he said.

She felt very uncomfortable as she took his arm and allowed him to lead her into the box. She couldn't understand what she had done wrong. Why had he not seemed pleased to see how well Milly could behave in polite company after only a few lessons in etiquette? There had been a kind of suppressed excitement about her, but she did not think anyone who did not know the whole story would have been able to detect anything untoward in her demeanour. Why was he not bursting with pride at her accomplishment?

And then she wondered if she had been terribly insensitive. He looked as though he was just barely keeping the lid on a seething cauldron of various hurts and resentments at a time when he was still, to judge by the pallor of his complexion, very far from well. The poor man had no idea that she was trying to prove to him, and the world, that Milly could easily take her place at his side, given a little instruction. Having her thrust under his nose like this, when he clearly still believed he could never marry her, looked very much as though she had twisted the knife in the wound, which was the very last thing she'd wished to do.

'You already know Beresford and his sister,' he said as they acknowledged her.

Lucy was not behaving half so well as Milly. She was so excited to be one of such a select party that it looked as though her brother was only just preventing her from prostrating herself at Lord Ledbury's feet.

'And now I must introduce you to one of the few military men still fortunate enough to be stationed in London,' he said, ignoring the adoring way Lucy was gazing at him. 'Lieutenant Kendell.'

Then Harry, who had been hovering in the shadows cast by the pillars holding up the tiers of boxes, stepped forward, bowed smartly, and said, 'Honoured to make your acquaintance.'

Her stomach lurched. She found herself hoping, as she curtsied and held out her own hand, that she was managing to conceal her reactions half so well as Milly had just done, when Harry took her hand, tucked it into the crook of his arm, and tugged her away from Lord Ledbury.

'Allow me to help you to your seat,' he said aloud. In her ear, he murmured, 'This is intolerable. He pursued me to the barracks. Now the devil has me on such a short leash there is no way I can escape him. He will ruin me if I step out of line.'

Lord Ledbury clenched his fists as he saw Kendell bend down to whisper in Lady Jayne's ear. The system that sent good men off to die while no-goods like this Kendell remained behind to prey on vulnerable heiresses was monstrously unfair. Not that the boy would be much good on the battlefield, he sneered. He wouldn't want that handsome face bashed about, or his uniform sullied.

He indulged himself with a vision of striding across the box and planting Kendell a facer to stop the man taking the chair next to Lady Jayne's. The fool! Could he not see that not only was he drawing attention to them by behaving in such an obvious manner, but he was also making her uncomfortable?

Well, he couldn't rearrange the man's face, but he could spare Lady Jayne's blushes by distracting his other guests from what was going on.

Turning his back on them, he devoted himself to doing just that.

'My darling,' Harry murmured, 'we cannot go on like this. It is such torment.'

'Oh, Harry,' she said, gazing mournfully into his ardent face.

She dreaded having to tell him it was all over. But it was wrong to keep him dangling like this, in a mix of agony and hope. The longer she put off the moment of parting, the worse it would be for him.

'Come to me where we met before,' he begged her. 'This time I shall have a carriage waiting, so that we can escape from them all. Forever.'

'No!' Oh, this was dreadful. He was still thinking in terms of making a runaway match, while she was looking for an opportunity to sever the connection entirely.

'You need not be afraid,' he said cajolingly. 'I understand how badly Lord Ledbury frightened you, coming upon us like that and uttering all those threats, but I swear I shall never let him hurt you. Once we are married I can protect you from him, and all those like him. My treasure…'

'It is not that,' she snapped. There were so many things wrong with that statement she did not know where to start. She was not afraid of Lord Ledbury. And she did not need Harry to protect her from him or anyone. And how dare he accuse her of being too timid to run away with him? If he thought her so lacking in nerve then he did not know her at all! If she had really loved him nothing would have made her hesitate. Nothing!

She glanced round at the other occupants of the box. Lord Ledbury was standing next to Milly, including her in a conversation that also encompassed his other guests. Whilst also managing to distract Lady Penrose from the fact that she and Harry were standing far too close, and whispering…

'Then what is it?'

She would scarcely get a better chance than this, whilst everyone else was busy exchanging greetings and deciding which chair to take. Now was the time to tell Harry it was over.

Time to stop making excuses for herself. Time to grow up and shoulder responsibility for her actions, not feebly hope somebody else would sort out the mess she'd made. She should never have taken up with Harry when he came to London searching for her, no matter how wonderful it had felt to have him persist in his pursuit of her in the face of her grandfather's objections.

She took a deep breath, looked him straight in the eye…and pictured the aftermath. Harry would be devastated when she told him it was over. Nor would he be able to disguise his hurt, or the fact that she had caused it. He was not made of such stern stuff as Lord Ledbury. Nobody, to look at *him,* would ever be able to guess he was experiencing such deep emotional as well as physical pain.

In fact at that moment she *did* look at him, and it struck her that now she had owned up to not being even slightly in love with Harry that Lord Ledbury cast him completely in the shade. The very perfection of Harry's features, when compared with Lord Ledbury's battle-scarred visage, made him look…well, like a pretty youth play-acting at being a soldier. While Lord Ledbury was the real thing.

'Oh, Harry.' She sighed again, shaking her head. She could not do it. Not here. It would be downright cruel of her to dash all his hopes in front of these theatre-goers. 'I…I just want to talk to you, that is all. Alone.'

She needed to tell him it was over in a private place, where his grief would not expose him to any loss of dignity. And if that meant breaking her pact with Lord Ledbury, to see him only where he could watch over them, then so be it. She owed Harry that much.

'I don't suppose…' She caught her lower lip between her teeth as a plan began to take shape in her mind. 'Can you get an invitation to Lord Lambourne's masquerade ball next week?'

'I dare say I could. And everyone will be in costume anyway, so the hosts won't know if I'm someone they've invited or not if I tag on to another party. It will be perfect. You are a clever girl…'

Lady Jayne cringed. Harry was the only man who had ever given her such unstinting praise. How she wished she could return his regard.

Seeing her pained look, he became all solicitude. 'It

will be difficult for you, though, escaping from your
dragon of a chaperone, will it not?'

Actually, she did not think it would be as hard as
all that. They had already discussed the event at some
length. They both knew that her grandfather would
never approve of her attending such an event. But Lady
Penrose had admitted that she thought it was a pity,
since it was just the sort of thing for a girl of her age.

'I shall contrive something,' she said, biting back her
impulse to defend Lady Penrose from the slur on her
character. 'Don't I always?' To her shame. She really
had to stop going behind her chaperone's back.

And she would!

Once she had freed herself from Harry.

'Yes!' Harry hissed in triumph, seizing her hand and
giving it a squeeze. 'I shall count the hours until we can
be together again. Truly together...'

Lord Ledbury saw the proprietorial way Lieutenant Kendell grasped Lady Jayne's hand and wanted to
knock the bounder's teeth down his throat.

He broke off the conversation in which he'd been engaged quite rudely and strode across the box. He had no
idea what the young man had been saying, but he could
see he was making Lady Jayne uncomfortable. And,
even though he knew she would resent his interference,
he could not stand by one second longer, doing nothing.

'Have a care,' he growled at Harry. 'You ought not
to be standing so close. Are you trying to draw attention to yourselves? Do you want Lady Penrose to suspect you might be the very man Lady Jayne was sent
to London to avoid?'

Harry flushed, and let go of her hand.

'Miss Brigstock,' he said, beckoning Milly over. 'The

performance is about to begin. Do take this seat next to your friend.'

Harry glared at him, but could hardly object to his host ordering the seating arrangements—particularly not when he was only just supposed to have been introduced to Lady Jayne. With bad grace, he took a seat behind the girls. And Lady Penrose herself sat beside him.

It was a good seating arrangement from Lord Ledbury's point of view. Milly soon took Lady Jayne's mind off her own woes by mercilessly making fun of the actors on the stage, who were very far from being the most talented he'd ever watched. Before long, Lady Jayne was giggling behind her fan.

He had never seen her looking so carefree.

That was when he understood why Lady Jayne had taken to Milly so quickly. Her parentage was irrelevant. They were both about the same age. And Milly had brought sunshine into her life.

He was just congratulating himself for being indirectly responsible for chasing away the shadows that her entanglement with Kendell had cast over her, when Milly did something that made his blood run cold.

Chapter Five

She laughed. That was all. But Milly had the most in-
fectious laugh he'd ever heard. It was what had drawn
him to her in the first place. What had drawn many of
the younger officers to her father's billet.

Anyone who'd ever heard that laugh would never forget it. They would take a second look at the shapely and
assured young woman at Lady Jayne's side and perceive
beneath the Town bronze the ragged girl with the dirty
face who'd been the regiment's darling.

A shiver of foreboding went down his spine. Even
though most of the men who might have recognised
Milly had already been deployed, she could still pose a
threat to Lady Jayne's reputation. It would only take one
of the more curious amongst the idlers loafing around
the gentlemen's clubs to investigate his background and
discover that he'd been living under the same roof as
Milly for over a year. That once he'd moved into Lavenham House he'd had set her up in her own dwelling and
given her a generous allowance.

And assume she was his mistress.

People were already casting speculative looks towards the occupants of their box. There would be no end of conjecture about each of his guests, and why he had invited them to form such a small, select group.

What conclusions would they draw about how his 'mistress' had come to be on terms of intimacy with Lady Jayne?

He cursed himself roundly. He'd been annoyed with Lady Jayne when she'd criticised his strategy, since he'd proved himself a skilled tactician time and time again on the battlefields of the Peninsula. But perhaps she'd had a point. He wasn't used to manoeuvring through the morass that was polite society, or considering the fragility of a woman's reputation.

At that moment Lieutenant Kendell leaned forward and said something in Lady Jayne's ear. She forced her lips into the semblance of a smile, but it was a far cry from the natural gaiety she'd been expressing before. She was so good at masking her feelings that everyone else would probably conclude that she was freezing out an importunate young man who was trying on his charm with her, the same way she always did. But he detested the effect her lover was having on her.

If he ever found any evidence to prove the fellow did not really love Lady Jayne, he would make damn sure he never got near her again.

He glowered across the box and Kendell sat back, leaving Lady Jayne in peace for the present. It was the best he could do for now with regard to Kendell, but he could definitely deal with the potential for disaster he'd created by introducing her to Milly.

When it came to the first interval he made his way to Lady Jayne's side and with a jerk of his head dismissed Kendell.

She was so glad he'd come to her rescue. She did not think she could take much more of Harry's endearments. They made her squirm with guilt.

And, from the way Lord Ledbury had been glaring at them, Harry had been far too obvious in spite of the earlier warning. She lifted her chin, bracing herself for the scold she was sure he was about to give her, though for the life of her she could not think how she could have prevented Harry from making a spectacle of himself. Surely it was Harry to whom he should be addressing his concerns?

'This association with Milly is getting out of hand,' he said the moment Harry had moved out of earshot. 'I never imagined, when I asked you to give her a touch of style, that you would take her up this way.'

'What?' It was the very last thing she had expected him to say.

'She is not, and never has been, a proper person for you to know…'

That sounded so very like the kind of criticism her grandfather would have levelled at her that her surprise turned to anger.

'Well, you introduced me to her. You asked me for my help, and—'

'Yes, I know,' he said more gently. 'But I had no notion then, what a warm-hearted person you are. Or how lonely.'

She blinked. She would never have thought such a hard-faced man could be so perceptive. He'd seen right to the heart of her. And put his finger on who she wanted to be but was never allowed to be.

'I thought you would spare her a few hours to take

her shopping, discreetly, not...fling yourself headlong into such an inappropriate friendship.'

'Oh.' His unexpected compliment had touched her so deeply that the warm glow it created melted her anger away. 'But... Milly is a perfectly lovely person. I do not consider a friendship with her inappropriate at all. In fact—'

'That's enough,' he said, the flinty look returning to his eyes. 'In the long run, this association can only be bad for you both.'

'Bad for both of us? Are you suggesting that I am a bad influence on Milly?'

'Not intentionally. And so far you have done her a great deal of good. She has taken advice from you regarding her dress and manners that she would never have taken from me. But was it wise to bring her here, tonight, for example? Is it really kind of you to introduce her to a world in which she can never have so much as a toehold?'

She firmed her mouth mutinously. Milly could have very much more than a toehold if he would only relinquish his absurd belief that he ought to be making a splendid dynastic marriage. If she became his countess people might talk for a while, but the novelty would soon wear off. There would be some other scandal brewing, somewhere, to make them lose interest—particularly if she behaved well.

'You must have noticed how many looks have been directed at our box tonight,' he persisted. 'Everyone wants to know who my guests are. And if they don't know, they will make it their business to find out. You know what nasty minds people have. How long do you think it will be before somebody jumps to the conclusion that I have foisted my mistress on you? You would become a laughing stock.'

'Much I care for that,' she said, militantly lifting her chin.

'Your loyalty is commendable, but in this instance it is not very wise.'

She supposed she could see his point. People would want to know who Milly was now that she had been seen in public in such elevated company. And people *were* always prepared to think the worst. They would never credit any man behaving with such generosity towards a woman of lowly birth unless she was his mistress. And he had gone to such pains to shield Milly from precisely this sort of conjecture.

'Oh…' No wonder he'd been so cross with her for bringing Milly along tonight. All that talk about not wanting *her* to become a laughing stock was so fustian. It was Milly's reputation he was trying to protect.

'This ruse has gone far enough. I cannot permit the association between you two girls to continue.'

'What?' She had been on the verge of apologising for exposing Milly to public scrutiny, and promising she would carry on the friendship with more discretion in future. But now he expected her to drop Milly altogether? Just when she was going to be most in need of a real friend?

Breaking off with Harry was going to be the hardest thing she'd ever done. But at least she'd thought she would have Milly to turn to for consolation in the aftermath.

But if Lord Ledbury had his way her life would descend into that same dreary round that had pitched her into Harry's arms in the first place. Only now it would be far harder to bear because for a short while she'd discovered what it felt like to have a friend, a girl of her own age, who had given her a glimpse into a world she'd only ever been able to dream of.

For years she had yearned for some kind of adventure. She had sometimes wondered, wistfully, what it would have been like to have been the Earl of Caxton's other granddaughter. The one who had got away from England and its stuffy rules and restrictions altogether. Lady Jayne might not actually be having an adventure now, but hearing Milly talk about hers was almost as good.

And then again, once Harry was out of the picture, Lord Ledbury would no longer need to pretend any interest in her, either. He would openly court other women whilst cutting her dead. Not that she wanted to marry him, or anyone else—not this Season. That was not the point.

The point was... Well, she couldn't think what the point was when he made her so cross. She was sure she didn't know why being set at a distance from him should bother her in the least, when he was so overbearing and critical...and...and he had no right to tell her with whom she might be friends! She had defied her own grandfather when he'd tried to dictate to her on just such a matter. Should she meekly fall in with Lord Ledbury's orders?

Absolutely not!

She was not going to give Milly up, and that was that.

Oh, how glad she was that she'd already arranged to meet Harry behind his back.

She would show him that she was quite capable of running her own life *and* choosing her own friends.

With a toss of her head she turned away, without vouchsafing him a single word, and took a seat next to Lady Penrose.

Just as she had predicted, it was not very hard to persuade Lady Penrose to allow her to attend the Lambournes' masquerade ball. The very day after the theatre trip, when they had been discussing how much they had enjoyed it, and how much Milly had added to their enjoyment with her witty remarks, all she'd had to do was sigh wistfully and say what a shame it was she would never be able to take her to a ball. Then she'd picked up the invitation, and said, 'This is the only sort of thing where we might get away with it, since everyone would be masked and nobody quite sure of anyone's identity.'

Lady Penrose had looked at her through narrowed eyes. 'You really wish to attend this masked ball, do you not?'

Lady Jayne had nodded.

Lady Penrose had frowned thoughtfully.

'I suppose I ought not to be surprised. It is exactly the sort of thing to appeal to you young things rather than the staid parties which suit me. And do you know,' she had said, her lips pressing together in an expression of annoyance, 'I think you *ought* to be allowed to enjoy your first London Season. You have not uttered one word of complaint about the limited events to which I have taken you, though I can tell they have not always been to your taste. You are such a good girl, Jayne, that I cannot think why your grandfather feels he needs to be so strict with you. This is exactly the way he treated your aunt Aurora, you know. No wonder she ran off in the end. It would have been much better if he'd allowed her an outlet for her high spirits, rather than trying to crush her. Not that you are anything like her. Dear me, no. Whilst you have lived under my roof you have always behaved exactly as you should. If you really wish to attend this ball, then I... Yes, I do believe I shall allow you to go. You deserve a treat.'

Lady Jayne had been ready to curl up with shame. She had not behaved as she should—not at all! She had sneaked away to meet Harry in libraries, or out on chilly terraces, and had even climbed out of her window to meet him in the park.

Well, she'd make it up to Lady Penrose by *really* being a model of decorum once the masquerade was over. Aside from the matter of defying Lord Ledbury's decree with regard to Milly, which did not count. If Lady Penrose did not object to Milly, then that was all that mattered.

But she soon discovered that though it was all very well tempting to put right all the wrongs she had done with regard to Harry, in order to reach the moral high ground she had to scramble through some very treacherous territory. She even turned Lady Penrose into an accomplice!

'You will need a disguise, not a costume,' Lady Penrose declared. 'A mask will not be enough. If you wear a dress that is too memorable somebody might look too closely at you and recognise you, which would never do. Wear something plain. The plainer the better. Something you have never worn before and will never wear again. And you must definitely cover your hair,' she said, eyeing Lady Jayne's golden ringlets with a frown. 'It is so distinctive.'

She'd ordered Josie to scrape it away from her face, fix it in tight braids and, as an added precaution, cover it with a white sort of bonnet thing, so that even if the hood of her pale blue domino should slip nobody would catch so much as a glimpse of a golden ringlet.

But the most daring part of her disguise would be Lady Penrose's absence.

'Nobody will believe I would ever let you out of my sight, so strictly have I adhered to your grandfather's terms up until now,' she said with a gleam in her eye. 'And they also know that if I were to go I would never, absolutely never, do anything so vulgar as dress up as a shepherdess or a Greek nymph.' She shuddered at the very thought. 'No, if I were to chaperone you I would do so in a proper evening gown, with perhaps a loo mask as a concession to the theme of the event. So even if somebody should suspect you look a bit like Lady Jayne Chilcott, the fact that I am not there will persuade them they are mistaken.'

She raised a hand to her throat and gave a nervous laugh. 'My goodness, I am become quite a rebel! I do not know whether to congratulate myself for finally showing Lord Caxton that he has no right to dictate to me about which venues I consider suitable for you to attend, whilst I have the charge of you, or whether to give myself a stern talking-to for allowing you out of my sight. Though I cannot be sorry,' she declared, 'that *someone* from our family is attending, even if nobody knows who you are. As you know, I had wanted to support Lord Lambourne's return to Society. He made mistakes, but I hope we all know our Christian duty well enough to extend a spirit of forgiveness now that he is reconciled with his wife.'

But, in spite of the delight they took in planning their rebellion against Lord Caxton, by the time it came to Tuesday night both ladies were in quite a state. Lady Jayne gave up waiting decorously on the sofa and stood at the window, watching out for Milly's arrival.

Lady Penrose simply paced the floor.

'Oh, dear,' she said, for the umpteenth time. 'I should not be doing this. If anything were to happen to you, your grandfather would never forgive me.'

'What could possibly happen to me? I shall only be at a masquerade ball. In a private house.'

'These events sometimes degenerate into sad romps. It is why your grandfather would disapprove.'

'Miss Brigstock and I will have a male escort, Lady Penrose.'

'Yes, but we hardly know this Lieutenant Kendell.'

'Surely he must be perfectly respectable,' Lady Jayne replied mischievously, 'since Lord Ledbury introduced us to him.'

She had taken great delight in getting her seal of approval for the male escort in question by emphasising his connection to Lord Ledbury. The mere mention of his name always soothed Lady Penrose's ruffled feathers. And Lady Jayne hadn't been able to help enjoying using him to enable her to go through with an enterprise he would roundly condemn, should he ever find out about it. It was a fitting revenge for the way he'd tried to dictate with whom she could be friends.

At last the long-awaited carriage drew up outside. They had decided to hire a hack, since travelling in Lady Penrose's town carriage would betray their identity at once.

She saw Milly getting out and so, before Lady Penrose had time to think better of letting her go out without her, she flew across the room, gave her a swift hug, promised that she would be very, very careful, and ran from the room.

'This is so exciting,' said Milly as Lady Jayne bundled her back into the hired cab and climbed in after her.

Exciting was not the word Lady Jayne would have chosen to describe the emotions churning round her stomach. She was riddled with guilt at not only deceiving Lady Penrose, but making her an accomplice. She was dreading giving Harry the news that would break his heart. This evening was going to be quite an ordeal.

A bit like lancing a boil. Quite painful, and messy, but once it was done she would be able to return to a more healthy state of mind. Eventually.

'You look adorable,' said Harry, who had been sitting in one corner, hidden from the inquisitive eyes of the footman who had opened the carriage door for her. He had gone to pick up Milly first, thinking it would be best for them all to arrive together, rather than waste time trying to locate each other whilst heavily disguised if they made their way to the ball separately.

As he ran his eyes over her with smouldering intensity her discomfort increased all the more. For one thing, it was hard to accept compliments and admiring looks when she was about to break things off with him.

For another, she knew she did not look in the least adorable. She looked like a nun in a wimple.

'What do you think of my costume, Lieutenant Kendell?' Milly twitched aside the heavy cloak she wore, drawing Harry's eyes away from Lady Jayne.

'My word,' he said, his mouth spreading into an appreciative grin. 'That is quite something.'

Indeed it was, thought Lady Jayne with a spurt of feminine jealousy. Milly had told her that she had once seen a Spanish woman wearing a dress of red satin, with hundreds of ruffles round the skirts, which had looked so incredibly opulent that she had vowed if ever she had any money she would buy such a dress for herself. She knew, of course, that such a style would normally be quite unsuitable for everyday, but it would be perfect for a masquerade ball. Red satin she had promised herself, if ever she had the means, so red satin she would have.

Her own plain white muslin gown, and the blue silk domino that covered it, were positively insipid in comparison with Milly's flamboyant costume. Particularly since it moulded to Milly's figure as though it had been painted on. She even had a red mask—Lady Jayne sighed enviously—studded with tiny red beads to resemble jewelled eyebrows.

She had to remind herself quite sternly that it was ridiculous to feel jealous when the whole point of her nondescript outfit was to deflect attention, not to attract it.

Their host and hostess were waiting, arm in arm, at the head of the stairs to greet their guests as they arrived. Lord Lambourne was dressed in some kind of military uniform, while his wife was dressed in a costume very similar to Milly's. Spanish ladies were obviously in vogue for masquerade balls this Season.

Their party passed on into a ballroom where dancing was already underway. No sooner had they got there than a rather portly man in black silk, sporting a pair of red devil's horns, lurched up to them.

'Do I know either of you fair maidens?' He peered at Lady Jayne and Milly in turn. 'My, but I am going to enjoy endeavouring to penetrate your disguises.'

The lascivious tone of his voice made Lady Jayne pull her domino tight to her throat and shrink closer to Harry.

But Milly gave a sultry gurgle and replied, 'And I shall enjoy fielding your efforts to do so.'

He couldn't tear his eyes from the front of Milly's very tight and daringly low-cut bodice when he asked her to dance.

Had Lady Jayne been on the receiving end of such a lascivious look she would have slapped the portly devil's face, but Milly did not appear to feel in the least bit insulted. On the contrary, she laughed with apparent delight and went off to dance with a perfect stranger...

Leaving her alone with Harry.

Chapter Six

While Lady Jayne was trying to think of some way to rescue Milly, even though she did not look as though she wanted rescuing, Harry swept her onto the dance floor.

As he twirled her round and round she remembered exactly why she had begun to look out for him whenever she had attended any of the assemblies that the locals had put on to welcome his regiment to their part of Kent. He was such a good dancer.

It was sad to think this would be the last time they ever danced together. She was going to miss dancing with him. Well, the truth was she was already missing dancing altogether. She bitterly regretted the fact that she had been so adamant in rejecting all offers to dance with anyone when she had first come to Town. It would make it very awkward to accept anyone now. Though she could not think of anyone she was likely to enjoy dancing with anyway—except perhaps Lord Ledbury, who would not read more into it than was really there. Only he never danced, either. She was not sure why. He scarcely limped at all. Though he did sometimes look very fatigued. And it was at those times that he became particularly crotchety with her.

According to Milly, he got crotchety with her, too. Apparently, during the year she'd acted as his nurse, they had frequently bickered. Though Lady Jayne found that hard to believe. Milly was such a sunny, good-natured person that it was hard to imagine her bickering with anyone. Even Lord Ledbury. Although admittedly she was never in his vicinity for long before something he said or did annoyed her.

'You feel it, too, don't you, my darling?' Harry murmured into her ear, bringing her back to the present with a jolt. 'Being forced to meet only in secret is breaking your heart, is it not?'

'Oh, er...' Far from worrying about Harry, she had just spent the entire dance thinking about another man.

Lord Ledbury was invading her thoughts far too often. She would be glad when this evening was over and she would be free of him, as well as Harry. She *would,* she told herself sternly as her spirits inexplicably plunged at the prospect of seeing him heave a sigh of relief as he realized that he could bow out of her life for good.

Harry slid his arm round her waist and towed her from the dance floor. 'Enough of this. Though it is delightful to hold you in my arms, I need to talk to you.'

He took her along a short corridor and into a conservatory. Seeing that it was already occupied by a couple of pairs of lovers, tussling on most uncomfortable-looking benches, he led her past them and out through French windows onto the terrace beyond. Then he turned and shut the doors behind them, so that she could scarcely hear the music from the ballroom any more.

She clasped her hands at her bosom, her heart pounding as she prepared to give him the little speech she had prepared in which she planned to tell him that she had mistaken her feelings, beg his forgiveness and urge him to forget her.

But then he seized her hands and said, 'I cannot bear sneaking around like this. Give me the right to call you mine. Marry me. I know it will mean eloping, but...'

'Harry, no...'

'Darling, yes. We could just walk out of this ballroom, get into a cab and run away together.'

'No, we could not...'

'Ah!' He smiled at her fondly. 'You are thinking of the practicalities. You are right to do so, my clever darling. We must have the money to pay for a licence and so forth. You will have to go home first, and get hold of whatever you can...'

She could not help it. She snorted.

'Well, my pin money is not going to get us very far.'

'But surely your grandfather does not keep you short? You dress so well. And your jewels alone must be worth a fortune.'

'I dress well because I have accounts all over Town and the bills are all sent to his man of business to settle. I have very little actual money to spend. But let us not talk about money. Harry, I have something I need to tell you...'

'It will be different once we are married, though, will it not? There must be some kind of settlement which will mean that your husband will have charge of your fortune?'

'What fortune?' she scoffed. 'If I marry a man of whom my grandfather disapproves I shall be cut off without a penny.'

'I am sure he would not be so harsh...'

'That's because you don't know him. He has already cut off his own daughter without showing a single sign of remorse. How much easier will it be to do the same to me?'

'Daughter? What daughter?'

'Oh. Well, it is not known outside the family. And even within it we only speak of my aunt Aurora in whispers. But she ran off with a penniless local youth, and Grandpapa not only banished her from the country but forbade anyone to speak her name in his presence.'

A look of confusion flashed across his face. 'But surely your *father* must have settled something upon you. You cannot be entirely dependent upon your grandfather?'

'I suppose we could live on the pittance that he set aside for me. But the bulk of his fortune, along with all the land, went to the new holder of his title.'

'You mean you have *nothing?*'

That was not strictly true. The lawyers had drawn up what they considered a reasonable settlement when her mother had married the Marquis of Tunstall, to provide for any female offspring of the union. But in comparison with what a son would have had Lady Jayne considered her inheritance from him to be a paltry sum.

His face distorted with fury, Harry thrust her roughly away from him.

'You bitch!'

She was not sure what hurt most. Her hip, where it had caught on the corner of the balustrade, or her feelings at being called by such a vile word. Or the expression of complete loathing on Harry's face.

'All this time you have been leading me on when you knew full well there was never any chance I could marry you!'

This was terrible. She had known he would be hurt when he learned it must end, but she'd never expected him to think she'd deliberately deceived him. No wonder he was furious.

'I did not mean to lead you on,' she said, stretching out her hand as she begged for his understanding. 'I simply did not think.'

He seized her by the upper arms, his fingers digging into her flesh.

'Well, if you think,' he snarled, thrusting his face into hers, 'that I am going to keep hanging around on the off-chance your grandfather might change his mind about me, then you are very much mistaken. This is farewell, my lady.'

Then his mouth came crashing down on hers. And it was horrible. Far worse than the last time he'd kissed her. It was as though he was trying to punish her. She could taste his anger in the metallic tang of blood when his teeth ground against her lips. Though she did not try to fight him off, as she had the last time he had pounced on her and taken liberties. She just stood there, rigid in his embrace, accepting the punishment she felt she fully deserved.

'My God,' he said, abruptly letting her go. 'What a narrow escape I've had. You don't even have what it takes to keep a man warm at night.'

She groped behind her for the balustrade. Her legs

were shaking so much it was all that kept her from slumping to the ground.

'They call you Chilblain Jayne—did you know that? Because though you look delectable enough to heat a man's blood to boiling point, the minute he tries to put his hands on you the frost you exude will freeze *all* his extremities.' He laughed mockingly as she flinched. 'Frankly, I don't have the patience to try and thaw you out. Nobody would even attempt to without the lure of the Earl of Caxton's fortune. You are just not worth the effort.'

And then he turned on his heel and stalked off into the house, leaving the French doors swinging wide behind him.

She pressed her hand to her bruised lips, feeling sick.

It had all been a sham. He had been pretending. Deceiving her because he wanted her money. Not her. Never her.

But then, when had anyone ever wanted her?

She felt like curling up into a ball and keening with pain. But she could not. She just could not bear to think someone might witness her humiliation.

She had to find Milly and get home.

She blundered her way back to the ballroom, half blinded by the tears she could not even wipe from her eyes because of the mask she dared not remove lest anyone recognise her.

But before she'd made it through the door a pair of arms shot out and grabbed her. A man, a very large and very strong man, whirled her right off her feet and carried her, kicking and struggling, back into the conservatory.

* * *

Lord Ledbury's spirits had been steadily sinking since the night of the theatre trip. But they had hit rock bottom the night before, when he'd seen the bet written down for all to see. Two so-called gentlemen had staked a tidy sum on the precise amount of time it would take Morty's successor to thaw out 'Chilblain Jayne.' His insistence that she appeared to welcome his suit had blown up in his face. Spectacularly.

He had only taken her for a drive once in Hyde Park—but she had never gone driving with any other man. Whenever he approached her in a ballroom he got a polite smile, and the pleasure of her company for a stroll about the room—whereas she sent every other petitioner about his business.

And then she'd accepted a seat in his private box at the theatre. He should have known from the amount of interest each of them had garnered individually at Lucy Beresford's come-out ball that speculation would rise to fever pitch when they were seen together.

He had wanted to hit somebody. Thrash them. Only he was not quite sure upon whom to focus his anger. The men who'd made the repulsive wager, himself for making her the subject of vulgar speculation or Lieutenant Kendell for being the man with whom Lady Jayne was secretly already in love.

Ever since that night he'd stood beneath her window, savouring the miraculous effect she'd had on his manhood, he'd been having the most disturbingly explicit dreams about her. Dreams from which he woke in a tangle of sheets, covered in sweat and rock-hard. And every time they'd met since then his physical response to her had grown stronger.

But it wasn't merely lust. The more he got to know her, the more he liked her as a person, too. Even when her behaviour irritated him he could see that she was acting from motives he couldn't help admiring.

Worst of all was the fact that every other woman paled into insignificance in comparison with her. He'd hoped that since she'd resurrected his interest in sex he might be able to divert it to some other suitable female.

No such luck. She was the only woman he wanted to haul into his arms and kiss into submission.

And, to his annoyance, just lately he'd begun to daydream about the various ways a man could permanently dispose of a rival in a crowded city like London. Kendell would not pose much of a challenge. He might wear a uniform, but he'd never got it dirty. And he wouldn't be expecting a physical attack...

Though his murderous daydreams always ended the same way. With Lady Jayne finding out what he'd done—for she was so bright she was bound to—and cheering as he was led to the gallows.

And she would. She didn't like him. He'd thought she had begun to soften towards him a little, but since the theatre trip there had been a definite withdrawal. The few times he'd managed to insist they spend some moments together her smiles had been forced, rather than natural. And, no matter how much he'd goaded her, he hadn't been able to rouse her from her abstraction.

Why should it feel so important to try, anyway? He'd come to Town to find a wife. Surely amongst the gaggle of girls on the catch for a husband there must be *one* who could oust Lady Jayne from the forefront of his mind?

But he could not face another night of searching in

vain for some elusive quality that would raise one of this Season's debutantes above the average. He could not stomach one more stuffy *ton* event, where everyone was on their best behaviour and nobody said or did anything *real*.

For just one night he needed to behave disgracefully. To get more than a little drunk and dance with a dozen women of the kind who would not take his interest in their charms as a prelude to a marriage proposal. Maybe even kiss one or two of them if he felt like it and they showed willing. And hopefully break the incomprehensible hold Lady Jayne had over him.

The Lambournes' masquerade promised exactly the kind of mild debauchery he was seeking.

Almost immediately upon his arrival he'd begun to pursue a shepherdess whose main attraction had been a gown that was so low-cut he could actually see the outer edges of her nipples. He'd just persuaded her onto the dance floor and into his arms when he'd heard Milly laugh.

Since he hadn't expected her to gain entry to an event like this he'd turned round, in some surprise, to see who had escorted her here.

He'd frozen when he'd seen the woman standing on the edge of the dance floor beside her.

Lady Jayne. With Kendell.

Well, if she held him in such disdain she thought she could flout their agreement, then to hell with her!

He'd pulled the shepherdess hard against his loins and resumed dancing in a way that paid no heed to the proprieties. But in spite of the gratifying response the shepherdess gave him he was painfully aware of Lady

Jayne, swirling round the dance floor with Kendell, a look of dreamy absorption on her face.

When they left the ballroom, arm in arm, they took with them any last remnant of desire he'd fleetingly felt for the wanton little shepherdess. The thought of Kendell holding Lady Jayne in his arms, kissing the lips that *he* dreamed of nightly not fifty feet from where he was standing, made him feel physically sick.

He broke out in a cold sweat. Suddenly it all made sense. When some of his fellow officers had talked about falling in love they'd described the same symptoms from which he was suffering. They'd said it made them blind to the attractions of all other women. To think he'd scoffed at them, insisting all cats were grey in the dark.

Well, he knew better now. He hadn't seen it sneaking up on him, but he'd been well and truly ambushed by the one emotion he'd never thought would come into his life.

He'd gone and fallen in love with the most unsuitable, unattainable woman in London.

He rather thought he must have groaned, because the shepherdess looked up at him with concern.

'You ain't gonna cast up your accounts, are yer?'

He managed a strained smile. 'I hope not. But just in case…' He pried her arms from about his neck. She readily took the hint, patting him on the shoulder sympathetically before skipping off in search of a fresh partner.

Goddammit. In spite of just saying Lady Jayne could go to hell as far as he was concerned, he'd been lying to himself. He was the one in hell. He turned to glare at the door through which she'd wafted with Kendell—

only to see the man himself come storming back into the ballroom with an ugly look on his face.

But without Lady Jayne.

He waited for her to appear in his wake, and when she did not he just knew something dreadful must have happened.

He pushed his way through the swirling crowd of dancers. He had to find her. She was alone out there somewhere, and unprotected, at the kind of event she should never have come to in the first place.

He'd barely got through the door when she ran full tilt into him and, before he'd had a chance to identify himself, began lashing out at him in a panic.

There was only one thing to be done. He picked her up, placing one hand over her mouth to stifle her protests, and carried her into the conservatory.

'Hush,' he said once he'd set her on her feet. 'You're safe now. I'm here.'

She looked up at him then, but if anything her eyes grew even more panicked.

'Don't you recognise me?' he said softly, when it looked as though she was desperately thinking of some way to dart past him.

Lady Jayne looked up at the face of the masked man who'd just picked her up and hauled her into this darkened alcove with such ruthless determination. When she'd tried to scream for help he'd put his hand over her mouth. He hadn't appeared even to notice when she'd kicked out at him with her flimsy evening slippers. It had felt like trying to wrestle with a walking…oak tree. What kind of a party was this? No wonder Lady Penrose had had second thoughts about allowing her to come here. She must have known the kind of disgraceful things that went on.

The oak tree had put her down eventually, but with her back to the wall. And his shoulders were so broad they blocked her view of the rest of the room. Though she already knew that the other occupants of the conservatory were so intent on their own pleasure that they had not even noticed a struggling nun being carried into the room by a...corsair! For that was what he looked like. She could see now that he'd set her down. He wore a mask, and a red bandana over his hair. He had a cutlass tucked into the belt that spanned narrow hips clad in indecently tight breeches. His ruffled silk shirt was open to the waist, and a pair of thigh-length sea boots completed the outfit. He took his hand from her mouth the moment she stopped struggling. Not that she would yield to the rogue! But he was so big and powerful she would never be able to escape him—except perhaps by persuading him to let her go.

'Lady Jayne...'

The gentleness of the voice saying her name pierced right through her mounting panic. She looked properly into the eyes that were regarding her through the slits in his black mask. They were grey. And full of concern.

As they had been that night he'd wiped the tear from her face.

'L-Lord Ledbury?' The rapid pounding of her heart steadied and slowed when he nodded and took his arm from her waist. But thankfully he remained exactly where he was. Shielding her from view.

Protecting her from possible exposure.

It was not some lecherous stranger, intent on making sport of her. It was Lord Ledbury come to...to tell her off for behaving so badly, no doubt. But, even so, she had never been so glad to see anyone in her life.

'I was so careful with my disguise,' she began to excuse herself. 'How on earth did you recognise me?'

'How did I recognise you?' He shook his head ruefully. Her image was imprinted on his brain. Though she was covered in the most unflattering garment ever devised, she could not hide her height, or the shape of her figure.

And her mask did not cover her mouth.

He dreamed about those lips. What they would taste like. How they would feel pressed on various parts of his body.

'Your mouth,' he grated and, because he couldn't help himself, he reached out, meaning to trace the outline of those lush lips with the tips of his fingers.

And that was when he saw the smear of blood, the cut, the puffiness that spoke of a bruise already forming below the tender skin.

'What the hell did he do to you?' He had a pretty good idea. He'd witnessed the fool trying to force himself on Lady Jayne in the park. And it looked as if her reaction tonight must have been the same as then. It was one thing for a girl of her age and sheltered background to indulge in romantic dreams, but Kendell ought to have learnt that she wasn't ready for unleashed passion. 'This is why I did not want you meeting him without me around. I would never have let something like this happen to you.'

'Y-yes, I know. It was all my own fault.'

She'd brought it on herself. And now Lord Ledbury was angry with her, too. That he was also angry with Harry was of scant comfort. She could not endure a

lecture—not now. Not after Harry had turned into a
stranger in the blink of an eye. A frightening stranger
who had torn down the romantic fantasies she'd been
weaving round herself, leaving her naked, bereft and
bleeding.

'B-but, please, d-don't...'

'Lady Jayne,' he said, gently brushing something
from her cheek. 'Don't cry.'

'I'm not crying. I n-never cry.' She hiccupped.

'Then he must have really hurt you,' he said fiercely,
'because you most certainly are crying.' Very gently he
lifted her chin and examined her lower lip, which was
swelling rapidly round a jagged tear.

'He w-wanted me to...' She shook her head.

His blood ran cold. Had it been worse than ardour
getting out of hand?

'But when I said I would not, he...' Her face crumpled. 'He was just...it was...and now it is over...'

Then she flung her arms round his waist, and hid
from the questions in his eyes by burying her face in
the solid warmth of his chest.

'Just take me home,' she sobbed. 'Please take me
home!'

It was over! He put his arms round her and rocked
her while she wept. Or were they rocking together? He
hardly knew. He was sure of only two things.

Kendell was out of the running.

And she was in his arms.

He felt as though he was being torn in two. Until
now there hadn't been any choice. But now his body
was pulling him one way, demanding he abandon all
aspirations to find a *suitable* wife and commit to this

woman, the only woman it wanted to possess. And to hell with all his carefully laid plans. And the future he'd envisaged, with his glorious countess at his side, helping him improve his estates and leaving such a legacy that generations to come would speak in awe of the seventh Earl of Lavenham and his redoubtable wife.

It was all he could do to prevent himself from blurting out that she was better off without a no-hoper like Kendell. That he was ready to take the fool's place like a shot...

And then he was no longer in a dilemma. He simply couldn't imagine her looking up at him in dawning wonder and then them kissing and it all ending happily ever after. His life had never resembled any kind of fairy story. His reality was that she was only clinging to him because he happened to be there, and she'd learned enough about him in their short acquaintance to know she could trust him.

She only wanted one thing from him. She wanted him to take her home.

Well, he could do that much for her.

It would mean letting her go, that was the trouble...

No, dammit, it wouldn't! Keeping one arm round her shoulders, he guided her into the hall, snagged a cloak from a footman who happened to be passing with guests' discarded outerwear and, wrapping it round her to shield her from view, got her outside and into the first available hack he could hail.

She did not object to any of it. On the contrary, she clung to him throughout as though her life depended on it, weeping as though her heart was broken.

It probably was. His mouth flattened into a grim line. Thank heaven he hadn't made a complete fool of himself by blurting out all that nonsense about taking Kendell's place. He'd had enough of standing in for some other man since he'd come back to England. Besides, what good would it do her for him to make a declaration he had no intention of following through? He might be dazzled by Lady Jayne. He might want her so much he felt sick to think of her in another man's arms. But that didn't mean he had any right to burden her with the news.

Especially not when he hadn't come to terms with it fully himself.

No, what she needed right now was somebody she could just lean on.

So when she slumped onto the seat of the hired hack, looking utterly forlorn, he took the risk of putting his arms round her again. Far from rebuking him, she burrowed into him again, clinging like a limpet while the storm of sobs continued unabated.

He held her tight. Inhaled the scent of her hair. She smelled like roses and honeysuckle. Every time he smelled a rose from this day forward he would remember this moment and savour the memory of holding her delicious curves against his body. He knew his dreams would grow even more vivid now that he had reality to mingle with his fantasies. But he was willing to pay that price. For who knew when he would ever get another opportunity like this? It was not as if he was taking advantage of her moment of weakness. She was drawing comfort from his embrace. And he was taking damn good care to make sure that source of comfort did not become distasteful to her by not letting her suspect exactly how her proximity affected him.

It was quite some time before she unwound her arms

from his waist, looked up, sniffed and asked, 'Where is Milly?'

He cupped her cheek with the palm of his hand, marvelling at her ability to think of another when she was in such distress.

'Do not worry about Milly,' he said gruffly. He could cheerfully wring Milly's neck. What had she been thinking, to aid and abet Lady Jayne in meeting Kendell behind his back? But, since he wanted to soothe her fears, he explained, 'Milly is a daughter of the regiment. She is well used to looking out for herself.'

Lady Jayne's self-esteem shrivelled even further. She'd thought Harry's confession that he would not have bothered with her were she not rich had been bad enough, but now Lord Ledbury was treating her as though she was as fragile as porcelain, while having complete confidence in Milly's ability to look after herself.

In spite of being plain and poor, Milly had managed to capture the heart of the man who was holding her in his arms—much against his inclination, if the stiffness of his posture was anything to go by. She cringed to think of how proud she had been to have influenced Milly's dress sense. As if that mattered. Lord Ledbury loved her just for being herself. Because Milly had something about her that far outweighed her own rank and wealth.

But then, had not Harry just explained that there was *nothing* about her that could attract a man apart from her money? She did not even know how to kiss properly!

She swiped at the tears dripping from her chin with the backs of her hands. Why had she believed his lies in the first place? She'd always known she was worthless.

Her father had never let her forget that she had disappointed him by not being a boy. He'd regarded her very existence as her mother's unforgivable crime. And then her grandfather had confirmed her worst fears by taking one look at her, reeling in horror, and paying legions of professionals to change her into something he would not find quite so obnoxious.

The last thing anyone had ever wanted her to be was herself.

And yet when Harry had told her all those lies about how much he adored her she'd believed him. Why had she been so stupid?

Because she'd wanted *somebody* to love her. Anybody. Even somebody whose regard she could not return.

And that was when she remembered that the whole point of meeting Harry tonight had been to tell him that very fact. She didn't love him. She'd never loved him.

And then she realized that the only reason the things he'd said had hurt her so badly was because they had struck directly at wounds she already bore. She didn't care what *he* thought of her. Not one bit! Not now she knew what a lying, deceitful...*toad* he was. Fancy taking such ruthless advantage of an insecure girl. Just to get his hands on her money.

And to think that for the last few weeks she'd been racked with guilt over the prospect of hurting his feelings.

Well, she wasn't going to waste one more moment feeling any guilt whatsoever in regard to Harry Kendell. She was just glad she'd never fallen completely under his spell, and that now she'd broken free.

She reached into her reticule, got out a handkerchief and blew her nose with some force.

Her mother had warned her never to let any man crush her spirit. Days after her father's funeral. She'd been too weak to rise from her bed for several months, and though she'd never been robust enough to let a boisterous child invade her rooms, she'd suddenly summoned Jayne to her side.

'I outlived him,' she'd whispered hoarsely. 'It was the only victory I could gain, but I did it. Before I go, I want your promise that you will never let a man crush you, either. Remember you are a Vickery. We always rise above whatever adversities life thrusts upon us.'

Mama had certainly risen to the challenge of being married to the odious Marquis of Tunstall. She had gone down fighting him to her last breath. His only wish, for years, had been that his invalid wife would die, so that he could remarry and get the heir she had failed to give him.

She shuddered. Did relations between men and women always have to be a battle?

Lord Ledbury, feeling her convulsive movement, put his arms round her again.

And brought her back to her senses.

What must he think of her? And, oh, Lord, how many times had he made the driver go round in circles while she wept into what little there was of his shirt-front?

It had been kind of him not to take her straight home, but still… She sat up straight, making it clear she no longer needed his support.

'I beg your pardon,' she said. 'I have finished crying now.'

For a moment he considered telling her that he would not care how long she cried if it meant she would stay in his arms. Except that it tore him up inside to see her so wretched.

Reluctantly, he released her and let her sit up.

Hating the physical distance she put between them as she inched along the seat, he reached for her free hand and held it between both of his own.

'Lady Jayne, I shall not pry. But if it would help you to talk about what happened I swear I would never betray your confidence. And if there is any way I may be of further service, you have only to ask.'

She wiped her nose. She had no intention of admitting what an idiot she'd been to fall for Harry's glib lies. But on the other hand he was being so kind...

And, in a way, she did owe him something of an explanation for dragging him away from the ball where, by the looks of that costume, he'd gone to have the kind of fun nobody ever got at the events where she usually met him.

Strange... She'd never thought of him as anything but a creature of duty. But seeing him in that outfit showed her there was more to him than met the eye.

What a pity she'd not gone to the masquerade with him. He looked as though he would have been a much more entertaining escort than Harry. And he wouldn't have crossed the line, either....

She shook herself and lowered her eyes to where he was holding her hand between his own.

'Harry had been trying to persuade me to elope with him for some time. Tonight, when he saw that nothing he could say or do would ever persuade me to take such a reprehensible step, he became very angry. He... Well, let us say he left me in no doubt that he never cared for anything about me but my fortune.'

'I knew it!' He'd known a man who was truly in love could never have enticed a lady into a series of such scandalous escapades. It was disrespectful. If Harry had really loved her, wouldn't he have begged her to wait for him, rather than urged her to elope? If *he'd* gained a place in her affections, when he'd been a mere lieutenant living on his pay, he would have waited forever. Done whatever necessary to prove his worth to her family by his conduct within his regiment, if nothing else. Lady Jayne was the sort who would stand by her word, once given. She would never have married anyone else.

But to find out that the man for whom she had taken such risks had only been toying with her... He frowned down into her bleak little face. And his heart turned over in his chest. She did not deserve to have her trust shattered like this.

By God, if he ever got his hands on Kendell...

Lady Jayne flinched at the murderous expression that came over him. Though how it was possible to hurt any more, after hearing him say he'd always known no man could really be in love with her, she wasn't sure. But there was definitely a pain in her chest. It was so sharp it hurt to draw air in past it. She had to get away from him before she broke down all over again.

'You may set me down at Lady Penrose's house now.'

He saw her face close up and bitterly regretted the fact that she was turning back into the lifeless little puppet he'd first encountered at Lucy Beresford's come-out ball.

'Not yet,' he said. 'Your eyes will still be red. And your nose...'

'Lady Penrose is hardly going to miss this, is she?' She indicated her torn lip. 'I shall have to give her an explanation. And,' she said, drawing herself upright, 'I am now ready to give it.'

He almost gasped with admiration. She must have an inner core of steel.

'Do you wish me to come in with you? Would it help at all?'

She shook her head. 'I have taken up far too much of your time as it is.'

The polite tone of her voice as she tugged her hand free of his was worse than anything that had gone before.

Do not withdraw from me, he wanted to beg her. *Do not shut me out.*

In the event, what he said was, 'As you wish.'

She clearly wanted to be on her own. He could understand that. Her pride made her reluctant to reveal her weaknesses. People who had not glimpsed her real self looked at her frozen expression, the one she was wearing now, and assumed she was cold all the way through. But it was as much a mask as the little scrap of satin she'd donned to attend tonight's masquerade. Only she put it on to conceal the depth of her hurt, not merely her identity.

Nobody, apart from himself and Lady Penrose, would ever know anything about this night's work. And he would hazard a guess that she would tell her duenna as little as she possibly could. He would be the only person to know that tonight she'd had her heart broken.

And all he could do about it was take her home and hope that Lady Penrose was kinder than she looked.

Chapter Seven

'I had not expected you back quite so early,' said Lady Penrose, looking up from the book she was reading. Her eyes narrowed upon Lady Jayne's lower lip, and her hand flew to her own mouth. 'I knew I should not have let you go to such an improper sort of party! They always get too boisterous. And there is always some man who gets out of hand.'

She braced herself for a scold when Lady Penrose shut her book with a snap.

'My dear, I am so sorry. You have led such a sheltered life. Nothing can have prepared you for the vile behaviour in which some men indulge when in their cups. But how did it come about? I thought you would stick close to Miss Brigstock all evening.'

'Oh, I…er…slipped away from her for a moment or two…'

'That is all it takes,' said Lady Penrose acidly. 'Men need no encouragement at the best of times, and when they are masked, and think they can get away with taking liberties without anyone knowing quite who they are… But what of the gentleman who escorted you there? I trust he came to your rescue?'

'No, he…he turned out to be a very great disappointment. In fact,' she said bitterly, 'he abandoned me not long after we got there.' Which was as much of the truth as she felt able to confess.

'But then however did you get home? I heard a carriage. Is Miss Brigstock with you?'

When Lady Jayne shook her head, Lady Penrose turned pale.

'Never say you had to get *yourself* a cab?'

'Oh, no. Fortunately Lord Ledbury…er…recognised me, saw that I'd had to extricate myself from a…predicament, and…um…escorted me home.'

Lady Penrose sagged with relief. But after only a minute's reflection, she sat up straight again. 'Lord Ledbury? He was there? And brought you home? The two of you were quite alone in a hired hack? I am not sure that this is not worse… Can we rely on his discretion, do you think?'

'You need have no worries on that score. Lord Ledbury will not tell anyone.' The last thing he'd want would be for anyone to know they'd spent the last half an hour locked in each other's arms.

Lady Penrose looked at her sharply. 'You trust him that much?'

'Yes. I do.' She was being unfair to accuse him of wanting to hush everything up for his own sake. He had shielded her from scandal once already. And he'd had nothing to gain that time.

He was innately chivalrous. She could never, not for one instant, imagine *him* trying to inveigle his way into an heiress's affections, then urging her to elope with him. Not that he needed an heiress. He was wealthy enough in his own right.

Nor was he the sort of man to humiliate a woman by telling her what vile nicknames people called her. Though he would probably know they called her Chilblain Jayne. Of course he would.

Oh, God. Had *he* ever referred to her by that name? A shaft of pain seared through her.

'Well, then, we must hope no real harm has been done. You have already paid dearly enough for learning about the true nature of men.' Lady Penrose looked at her lip. 'My advice to you is that you look upon this evening in the light of an educational experience. And we need say no more about it.'

It had definitely been educational. Harry had taught her a lesson she was not about to forget in a hurry. A lesson she should have learned years ago. She was unlovable. Completely worthless.

'May I go to bed?' she asked in a small, chastened voice.

'Of course,' Lady Penrose replied kindly. 'And do not repine too much. Just try to remember what you have learned so that you will not repeat the same mistake again.'

'Yes, that is what I shall do,' she said.

She would certainly never let another man fool her into believing he was interested in anything but her fortune.

She climbed the stairs slowly, trailing her hand along the banister. How could she have been so stupid? And she wasn't just thinking about falling for Harry's lies now, but her whole attitude since coming to London. She'd been so hurt and angry at the way her grandfa-

ther had treated her that she had rebuffed all the overtures of friendship made. Not that she liked any of this
year's crop of debutantes all that much anyway. They
were all so keen to get husbands, and their conversation revolved so exclusively around that topic, that five
minutes alone with any of them would have made her
boiling mad. But if she only had a circle of friends…

But there was no way back from the stance she'd
taken. Not now. She would just have to carry on as
though nothing had changed. When she got to her room
she would be able to remove the mask and domino she'd
worn tonight, but she could never let down her guard
with the people among whom she moved in Town. Or
they would start to wonder what had happened to wreak
such a change. And ask questions she had no intention
of ever answering.

She paused on the landing, head bowed. She was
trapped in a disguise she'd made for herself. And
the only people who would persist in trying to break
through it would be the truly desperate fortune-hunt-
ers. The ones who wanted access to her money badly
enough to put up with the chilblains they'd get from the
frost they said she exuded.

And she had nobody to blame but herself.

Over the next few days she found that she was glad
Harry had bruised her face. For each day Lady Penrose
would take a long hard look at her and decide that it
would be better to stay in her room and inform callers
that she was indisposed. It gave her a legitimate excuse
for staying out of circulation while she came to terms
with what an idiot she'd been. Though it might be a long
time before she felt ready to face anyone.

The first posy of flowers from Lord Ledbury arrived the very morning after the masquerade. And every day he sent her another.

Lady Penrose became so excited about the daily delivery from the florists that Jayne wondered whether she ought to explain that Lord Ledbury was just being kind. She didn't want her to get her hopes up for nothing. For, though flowers usually signified romantic interest, she knew he couldn't possibly have any romantic feelings towards her, having seen her at her worst. Though she would always treasure the memory of receiving flowers from Lord Ledbury, she was sure his concern was a transitory thing. It would wane just as surely as the flowers he sent withered and died.

One afternoon, Lady Penrose came to her room, took a chair, and gave her a stern look.

'Now, I know you have not come down to receive any callers, and I agree that that has been the best policy up till now. But today there is a visitor I think you would like to receive...'

Her heart leaped. Had Lord Ledbury done more than just send flowers via his footman today? Had he come in person? He had already seen the bruise on her mouth, so Lady Penrose would not feel she had to hide it from him.

'She has always acted like a tonic upon you,' said Lady Penrose, quashing her hope even before it had fully formed, 'and so I have said I will ask if you would receive her up here, in your room. Otherwise, you know, she might think you have fallen out with her over the masquerade. And, although you were both rather silly that night, I do not think what happened there was her fault, was it?'

Lady Penrose's gentle reproof struck her to the core. She had been so wrapped up in her own misery that she'd not spared a thought as to how Milly had got home. Lord Ledbury had said she could look after herself, and she'd been so jealous of the complete confidence he placed in her that she hadn't questioned that assumption.

'Of course I will see her,' she said.

Lady Penrose smiled approvingly, and went away to let Milly know she could come up.

'Richard,' said Milly, the moment she came through the door, 'was that mad at me for going to the masquerade with you. Rang a peal over me as if whatever it was that happened to you there was all my fault!' She sat down on the bed, untying the ribbons of a very fetching bonnet as she did so.

'Oh, no. I am so sorry...'

Milly shrugged her shoulders. 'It's not your fault he's got so stuffy since he come—I mean *came* into that title. And, anyway, he was there, too, wasn't he? Looking much more like his old self. He used to be such a great one for dancing and kicking up larks. You should have seen him doing the fandango when he was just a captain. Not many of the British officers ever mastered the steps properly, but he kept on and on at it, practising with the Portuguese women until he was as good as any of the muleteers.'

Somehow, Jayne could see it. Well, she could now she'd seen him in that corsair outfit, anyway. Putting on that costume had given him the liberty to be that dashing young officer Milly had just described once more. She'd got used to seeing the grim expression he wore in Society settings—but who wouldn't look grim if he had to go about looking for a suitable wife when deep down he didn't want any Society lady at all?

'So, why have you come today? Has something happened? I know Lord Ledbury does not want us to meet again, so...'

Milly made a rude noise, flapping her hands in a dismissive gesture. 'You weren't going to pay any attention to that silly notion of his, were you? That wasn't the impression I got when we planned getting into the masquerade, anyhow.'

Lady Jayne sat down on her dressing-table stool. When Lord Ledbury had first told her she was not to meet Milly again she had been incensed, and vowed he had no right to dictate with whom she might be friends. But in the aftermath of Harry's defection she'd begun to question her own judgement. Maybe she ought not to be so ready to flout authority. Or at least perhaps she ought to try and cultivate the habit of sitting down and thinking before reacting rebelliously to a stricture she found perfectly ridiculous.

Tentatively, she suggested, 'I expect he is only trying to protect you...'

'Protect me?' Milly gave her a searching look. Then, with a conspiratorial grin, she said, 'You don't really believe that, do you? It's been my experience that the stupid notions men have about how they want their women to behave only end up making everybody miserable.'

'Well, I can't argue with you there,' said Lady Jayne, thinking of how miserable all the men in her own life had made her.

'They're all self-serving bastards.'

'Not Lord Ledbury! You don't mean him, Milly.'

Milly pouted. 'Yes, I do. I know I can't ever marry

him. Not now he's come into that title. But he's got so starchy nowadays that he won't even make me his mistress.'

Lady Jayne was not used to such forthright speaking. Her cheeks a little warm, she said, 'It is not the thing to *want* to be a man's mistress. It isn't at all proper.'

But if she were in Milly's shoes how would she feel? If she knew she could never marry him, she rather thought she might be prepared to take whatever small crumbs Lord Ledbury scattered her way. After having been held in those strong arms, she knew she wouldn't feel the least bit revolted if *he* wanted to kiss her. If she'd been meeting him in the park, rather than Harry, she would definitely have wanted to kiss him back. And if *he'd* suggested eloping...

She pulled herself up sharply. It was *Milly's* relationship with Lord Ledbury they were discussing.

It was funny, but when she'd put herself in the theoretical position of being Lord Ledbury's forbidden love she'd seen herself getting swept away. But as soon as she tried to imagine Milly on the park bench kissing him she felt most uncomfortable. And her mind shied away from thinking about them going to bed altogether.

'Oh, let us not get into a quarrel about that. I have been so wretched since the night of the masquerade. And I am really glad you've come to see me.'

'In spite of what Richard might say if he found out?'

'Even then.'

Lord Ledbury clearly had his reasons for wanting this friendship to cease, but neither she nor Milly agreed with him. It was two to one.

Milly grinned. 'So come on, then, tell me all about it. I've been dying to find out what really happened between you and that handsome soldier of yours, and Richard just closes up like a clam whenever I ask him for details.'

The hour flew past, and by the time Milly left Lady Jayne's the mood had lifted considerably. Her bruise had almost disappeared, and her spirit, too, was reviving. It would not be much longer before Lady Penrose decreed she was fit to return to Society. And she would be ready.

She was a Vickery, after all. And Vickerys were never crushed by adverse circumstances. She was not, most definitely not, going to appear as though there was the slightest thing troubling her.

She took extra care over her appearance on the night of her first ball after the break with Harry, choosing a gown that had never had an outing before. When she'd had her last fitting she had adored the spangles on the overdress, and thought the white embroidery on the satin underskirt raised the outfit above the ordinary. But as she stood in front of the mirror she was appalled to see a glittering ice maiden looking back at her.

'Not the diamonds, Josie,' she said with a shiver. 'The sapphires tonight.'

'Yes. They will bring out the colour of your eyes.'

She didn't care about that. But at least they did not add to the impression of coldness that made everyone mock her.

Not that she cared. She lifted her chin as she walked into the ballroom later, telling herself she was ready to face them all down.

But in the event she did not notice who else might have been there. Because she saw Lord Ledbury, and for a moment all she could think about was how good it had felt to fling herself into his arms and let him hold her while she wept. Nobody in her whole life had held her like that. Nobody.

She tore her eyes away from him and made a great production of finding a chair, settling herself and Lady Penrose, arranging her skirts and flicking open her fan. She needed to cool her heated cheeks. How could she have considered running across the crowded room and flinging herself at him? He would be appalled. He had not minded coming to her assistance in a moment of need. When he was masked and nobody knew who he was. But he set such store by appearances that he wouldn't even let anyone see him take Milly to a modiste. He would detest being made a spectacle of at a *ton* event.

From across the room Lord Ledbury watched her surreptitiously as she pulled her dignity around her like a suit of armour. It set her apart from the frivolous gaiety of the rest of the guests. She might as well have been holding up a placard saying Keep Away.

To her right, he observed Miss Beresford look at Lady Jayne and giggle at something her friend Lady Susan Pettiffer whispered behind her gloved hand. Rage roiled up inside him. Yes, tonight she might look as though she deserved the nickname that some wit had coined for her, but they had no idea how bravely she was dealing with Lieutenant Kendell's perfidy. He would like to see Miss Beresford's reaction to such a betrayal. She would not get up and go about as though nothing had occurred. She would, no doubt, make a grand drama out of it, involving maids and her mama, recourse to the vinaigrette, and probably a doctor or two, and then a retreat to some seaside town for a rest cure.

He'd had no intention of drawing attention to how he felt about her by singling her out tonight. And he'd taken great care, while she had been absent from Society, to try and deal with it by searching even harder for a woman who would actually want to become his wife.

The trouble was, he was beginning to wonder why he'd ever thought it so important to prove himself to what remained of his family by marrying a woman who would impress them. He couldn't stop thinking about how it had felt to hold *her* in his arms.

And then the moment she'd walked in the door all the merits of the other girls he'd been…interviewing over the past week had faded away to nothing.

She was the only woman he really wanted.

Then almost at once his own needs were swept aside by the conviction that what *she* needed at this moment, more than anything else, was a friend.

He strode across the room, and bowed over her hand.

'I am pleased to see you have recovered from your indisposition,' he said, conscious that others would be listening.

'Thank you,' she said politely. 'I am completely re-covered now.' It was the only way she could think of to tell him that she had learned her lesson where Harry was concerned. That she would never be so stupid again.

He glanced at her mouth, concern briefly flaring in those smoky grey eyes.

'Would you care to take a walk with me, Lady Jayne? Outside on the terrace? The gardens of this house look particularly enchanting by moonlight, and the air is mild tonight.'

Her heart stuttered in her chest. She had thought he would distance himself from her, since he no longer had to seek her out to inform her when the next meeting with Harry could take place. And, since he would also assume her association with Milly was at an end, they would have very little to discuss. She'd braced herself for the conjecture that would arise. She'd imagined people whispering that he had not the stamina to *thaw* her. The only thing they might wonder at was that he had persisted for this long. Yet he'd marched right over, the moment she'd set foot in the ballroom, exactly as he'd always used to.

She wondered what he wanted to talk about tonight. Not that she had any intention of refusing his request. She had never done so before, and to do so now would only create speculation about what might have changed between them.

'May I, Lady Penrose?'

'Of course, my dear.'

Rising gracefully to her feet, she threaded her hand through his extended arm and strolled outside with him.

'How are you, truly?' he said, the moment they were out of earshot of anyone else.

'Completely recovered, as I told you before. Well,' she said with a brittle smile, 'to *you* I will confess that occasionally I still feel a little sorry for myself. But now the bruise has healed I have no excuse not to go about in Society again. And let me tell you I have no intention of sitting at home and repining over a man who proved himself to be completely unworthy of my regard. I would rather die,' she admitted, with some vehemence, 'than let anyone know what a fool I have been.'

Her voice was hard. Her face a mask of hauteur. He did not think he had ever seen a more tragic little figure in all his life.

'Fortunately Harry will not dare to breathe a word of what he was up to, lest he gain a reputation that would hamper future enterprises of the same sort,' she said, with a perspicacity that amazed him.

He wished he knew the right thing to do, or say. He could not stand to see her in such pain, yet walling herself off from it with this show of not caring. But the very worst thing he could do would be to offer her sympathy. She would hate him if he were to cause that wall of ice to crack and make all her grief come pouring out in such a public place. But he was still compelled to let her know that, in him, she had a friend who would always remain tactfully silent, yet stolidly faithful.

'You know, I hope, that you can trust me not to reveal what went on?'

'Of course I trust you,' she said, looking up into his stern face. She would trust this man with her whole future. He would never let her down.

And just like that she understood *exactly* what it was that had made her aunt Aurora defy convention to run off with the man she loved. If she ever won the heart of a man like this she would follow him to the ends of the earth if he should ask it of her. She gasped at the audacity of even *thinking* such a thing, tore her eyes away from him and fanned her heated cheeks briskly.

He took a step back. Dammit, he had been standing too close to her. Just because she'd let him hold her in his arms when she'd been distressed, it did not mean she was ready to repeat the experience.

A friend. That was all she wanted him to be.

'May I take you for a drive tomorrow?'

'Are you sure? I mean, there is no need.'

'There is every need. You have more need of me now than at any time since we first met.'

'I do not *need* anyone,' she retorted. Then hung her head. 'But, yes, I would enjoy going for a drive tomorrow.'

No, she did not need anyone. He'd watched her pulling herself together after Kendell had betrayed her trust, marvelling at her inner strength.

He would be a fool to think he might be able to make her fall in love with him, even if he knew how to begin courting her.

But then… He hadn't expected *whichever* woman he eventually decided to propose to to love him, either.

His heart began to beat very fast.

Was there a chance for him after all?

He certainly had one advantage over every single other man she knew, and that was his knowledge of the affair with Harry. He knew she was unhappy, and why, and he could at least offer her an escape. He could take her away from Town, and all its unpleasant associations, and give her the opportunity to recover.

And, as an added benefit, he could offer her the freedom she craved.

The freedom to be herself. That had to be worth something, didn't it?

Ye gods. He was seriously thinking about proposing to Lady Jayne Chilcott.

'Then I shall see you tomorrow,' he said curtly, and led her back to her seat beside Lady Penrose.

For the rest of the evening Lady Jayne surreptitiously followed Lord Ledbury's movements. He sat out the quadrille in the company of a plain, plump girl she didn't know. He took a walk round the perimeter of the ballroom with Lady Susan Pettiffer during the first half of a set of country dances. And he escorted Lucy Beresford into supper. At least, Lucy would have liked to think so. The truth was closer to being that they were in the same party, which included her brother and the plain plump girl.

It appeared that his search for a suitable bride had been continuing apace while she had been out of circulation. Well, what had she expected? He was the kind of man who, when set a task, did it to the best of his ability. She only had to think of Milly's description of how determined he had been to learn the fandango.

It was as if he regarded his whole life as a contest which he was determined to win. She'd noticed his belligerence the very first night they'd met, though she hadn't understood its cause. He'd walked into that ballroom and glared round as though defying anyone to question his right to be there. She smiled ruefully. Now she knew him better she wouldn't be a bit surprised to learn that part of what drove him was the need to prove to his family that he was a better man than they took him for.

Her smile faded away. That made it especially kind of him to continue with the pretence on which they'd agreed—that he was interested in her and she was responding to his suit. If he wouldn't even marry Milly, the woman he loved, he most certainly wasn't really going to consider a silly chit who'd almost been seduced by a man with nothing to recommend him but a handsome face. Who was a harum scarum creature that he'd watched getting into one disgraceful scrape after another.

Not that she wanted to get married anyway. She'd promised herself she wouldn't.

So why did she suddenly feel so depressed?

'I am growing quite tired, Lady Penrose,' she said morosely, plying her fan to stir the stuffy air of the ballroom. 'May we leave soon?'

'Of course, my dear,' said Lady Penrose. 'You need to recoup your strength so that you look your best for your outing tomorrow.'

Lady Jayne's heart sank still further. Her chaperone was convinced Lord Ledbury was developing a tendre for her. She was going to be so disappointed when it all came to nothing.

Chapter Eight

'What you need,' Lord Ledbury said, the moment his groom had set the carriage in motion, 'is a change of scenery.'

'Yes. Thank you. It was a lovely idea of yours to take the air in the park this afternoon.'

'No, no, I didn't mean that.' He turned his upper body to face her. 'You were drawn tight as a bowstring last night at that wretched ball, trying to preserve a calm facade so that nobody could tell how badly you are suffering. It would do you good to get out of Town altogether for a space. Spend some time recovering in the countryside.'

For a moment she was quite worried. She had thought she had done such a good job of concealing her lowness of spirits. She darted a glance at Lord Ledbury, who was gazing at her with one of his searching frowns. She relaxed, remembering she had confided as much to him last night. And was touched to see he'd been thinking about what she'd said, and was offering his advice.

'It is kind of you to be concerned for my welfare. And, to be honest, I should dearly love to return to

Kent, in some ways. Only...' She pulled at the fingers of her gloves. 'I really, really don't want to let this business with Harry defeat me. Going home *would* feel like a defeat. Besides,' she continued with a wry smile, 'I cannot think of anything that would induce my grandfather to have me back.'

'I did not mean to imply I thought you should go home. Far from it.'

He took a deep breath and took the gamble of his life. He knew she was the wrong woman in so many ways, and yet if he wrote her out of his life irrevocably, without even trying... Well, he would always regret it.

'I would like you to attend a house party I mean to get up at Courtlands, the family seat in Buckinghamshire.'

While she was maintaining her defences so rigidly, to conceal the depth of her hurt, he stood no chance of ascertaining what her feelings towards him had the potential to become. But in the less formal atmosphere of a country house party there would be plenty of opportunities for breaching the rigid etiquette Society enforced. Rides in the woods, strolls through the shrubbery, picnics by the lake...

'A house party? So early in the Season?' People did not normally start deserting the capital until the weather started to grow uncomfortably hot.

Unless they wanted to introduce a prospective bride to the head of a family, and give them a glimpse of the property of which they might one day become mistress.

Was he that close to making a decision? A shaft of pain went through her. How on earth could he think it would *do her good* to watch him make his selection from whichever other girls he invited down there, whilst discounting her from the running altogether?

She averted her head sharply while she grappled with her emotions. He wasn't being deliberately cruel. Not Lord Ledbury. It sounded as though he really just wanted to offer her some respite from the nightmare that her Season had become. He could have no idea that he was catapulting her into an altogether different kind of nightmare, since she'd taken great care not to let him know how very much she was beginning to... admire him.

'The grounds of Courtlands are quite lovely at this time of year,' he said. 'But, to tell you the truth, I need an excuse to get out of Town, too. You are the one person to whom I can confess this, but I feel almost like a traitor, doing nothing but going to balls, or performances at the theatre, when it looks as though the whole of Europe is about to be plunged into yet another war.'

She could have kicked herself. Why did she always only look at things from her own point of view? Every day the papers reported more regiments sailing for the Low Countries, and poor Lord Ledbury was stuck in England, obliged to find himself a suitable bride— whilst his heart belonged to Milly.

'It must be terribly frustrating for you,' she said. 'Everyone who has any military experience at all seems to be scrambling to get across to the continent and join up. If I were a man, and I had been used to being in the army, having to kick my heels in London whilst others went off to trounce Bonaparte would make me want to scream with frustration.'

That surprised a wry laugh from him. 'I would never scream, no matter what the provocation. But I admit that sometimes it is all I can do to keep a civil tongue in my head when people who have never been involved make stupid remarks about...oh, how shocking it is that Bonaparte's former marshals won't arrest him, for instance.'

'As if they would! On fat Louis Bourbon's orders!'

'That is a remarkably perceptive thing for such a... I mean, you follow the news? The political news?'

She supposed she should be glad he'd swallowed back whatever derogatory remark he'd been on the verge of making. 'Why should I not read the newspapers?'

'Not many ladies would. I'm pretty certain that most would not consider it a fit topic of conversation, either.'

She wondered whether that was a rebuke, as well. Except he didn't look the least bit cross with her. And that encouraged her to admit, 'Well, I don't say that I always understand everything I read, especially when a report seems to contradict the one that went before it, but...'

'War can be a confusing business. Nobody can ever really know the truth of any battle unless he was there,' he said grimly. 'And as for what gets printed in the papers...' He drew a deep breath, as though deliberately distancing himself from whatever thoughts had put such a grim expression on his face.

'Let us not speak of such matters on such a lovely day.' She laid her hand tentatively upon his sleeve, the only way she could think of to express her sympathy.

He felt the pressure of her hand, and the rather sad little smile that accompanied it, like a benediction. Sometimes it was as though Lady Jayne could see into his very soul. Nobody had ever intuitively understood him the way she did.

He wished he could snatch up her hand, carry it to

his mouth and press his lips upon it in homage. His fingers flexed as he willed himself not to behave in such a rash manner. She wasn't ready to think of him in those terms. Besides, they were in a public park. He must not do anything to add to the speculation that had resulted in that bet being written down. He wanted to protect her from that kind of nastiness, not make her situation more uncomfortable than it already was.

Besides, he needed to persuade her to come down to Courtlands—not frighten her into refusing the invitation.

'Come, Lady Jayne. You have admitted that you would rather be in the countryside than in Town. And Kent is not an option. I am offering you Courtlands.' Perhaps in more ways than one. 'Please say you will come.'

His expression turned exceptionally earnest. As though it really mattered to him that she should be there. Though she could not imagine why. Except... She was the only person who understood how hard it was for him to pick a bride of whom his family would approve when his heart really belonged to Milly. Did he want her there to lend him moral support?

'I...I don't know,' she prevaricated. Was she up to putting aside her own hurt and supporting him this way? Nobody else had ever asked for her support. It was a huge compliment. To avoid having to make a definite answer either way, she asked, 'Who else will be going?'

'Berry, with whom I was at school. He renewed our acquaintance when I first moved into Lavenham House. And his sister Lucy. We first met at her coming-out ball, if you remember?'

Lady Jayne's mind flew back to that night. How she

had thought him grim and unapproachable as she'd watched him fending off the advances of ambitious matchmaking mothers. And then how later he'd come so magnificently to her rescue. Still looking grim, to be sure, but not in the least bit unapproachable. She'd somehow poured out her whole life story, telling him things she'd never shared with another living soul.

He was looking at her as though he was remembering that night, too. Little shifts in his expression told her that he was reliving it all just as she was. The shock of coming across her in the park, his anger with her for behaving so disgracefully, his sympathy for all the people she'd dragged down into the mire with her...

She tore her eyes from his and said, 'Yes—and who else, pray?'

'Another young lady who happens to be a friend of hers, Lady Susan Pettiffer, and a couple you may not know: Tom Waring—Lord Halstead, as he is now—and Miss Julia Twining. But does it really matter? Courtlands is a vast building. You need not even speak to any of them, should you not wish to. Please, think about it seriously.'

Serious? Could there be anything more serious than to hear that *these* were the women from whom he meant to make his choice?

Admittedly Lucy Beresford must *seem* as though she would make a good countess, in that she had a zeal for charitable works. Oh, yes, she could just picture her swanning into the houses of the *deserving poor* on his estates, distributing largesse with a self-satisfied smile.

And, yes, admittedly Lady Susan had a brilliant mind. She read extensively, attended lectures at all sorts of obscure scientific societies and could talk at great length upon just about any topic under the sun. He could probably see her presiding over fabulous dinners...where she would cut the less brilliant among them down to size with her rapier wit.

And, in spite of what he thought, she did know who Miss Julia Twining was. She'd found out last night on the way home, when she'd asked for the name of the plump girl with whom he'd sat out the quadrille, attempting to draw her into conversation. A lot of men found her voluptuous curves very attractive, Lady Penrose had informed her. And the fact that she was shy was no drawback. Men often liked a woman to have a meek and biddable disposition.

Some men, yes. But surely not a man of Lord Ledbury's temperament? He would walk all over her. And grow bored with her. And make her dreadfully unhappy. For how could the poor girl do anything but fall in love with him if she married him?

He wouldn't grow bored with Lady Susan, she admitted. She was so clever there would never be any lack of things to discuss. But they could never be in total harmony, for Lord Ledbury was basically kind and Lady Susan was...not.

Lucy was beginning to look less unappealing in comparison with those two. She did at least appear to have a kind nature. Grudgingly she conceded that Lucy Beresford might not make too bad a fist as Countess of Lavenham when the time came. She would see to the welfare of the tenants—albeit in such a way that they would all feel crushed by her condescension. But what kind of wife would she be? Not a loving one.

And Lord Ledbury ought to have a wife who loved him. When she thought of how hurt he must have been when his family ignored his sufferings after his injury at Orthez... And how he had more or less expected it...

No. She couldn't bear to think of the rest of his life being as grim and cheerless as his youth must have been. She must warn him what these three girls were really like. There was plenty of time to find someone else—someone with whom he stood a chance of finding some measure of happiness.

She turned to him, intending to warn him that if he married any one of these three girls he would regret it for the rest of his life. She even drew a breath to form the words.

But she never spoke them aloud. For she could not believe he would heed any warning *she* might give him. Not the girl he'd caught making a total fool of herself over a man like Harry. She'd demonstrated she was an exceptionally poor judge of character by being so completely taken in.

Oh, this was awful. Her own unhappiness seemed so small and petty in comparison with the misery upon which he was about to embark.

What on earth was she to do?

She wasn't sure she could bear to go to Courtlands and witness him proposing to one of those girls, knowing it would lead to a lifetime of misery for him.

But if she didn't go she would feel as if she'd abandoned the one person who'd selflessly come to her aid not once, but several times in the few weeks since they'd met.

'I will think about it,' she said, her throat feeling as though she had swallowed broken glass.

'Then I suppose I shall have to be content with that,' he said, looking anything but.

* * *

The formal invitation arrived four days later. Lady Penrose took one look at it and let out a little cry of delight.

'Oh, my dear! Just think what this means! Nobody who has witnessed the very close attention he has been paying you could possibly mistake Lord Ledbury's intention.'

Well, clearly they could, thought Lady Jayne bitterly. The fact that she was on the guest list did *not* mean that he wanted to marry her. He was just killing two birds with one stone. Forging ahead with his campaign to make a brilliant match, whilst doing his chivalrous best to offer a friend for whom he felt sorry some respite from the nightmare her Season had become.

'Naturally you will not be the only young lady who has been invited,' Lady Penrose continued. 'That would look too obvious. But I am sure you are the one he intends to offer for. Only think of the gallant way he came to your rescue after that masquerade. The posies he sent you every day...'

'I do not think I wish to attend.' She had thought long and hard about it, and come to the conclusion that there was nothing she could do to sway a man of Lord Ledbury's determined nature. All she would achieve by attending his wretched house party would be to make herself more miserable than she already was.

Lady Penrose's mouth gaped. 'You cannot mean that!' She looked intently into her face. 'Or perhaps you do.' She laid her hand briefly over Lady Jayne's. 'It was your grandfather's idea you should find a husband this Season. Not yours at all. And if you do not wish to marry Lord Ledbury then you are quite right.

We ought to refuse this invitation. It would not do to raise false hope in his breast. That would be unkind.'

'It is not that…' There was no hope in his breast at all. But how to explain her certainty without confessing the nature of their entanglement?

Lady Penrose clucked her tongue and shook her head. 'I see. You enjoy his company but you are not ready to make such a momentous decision. Well, I never did think you were old enough for a London Season. I told your grandfather that it would have been better to take you to Bath, or Harrogate, or perhaps a seaside resort this year—just to try your wings in public, without all this pressure to settle down—but there. What could I do?'

Lady Penrose laid the invitation aside with evident regret.

'Now, while we are on the subject of your grandfather, I think I had better tell you at once that I have received a rather…unsettling letter from him.'

Her heart sank. He must have finally announced that she had fabricated prior knowledge of Milly, and Lady Penrose was going to take her to task for the deception.

'I am sorry if he is angry with you about Milly. But you see, I…'

'Milly? How can he possibly be angry about Milly when he knows nothing about…' Lady Penrose trailed off, looking a little uncomfortable.

'You did not mention my friendship with her?' Lady Jayne was astounded.

'No.' She flushed. 'I knew full well that your grandfather would disapprove of her. But he left you here under my care. And in my judgement the fact that she is of lowly birth is outweighed by the fact you enjoy her company so much. I have noticed that you do not make friends easily. That, of course, is because your grandfather would not allow you to mix with anyone except long-standing connections to the family.' She pulled a disapproving face. 'Only when you are with Miss Brigstock do you unbend and become the carefree girl you ought to be at your age. She makes you laugh. For that alone I would defy a hundred cross old earls. But that has nothing to do with the case. Here,' she said, thrusting the page towards Lady Jayne. 'You might as well read it for yourself.'

Lady Jayne's astonishment increased. Lady Penrose had never permitted her to look at any of the letters her grandfather had written before, even though they referred to her. But then she was clearly still a bit flustered after her admission that she'd deliberately defied Lord Caxton by omitting to mention Milly to him.

Well, well. It seemed Lady Jayne was not the only one who instinctively rebelled against her grandfather's high-handed attitude.

With a little smile upon her face, she bent her head to peruse his letter. But after she had scanned only the first few lines she felt as though her world had been turned upside down.

He had received confirmation that her scandalous aunt, Lady Aurora, had died some years previously. But her daughter had recently returned to England and, due to what Grandfather referred to as a stroke of good luck, had been made known to him. Her breathing grew faster, and more shallow, as she read with increasing resentment how this girl, Aimée, had spent her childhood jaunting all over Europe, having—just as she had imagined—all kinds of adventures, before marrying the Earl of Bowdon and making her home in Staffordshire.

But what hurt her beyond anything else was the list of instructions he gave Lady Penrose regarding Jayne's reception of this Aimée when she came to Town.

As if she was not quite capable of knowing how to behave!

And to think of this cousin, experiencing the delights of Rome and Paris and Naples, whilst she had been immured in Kent, hedged about with draconian governesses! Or occasionally escorted to the houses of families she had known from birth, where she was not even permitted to walk down a corridor without a maid to dog her footsteps. And now he *admonished*—yes, that was the word he had used—*admonished* Lady Penrose to ensure her compliance with his plans to reinstate cousin Aimée into Society. The family had to stand together in this, he had insisted, underlining the word *together* twice. The girl was not to be held accountable for the sins of her parents.

Suddenly she knew exactly how the stay-at-home brother had felt when his father killed the fatted calf to welcome the prodigal home. She had always thought him a rather mean-spirited sort of fellow when hearing the parable expounded before, but here was her grandfather, expecting her to drop everything and— and *perform* for him like some kind of trained poodle, with Lady Penrose flicking the whip to guarantee the quality of her performance. Well, she would not have it!

'This is rather inconvenient, is it not?' she said coldly, handing the letter back to Lady Penrose. Inside she was seething with resentment and hurt. But nobody would ever have guessed. She did not know it, but she had never resembled her father so much in her life.

'Inconvenient?'

'Well, yes. Because, having given it careful thought, I have decided I ought to accept the invitation to Lord Ledbury's house party. So I will not be in Town when this long-lost cousin arrives, will I?'

Lady Penrose looked at the letter, then to Lady Jayne's face, and to the writing table by the window on which all the invitations lay scattered.

'You have changed your mind about the house party...?'

'*Made up* my mind, Lady Penrose. Don't you think it is positively my *duty* to go? After all, Grandfather sent me to London for the express purpose of finding me a husband.' *Get the chit married off,* had been his exact words, she recalled bitterly. 'And I do seem to have captured the interest of a man of whom he would thoroughly approve. If I do not attend this house party,' she said airily, 'Lord Ledbury might slip right through my fingers.'

A smile of comprehension spread slowly across Lady Penrose's face. 'Oh, indeed, yes. It *is* your duty to do all you can to attach the kind of husband of whom your grandfather would approve. And I,' she said, taking up her pen with an air of unholy glee, 'am going to take great pleasure in writing to inform him that his plans to come to Town and make us all dance to his tune will just have to wait a week or two.'

Chapter Nine

Lady Jayne twisted her hands together in her lap. She couldn't believe she'd done it again. Had she learned nothing from the scrapes she'd got into in London?

Making Lady Penrose her accomplice to get her into the Lambournes' masquerade was as nothing compared to this. It made not a scrap of difference that her chaperone was thoroughly enjoying flouting her grandfather's wishes. She had let her temper get the better of her, and not only was she going to Lord Ledbury's house party but...

She darted a glance at the other occupants of the carriage, who were chattering away as though neither of them had a care in the world.

She should never have dragged Milly into it. And yet at the time, with her temper raging so hot, it had seemed like the perfect solution. Well, that was because she hadn't stopped to calm down and think rationally. She had just told Lady Penrose that she would enjoy the house party much more if she had her dear friend with her, and her chaperone had made all the arrangements.

With the result that here they all were, travelling down to Courtlands together.

She turned her head sharply and looked out of the window, lest the other two should attempt to include her in their conversation. She didn't know what to say to them. How to deal with the guilt she felt at the disaster that was looming. Lord Ledbury was going to be so... angry. Confused. Hurt.

Why hadn't she taken his reaction that night she'd taken Milly to the theatre into consideration? When she had thought it would be a lovely surprise for him to see how beautifully Milly could cope with polite society. But it had been no such thing. She might as well have taken a dagger and plunged it into his heart. And this... this sneaking of her into Courtlands would be ten times worse. For he was actually steeling himself to propose to someone. Only of course she hadn't thought of that in the moments immediately after reading her grandfather's letter. She had just thought that men were so *stupid,* and so *tyrannical* that what could any woman with an ounce of spirit do but thwart them at every turn?

It wasn't even as if she had been angry with Lord Ledbury, either. But somehow her determination to thwart male stupidity had spilled over into her muddled thoughts about his house party and before she knew it she'd decided to get Milly down there to stop him proposing to any of those women who were bound to make him miserable. She knew he wouldn't listen to any arguments she might put forth. But he surely couldn't withstand the appeal of Milly herself? Surely he couldn't do anything so cruel as to propose to another woman whilst Milly was under his roof?

And before she knew it not only was Lady Penrose

up to her neck in schemes to defy their menfolk, but Milly, too, was gleefully anticipating seeing the look on Lord Ledbury's face when she walked into Courtlands through the front door.

So even when she'd begun to have second thoughts she hadn't been able to back down. Milly would have been so disappointed if she'd tried to put her off. But it hadn't been until they'd actually climbed into the coach this morning that she'd begun to consider there would be even further-reaching consequences. For that poor cousin of hers.

It was not going to be easy for Aimée to carve out a place for herself in Society, even if she had now married an earl. And, had Grandpapa not ordered her about in his usual overbearing, not to say insulting manner, she would have been thrilled to be meeting her and hearing all about her adventures.

Oh, bother her temper! Well, she would make it up to her cousin once this house party was over. She would most definitely not stand for anyone turning their noses up at her just because she was unfortunate enough to be the product of a runaway marriage. Really, the rules that governed Society were ridiculous! If not for those rules her aunt Aurora would never have had to elope in the first place. And Lord Ledbury could just marry Milly, and then there would have been no need for her to have resorted to such underhanded tactics.

Though it was no use trying to lay the blame elsewhere. She held herself entirely responsible for the disaster that was about to unfold. Lord Ledbury was going to be so angry with her for meddling. He had been most tolerant of her behaviour up to now, but this latest escapade was completely unforgivable…

And then it was too late, for the carriage was slowing for the turn between the two gateposts guarding the entrance to Courtlands.

Milly fell silent. Both girls pressed their noses to the window, straining for their first glimpse of Lord Ledbury's ancestral home.

It didn't disappoint. Not that it was anywhere near as imposing as Darvill Park, her grandfather's mansion in Kent, for it was a scrambling mixture of styles, as though it had been added to by successive generations in accordance with the architectural style of the day. But it did look welcoming.

Even the immense grey-stone *porte-cochère,* under which their carriage drew up, looked as though it had been added for the comfort and convenience of guests, rather than to blend in with the ivy-clad redbrick frontage of the house.

She was glad of its shelter, for it had been raining steadily all day. But her knees were trembling as she climbed out of the coach, dreading Lord Ledbury's reaction.

She grasped Milly's hand as they climbed the four shallow steps to the front door. Her guilt redoubled. Milly had far more to risk from this venture than she did. What had she done?

She went quite faint with relief when she saw a housekeeper standing in the open door, rather than their host. It only delayed the inevitable confrontation, but once Mrs Hargreaves had shown them up to their suite of rooms at least she no longer had to fear the prospect of being turned away altogether.

'This is lovely,' said Milly, wandering over to look

out of Lady Jayne's window, which was right over the *porte-cochère,* at the front of the house.

'What is your room like?' Lady Jayne crossed their shared sitting room and opened a door on the far side. 'It is a bit small.'

'I've slept in far worse,' said Milly with a grin. 'And at least we've got this—' she indicated the sitting room '—to escape to if things get a bit uncomfortable downstairs.'

'Oh, Milly, I'm beginning to think I should not have brought you here. Lord Ledbury is bound to be angry. What if I've ruined everything for you?'

'I wanted to come here,' said Milly, and turned away with a pained expression on her face. 'At least I can see what it would be like to live as a fine lady, if only for a few days.'

Lady Jayne recalled Lord Ledbury's words on the night of the theatre, that it wasn't kind to show Milly a world in which she could never have so much as a toehold. And she felt more ashamed of herself than ever.

They had both washed and changed out of their travelling clothes by the time Lady Penrose came to their room. She had her own suite of rooms, she told them, on the same corridor, but with quite a different view. And not nearly so large.

'But then, I have it all to myself,' she said, with a smile for both girls. 'Are you ready?' She ran her eyes over their outfits, though Lady Jayne knew she would find nothing about Milly's appearance with which to find fault. Only Lord Ledbury would know she was not a perfectly respectable young lady, brought along to act as her companion. What was more, it was not only her appearance that Lady Jayne had changed. She had spent hours drilling her, so that she now knew as much about how to behave during a country house party as any young lady who'd been bred to it.

Lady Penrose gave her nod of approval and rang for a footman to escort them all downstairs to the rose salon, where Mrs Hargreaves had told them guests assembled before going in to dinner.

Lady Jayne's heart was pounding erratically by the time their footman opened a door, bowed and withdrew, to indicate they had arrived. She peeped anxiously past Lady Penrose's shoulder. Lord Ledbury was standing just inside the door.

When he saw Milly, the bland smile of welcome died from his lips. His hand clenched convulsively on the back of the chair on which he'd been leaning, his knuckles turning white. While he said all the correct things to Lady Penrose, Milly sidled past him and scuttled into the room. Lady Jayne could not blame her for running for cover. He was quite fearsome when his eyes turned all wintry like that.

When he'd finished greeting Lady Penrose, he turned the full force of his disapproval upon her.

Out of long habit of enduring blistering scolds from her grandfather, she composed her features and looked straight back at him. Though she fully accepted she was the one Lord Ledbury would blame for leading Milly astray, she had no intention of cringing or making excuses. Not here, in the doorway, with all those beady eyes watching avidly from behind their languidly waving fans.

'Lady Jayne,' he said, through gritted teeth that from a distance might have passed for a polite smile. 'I had no idea you would be bringing Mi...Miss Brigstock.'

He leaned in closer and whispered right into her ear, in a furious undertone, 'What on earth possessed you to do such a thing? Are you mad?'

She smiled up at him, and playfully tapped his shoulder with her fan, as though he had made some flirtatious remark. 'Determined,' she replied.

'Determined to do what?'

She shook her head and wagged her finger reprovingly. 'You will thank me later. I know you will. So don't pretend to be cross.'

'I am not pretending, da…dash it all. Oh, this is intolerable,' he hissed, darting a glance over his shoulder to see exactly how many of his guests were watching their interplay. Leaning in close again, he growled threateningly, 'We will have to speak privately about this. Later.'

She smiled up at him enigmatically, hoping he would take the look as acquiescence. For she had no intention of getting into a tête-à-tête with him.

'I shall get a message to your maid. My God,' he said, closing his eyes briefly and shuddering. 'To think I once said I would *never* sink to the level of smuggling notes to you via your maid. And now you have got me saying I shall do exactly that. The minute you set foot in my house, you have…' He opened his eyes and stared down at her. 'You are just like one of Congreve's rockets. So small and innocuous-looking, but if a man takes his eyes off you there is no telling what direction you will veer, or where the next explosion will go off.'

Since she'd spent the entire journey bewailing her lack of control over her temper, she could hardly argue with that assessment. So why did it hurt so much to hear Lord Ledbury say it out loud?

'One day you will apologise for speaking to me like

that,' she said vehemently. And, raising her chin, she stalked past him and made straight for the sofa on which Lady Penrose was sitting.

She sank onto the cushions with more necessity than grace. And it took her some time to stop trembling. The confrontation with Lord Ledbury had taken more out of her than she'd expected.

If she weren't so well-trained she would fling herself back amongst the cushions, cover her face with her hands, and wail with misery. For there were still five days of this to get through.

Instead, she consoled herself by observing that the other young ladies already down, Miss Twining and Miss Beresford, were also sitting beside their own chaperones, looking just as edgy as she felt.

The gentlemen of the party were all standing by a window which, to judge from the snatches of conversation she could overhear, overlooked the stables. Amongst them was a tall, bulky, elderly gentleman who was telling them about the various rides to be had in the vicinity. She assumed he must be Lord Ledbury's grandfather, Lord Lavenham.

Lord Ledbury was welcoming a latecomer to the room when she eventually gave herself permission to look his way again. Lady Susan Pettiffer was smiling up at him. And he was smiling right back, as though he didn't mind *her* flirting with him. He wasn't telling *her* she was like an unexploded bomb he dared not take his eyes off, or castigating *her* for polluting his orderly house with her unruly presence. Her fingers curled into claws. *I shan't let you have him,* she vowed under her breath.

And began to feel much better. All the people who'd

come here were playing their own game. And hers was no worse than anyone else's. That cat Lady Susan did not love Lord Ledbury in the least. She just wanted to be a countess.

At least she was not plotting anything for selfish reasons. She resolutely ignored the little voice that whispered how she always said it was for a good cause when she was about to embark on some course of action she knew was questionable. It had been her temper that had led her into this, not duplicity! She'd gone and committed herself to this house party, and when she'd known there was no way out of it she'd wished she could find some way to prevent him from becoming a sacrifice on the altar of family duty. She couldn't have borne to watch him pledge himself to anyone but the woman she knew he loved. Knowing she'd secured his happiness was the *only* thing that would console her for knowing *she* did not even make the running. The one comfort she would take with her into the future she saw unfolding before her. The future where she dwindled to an old maid, living the life of an eccentric recluse, since *nobody* would ever want to marry Chilblain Jayne.

She managed to eat a respectable amount at dinner, considering the tension that had her strung tight as a bow. Milly helped by behaving impeccably. She conversed in turn with each of her dining partners, making Lady Jayne want to nudge Lord Ledbury, and say, *See?*

Only he was not seated near enough for her to do any such thing. And whenever she looked his way he studiously ignored her. Though from the way he chewed his food and threw his wine into his mouth he was barely keeping a lid on his own temper.

It was only after dinner, when all the ladies withdrew, that Lady Jayne perceived Milly was not entirely at ease at all. It was when she came straight to her side, clutching her fan, white-knuckled, that she appreciated just how much of an ordeal this must be for her. She had warned Milly that after dinner the ladies would all be expected to perform for the gentlemen. And Milly had confessed that she had never learned to play a musical instrument.

It had taken some planning and hours of practise to surmount this obstacle. Fortunately Milly had a good strong singing voice. After putting their heads together, they'd come up with several ballads with which they were both familiar. Lady Jayne would play the music as she sang, with Milly accompanying her and, with the help of subtle prompts, turning the pages so that it looked as though she knew how to read music. They had only gone through the pieces a couple of times before Milly began to improvise a very pleasing harmony to the melody Lady Jayne was to be singing. To her delight, although Milly lacked formal training, she had certainly heard far worse from girls who'd had the benefit of years of expensive tuition.

The only thing that might let them down was Milly's nerves.

Lady Jayne need not have worried. After a slightly wobbly start, which only served to make Milly look appropriately bashful, their performance went without a hitch. And, judging from Miss Beresford's look of acute annoyance when the gentlemen of the party applauded their duet with what she thought sounded like genuine appreciation, they really had done themselves proud.

Lord Ledbury alone did not applaud. He kept his

arms folded, glowering at them both tight-lipped. He'd
clearly realized that to perform so well together they
must have put in hours of practise. Which meant they
had both flouted his orders not to meet each other. She
returned to her seat in a subdued frame of mind. Yet another crime for him to lay at her door. Although, from
what Milly had told her, Milly herself had never been all
that biddable to start with. She thought nothing of going
behind Lord Ledbury's back, or *acting on her own ini-
tiative,* as she phrased it, when she disagreed with him.

But justifying her actions by mentally accusing Milly
of being as intractable as she was did not make Lady
Jayne feel any less uncomfortable.

Nor did the look of malicious triumph Lady Susan
shot her. Nobody could possibly guess what had pro-
voked Lord Ledbury's simmering fury, but it was
enough to encourage her pretensions. Because he had
applauded everyone else's performance.

The evening only grew more uncomfortable after
that. The other prospective brides were trying too hard
to impress Lord Ledbury. And since he was in a foul
mood, due to her bringing Milly along, their efforts to
please him were only making them look increasingly
desperate.

Eventually the arrival of the tea tray heralded the imminent cessation of hostilities. She went to fetch a cup
of tea for Lady Penrose, since she had become deeply
engrossed in conversation with Miss Twining's duenna.
She was not all that surprised when, the moment she
reached the table where Mrs Hargreaves presided over
the teacups, Lord Ledbury materialised at her side.

Before he had the chance to lay into her, she smiled

up at him brightly and said, 'Yes, thank you, I am having a lovely time. *Such* congenial company.'

'Sarcasm does not become you.'

'I am not being sarcastic. Well, not wholly. I like the look of your grandfather.' She regarded the rotund old gentleman wistfully. He was laughing heartily at something Lady Susan had said. She did not think she had ever seen her own grandfather laugh like that. Least of all at any sally a girl as young as that could make. He would be more likely to treat her to one of his withering stares and remove himself to the card room. 'He looks so jolly.'

'He looks,' Lord Ledbury retorted with disgust, 'like a man who is getting his own way. You should have seen the way he reacted when I asked if I might hold this house party and have a few of my friends to spend a few days here. He has very generously offered to run his eye over every female I have considered as a potential bride and give me the benefit of his advice. As if I was not perfectly capable of choosing my own wife!'

Some of Lady Jayne's tension dissolved at the realisation that not *all* of his anger stemmed from something she had done. In fact, she found it very encouraging that he was confiding in her like this. It proved that he found it as easy to talk to her as she did to him. Something inside her settled, like a knot coming unravelled. Even though they had quarrelled, he still considered her a friend.

But she was not going to offer him her sympathy. Apart from firmly believing he *was* going about finding a wife in completely the wrong way, the last thing he would want was to think she pitied him.

'Well, I must say,' she said quite frankly, 'judging

from the people you have invited, I tend to agree that you are in dire need of somebody's advice.'

'What do you mean? I have very good reasons for inviting each and every one of my guests.'

Not that he had any intention of explaining those reasons to her now, with so many of them within earshot. Possibly not ever.

For it was a bit galling to have to admit that Lady Susan and Lucy Beresford were the only two women he'd met so far this Season that he could actually remember anything about when they weren't in the room. Lady Susan was, in fact, exactly the sort of woman he'd had in mind before he'd met Lady Jayne. She was bright, witty, capable and well-connected. She was sure to leave her mark on the world.

And as for Lucy—well, as Berry's sister he couldn't very well *not* remember her. He'd decided he might as well invite her down here, to see if he could learn to find something about her to appeal to him as a man.

Which had led him to invite Miss Twining, too. For he had noticed that Berry was developing quite a tendre for the girl. Unfortunately she was so bashful it was well nigh impossible to tell whether she returned his regard. Only once or twice had he noticed her casting Berry glances that indicated his feelings might be reciprocated, if only he would pluck up the courage to make the first move. So Lord Ledbury had decided to give them a helping hand. A few days down here should resolve matters between them. Because between them he and his grandfather had organized a whole series of activities conducive to courtship.

That had made quite a small party, so he'd cast his net a bit wider and thought of Lord Halstead, who had apparently gone to Milly's assistance during the Lambourne masquerade. When he'd gone round to give Milly a piece of his mind for exposing Lady Jayne to danger by encouraging her to see Kendell behind his back, she'd angrily retorted that Lady Jayne had not been the only one who'd needed help that night. 'If it had not been for Lord Halstead I don't know how I would have got home safe. Not in that outfit.'

Not that he'd admitted to the fellow that was why he'd been invited. It was damned risky, having him here as well as Milly. He rubbed his hand over the crown of his head. Hopefully he hadn't seen Milly anywhere near Lady Jayne that night and would continue to think he'd been invited to make up the numbers. He certainly hadn't questioned the reason for his invitation at the time. Just jumped at the chance to spend a few days in the countryside on a repairing lease.

'More to the point,' he said to Lady Jayne, having shot a significant look in Milly's direction, 'I had very good reasons for *not* inviting others.'

She pursed her lips. She was doing it to express exasperation with him, no doubt, but to his way of thinking it looked just as though she was puckering up for a kiss.

'They are not good reasons,' she said mutinously. 'They are absolutely stupid reasons.'

He stopped wanting to kiss her. No, what he wanted to do now was grab her by the shoulders and shake her. Had she no idea what damage could be done to her reputation if it once got about that she had introduced his mistress into Society? Not that Milly *was* his mistress, but that was what everyone would think if they discovered his connection to her.

And he'd warned her that it was dangerous.... But

she'd said she didn't care. That was the thing about Lady Jayne. She was loyal to a fault. He could not fathom why she'd brought Milly here, and the cryptic remarks she'd made earlier about making him grateful had made no sense at first. But he was beginning to wonder if she didn't consider herself on some sort of crusade.

'We have got to have a serious talk,' he said grimly. 'Somewhere nobody else can overhear us, so that you can explain yourself. At the side of the house there is a shrubbery. You can get out to it by going out of the library doors and down the steps at the end of the terrace. Meet me there tomorrow, before breakfast.'

He turned and stalked off, having delivered his orders as though he expected her to snap to attention, salute and say, *Yes, Sir!*

Well, if he thought he could order her about like that, he had another think coming! Besides, she had no intention of getting into a potentially compromising position with him. The whole point of coming down here was to promote Milly's case with his family. If only she could have a few days' grace, to prove how well she could fit in, then he could announce that his search for a bride was over. Once they'd got to know her for the sunny, charming person she was, surely they would have no objections to him making her his countess? Why, in comparison with the other girls he'd brought down here Milly was like a rose among thorns.

Yes, within a few days he could introduce Milly to the world as the woman he loved, and they would all live happily ever after.

Well, Lord Ledbury and Milly would, anyway. She shivered as she had another vision of the bleak future awaiting her, and added an extra spoonful of sugar to her cup of tea. As she walked across the room to join Lady Penrose she consoled herself with the reflection that her chaperone lived alone, unmarried and was perfectly content.

She would be, too.

So long as she knew that Lord Ledbury was happy.

Chapter Ten

The next morning, when she went down to breakfast, she only had to glance at Lord Ledbury, who was savagely sawing away at a slice of sirloin, to see that he was furious with her for not keeping their assignation in the shrubbery. She lifted her chin as a footman held out a chair for her and took her place at the table. He would thank her one day. She just had to have the determination to ride out his annoyance and stick to her guns.

Why did one talk about sticking to guns? She had often wondered. It sounded like such an absurd thing to do. Guns recoiled after being fired, and if one stuck to them surely one would be flung about most uncomfortably? She would ask him to explain it to her one day. Since he had been in the army for such a long time he was bound to know what the expression really meant.

She lifted her head to look at him, anticipating the conversation, and was shocked by the chill with which he met her gaze.

Jolted by the searing pain that shot through her on receipt of that look, she lowered her eyes to her place setting. What if he never forgave her for meddling in

Play the Lucky Hearts Game

and get...
2 FREE BOOKS and
2 FREE MYSTERY GIFTS...
YOURS TO KEEP!

yes! I have scratched off the gold card.
Please send me my *2 FREE BOOKS* and
2 FREE MYSTERY GIFTS (gifts are worth about $10).
I understand that I am under no obligation to purchase
any books as explained on the back of this card.

Scratch Here!
Then look below to see what your
cards get you...2 Free Books
& 2 Free Mystery Gifts!

246/349 HDL FJCQ

FIRST NAME

LAST NAME

ADDRESS

APT.#

CITY

STATE/PROV.

ZIP/POSTAL CODE

Visit us online at
www.ReaderService.com

Twenty-one gets you
2 FREE BOOKS and
2 FREE MYSTERY GIFTS!

Twenty gets you
2 FREE BOOKS!

Nineteen gets you
1 FREE BOOK!

TRY AGAIN!

Offer limited to one per household and not applicable to series that subscriber is currently receiving.

Your Privacy—The Reader Service is committed to protecting your privacy. Our Privacy Policy is available online at www.ReaderService.com or upon request from the Reader Service. We make a portion of our mailing list available to reputable third parties that offer products we believe may interest you. If you prefer that we not exchange your name with third parties, or if you wish to clarify or modify your communication preferences, please visit us at www.ReaderService.com/consumerschoice or write to us at Reader Service Preference Service, P.O. Box 9062, Buffalo, NY 14269. Include your complete name and address.

© 2011 HARLEQUIN ENTERPRISES LIMITED. Printed in the U.S.A. ▼ DETACH AND MAIL CARD TODAY! ▼

H-H-11/11

The Re

Accepting
books
you ju
is jus
6 m

*Te
cha
be

BUSINESS REPLY MAIL

FIRST-CLASS MAIL PERMIT NO. 717 BUFFALO, NY

POSTAGE WILL BE PAID BY ADDRESSEE

THE READER SERVICE

PO BOX 1867

BUFFALO NY 14240-9952

NO POSTAGE
NECESSARY
IF MAILED
IN THE
UNITED STATES

his search for the perfect bride? He was the one person, apart from Milly, with whom she had ever been able to converse openly.

She spooned some jam disconsolately onto the side of her plate, though her appetite had vanished completely. She had meant well, but perhaps it would have been better not to have meddled in his love life?

Better for her. Yes, it would have been easier for her to just keep out of it. That would have been the sensible thing to do, and the course she had been tempted to take. But could she have lived with herself if she had stood back and let Lord Ledbury marry the wrong woman? No.

She firmed her mouth, picked up her knife and, with great deliberation, spread the jam onto a warm roll. Lord Ledbury deserved to find some happiness. And she would do whatever she could to help him achieve it.

'It looks as though the weather today is going to be fair and warm,' Lord Lavenham suddenly announced in a voice loud enough to carry above the muted conversations going on around the crowded breakfast table.

She would never have believed every single one of the girls invited would be such early risers. Clearly none of them had any intention of letting any of the others gain so much as five minutes' advantage in their pursuit of Lord Ledbury.

'I should be pleased to give as many of you as would care for it a tour about the estate. We shall convene in about an hour, in the stable block—if that gives you ladies enough time to get ready,' he said with a chuckle. 'I shall be able to match you all up with suitable mounts.'

The gentlemen, she assumed, would have brought their own horses.

'Now, I know that the ground will be a bit soft after all the recent rain, but I do not want you to worry about muddying your riding habits. For those of you who do not wish to ride this morning, I shall provide other transport.'

She met Milly's eye. What a stroke of luck! Milly did not know how to ride side-saddle, so the offer of a carriage ride to preserve the ladies' clothing was a wonderful cover for her lack of that particular accomplishment. So far, things could not be going better.

She felt more cheerful than she had for an age when she entered the stable block about an hour later. One of the things she had hated most about London was not being able to canter through the woods at Darvill Park in the misty dawn, or indulge in a breakneck gallop across open fields. In anticipation of just such a treat, when she had decided to come to this house party she had purchased a new riding habit. In honour of Lord Ledbury's military service she had gone for a severely tailored midnight-blue jacket with silver frogging round the buttons and silver-lace epaulettes. The hat she wore with it was one of those so popular at the moment, which looked a bit like a soldier's shako with a little white cockade.

Lady Penrose walked across to the barouche in which Miss Twining's chaperone was already sitting. The hood was pushed back, to allow them to get a good view of the estate, but it could be pulled up in the event of further rain.

Lady Susan, Miss Twining and Miss Beresford were already making their selection from the line of horses being held by some grooms. She had no idea how keen they really were on riding, but since the older ladies in the carriage would be obliged to stick to the roads, no husband-hunter worth her salt would pass up such a golden opportunity to shake off her chaperone. On horseback, the girls could disappear into a copse, or over the brow of a hill, for minutes at a time without incurring too much disapproval.

Lord Ledbury was lounging against the stable wall, his arms crossed, but when he saw her party he pushed himself upright and made towards them, his expression as forbidding as she had ever seen it.

Milly detached herself from Lady Jayne's side, made straight for the curricle in which Lord Halstead intended to drive himself and wasted no time in clambering up beside him.

Lady Jayne could not blame her. It would take a very brave person indeed not to quail before the look in Lord Ledbury's eyes as he stalked across the stable yard.

'Allow me to help you choose your mount,' he said through gritted teeth. When he crooked his arm, she dared do nothing but meekly take it and let him lead her across the yard to where the horses were lined up.

The other ladies looked daggers at her to see her receiving such special attention from their quarry. She looked straight through them. She did not care how much they hated her so long as she could prevent any of them from getting their claws into Lord Ledbury.

Since she was the last down to the stable yard there was little choice left. But the spirited-looking bay mare which Miss Twining had just rejected, after it had tossed its head and rolled its eyes when she reached out to pat its neck, looked as though it would suit her perfectly. The groom was having to hold its bridle with some determination to prevent it from skipping sideways across the cobbles. It was itching to get out and have some fun.

Well, so was she!

While she was making friends with the creature—whose name, the groom informed her with a meaningful look, was Mischief—Lord Ledbury strode away and, somewhat to her surprise, himself mounted up. True, the creature on which he was now sitting looked weary to the point of somnolence, but he was on horseback.

She had never seen him ride before. In fact, from the way he'd talked about his injuries, she'd suspected he might spend the rest of his life as a semi-invalid.

But he was fit enough to ride with them this morning. Which was absolutely wonderful.

She mounted Mischief and spent some time rearranging her skirts to give herself time to get her feelings under control. Had there been nobody else about she thought she might have rushed over and hugged him. Or broken out into a loud cheer. Or…something. She did not know what.

She had still not quite succeeded in regaining full control of her sheer delight by the time he positioned his beast beside hers as they began to exit the yard. In fact, she turned and beamed at him.

'How do you have the nerve to smile at me like that?' he snapped, dousing her joy at the sign of his return to health. 'Do you know how long I waited for you outside in the cold this morning? And don't tell me you never leave your room before breakfast. I know full well you can get up and dressed and go out to meet men when it suits you,' he finished bitterly.

There was nothing that would stop her from doing anything she put her mind to. He had seen her scramble up a tree like a monkey, having donned breeches under her dress, so that she could sneak out and dally with Lieutenant Kendell in the park at dawn.

'I could not help it,' she said, though she was not smiling any more. 'Are you not pleased to be on horse-back again, too?'

He sighed. She had no idea how badly she had hurt him by not keeping their assignation. Well, it had taken him by surprise, too. Another proof, as if he needed any, that he was in love with her.

Falling in love was a damnable business, he thought, scowling. A bit like being at sea. When he'd seen her sauntering towards him in that outfit, with that smile on her face, his heart had soared. Then as abruptly plunged to his boots when he realized she hadn't chosen a mili-tary style for any reason that had anything to do with him. It was probably just the current fashion.

Yes, just like being at sea. Whether his mood was on the crest of the wave, or plunging into a trough, he never stopped feeling sick at heart.

Perhaps he ought to abandon this particular ship. He would certainly feel as if he'd got his feet back on firm ground if he stopped wondering whether he might ever induce Lady Jayne to marry him.

He could set off back on his original course. The one which would lead him to make a practical union with a woman who would bring lustre to the family line.

Only he'd lost any enthusiasm for going down that route. Oh, yes, he'd be on an even keel again. But he suspected it would be like slogging across a flat, bar-ren, joyless landscape, with him frequently looking over his shoulder at what might have been.

'Pleased to be on horseback?' He turned his pessimistic mood on the poor unfortunate beast he'd just mounted. 'I would hardly grace this animal upon which I am sitting with the appellation of *horse*. In fact I do not think I have ever sat a creature which more nearly resembles an armchair in all my life. Even as a boy the first pony I was put up on by my groom had the energy to break into a trot upon occasion.'

Lady Jayne giggled. And it felt as though the sun had come out. It was the first time anything he had said had actually amused her. To hell with any thought of abandoning ship. This was progress. Real progress.

'Well, I expect it will be some time before your leg is strong enough to warrant mounting anything with too much spirit,' she observed, running her eyes along the length of his thigh.

Dear God, how he wished it was her little hands making the journey. He had never met any creature with more spirit, or more worth mounting, than the deceptively dainty-looking Lady Jayne.

To keep his mind off erotic images of Lady Jayne writhing beneath him with the kind of enthusiasm a man yearned for but very rarely found in his bed partner, he urged his recalcitrant mount into a forward motion.

Lady Jayne, by contrast, appeared to be exerting all her strength in holding Mischief back.

'Will it… I hope you do not mind me asking…. Will it mend completely, do you think? You do not limp as much as you used to. And you do not seem to need your cane very often now, either.'

'My leg wants only exercise to resume its former strength. Just like the rest of me.'

From the corner of his eye he saw her frown pensively.

'Yes, Milly told me you had a recurrent fever that laid you low throughout the winter.'

Hmm… The girls talked about him, did they?

'I cannot imagine a gently bred young lady being truly interested in hearing all the gory details of a protracted illness.' Unless she was interested in the patient.

'Oh, well…' She couldn't admit that she greedily devoured any tidbits Milly ever divulged about his past life. 'Do you object?'

Mischief shook her head irritably from side to side, indicating Lady Jayne's grip on the reins must have confused her.

'I suppose,' she said in a rather contrite tone, 'it must sound as though we have been gossiping about you. But, truly, neither of us meant any harm. It is just that sometimes, when we first met, you did not seem very well, and I did not quite dare ask *you*…'

She looked mortified, but he was heartened by her admission that she was, indeed, interested in the patient.

'When we first met,' he said, 'I was still far from well, it is true. Had I not felt it my clear duty to embark on the hunt for a wife I would not have attempted to take my place in Society at all this Season.'

He didn't look cross with her. So she plucked up the courage to add, 'You often looked very pale.'

'You noticed?' Lady Jayne had finally managed to settle Mischief to a walking pace his own mount was capable of matching. As they left the shelter of the last of the stable buildings he felt emboldened to admit, 'I thought I'd taken such good care to conceal my condition. I leaned on that cane and let people assume it was my leg that was the problem.' He laughed, a little self-deprecatingly. 'Rather that than risk my pride getting dented by passing out in the heat of a stuffy ballroom. But I don't mind admitting the truth to you, Lady Jayne.'

'You don't?'

The smile she darted at him put him in mind of a child who'd just been given an unexpected treat.

'No. I want you to know the truth about me, Lady Jayne. I want you to know who I am. All of me.' He frowned, as though choosing his next words carefully. 'The life of a soldier is harsh, Lady Jayne. Far harsher than a sheltered lady like you can possibly imagine. In summer we burn like biscuits in the heat of the sun as we march. In winter, if we cannot get shelter overnight, our blankets stick fast to the ground with ice. If we progress too fast, and the supply trains cannot keep up with us, we starve. And then, when it rains, we live in sodden clothing for days on end. Illness runs rife through the ranks, killing far more men than battles do. Even before I got my leg broken at Orthez, my constitution was pretty worn down. And then suddenly I had to stroll into ballrooms, and behave as though I was some great lord. I had never felt less like a lord in my life.'

No, she mused. He was far more like the corsair he'd dressed as the night of the masquerade. A man who helped damsels in distress to climb back in through their bedroom window rather than knock on the front door and hand them over in disgrace to their guardians.

'Th-thank you for telling me all that,' she said. He had paid her a very great compliment in confiding things to her that he deliberately concealed from everyone else. And his telling her about what it had been like to be a soldier helped her understand why he seemed so much more real than anyone she had ever met before. He had lived the kind of life most people only read about in books.

No wonder he often betrayed impatience with the pampered, shallow creatures who inhabited her world.

He heard her sigh, and saw her eyes filled with a look he found hard to interpret. Damn! He hoped he had not made her feel sorry for him. He had just wanted her to know him and…love him for himself? His mouth twisted in self-mockery. He was a lost cause. What was he doing, thinking he could win a prize like Lady Jayne with tales of warfare and injury? He wanted his head examining.

'I began to move in Society before I was ready, it is true,' he said. 'When I first went to Town doing hardly anything at all exhausted me to the point where I often went light-headed. But I have not needed that damn cane for the past couple of weeks.'

Now she came to think of it, that cane had been conspicuous by its absence on the night of the masquerade.

'The fact that you see me up on horseback, even though it is such a slug, is testament to my convalescence. The more exercise I can take, the quicker my weakened muscles will regain their full strength, I am sure.'

His full strength? What was that she had been on the receiving end of at the masquerade, then? When he'd picked her up and carried her into the conservatory it had felt as though she was wrestling with something very like a walking oak tree.

And yet he didn't consider himself to be back to his full strength?

Gracious.

And then, with a wrench—and because if she didn't

get back to the matter at hand she might spend the rest of the ride gazing in fascination at the muscles of his thighs, or remembering the feel of his arms clamping round her as he'd lifted her effortlessly off her feet—she said, 'M-Milly said that during last winter you were so poorly she sometimes despaired...'

'Yes, yes,' he said impatiently, the mention of Milly's name reminding him of the danger Lady Jayne was courting. 'You don't need to remind me how much I owe Milly. But that does not alter the fact that you should not have brought her here. Which was why I wanted to talk to you alone this morning.'

His expression turned so grim Lady Jayne's courage deserted her. She loved the way he'd opened up to her. It made her feel as though she was special to him. It would make his censure even harder to bear.

'Oh, dear,' she said, slackening her grip on the reins. 'I do not think I can...'

Mischief, sensing freedom, flung her head up and down, curvetted, then shot away at breakneck speed.

She aimed her towards a long, slow rise, crested by a belt of woodland into which she intended to disappear, trusting that the horse Lord Ledbury was riding would have neither the inclination nor the stamina to follow.

The dash up the hill took the edge off Mischief's pent-up energy, just as she'd known it would, and they entered the woodland at a steady canter. Even so, she had to bend low over Mischief's neck to preserve her hat from overhanging branches.

Since Mischief knew the terrain, Lady Jayne did not attempt to guide the creature too strictly, and was soon rewarded by her faith in the animal's instincts when they emerged into a clearing on the far side of which was just such a broad ride as she had hoped to find.

But, instead of finding herself completely alone, she heard hoofbeats thundering up behind her. When she looked over her shoulder, to her complete astonishment she saw Lord Ledbury was only a few yards away. She could not believe he had managed to get that sluggish creature to keep up with Mischief!

Though she knew why he had done so. He was determined to give her a scold. Not only for bringing Milly into his home but also for letting him think she would meet him in the shrubbery and then cravenly staying away.

She wheeled Mischief round to face him.

'I know. I am sorry. I should have let you know I was not going to meet with you this morning,' she blurted, before he had the chance to reprove her. 'I know you must be furious with me. But think, my lord. You cannot possibly want to be caught in a compromising position with me.'

She meant, he thought moodily, that it was the last thing *she* wanted. She had not been so pernickety about getting caught out with Kendell.

'As if you care a rap for propriety!'

She flinched at his condemnation of her behaviour.

'Well, I do, actually,' she replied earnestly. 'Especially when it comes to you,' she admitted, blushing. 'I would never do anything to embarrass or hurt you.'

He allowed his horse to shudder to a standstill. It dropped its head to the ground, its flanks heaving wheezily.

'Are you telling me you had no intention of punishing me for the way I issued you with orders to meet me?'

'No! It was not like that. I did resent the way you spoke to me, but I had no deliberate intent to punish you. I suppose it cannot have been very pleasant for you, waiting outside for me.' She glanced at his leg, then at his face. 'I did not think.'

She looked so contrite that he could not doubt she spoke the truth. Though she was often impulsive and thoughtless, in all the time he had known her he had never seen her be deliberately unkind to anyone.

'Very well. I acquit you of attempting to punish me.' When her face lit up he almost forgot why he had been so determined to get her alone. It took him quite an effort to say, 'But that does not mean I am not still very angry with you for bringing Milly here, when it is the last place I ever wanted to see her.'

'No!' She looked shocked. 'You cannot mean that.'

'Of course I mean it!'

'Oh, but Richard, can't you see that once your grandfather has seen with his own eyes how lovely Milly is he can surely have no further objection to you marrying her?'

'*What?*'

Lady Jayne thought he wanted to marry Milly? And that his grandfather objected? How the hell had she reached such a staggeringly inaccurate conclusion?

He swiftly reviewed that initial interview, when he'd asked her to take Milly shopping a few times, and shook his head. Had he said something that had misled her?

He looked down into her earnest little face and something inside him settled. She had not brought Milly here to deliberately flout him. To show him that she would be friends with whomever she pleased and to hell with him...

Quite the reverse.

She thought she was assisting a pair of star-crossed lovers. She had spent hours teaching Milly how to look as though she was a real lady, or at least a woman who could pass as a lady's companion…when she had not, initially, even wanted to come down here. Because she wanted him to find the happiness that had been denied her and Lieutenant Kendell.

She had put her own problems to one side in order to try and solve his.

It didn't matter to him that she'd got hold of completely the wrong end of the stick. She'd flung herself into this madcap enterprise with the sole aim of making him happy. Nobody in his entire life had ever cared if he was happy or not. Let alone gone to such lengths to attempt to secure his happiness.

How could people think she was cold and call her such vile names? She was not cold. She was warmhearted. And so beautiful, through and through.

There was a splash of mud on her face, and her hat had come askew at some point during her mad dash for the trees, releasing one golden curl from its confines. And there was nobody in the whole world to match her.

'You are such a darling,' he said huskily.

She was still looking at him warily, chewing on her lower lip.

That luscious lower lip.

Be damned to his ambition, and his search for a bride that would impress his family. Be damned to propriety, too. He wanted Jayne, and he was blowed if he was going to carry on resisting her allure for one more second.

He leaned across the space between their two mounts

and before she had time to guess his intention, before she had time to object or take evasive action, he kissed her.

He only managed to brush his lips across hers before Mischief fidgeted and jolted her out of his reach, but she felt it all the way down to her toes.

She had never dreamed one such brief kiss could do that to a girl.

She couldn't for the life of her think what on earth had prompted him to do it. But then her wits were so badly scattered that it was taking all her concentration to prevent herself from sliding out of the saddle and melting into a puddle on the forest floor.

Fortunately she was spared the necessity of having to attempt to make any kind of verbal response, because at that very moment Mr Beresford and his sister arrived on the scene.

'I say, Lady Jayne, are you unhurt?' called Mr Beresford.

'You must be terribly shaken after the way that horrid horse bolted with you,' said Lucy, looking, Lady Jayne thought, a little disappointed not to see her lying on the floor with at least one limb broken.

'Mischief did not bolt,' she returned coldly. 'I gave her her head. We both enjoyed the gallop. And now, if you will excuse me, my lord...'

Completely unable to look Richard in the face after that bone-melting kiss, she simply indicated to her mount that she was more than ready for some more exercise. He would not pursue her. Not even should he want to—which she doubted. How on earth he had managed to get such a turn of speed out of the horse he was on she would never know, but of one thing she was sure. He would not be able to reproduce such a miracle.

Mischief needed very little prompting. Glancing over her shoulder as she galloped out of the clearing and onto the broad ride, she saw Mr Beresford urge his own mount in hot pursuit—determined, she supposed, to do the gentlemanly thing by sticking close and thus being able to report the spot where she finally parted company with Mischief—leaving his sister alone with Lord Ledbury.

Not that it would do Lucy any good. His heart belonged to Milly.

While hers, she realized in a moment of startling clarity, belonged to him.

That was why she could not bear to think of him being miserable.

That was why she had visions of dwindling into an eccentric spinsterhood once she'd pictured him happily married off. It wasn't that nobody would want to marry her. It was that she couldn't imagine marrying anyone but him.

And *that* was why the merest brush of his lips upon hers had been enough to have her practically swooning, when all Harry's most vigorous efforts had done nothing but irritate her.

And was that the real reason she'd brought Milly here, too?

Was she so sure, deep down, that his family would never let him marry a girl from such humble origins that the only result of having Milly here would be to scupper his plans to marry anyone else?

Had she become so possessive of him that she could not bear to let any other woman take the place she had not admitted until this very moment that she wanted for herself?

And that awful sensation she'd had when she'd imagined him making Milly his mistress… Had that been jealousy?

She spurred Mischief on, needing speed to distract her from the dreadful pain of facing up to her deepest, most hidden desires. Desires she'd refused to acknowledge even to herself.

But now that she had acknowledged them she began to wonder when it had started.

From the first moment they had met, at that ridiculous come-out ball of Lucy Beresford's, where she had sat sulking on one side of the dance floor and he on the other, she had felt a connection. It hadn't been the fact that they were the only two there of comparable rank. No, she had sensed in him an irritation with the way people treated him that marched with her own.

And then he'd rescued her from Harry and taken her home when he could have landed everyone involved in hot water. And instead of bowing out he'd plunged right into the mess she'd been in with Harry and done his level best to prevent it all getting any worse. He'd been protective. And even when she'd interpreted that protectiveness as being overbearing and dictatorial, and told herself she resented him, she'd been *aware* of him. She always knew the moment he entered a ballroom without having to look up. And once he was there it was as if he and she were the only two people in the room. Nobody else had any real substance.

And since he'd held her in his arms as she'd gone to pieces over Harry's brutal honesty she could not stand anywhere near him without feeling the urge to…well, to wind her arms and legs right round him.

She'd told herself it was because of the comfort she'd found in his arms. And, despising herself for being weak, thinking she needed comfort, she'd ruthlessly repressed the urges and refused to so much as examine them.

But it wasn't comfort she wanted from him at all. The way her whole body had fizzed, then melted at the merest brush of his lips upon hers, had really opened her eyes.

Somewhere along the way she'd fallen in love with him.

She supposed she hadn't correctly identified the nature of her feelings because she didn't have any experience of love, first-hand. She'd thought that the fact that Richard stood in a class of his own, in her estimation, was because she'd never met anyone like him before—never had a relationship with anyone, male or female, with whom she'd shared so many intimacies or entrusted with so many secrets. She'd told herself that was why she thought about him so often. Why, when she wasn't with him, she wondered what he was doing. Why any event he attended stuck in her memory, and when he wasn't there the evening was unbearably flat.

But now that she knew the truth she did not know how she would be able to face him again.

Nor Milly. Her friend.

Her rival.

Chapter Eleven

She was avoiding him. Ever since she'd bolted from him Lord Ledbury had been kicking himself. He'd startled her with that kiss. And so, even though they were all confined to the house that afternoon because of the weather, in the end he had to recruit help to outmanoeuver her.

First he persuaded Lord Halstead that he would enjoy giving the ladies some instruction in billiards. As usual, Lady Susan and Lucy Beresford managed to exclude Miss Twining from the activity. And, after several minutes of watching from the sidelines, she was delighted to accept his invitation to take a walk in the long gallery so that he could show her the portraits of his many ancestors.

He heaved a sigh of relief as Miss Twining laid her arm on his sleeve and they set off. She was not given to conversation, which left him free to work out how to make Lady Jayne understand the almost blinding revelation that had led him to kiss her that morning. He had to explain that in that one moment he'd changed his mind about marrying some paragon who would impress his family for generations to come. He just wanted *her*.

No... That didn't sound right.

He would have to marshal his thoughts into better order before blurting out something clumsy like that.

Firstly, then, he would disabuse her of the notion he was in love with, or had ever been in love with, Milly— and, while he was at it, he needed to warn her that Milly was up to something. He wasn't sure quite what it was yet. But when he'd heard them singing that ballad he'd hardly been able to believe his ears. Oh, it was innocent enough on the face of it, but in their regiment they'd sung a version of it so bawdy it would have scandalised even the gentlemen present in that drawing room. He could have wrung Milly's neck. How could she repay all the kindness Lady Jayne had shown her by encouraging her to sing a song that would have made her a laughing stock if anyone with a military background had been there?

Admittedly, so far Milly had not actually done anything to harm Lady Jayne. But she could. Very easily.

Once he'd warned her that she ought not to be quite so trusting where Milly was concerned, he could move on to telling her that he'd changed his mind—no, that *she'd* changed his mind—about what he wanted from a wife. He'd been a stranger to love until he'd met her, so naturally he had not considered it as an important ingredient in any marriage he might contract. But she'd taught him it was vital. Vital. Yes, that sounded much better.

As he mounted the stairs he repeated the phrases in his head, hoping to fix them in his memory. At times like this he could understand what Berry saw in Miss

Twining. She was the most undemanding of women. They'd walked the entire way in complete silence, and she had not once attempted to interrupt his train of thought. He glanced at her as they reached the gallery, wanting to take note of her reaction when she saw Berry already there with Lady Jayne.

If he had not been paying close attention he would have missed it. It wasn't so much that she smiled, more that her whole face softened and her eyes warmed. And her fingers tightened on his sleeve, ever so briefly.

She was more than willing to accept Berry's suggestion that the men—as pre-arranged—should swap partners.

It was harder to read Lady Jayne's mood. Though she voiced no objection, neither would she take his arm as they strolled along the corridor. But still, by dint of stopping at each portrait to expound that person's life story, while Berry inexorably drew Miss Twining along to the next, it was not very long before he had managed to put some distance between himself and the other couple.

She was uneasy with him. But at least with Berry and Miss Twining within hailing distance she had no excuse for fleeing the scene altogether. And, since Berry wanted a modicum of privacy as much as he did, they were soon far enough away to converse without being overheard.

Which was good, because he had no intention of wasting this carefully staged meeting by sticking to polite nothings. He knew her well enough by now to see that the only way he would break through her reserve would be by a full frontal attack.

'It is no use,' he said firmly. 'I am not going to take the hint and pretend that kiss this morning never happened. You have been so distant with me ever since that I can only assume I offended you.'

'Offended me? Oh… No, not at all,' she said, so politely it made him grind his teeth.

'I must have done. It was not the act of a gentleman to take advantage like that.'

She still wouldn't look at him.

'Please believe me. I just couldn't help myself. No, dammit, that's no excuse, is it? When I saw Kendell pawing you about in the park I wanted to rip his arms off.'

They came to a standstill. He could not believe he had said that out loud.

She blushed and walked across the corridor, where she turned her back on him, ostensibly to look out of the window.

'It…' Eventually she managed to speak, in a very low voice. '…It was not at all the same.'

For one thing, she had enjoyed it. That slight brush of his lips had made her yearn for more. She had wanted him to put his arms round her and prolong the contact. She wouldn't have fought him off the way she'd fought Harry. Because he would not have crushed her. She couldn't imagine Lord Ledbury doing anything so maladroit when he took a woman in his arms. No, the woman lucky enough to have Lord Ledbury really kissing her would know only pleasure….

'It is generous of you to say so,' he replied, heartened by her verbal forgiveness, though she was still pretending to admire scenery that was scarcely visible through the rain-lashed window rather than facing him.

'Not at all. I could tell you were just overcome by… some momentary impulse…' A perplexed frown pleated her brow, as though she could not understand what on earth could have motivated him. 'Whereas when Harry kissed me it was all part of a deliberate, cold-blooded scheme....' She shuddered. 'Looking back, I could almost wish you *had* ripped his arms off.'

She turned and shot him a rueful smile over her shoulder.

Well, that was better. 'I am glad that I could not sleep that night, then, and decided to take a walk.'

He hitched his hip onto the windowsill, so that he could look at her profile, at least, since she had turned her head away again, and begun to fiddle with the tassels on the curtains.

'Actually, Lady Jayne, this is a good time to tell you that I have long since decided I am glad the solicitousness of those London servants drove me outside to seek fresh air, or I might never have met you.'

'I am glad, too. You came striding down upon us like some kind of avenging angel—even though, at that time in your life, you were still far from well.' She blushed again. 'D-do you still find it difficult to sleep? Or have you found some remedy for that particular ailment?'

Far from it. But the sleepless nights he'd suffered since had been mainly on her account.

He rubbed his hand over the crown of his head and got to his feet again. She was fencing with him. Deliberately keeping him at a distance.

'Lady Jayne,' he said, remembering his feeling that the only way to breach her defences was by full-frontal attack, 'I am trying to tell you something of great importance. I am trying to explain that I kissed you because... Well, the truth is that you have saved me from making a terrible mistake.'

He turned her round and took her by the hand, so that he could be sure she was attending carefully.

'When we first met, I told you about the kind of marriage I intended to make. Thinking like a soldier, I made a list of my objectives, drew up the plan of action most likely to achieve a swift outcome, moved myself into a strategic position, armed myself to the teeth and started making forays into what I looked upon almost as hostile territory. Before I met you it never occurred to me that I ought to feel more than respect for any woman I considered marrying. But over the last few weeks, and particularly since you have come to Courtlands, I…that is… You have shown me that a marriage without affection…that is…without…love would be…a travesty. Lady Jayne, you yourself said that love is the only reason a man and woman ought to marry…'

'Yes, I did, didn't I?'

She was pulling her hand away.

And it occurred to him that just because she wanted to make him happy, it didn't mean she was willing to sacrifice herself. She cared enough to see him happily married to someone else…which led him to the point he ought to have made first.

'Now, about Milly…'

She flinched, and began to chew at her lower lip.

'No, I am not about to scold you for bringing her here. You meant only to help, and although…'

She looked so uncomfortable he couldn't continue with the warning he'd meant to give her. In fact, it would be better to tackle Milly herself. Ask her what the devil she was playing at and warn her that if she ever did anything to harm or even embarrass Lady Jayne, their friendship, such as it was, would be at an end.

'Well, there is just one benefit of your bringing Milly to Courtlands,' he said, wondering where his plan to stick to his well-rehearsed script had gone. 'My former army servant, whom I left with her to see her settled into her new house, came here hotfoot to let me know she had run off.'

Fred had been frantic with worry over her apparent disappearance. He'd almost wept with relief to know she was safe and well.

'Fred *is* most welcome. He knows just how I like things done, and, since there is nothing for him to do in Town with Milly being here, he has agreed to stay and resume his role as my valet for the time being.'

'Fred?' She looked up at him with a puzzled frown.

He was almost as puzzled himself. He couldn't think how he'd ended up talking about his former batman when what he wanted to say was so important. He supposed it must have come from her asking about his inability to sleep....

But before he could wrest the conversation back into line, they were interrupted.

'Now, now—cannot have you monopolising Lady Jayne all day,' boomed the voice of Lord Lavenham.

He looked up with a flash of irritation to see his grandfather striding towards him, a brace of spaniels frolicking at his heels.

'Must mingle, my boy. Duty of a host to mingle. And numbers down in the billiard room are uneven. Get yourself down there and even them up, what? *I* shall show her ladyship the family portraits.'

'As you wish,' he said flatly, bowing and turning on his heel. He had not been making much headway with Lady Jayne anyway. He had started off well enough.

But then she'd started chewing her lower lip. And the ability to think about anything except kissing her had abruptly deserted him.

Time for yet another tactical withdrawal.

Lady Jayne noted the stiff set of his shoulders as he walked away and felt a surge of anger on his behalf. How *could* the old man treat him like an errant school-boy? Demean him like that in front of witnesses?

Lord Lavenham held out his arm with one of his ge-nial smiles which, now she was on the receiving end of it, she beheld to be totally false.

She was not in the most receptive of moods to begin with, and over the course of the next half-hour, during which he not very subtly interrogated her upon her suit-ability to become the next Countess of Lavenham, she grew increasingly annoyed with him. But at least her irritation with his intrusive questions, coupled with the way he would keep running his eyes over her as though she was a brood mare, kept her from succumbing to the dreadful temptation to sit down, bury her head in her hands and burst into tears.

Lord Ledbury had decided to abandon his cold-blooded search for a titled, accomplished woman to marry. He was going to follow his heart instead. That was why he'd kissed her that morning. He'd had some kind of…epiphany. And it was all her doing. By bring-ing Milly down here she had in fact accomplished ex-actly what she'd set out to do. That was what he had been trying to say just now. Awkwardly, because he had been a soldier and was not used to talking about feel-ings of a romantic nature.

And when he'd said he was glad he'd met her it had not been because he found anything about her in the least bit appealing. Nobody could possibly just be glad to know her for herself. Had not the last few weeks seared that knowledge into her consciousness?

But she *had* shown Lord Ledbury that there was more to life than honour and duty. *That* was why he was glad he'd met her. She'd persuaded him that being in love with the woman he was going to marry was more important than any other consideration.

At the very moment she'd discovered she was in love with him herself, she was going to have to watch him casting everything aside in order to be with another woman.

She didn't know how she was going to bear it.

That evening Lord Ledbury went to his grandfather's study, where he knew he would find him taking one last drink before turning in for the night.

'Ah, Richard, my boy, take a seat.' He waved to the chair opposite the fireplace, where he was ensconced with a large glass of brandy. 'Come to discuss the girls, have you, now I've had a chance to look 'em all over?'

'Not exactly.' Not in the least. For he did not give a damn what his grandfather thought. He sat down, crossed his legs, and leaned back before saying, 'I just thought it would be polite to let you know that I've made up my mind regarding whom I intend to marry.'

'So soon? Well, whichever one it is, I must say I admire the way you've gone about the task I set you. No shilly-shallying.'

Well, that was hardly to his credit. He hadn't cared much who he might end up married to when he'd first accepted that his duty was clear. It had only been after Lady Jayne burst into his life like... Well, as he'd told her, just like one of Congreve's rockets, that he'd discovered there was only one woman with whom he wanted to spend the rest of his life.

'Miss Beresford, is it?' Lord Lavenham leaned back in his own seat and twirled his brandy round in its glass. 'Out of all the girls you've brought down here she is the one I can see making you the most comfortable sort of wife. You get on well with the brother, at least. Can be devilishly uncomfortable if you don't get on with the extended family.'

'No, not Miss Beresford. I intend to ask Lady Jayne to be my wife.'

Lord Lavenham looked up at him sharply.

'Lady Jayne Chilcott?' He shook his head. 'Richard, I can quite see why you considered her, given the qualities I urged you to look for in a bride. Highly born, and with a substantial fortune to bring to the table. And a good seat. Yes, I liked the way she handled Mischief this morning, and that's a fact. But you must have noticed how cold she can be?'

'Her manner may be cool, sometimes, but she is not cold at heart.'

'I have noticed that there is a distinct thaw in her attitude towards *you*. But I have to tell you, after spending half an hour in her company this afternoon I had to come in here and call for Watkins to light the fire.'

He shivered.

'Only met one person before with the capacity to freeze the blood in m'veins with one look, and that was her father. He was a cold-hearted blackguard, was the Marquis of Tunstall. Could be downright nasty if you got on the wrong side of him. Before your time, so you wouldn't know, so it's my duty to warn you, boy, to think very carefully before getting yourself hitched to any child of his.'

Richard sat forward, his hands clasped between his knees.

'I think I know what you mean, sir. I have watched her retreat within herself when she is upset or offended. But I find her dignified withdrawal far preferable to the behaviour of girls who lash out in anger when they are crossed. Or make spiteful remarks behind an unsuspecting victim's back.'

'Like Lady Susan.' His grandfather nodded. 'I am inclined to agree with you there.'

Well, that was something.

'If I can persuade Lady Jayne to accept me, I am confident that she will do her best to make me happy.'

Lord Lavenham frowned.

'So long as you have no sentimental expectations regarding a match with one of the Chilcotts, I suppose it might answer. And you don't strike me as being the sentimental sort, so... No, I suppose I cannot raise any objections.'

Expectations? No, he had no expectations. Expecting a woman to love him was not the same as hoping that one day she might feel something stronger than fondness towards him.

'When I set out to find a wife, you must know, sir, that sentimentality had nothing to do with it.'

'Indeed,' said the earl thoughtfully. Then he sighed. 'Well, whomever you marry, I cannot believe you could do worse than your own father, or either of your brothers.' His expression soured. 'They all disappointed me. Whereas you—' he looked at him squarely from beneath his beetling brows '—you never have. I have followed your career with great interest.'

'You have?' Why was this the first he'd heard of it? As far as he knew, his grandfather was only interested in his horses and his hounds.

'Yes. Upon several occasions your gallantry has brought distinction upon the name of Cathcart. Been proud of the way you earned your promotions. In short, I am not at all sorry that you will be the one to take up the reins when I am gone.'

At one time Richard would have given anything to know that one of his family was watching his military career. His father had acted as though he'd done him an immense favour by purchasing him a commission for his sixteenth birthday, but he'd always assumed the fact that it was in a regiment serving overseas had been a deliberate attempt to deal with the problem of the middle son for whom he could feel neither love nor hate. And he'd never, not once in his life, received a letter from his own mother—not once he'd left home. And he wasn't talking about his military service. She'd washed her hands of him the moment he'd gone away to school.

But his grandfather had followed his career? How he wished he had known that when it might have meant something. Now it was…not something that affected him as much as he would have expected.

When he'd vowed to do his duty by his family, in resigning his commission and marrying a woman worthy of raising the next generation of Cathcarts, he realized he'd done it because it was in his nature to do his best—not to win anyone's approval.

'Now, tomorrow,' said Lord Lavenham, 'I thought it

would be a good idea to take 'em all out to The Work-ings.'

'A good idea,' replied Richard, relieved that his grandfather was moving the conversation away from the personal to the practical.

'Chaperones in carriages. The rest of you on horse-back. A pretty spot, some nice views, and you young things can all picnic. Play cricket in the afternoon if it is fine. Parlour games if not.'

Richard nodded. The Workings was an ideal loca-tion for an afternoon's entertainment during unsettled weather. Some twenty-five years previously his grand-father, this crusty old man who had such trouble talk-ing about emotion of any sort, had built his own wife a substantial pavilion on the brow of a hill from which she could watch the progress of the canal which was being cut along one of the farthest-flung borders of the estate. It had been his way, Richard supposed, of show-ing her that he loved the woman his own parents had arranged for him to marry, since she'd become inexpli-cably fascinated with everything to do with the work-ings in the valley.

He'd even had the estate carpenter make her lady-ship a working model of a lock staircase, though there was not one along this stretch of the canal. As a boy, Richard had loved going down to The Workings with a jug of water and navigating twigs, leaves or anything he could find that floated, through the series of locks. If the contraption still worked, it was just the sort of thing to keep all his guests amused for ages.

He left his grandfather's study wondering how, amidst all the bustle of the proposed activities, he would be able to draw Milly to one side and put a stop to her mischief-making.

Or, better yet, get Lady Jayne in some secluded spot where he might be able to coax her into letting him kiss her again.

Only this time it wasn't going to be a brief touch of lips. No, this time he was going to make sure she knew she'd been well and truly kissed. He was going to make such a thorough job of it that she wouldn't even be able to remember Lieutenant Kendell's name, never mind what he looked like.

He might have known she wouldn't make it easy for him. In fact, the day which he'd hoped would accomplish so much had been one of unmitigated torture.

Surrounded by chaperones, grooms, footmen with tables and chairs and boxes of other sundry equipment, maids with hampers of food, not to mention the other house guests all intent on getting a piece of him, Lady Jayne had had no trouble whatsoever avoiding him completely. To round things off nicely, now, when he'd rung for Fred, it had been Mortimer's valet who had answered his summons, with the intelligence that, so far as anyone knew, Fred had 'absconded to the nearest hostelry, in search of liquid refreshment.'

In one way, that news had come as no surprise. Fred had seemed ill at ease, if not downright morose, when he'd shaved him that morning.

For a moment he felt half inclined to go after him, so that they could drown their sorrows together.

Instead he dismissed Jenkins, deciding he would rather put himself to bed than endure his mealy mouthed ministrations.

But he got no further than pulling off his evening shoes, stockings and neckcloth before he sat down on the edge of the bed and buried his face in his hands.

Deciding to marry Lady Jayne was one thing. Telling his grandfather he was going to propose to her, no matter what he thought, was another. But actually saying the words to *her*...when like as not she would reject him...was turning out to be a great deal harder than he could possibly have imagined. How the hell did a man persuade a woman who was still recovering from a broken heart to look favourably on him? Last night it had sounded easy. Just kiss her and tell her he loved her. Or tell her he loved her, then kiss her and...

And that was the thing. He couldn't get the image of her struggling with Kendell, when he'd forced a kiss on her, out of his head. And she had loved *him* enough to agree to a secret assignation with him.

This kind of courting was damned complicated. He'd never been all that bothered about how the women he'd taken a fancy to might feel about him. A soldier took his pleasure where he could find it. But if he made one wrong move where Lady Jayne was concerned, and destroyed what goodwill she did appear to have for him, he did not know how he would bear it.

He shot to his feet, wrenching his shirt from his waistband and tearing open the neck, though the action gave him scant outlet for his frustration. He could not risk taking any course of action that might alienate her altogether. But if he sat about doing nothing she might still slip right through his fingers. He was going to have to—

What was that? He'd heard a most peculiar noise— a kind of rattling as of hailstones against the window, though there was not a cloud in the sky. It made the hairs on the nape of his neck stand on end, just as they always did when he scented danger.

Another, sharper sound, as of a bullet striking the masonry, had him flinging himself to the floor in a move so instinctive he was face to face with his chamber pot before he rightly knew what he was doing.

Who the devil could be taking potshots at him through a first-floor window, of all things? He swarmed on elbows and knees to his dresser, reached up and pulled his pistol from the top drawer, whilst wondering what kind of enemy would have waited until now to fire upon him, when he had been strolling about the park all day, a much easier target—especially when he had stood on the brow of the hill….

Well, he was not going to make it easy for him to put a period to his existence. He loaded his weapon, crawled to the window, sat up next to it and took a cautious peek over the edge of the sill.

Lady Jayne had been growing more and more miserable all day, waiting for Richard to propose to Milly.

But Milly still seemed to be under the impression he was angry with her, and had been keeping well out of his way.

Just as assiduously as she'd been avoiding Milly.

She should have gone straight to Milly yesterday and told her what Richard planned. But every time she braced herself to go through with it, and formed the words in her head, other words came welling up from deep, deep within. *Not you. He loves her, not you.*

And after the pain had come the shame that, instead of wanting Milly to be able to find happiness with Richard, she was all twisted up with jealousy inside. It was a rotten thing to do—fall in love with a man your friend wanted to marry.

It was no use telling herself she hadn't meant to do it. She *had* done it. And it made her feel like a traitor.

All day long everyone concerned had been utterly miserable.

She sighed.

Tomorrow. Tomorrow, if Richard had not managed it himself, she *would* tell Milly what she knew, and at least the two of them could be happy.

Only...

It sounded as though Milly was as unable to sleep as she, for some time now, had heard her moving about the room as though she was pacing up and down in agitation. In the end, though part of her wanted to pull the covers up over her ears and blot everything out, she pushed her own selfish desires aside, along with the bedcovers, got out of her bed, crossed the sitting room and tapped gently on Milly's bedroom door.

And stopped still on the threshold.

Clothes were strewn everywhere, as if somebody had got in and ransacked the room. But it must have been Milly who'd made all the mess. For she was standing amidst the wreckage, a small valise clutched in one hand, a bonnet in the other, and a mulish expression on her mouth.

And she was wearing a coat.

'Milly...'

Lady Jayne had been about to ask her what she was doing, but it was so obvious she intended to leave she would have felt foolish voicing the question.

'Milly,' she began again. 'Please don't leave. Not now, just when Richard—'

'This has nothing to do with him!' Milly's face hardened. She tossed the valise onto the bed and placed the bonnet on her head.

'Of course it has. Milly, I can see you must have given up hope to say such a thing, but—'

'There was *never* any hope for me with him,' she said as she yanked the ribbons into a bow under her chin. 'But at least now I've met a man who does see me as a woman. Tom's waiting for me right now. In the lane that goes up to The Workings. In his curricle...'

'Not... You don't mean Lord Halstead?'

'Why not Lord Halstead?'

'Well, because I...I can't believe he loves you. Not if he has asked you to run away with him like this.' She'd learned that much from her relationship with Harry. 'Besides, if you run off with another man it will break Richard's heart.'

'If you think anything I do might *touch* Richard's heart,' Milly said bitterly, 'let alone break it, you are very much mistaken.'

She turned to the bed and picked up her valise.

'Of course it will hurt him!' How could Milly be so obtuse? She had been devastated when Harry abandoned her, and she hadn't loved him at all. It was the betrayal, the lies he'd told. And it would be ten times worse for Richard, because he *did* love Milly. Was on the verge of proposing to her.

'Well, that only goes to show how little you really know him. That's 'cos he's only let you see him in the guise of a gentleman. But that's not really him. He's a soldier at heart. And an officer to boot. There's nothing soft about him to hurt. He's steel through to the core.'

'Even if that were true—' which she didn't believe for a minute '—you can't just go throwing your life away because you are upset.' It was the kind of thing she'd done in the past. Completely overreacted when she'd been hurt and angry. 'You don't really think Lord Halstead is going to offer to marry you if you run off with him tonight, do you?'

'Course not! What do you take me for?'

Lady Jayne gasped. She could just about see why Milly would have been content to become Richard's mistress. If a woman loved a man enough she might easily sacrifice her virtue. But this was not the same at all.

'Milly, have you taken leave of your senses? You hardly know the man!'

'I know enough,' said Milly defiantly. 'He's fun, at least. Since we've been down here I've had such laughs with him while he's been trying to work out if I'm really his Spanish lady from the masquerade. It was him as took me home, you know, after Richard spirited you away.'

'But...'

Milly's face softened. 'Look, I can see you're worried about what will become of me, but you needn't be. I'm not daft. I know this thing with Tom won't last long, but I'll survive. I've still got the house Richard gave me...'

'Milly! You cannot actually want to demean yourself by letting a man like that...use you? Then throw you away as though you were of no account?' For that was what men did with their mistresses, was it not?

Milly made an impatient gesture with her hand to silence her.

'Don't start preaching at me, Jayne. You don't un-derstand…*anything*. You cannot begin to know how awful it was, all those months when we didn't know if Richard was going to live or die. Fred was out foraging, and I was scrimping and saving and making do when his precious family wouldn't lift a finger to help. Es-pecially when you consider our regiment was having picnics and parties and balls all the way to Paris. And where was I? *Chatham!*'

She spat the word as though it was a curse.

'And then, when he did come into all this—' with a rather wild laugh she waved at the opulence of the room in which they stood '—and said he was grateful for all I'd done, and he was going to treat me right, I thought he was going to set me up in style. Give me a carriage and a pair of cream horses so I could go round the park like as if I was someone. Or a box at the theatre—now, that wouldn't have gone amiss neither. But instead of mak-ing sure I could start having some real fun he packed me off to Bedford Place and told me to be a good girl. But I'm not a girl,' she cried, stamping her foot. 'I'm a woman!'

Oh, how often Lady Jayne had wrought herself up to the same pitch as her friend was in now. Even though she could understand Richard's motives, she could *feel* every ounce of Milly's frustration. In just such a mood she'd vowed not to dance with a single man in London. In just such a mood she'd decided to go to that masquer-ade and meet Harry.

And who had been hurt? *Not* the person who'd pro-voked her into the act of defiance. Just herself.

'No!' cried Lady Jayne, stepping in front of Milly as she picked up her valise and made for the door. 'I won't let you do this. I can see you are very upset, but you have to stop and listen…'

'You really think you can stop me? I'm a head and a half taller than you, and far, far stronger if it comes to a fight. And I know tricks you couldn't even dream of.'

'I…I am quite sure you do,' she replied, lifting her chin. 'But I have something very important to tell you. It will change everything…'

But Milly did not stop. She did not listen. With a mulish pout, Milly simply pushed Lady Jayne aside and stalked into their sitting room.

She ran after her and seized her arm as she reached for the door handle.

'Milly, stop! I can't let you leave like this. I can't!'

'For heaven's sake, Jayney!' Milly dropped her valise, wrapped her arms round her waist, lifted her from the floor and flung her away from the door. 'Can't you see this will be to your advantage? Now you know I'm no competition, there's nothing to stop you going after Richard yourself.'

'What?' She straightened up, rubbing at her waist where she could still feel Milly's steely strong grip.

'Don't play the innocent with me. I've seen the way you come alive for him, when you can barely be bothered to be polite to any other man.' She thrust her face into hers. 'You go for the heroic type, don't you? That was what attracted you to your Hyde Park soldier. The uniform. The veneer of manliness.'

Lady Jayne retreated, shaking her head. It hadn't been like that with Harry at all!

'Well, take it from me, Richard is ten times the man Harry was. I've had my hands on every single inch of his body. And I can vouch for the fact he's got all the equipment necessary to keep a woman well satisfied.'

'Milly!'

'Even if it was true that my leaving might affect him, we both know he's on the hunt for a Society bride.'

'No! W-well he was, but he told me—'

'All you need do,' Milly interrupted, prodding her in the chest with her forefinger, making Lady Jayne take another step back, 'is flutter those great long eyelashes of yours, put your arms round his neck and let him kiss you. And I guarantee all will be right with his world again.'

'No. You've got it dreadfully wrong...' she protested, just as Milly shoved her hard in the chest and sent her reeling back.

And slammed the bedroom door in her face.

With every coarse remark, each jab of her finger, she had sent Lady Jayne retreating across the sitting room. She had been so shocked that Milly had known all along how she felt about Richard—especially when she'd only just untangled her web of emotions in his regard the day before—she had not noticed the moment she teetered on the threshold of her own room. But now she was on the wrong side of the door, while Milly was turning the key in the lock.

'Let me out! Milly! You must—' she slammed the palms of her hands against the locked door '—not leave!'

She grabbed the doorknob and tugged with all her might. It would not yield.

'Milly!' she yelled as loud as she could. But Milly's steps did not falter. And then she heard the outer door slam.

Oh, this was terrible. Not only was Milly ruining her

own future by acting on the kind of anger that Lady Jayne knew only too well, but she was also going to devastate Richard. This *affaire* would ruin any chance of him finding the happiness he'd only just started to reach for.

She kicked the annoyingly solid bedroom door just once, to relieve her feelings, welcoming the pain that shot through her toes. Because it was all *her* fault. If she hadn't gone to that masquerade Milly might never have met Lord Halstead. If she hadn't been such a selfish, jealous, coward she would have told Milly yesterday that Richard was going to propose, and then none of this would be happening.

There was only one way to make amends. With a determined glint in her eye, she marched across to the window.

Chapter Twelve

Lady Jayne opened the casement and leaned out, examining the climb she would have to make. For she had to get to Richard and warn him what was going on, and this window was the only way out of her room.

The apex of the *porte-cochère* was only a foot or so beneath her windowsill. The pitch of the tiles was quite steep and, since it had been raining earlier that evening, they were slick with moisture. The drop from the guttering that ran along the lowest edge of the slope to the ground looked to be another fifteen or twenty feet.

She had no fear of heights, since she had spent a great deal of her childhood, during the years when her father had just wanted her kept out of his sight, climbing trees. But this was not going to be an easy descent. That slippery slope had no handholds. And there was no way to avoid dropping the last bit.

She leaned out a bit farther. If she slid crabwise across the *porte-cochère,* to its lowest point, she might be able to find a toehold amongst the ivy. It covered the whole frontage of the house, and she knew from experience that a plant that vigorous would have some sturdy branches under all that thick foliage. Failing all else, she could grab a vine and let it slow her descent to the ground as it peeled away from the wall.

The image of getting a vine in her hand reminded her of a rope. A rope. Yes, if only she had a rope she could cling to it as she slid slowly down the sloping tiles. And then, even if it was not all that long, if she could hang from the end of it and reduce her fall by even a few feet it would make all the difference. If she only had to drop, say, ten feet, it would be like coming off a horse that was jumping a hedge, which she had done plenty of times.

You had to roll, her groom had taught her from an early age. Not just slam into the ground like a sack of potatoes, but crumple and roll. And then, though you still got bruises, you weren't so likely to break bones.

She turned round, scanning her room for something to fashion into a rope. Her eyes snagged on the plaited cords that tied back the silk damask hangings of her bed. She unlooped them and swiftly knotted them together as best she could. Then tied the end of the first one to the central stone pillar between her windows. Then gave a little tug, to make sure it was secure. She wished she had packed her breeches. But, since she had promised never to climb out of a window again, it hadn't occurred to her she might want them.

She clucked her tongue in annoyance. When would she stop making stupid, rash vows that she had no hope of keeping? Oh, dear. Was she doomed to end up like Milly? One day throwing her life away completely in a fit of…pique?

Not if she could help it. She firmed her lips and hitched her nightgown up round her thighs. She'd made mistakes in her past. Bad ones. But she wasn't so stupid she hadn't learned from them.

She knotted the yards of fine lawn in place with the belt of her dressing gown and swung her legs over the sill, clinging tightly to the plaited velvet cord.

There was a ripping noise.

She couldn't worry about whatever she'd torn just now. She had to concentrate on getting to Richard as fast as possible. To that end she turned to lie on her tummy on the tiles, skinning her knees in the process. Ignoring the pain, and the unpleasant sensation of wetness seeping through the front of her nightgown, she began to worm her way down.

It was when she was about halfway down that the rope went slack and then, to her horror, went slithering past her. Somewhere along its length it must have come untied.

Oh, why, she thought as she scrabbled in vain for purchase on the wet tiles, had none of those expensive tutors and governesses she'd had ever taught her how to tie knots?

After breaking several fingernails, she thought of kicking off her silk slippers. Maybe she could dig her toes into the steep and slippery slope. It didn't help at all. In fact, she felt as though she was sliding downwards even faster.

She shrieked as her feet went over the edge.

But then, by some miracle, she managed to grab hold of the limestone trough that acted as guttering. For a second or two she hung, suspended by her fingertips in midair.

And then she was falling through empty space.

Instinctively she curled into a ball as she hit the

gravel driveway. When she stopped rolling she lay quite still for a moment or two, taking stock and thanking providence for that groom. The one person who had taught her anything of real value.

It did not feel as though she had broken anything. With a determined grimace, she made herself sit up.

She was facing the massive, locked front door.

She could pound on the knocker, she supposed. Yes, and raise half the household. And then they would all know that Milly had run off with Lord Halstead after locking her in her room. Which was the last thing she wanted.

No, somehow she had to find Richard—and only Richard. Nobody else must ever know about this night's work.

She got to her feet and stood for a few moments, willing her legs to stop shaking, and wondered which out of the three storeys of closed, curtained windows this part of the house possessed was his.

And then she remembered him saying how hard he found it to sleep with the windows shut. But that Fred was here now. Fred who knew how he liked things done.

All she had to do was walk round the house looking for an open window. She didn't know anyone else who was likely to leave a window open at night, since most people believed that the night air was injurious to the health.

Although, she reflected as she made for the corner of the house, that did not stop anyone from staying out until dawn when they were in London. If night air was really that bad, surely it would be dangerous to go outside at night? She paused and scanned the windows on the west wing. All shut.

She set off again, going round to the back, where she came to a jumble of buildings that looked like kitchens and offices, which ran clear away to the stable block. He would not sleep down here.

So she retraced her steps to the front of the house, then continued round to examine the east wing, which had been tacked on to the earliest buildings at about the same time as the *porte-cochère,* by the looks of the stonework.

And felt a sense of jubilation when she spied, on the first floor, a single sash pushed up. It had to be Richard's room!

Only now that she'd found it how on earth was she to attract his attention? If she shouted for him she'd likely wake half the household.

She would have to throw something up at his window and hope it would wake him. She bent down, scooped up a handful of gravel from the driveway and flung it upwards.

Then squealed and scampered backwards as half of it came raining straight back down on her head. Gravel, she discovered, scattered in all directions when you threw it.

She'd have to find a pebble, then. But not too large a one. She did not want to run the risk of smashing anything. Broken glass would take too much explaining away in the morning.

A quick rummage through the urns that stood on the edge of the terrace proved unfruitful, the compost in them being so soft and crumbly she suspected it must have gone through a sieve. She trotted to the end, dived into the shrubbery and from beneath the very first bush managed to extract a couple of roughish small stones.

She threw the first one at the window, and almost stamped her foot with vexation when it went wide of where she had aimed it, striking the brickwork way to the left of the open window.

She stepped to the right half a pace and threw again. This time, to her immense satisfaction, the pebble flew right through the open window.

Only then there was a crash, as of breaking glass, and the sound of a man's voice cursing. Richard's head and shoulders appeared above the sill, as though he had been crouched beneath it.

'What the devil?' He stood up and leaned out. 'Lady Jayne? What do you think you are doing down there? My God! I almost shot you!'

'Oh, hush, Richard. Do not shout. Only come down quickly and let me in.' She gesticulated at a set of doors on the terrace. She thought she remembered him telling her they led into the library.

He nodded and disappeared.

She undid the belt of her dressing gown—the only knot that night that had held fast—so that her tattered nightdress covered the lower part of her legs once more. Then hopped from one bare foot to the other, wondering what they'd think when they cleaned the gutters out in spring and found a pair of ladies' slippers up there.

It seemed an age before the doors to the library swung open. When Richard stepped out onto the terrace, a furious scowl on his face, she wrapped her arms round herself in an involuntary gesture of self-defence. It was hard to be sure which aspect of the situation she found most intimidating. His scowl. The pistol he was still brandishing, even though he had warned her about the dangers of getting shot. Or the fact that he was barefoot and bare-chested, his open shirt billowing out behind him as he strode forward.

He'd looked very dashing at the masquerade, dressed up like a corsair. But tonight, she thought as she gulped, he looked as formidable as the real thing.

'What the hell is going on?'

'It's Milly.' Somehow she managed to drag her eyes away from that fascinating expanse of bare male skin and say, 'She... I'm so—so sorry, Richard, b-but she's run off with L-Lord Hals-tead.'

'You are freezing,' he said in response to her stammered sentence.

Yes, she silently agreed. It was *cold* that was making her tremble all over.

'Let's get you back indoors and into the warmth, and then you can tell me what on earth possessed you to go running about in just your night things.'

'Yes,' she said as he ushered her into the library. 'B-but you must hurry, Richard,' she said as he shut and bolted the doors behind him. 'If you get d-dressed quickly there might still be time to stop them. It won't take you long, will it? You already have your breeches on,' she said, eyeing his behind as he bent to ram home the floor bolts. 'You only need to do your shirt up and...'

She was gibbering. She could hear herself doing it. But she was standing here wearing only her nightdress. And everyone else in the house was asleep. Richard had not paused to take hold of a candle when he came down from his room, so the library was lit only by the moonbeams shimmering in through the doors. And, even though she could not make out very much of him beyond shapes now, she could still see, in her mind's eye, the wedge-shaped torso sprinkled with dark hair.

She'd never taken much account of the fact that a man's shape was so very different from her own. All hard, flat planes where she was soft, rounded curves...

'Stop them?' Why on earth would she think he wanted to stop them? If Milly had decided to throw herself away on a man like Halstead then there was nothing he could do about it. Good riddance to her! He had done all he could to ensure she stayed respectable. 'I know I can trust you not to make a whore of her,' her father had said. And he had not. *He* had kept his word.

But, no matter what hopes her father might have had regarding her future, Milly had a mind of her own. Of late she'd spent far too much of her time buying pretty clothes and showing them off at various pleasure haunts. Now it sounded pretty obvious that if virtue stood in the way of her enjoyment she had no compunction about shedding it.

But how could he explain that to an innocent like Lady Jayne?

'Look, let's get you back to your room, and we can talk about this in the morning.' By then he might have been able to think of some way to explain the way some women regarded relationships with men without shocking her.

'I *can't* go back to my room. It is locked. Milly pushed me inside and locked me in when I tried to stop her from leaving.'

'Then how the devil did you get down here? Don't tell me...' He made himself really look at her for the first time. He had been aware, from just one glance, that she was wearing only a nightgown. But he had tried to be a gentleman and not notice how wet it was, rendering patches of it transparent—how it clung to the swell of her belly and the fullness of her breasts. He forced his eyes not to linger on the dark shadows hinting at what lay beneath. 'Your dishevelled state tells its own story. You climbed out of the window.'

Why had she done that? Why had she thought it was so important to come to him, and…? Oh, Lord. He had never managed to explain properly that he was not in love with Milly. The darling little idiot had risked life and limb to come and warn him because she could not bear to think of him being hurt by Milly's defection.

Was there anyone so sweet-natured, yet so valiant?

Milly might have said she loved him, but he couldn't imagine her acting as selflessly or as recklessly as this. But then there was nobody quite like Lady Jayne.

'You might have broken your neck, you idiot,' he said, a shudder going through him just before he swept her into his arms and cradled her close.

'No, no, I would not. I am very good at climbing. I have had lots of practise.'

How could anything feel so wonderful when it was so wrong? It was her fault that Milly had run—both out of patience and off with Lord Halstead. And yet when Richard pulled her into his arms all she wanted was to put her arms round him and hug him back. Then press kisses onto the scars she had noted peppering the front of his left shoulder.

And it would not have been to offer him the comfort he was so obviously seeking in this moment of pain at Milly's betrayal. It was a purely physical response to being in his arms. Feeling his naked skin beneath her cheek. She just wanted him. In a way she did not fully understand with her mind. But her body—oh, her body knew what it wanted. It wanted more contact. Naked skin to naked skin. Her mouth wanted to taste and her hands to touch. It was all she could do to remain motionless in his arms, just breathing in the scent of him. It wasn't a scent she could put a name to. It was just... warmth and cleanliness and...Richard.

He felt her tense. 'Yes,' he said, relaxing his hold on her ever so slightly. 'All those times you climbed out of windows to meet with your Harry, I suppose.'

He had to rein himself in—and reminding himself she was still nursing a broken heart because of Harry was one sure way to do it. Though it was utterly delicious to feel her in his arms, now was not the time to let passion get the better of him.

She was not ready for moonlight kisses in the library. Especially not when they were both half-naked and he was growing steadily more aroused by the minute. It took every ounce of self-control he possessed, but somehow he managed to step back and let his arms drop to his side.

'Come *on,* Richard!' she urged him when he just stood motionless.

He clenched his fists. Lord, what would she do if she discovered how things really stood? He *had* to bring his arousal under control.

'You need to get back to your room and get some clothes on. Some boots on,' she corrected herself. 'And chase after her and stop her before it's too late.'

He didn't want to put his clothes back on. He wanted to take them off. And hers, too.

'Lady Jayne...' he grated. Now was the perfect time to tell her the truth. The bit that concerned Milly, at any rate. 'I don't really care if she has run off with Lord Halstead—' he began.

'You don't mean that! Richard, you mustn't give up on her! How will you ever live with yourself if you stand back and let her throw herself away like this?'

She seized hold of one of his clenched fists with both her hands.

'Don't you understand? She is not going to *marry* Lord Halstead. She… Oh, Richard, don't you see what will happen when he gets tired of her? She'll miss all the…what she calls *fun* she says she's been having with him, and she'll go out and get another…protector. And then another, and another.'

Her eyes were luminous with unshed tears.

'But she doesn't mean it. She isn't a bad person. She's just so angry and upset tonight that all she can think about is if she can't have you then why shouldn't she have cream horses and pretty clothes? Oh, Richard, you have to save her from making a mistake she will regret for the rest of her life.'

That was when it struck him that not all her distress was on his account. She was really upset at the thought Milly was making a mistake she would regret once her temper had cooled. A wry grimace twisted his mouth. If she were a man she'd already be down at the stables, saddling a horse and riding out after her. Once her friendship was given, she was loyal to the bitter end. And she would think less of anyone who demonstrated less than her own total commitment. Less of *him* if he stood back and did nothing to prevent Milly sinking into a life of vice.

'You are right,' he said. 'I must stop her.' Adding silently, *For your sake.*

'I *knew* that if only you could put aside your anger you would do the right thing. You always do.'

She was looking up at him as though he was some kind of…hero.

Even after she'd been betrayed by all the men in her life so far, she trusted him. She had complete faith in his ability to snatch Milly back from the abyss.

He felt ten feet tall. Because she believed in him.

'Very well,' he said, raising her hands to his mouth and kissing each one. 'Tell me where she has gone and I will go after her.'

Her whole body sagged with relief. 'She told me Lord Halstead would be waiting for her on the lane that goes up to The Workings. But she was on foot and carrying a bag. I'm sure you will be able to catch up with her.'

'Come on, then,' he said, grabbing her hand and heading for the door.

'Wh-where are you taking me?'

'Up to my room, for now.'

'Oh, there is no need for that. Just get after Milly.'

'As if I would leave you down here on your own— in the state you're in.'

He could hardly believe she would think he'd do that. What did she take him for? But one glance at her, and the way she was looking at him, was sufficient to re-assure him. It wasn't that she expected little from *him,* in particular, in the way of courtesy. That outlook had been drummed into her by the way everyone in her life had treated her so far. She simply did not expect *anyone* to care what became of her.

He felt a pang go through him. Lord, but he knew what that felt like.

He put his loaded pistol down on the table just inside the door when they reached his rooms, and led Lady Jayne to an armchair by the fire.

'Sit there while I fetch you a blanket.'

When he returned from his bedchamber she had drawn her knees right up to her chest and wrapped her arms round herself. But she was still shivering.

As he draped the blanket round her shoulders he noticed a bloodstain on her nightgown.

'You have cut your knee. And your poor feet,' he said, looking at the state of them. 'I should tend to your hurts. And get you some brandy…'

'Never mind me,' she said, grabbing the edges of the blanket and tugging them tight to her chin. 'I shall be all right. Just get after them. Hurry, Richard, hurry!'

Even now, she spared not a thought for herself. God, how he wanted to kiss her. But if he allowed himself to weaken now, while they were both wearing so little clothing, who knew where it would end?

Besides, by this time he'd come to the conclusion that she was right. It was essential for him to catch Milly and put a halt to her schemes. Otherwise, in the morning, everyone would hear that one of the young ladies—or at least a person they had all assumed was a lady's companion—had run off with one of the gentlemen. And it wouldn't stop there. Once the guests dispersed the scandal would be all over Town. It was just the sort of salacious gossip that people loved to spread: an apparent innocent seduced by a much older, experienced man at the house party where Lord Ledbury proposed to Lady Jayne Chilcott. And not just any innocent, but the girl who'd come as companion to Lady Jayne. And then how long would it be before someone unearthed the fascinating tidbit that Lord Ledbury had known said innocent even longer than he'd known Lady

Jayne? That he'd set her up in her own house, and given her an allowance?

It was the very scenario he'd been fighting to prevent ever since he'd introduced the girls to each other.

He would never forgive himself if it came to that.

'Help yourself to a drink, then,' he said gruffly, waving his arm at the table that held a decanter and glasses. 'While I go and get some boots on.'

By the time he returned to his sitting room, booted and half buttoned into his army greatcoat, Lady Jayne was sitting curled up in the armchair again, sipping a generous measure of brandy.

He went over and tugged the blanket back up round her shoulders snugly.

'I will be as quick as I can,' he told her. 'Just sit tight and keep warm. When I get back we'll see about cleaning up your cuts and scrapes and work out how to get you back to your room without anyone discovering you have ever been out of it.'

Then, because he couldn't hold himself back any longer, he bent down, seized her face between his hands, and kissed her hard—full on the lips.

'What did you do that for?' she gasped.

She looked puzzled, and a bit surprised, but not the least bit angry. Which filled him with elation. And hope.

'Because you are a darling,' he said, gently tracing the curve of her cheek with his forefinger. 'We shall have to have a serious talk when I get back. But in the meantime…' he bent and kissed her again '…behave yourself.'

And then he turned and left. Picking up his pistol on his way out.

Lady Jayne sat there in a daze. He had kissed her.

Twice. And called her a darling. She could still feel the imprint of his lips upon hers. And the echo of his hands cupping her face. A lovely, fuzzy warmth began to spread through her veins.

Only to come shivering to a halt when she recalled him adjuring her to *behave herself.*

He might be grateful to her for alerting him to Milly's flight, but he still only saw her as... Well, the best she could hope for was a friend. And he had not been able to resist saying something about her behaviour. He'd even brought up that dreadful episode when she had snuck out of Lady Penrose's house to meet Harry. The horrid, shaky feeling she'd had ever since she had fallen off the roof became a surge of real nausea.

She downed the rest of the brandy, then set the empty glass down on the floor by the chair with a snap.

Minutes ticked past.

It was awfully quiet, sitting up by the fire, in the middle of the night. She wondered where Richard was. Whether he'd caught up with them yet. And whether he'd shot Lord Halstead with that pistol he'd snatched up as he went out through the door. And whether Milly was flinging herself on his chest and weeping with gratitude...

She pulled her thoughts away from their reunion. Only to become increasingly aware of all the physical discomforts she'd told Richard did not matter. Her nightgown had absorbed a lot of rainwater when she'd slid down the wet tiles, so that in spite of the blanket round her shoulders she just couldn't get warm. Her knee hurt. As did the palms of her hands and her shoulders in the aftermath of hanging from the guttering. And her feet were filthy.

She'd feel much better if only she could have a wash and get into some clean, dry nightwear, rather than sitting here feeling sorry for herself because Richard had done exactly as she'd asked. Left her here alone, soaked, freezing and hurt, to go chasing after Milly.

But she could not go back to her room. Milly had locked her out.

No, she hadn't, though. She had locked her *in*. She had turned the key in the outside of the door. If she could just find her way back to the suite she would be able to get back in and, as Richard had said, nobody would be any the wiser.

Hitching the blanket round her shoulders, she tiptoed across the room and peeped out of the door through which Richard had gone. The corridor outside was pitch-black. Nobody would venture along here without a candle. And if she were to see any glimmer of light she could run and hide, surely?

She went and fetched a candle from Richard's bedroom. She felt a pang of guilt when she noted a mess of broken glass on his dressing table, where the stone she had flung had shattered the mirror. She also couldn't help noticing that his bed had not been slept in. He must have been getting ready for bed when she'd thrown the stone through his window. Which was why his shirt had been undone. Her mind flashed back to the sight of him, standing in the library doorway, barefoot and half dressed. And then her eyes fell to the rumpled coverlet of his bed. Had he been sitting just there, undoing his shirt, when her pebble flew through the window?

She backed hastily away from the bed, took the lighted candle from Richard's nightstand, and marched determinedly out of his suite of rooms.

If she turned to the left and walked until she came to the end of his side of the house, then turned left again, that would take her to the front of the house, where her own suite was situated.

The candlelight cast huge wavering shadows before her as she crept stealthily along the deserted corridors. How on earth did burglars have the nerve to creep through people's houses in the dead of night? By the time she reached the familiar sight of the door to the suite she had shared with Milly her heart was banging so hard against her ribs it was making her whole body shake.

She slipped inside, breathing a sigh of relief to think nobody had seen her, walked across to her room and stretched out her hand to unlock her door. But there was no key in the lock. Milly must have removed it for some reason, and she had not noticed because she had been making so much noise pounding on the door, demanding her release. With a sense of frustration she shook the handle, but it was no use.

There was nothing for it. She would have to go back to Richard's room and wait for him to return. It was what he'd asked her to do in the first place. If only she'd just stayed put!

She caught her lower lip between her teeth as she peered out into the darkened corridor. If only she'd just done as he'd requested, nobody would have known she was even out of bed. Richard would have got a spare key from somewhere and got her back to her room discreetly. But now, because she thought she knew best, she had doubled the risk of discovery by venturing along this same set of corridors twice over.

The nearer she got to Richard's room, the more nervous she became. She might have been able to explain away getting caught near her own room, but not all the way on the other side of the house.

When she finally reached the sanctuary of his suite she was shaking so badly there was nothing for it but to make straight for the brandy decanter. She sloshed a generous measure into the glass she'd used before, then sank onto the chair, draping the blanket she had left there round her shoulders—more for comfort than anything. Then she took a large gulp of the drink she'd poured, hoping the warmth that burned down her throat and into her stomach would soon radiate out through her limbs and help her stop shaking, as it had before.

Oh, what could be taking him so long? She peered at the clock on the mantelpiece. It was very blurry. She rubbed her eyes, but still could not make out the time. It was too dark in here. And her eyes did not seem to be able to focus on anything properly. And she was so tired.

She curled her legs up on the chair and tried to wedge her head against its high back, but it was very uncomfortable. It had not been so bad when she was moving about, but now she was sitting still she couldn't stop thinking about how cold and wet she was.

She wanted to lie down. And Richard's bed was just through that door. It had a huge bank of pillows where she could rest her head without getting a crick in her neck. And lots of blankets, topped with a quilt, that nobody was using right now. She picked up the candle to light her way into the room, the blanket slithering unheeded to the floor behind her.

She felt a sense of rightness when she returned the candle to the nightstand where she had found it. She ought to have just done as Richard had told her and waited for him here. And maybe used some of the water in that pitcher on his washstand to clean herself up a bit, instead of wasting all that time and effort running about all over the house.

She'd been really silly, tiptoeing up and down the corridors. She giggled as she recalled how, rounding one corner, she'd jumped when a grotesque shadow had loomed up—a shadow she'd created herself, because her hands had been shaking so much.

She threw the covers aside and saw the beautifully white starched sheets. It would be a terrible shame to soil them with all the slime and moss that was stuck to the front of her sodden nightgown. In fact, now she came to think of it, it was entirely the nightdress's fault that she was so cold.

'Ugh,' she said, pulling it off over her head. 'Nasty, wet thing.' She flung it away and then, completely naked, slipped into Richard's bed and pulled all the covers up to her ears. Oh, that was better. She would soon get warm now. She gave a huge yawn, shut her eyes and fell instantly into the deep sleep of total inebriation.

She had never partaken of spirits before. So she had no idea what effect two large glasses of brandy could have. She would never have dreamed that she might fall into such a deep sleep that not even dawn breaking could have the power to rouse her. Nor the sound of the maid coming in to draw back the curtains.

She did not even wake when the girl, spying a female head on her master's pillow, emitted a squeak of surprise. Not even when that girl, consumed by curiosity, tiptoed over to see if she could make out her identity, before gasping in amazement, and then running from the room, giggling.

Straight back to the servants' hall with the juiciest bit of gossip she'd ever had the privilege of broadcasting.

Chapter Thirteen

It was growing light when he got back to the stable yard, where he handed Ajax, a horse he'd inherited, like so much else, from his brother Mortimer, into the care of a sleepy groom.

He threw back his shoulders as he strode across the yard to the mud room.

He wouldn't have believed it would take so long. But he'd done it. He'd tied the entire affair up so neatly there would be no loose ends to come unravelled and bring so much as a thread of gossip to Lady Jayne's door.

And he'd learned something, too.

Shutting the mud-room door behind him, he bent to shuck off his boots. It had been when Milly had melted into Fred's arms the moment he'd confessed he was in love with her. If a confession of love was all it took to deal with all that spitting fury, all her rebelliousness, he'd thought, it was a great pity the idiot hadn't just told her he loved her months ago and saved everyone a whole lot of trouble. She didn't care a jot that the man had, as he'd put it in his own words, nothing to offer her but his heart. After all she'd said and done even

Milly could see that having a man who truly loved her was worth more than any amount of silk gowns a lord could give her.

Not a second later he'd seen that he'd been as much of an idiot as Fred. He'd thought he had nothing to offer Lady Jayne, either. But he did. His heart. It was hers. Had been completely hers from...well, to be honest, probably from the moment she'd begged him not to let her maid pay the price for her own misbehaviour.

His mouth firmed with determination as he removed his second boot and aligned it with precision next to its mate. The moment he got back to his rooms he was going to explain the situation with Milly in such a way that there would be no more room for misunderstanding. Then he was going to tell Lady Jayne straight out that he was in love with her. And ask her to marry him.

And if she refused—and he was almost certain she would the first time he proposed to her—then he was going to lay siege to her heart until she surrendered, however long it took. Because there was no question of him ever marrying anyone else.

He ran up the stairs two at a time, feeling as if he'd thrown aside a heavy cloak that had been hampering his sword arm. It had been as he was riding back to Court-lands that everything had fallen into place. He knew who he was at last. Not a soldier without a uniform. Or a lord with neither the training in estate management to be a success in the countryside nor the inclination to fritter his wealth away in the gaming hells of the capital.

No, he was just a man who was going to fight for Lady Jayne's hand, and her heart.

While he'd been removing his boots he'd been able to hear the rattle of pots and pans coming from the kitchens, and the smell of frying bacon assailed his nostrils.

It was going to be devilishly tricky getting her back to her own rooms undetected now that the servants were up and about their business. But he would make time to lay the bare facts before her, at least.

He flung open the doors to the suite that had once been occupied by his father, his eyes going straight to the chair where he'd left her.

She wasn't there. The blanket she had been using was crumpled on the floor, an empty brandy glass lying on its side next to it. But of Lady Jayne herself there was no sign.

Well, wasn't that just like her? The infuriating creature had slipped through his fingers yet again. He shook his head ruefully as he pictured her impatience mounting as the hours ticked by. Until she'd finally decided to take matters into her own hands. A slow smile spread across his face. He couldn't be annoyed with her for being resourceful and spirited. For behaving in the way that had made him fall in love with her in the first place. For being the ideal woman for him. Even if he'd still been a serving soldier she would have been perfect. The kind of dauntless woman who made an excellent officer's wife.

Well, since she was in no need of rescuing, he might as well go back to bed and catch an hour or two of sleep before breakfast. It went without saying that the pursuit and capture of Lady Jayne was going to be a challenging if not a downright exhausting business. But she was worth it.

He was still smiling as he went into his bedroom, shucked off his greatcoat and threw it over the back of a chair. He had not wasted time putting on a neckcloth before dashing off in pursuit of Milly, so all he had to do was undo the top few fastenings of his shirt and tug it off over his head.

He turned towards the bed as he unbuttoned the fall of his breeches, and froze.

Far from going back to her own rooms, Lady Jayne had solved her immediate problems by creeping into his bed. Seeking warmth and comfort, no doubt. He only had to look at her, with her hair in plaits, her hand tucked under her cheek, the very picture of innocence, to know she wouldn't have thought of anything else—more was the pity.

With deep regret, he refastened his breeches and went to wake her up. Much as he loved the sight of her lying in the bed where he'd spent so many hours dreaming of her, nobody else must ever know she'd been here.

He bent over her, a tender smile softening his features.

'Lady Jayne.'

The only response he got was a sigh redolent of brandy fumes. He winced, remembering the overturned glass on the sitting-room floor. How much more had she drunk while he was out haring all over the countryside? Quite a bit, to judge by the depth of her sleep.

He considered kissing her awake, like the prince in *Sleeping Beauty.* Only he didn't think he could be as restrained as a prince in a children's story. He wouldn't want to stop at just kisses.

He stretched out a hand to shake her instead. And paused, his hands hovering a scant inch over the curve of her shoulder.

Touching her, in any way, was just too great a risk

for him to take while she lay there looking so utterly tempting.

So he took hold of the coverlets instead, and swiftly twitched them off her, hoping the sudden cold might percolate into her consciousness.

And gasped.

She was completely naked.

For a moment he stood there, his fingers clenched on the coverlets, stunned to utter stillness by the perfection of her form. The early morning sunlight caressed the curve of her hip, slid lovingly along the line of her thigh, put a slight shadow between the bountiful fullness of her breasts…

He groaned as he went rock-hard.

And for the first time since Orthez he had complete confidence that, if she were willing, he could spend the entire day in bed with her without exhausting the possibilities.

He groaned again as he gently replaced the covers, in spite of wanting to just stand there, admiring her for as long as he could. She would be mortified if she ever knew he'd caught so much as a glimpse of her in all her natural glory. Which would not make her in the least receptive to a proposal of marriage from him.

Her eyelids flickered and half opened. She smiled up at him. And guilt assailed him. She would definitely not be smiling at him like that if she knew how long he'd been standing there, drinking in the sight of her without a stitch of clothing on.

'You're back,' she said. Then yawned, rolled onto her back and stretched her arms above her head. The covers slid down.

He grabbed them before they reached a point that

would have embarrassed her, and firmly tucked them up to her chin.

And backed away from the bed.

'Don't, whatever you do, sit up,' he warned her.

She frowned. 'Why?' A look of comprehension flitted across her face. 'Oh!' Her cheeks turned crimson. 'May I have my nightdress back, please?'

'If you tell me what you have done with it, I shall be only too happy to oblige.'

She pointed. He searched. And thrust the rather damp and grubby article of clothing into her outstretched hands.

'Cover yourself up quickly,' he urged her, turning his back, both to give her a modicum of privacy and to conceal his arousal. 'We need to get you back to your room before anyone notices you are missing.'

And they were running out of time. He ran his hand over the crown of his head, inwardly cursing at the realisation that explaining anything to her now, let alone proposing to her, was out of the question.

'Have you got a key, then? Tried to get back in on my own. Couldn't find the key.'

'Damnation!' He should have stopped off at the housekeeper's room and got a spare.

'Don't want to wear this.'

He looked over his shoulder to see Lady Jayne throwing the nightdress back onto the floor, her nose wrinkled in distaste.

His annoyance evaporated at the sight of her snuggling back down among the pillows, closing her eyes and sighing. She obviously had not quite slept it off, but damn if she wasn't the most charming drunk he had ever encountered!

He couldn't help smiling, but he still had to get her back to her room.

'If you don't like your nightdress, and I can hardly blame you,' he said, recalling the green smears coating the front of it, 'then you will have to make do with one of my shirts.'

He went to his clothes press and picked out a silk shirt.

'Come on, sleepyhead,' he said, giving her shoulder a nudge. 'Put this on and get up.'

'No,' she protested, squeezing her eyes tighter shut. 'My head feels funny when I move. I need to stay in bed.'

'Not in my bed, you don't.'

'No, Richard…' she protested feebly as he sat her up and began to try and thread her arms through the sleeves of his shirt. It might not have been so difficult if he had not felt obliged to keep her decently covered by the sheets at the same time.

'This is like wrestling a greased pig,' he chuckled as he pulled the edges of his shirt together under the sheets. Only that kind of activity would not have left him with such a painfully urgent erection. He might not be able to see anything beneath the level of her shoulders, but his hands could not avoid trespassing into forbidden territory. Besides, he knew she was naked. He had seen every glorious inch of her.

It was an exquisite form of torture, getting her decently covered in his shirt when all his instincts were clamouring for him to strip off his own clothes and join her in bed.

Especially when she flopped back onto the pillows the moment he let go of her and closed her eyes again.

No—*she* was the exquisite form of torture. Since the moment he'd met her she'd blown all his carefully constructed plans to smithereens, invaded his thoughts, robbed him of sleep, got him so tied up in knots he forgot what he was saying halfway through a sentence.

And made him feel more alive than he'd ever thought possible.

He stood looking down at her for a moment or two, hands on his hips. She had no idea what mayhem she was causing just by lying there. Tempting him.

Trusting him.

Hell's teeth—the only way to get her back to her room would be to carry her. Which would mean dealing with all that nakedness...

He swallowed hard.

'I'm going to pick you up now,' he warned her, just before rolling her over and over so that several blankets, as well as the eiderdown, enveloped her completely.

'Good.' She sighed as he hefted her into his arms. 'You are very strong,' she observed as she wriggled one arm free and looped it around his neck. 'Is this a dream? Are you going to kiss me again?'

She looked at his mouth and ran her tongue over her lips. And lowered her eyelids seductively.

There was only so much temptation, Lord Ledbury discovered, that a man could resist. With her still cradled in his arms, he bent his head and kissed her.

The little whimper of pleasure she gave ricocheted from his mouth to his groin, and the erection which had barely subsided since the moment he had seen her naked greedily sucked all the blood from the rest of his body, making his head spin.

He was shaking so much that he barely managed to

stumble into the sitting room before collapsing onto the armchair with her on his lap, though he did manage to keep their mouths fused together the whole time.

'We have to stop this,' he moaned eventually, tearing his mouth free. 'It is madness.'

'Don't be a spoilsport.' She pouted. 'It's lovely.'

And then her inquisitive little hand began to explore the breadth of his chest, and all the reasons why he ought not to make love to her, right there and then, flew out of the window.

He burrowed through the layers of bedding and slid his hand inside his shirt.

The one that *she* was wearing.

Her breast fitted the palm of his hand perfectly.

'Oooh…' She sighed, arching up into his caress. 'More of that, please.'

She wanted more? He would give her more. Pushing the silk aside, he bent his head and laved her nipple with his tongue. It was like having his dreams come true. Better. Tasting her for real exceeded all his fantasies. Soon he was lost to all but the feel of her under his hands and in his mouth, and the sound of her breathy little moans urging him on. So he sucked her nipple, rigid now after the attention he'd paid it, deep into his mouth. She let out a yelp—but it was of shocked pleasure, not protest.

At that precise moment the door to his suite flew open.

'Lord Ledbury!' a woman's voice screeched.

'Damn you, Richard, what do you think you are doing?'

He looked up to see Lady Penrose and his grandfather standing side by side, just inside his room. Lady

Penrose was white-faced and trembling. His grandfather red-faced and quivering.

He removed his mouth from Lady Jayne's left breast, thinking it must have been quite obvious what he was doing. He was wearing nothing but a pair of breeches, while Lady Jayne was... *Damn*. She'd somehow managed to kick aside every one of the blankets he'd so carefully wrapped her in.

Mindful of her dignity, he pulled the edges of his shirt together over her breasts, then grabbed the coverlet, draping it over the pale length of her legs.

Then Lady Jayne set the seal on things by looking at them in a bewildered fashion, and asking, 'What are you all doing in my room? And where is Milly?' She frowned up at Richard. 'Did you find her?'

'She's gone.'

'You mean you could not stop her? Oh, no!'

'Oh, I stopped her all right,' he said grimly. 'But I don't think this is the time to be talking about *her*.'

'Well, you are right about that much!' said his grandfather, giving Lady Penrose a shove between the shoulder blades that sent her tottering farther into the room, before turning and slamming the door shut.

'Put. Her. Down,' said Lady Penrose indignantly. 'Take your hands off her and put her down. This instant!'

'Just one moment,' said his grandfather. He strode across the room and into the bedroom. He did not stay in there long.

Richard groaned, knowing what he would see there. Tousled sheets. A torn, bloodstained nightdress lying on the floor. More bloodstains on the sheets. Which, he had noted when he picked her up, meant he ought to have taken care of that cut on her knee and her poor little abused feet before he went out. But which his grandfather was bound to take as evidence of a night of wild debauchery.

'You damned fool!' Lord Lavenham stood framed in the bedroom doorway, his face now mottled with purple.

'This is worse than mere foolishness,' said Lady Penrose, pointing at the overturned glass on the floor.

'You got her drunk?' Lord Lavenham bellowed. 'And then seduced her?'

He had thought it could not get any worse, but Lady Jayne set her hand to her head.

'Oh, please stop shouting,' she moaned. 'It goes right through my head.'

'Lady Penrose,' said Lord Lavenham, turning to her with a grim expression. 'You have my abject apologies. I did not believe that this one of my grandsons was as much a libertine as the others.'

'He is not a libertine,' Lady Jayne protested. 'He has not done anything that I did not ask of him…'

'That is quite enough!' Lady Penrose screeched, grabbing her hand and tugging her off Lord Ledbury's lap.

She stumbled on the mound of blankets strewn around the chair.

'I accept your apology, my lord,' Lady Penrose said stiffly to Lord Lavenham, whilst deftly rearranging the folds of the coverlet she'd snatched up with the expertise of one well used to ordering the demi-train of an evening gown. 'I could not believe it at first, either, when my maid came to me with the tale which she claimed is titillating the entire servants' hall. It was only when

I discovered that my charge was not in her room that I gave it any credence. In the same way, you needed to see the evidence with your own eyes.'

'What evidence?' Lady Jayne was blinking from one of them to the other. 'Why is everyone so cross?'

'The only thing to do is announce their engagement at once,' put in Lord Lavenham.

'Engagement? Why? We were only…'

'Be quiet, you foolish girl,' snapped Lady Penrose. 'There is no excuse for such carryings-on, even if the pair of you do wish to marry. Unheard of!'

'No…' protested Lady Jayne again. 'You have got it all wrong….'

She felt as though she was emerging from a lovely, vivid dream into a viciously muddled nightmare, where everyone was accusing Richard of the most vile behaviour. They seemed to think he had got her drunk and deliberately seduced her.

'Richard, tell them…' She turned to look at him. And her blood ran cold. If anything had the power to sober her up it was the sight of him, sitting on the chair, his head in his hands, his shoulders bowed.

The picture of despair.

As Lady Penrose seized her wrist and dragged her from the room she realized that she'd ruined his life.

Snatches of things that had happened flashed through her mind as she stumbled along the corridors in her chaperone's outraged wake. The look of shock on his face when he'd found her naked in his bed. The harshness of his voice as he'd ordered her to cover herself up. It had all been a bit hazy, but the next thing she knew he'd been grimly wrestling her into one of his shirts. And then he'd picked her up and forcibly carried her from his bedroom. Her cheeks flamed red as she recalled her wanton behaviour over the next few minutes. Having all that naked chest within reach had been more temptation than she could resist. She had rubbed herself up against it like a cat. Almost purring with pleasure.

And then she'd begged him to kiss her.

Well, he need not have complied quite so enthusiastically, the voice of reason reminded her. But then her love for him surged back with the excuse that *any* red-blooded male, propositioned by a naked woman who was running her greedy little hands all over his naked torso, might have succumbed to a momentary lapse of judgement.

But, oh, how badly he was regretting that lapse now! She only had to think of the way she had left him, sitting with his head in his hands, after learning that he was going to have to pay for what he'd said at the time was madness with a lifetime of wedlock to her!

The moment they reached her rooms she whirled round and said, 'Oh, please, you must not think Richard could possibly have done what his grandfather accused him of. None of what happened was his fault. It was all mine!'

Lady Penrose sat down upon a chair by the window that overlooked the *porte-cochère,* her back to the window.

'Indeed? Would you care to tell me what really happened?'

Lady Jayne sank onto the sofa and, pausing only once or twice to take sips of water to ease her parched throat, haltingly recounted the events of the previous night.

When she had finished, Lady Penrose made a gesture of annoyance.

'What on earth possessed you to drink so much
brandy?'

'It—it was only the two glasses,' replied Lady Jayne,
slightly mystified. She had done so many dreadful
things during the course of the night that it seemed
very odd that her duenna should take her to task for her
consumption of alcohol. 'I have often seen gentlemen
drink far more without it affecting them in the slightest.'

'They are well used to it, though. And before last
night, to my knowledge, you have never been allowed
to taste more than just a few sips of champagne.'

'That is so, but...'

'And it was Lord Ledbury who gave you that first
glass. Did he make you drink it all?'

'No! No...' She frowned, trying to recall the exact
sequence of events. 'In fact he did not give me a drink
at all! I helped myself while he was getting dressed to
go after Milly.'

'And I suppose you filled the glass to the top and
drank it down as though it were a nice cup of tea? Now
I can quite see how you came to think it was perfectly
logical to remove every stitch of your clothing and get
into Lord Ledbury's bed,' said Lady Penrose acidly.

Put like that, it did sound terribly wicked. Shamefaced, she nodded her head.

'Where you promptly fell asleep. And spent the rest
of the night. Alone.'

She nodded again.

'And you still maintain that the bloodstains on the
sheets must have come from the cut you sustained to
your knee sliding down the roof.'

'Yes.' She drew aside the coverlet to reveal her grubby grazed knees.

'I have to say that your explanation is the only one that makes complete sense. The others completely failed to account for the rope, and the fact that your room was locked from the outside.'

'The rope? It is still there?'

'Yes.'

For some reason the knowledge that the rope had not disintegrated completely was strangely comforting. Even if it was only in that one tiny detail, she had not made a *complete* mull of the whole affair.

'Your Josie came to my room in a dreadful state first thing, before I had even had my chocolate, with some wild tale about you eloping with a mysterious lover by knotting the curtain ties together to form a rope. Well, naturally I discounted that story straight off. If you had eloped you would have locked the door from the inside, to prevent your disappearance from being discovered as long as possible.'

'Wait a minute… How did Josie get into my room? I tried to return last night and the key was not in the door.'

'No, it was lying on top of the dresser next to it.'

'Of course! Why did I not think to look there?'

'Because you had already had one large glass of brandy,' snapped Lady Penrose. 'It was enough to dull your intellect to the point where all the subsequent choices you made were the wrong ones. Though for the life of me I cannot see what possessed you to climb out of your window by means of a makeshift rope in the first place. Why on earth did you not simply ring the bell for Josie to come and let you out?'

'I was trying to be discreet.'

Lady Penrose winced and closed her eyes. 'God help us all if one day you actually *try* to cause a scandal.'

Lady Jayne felt about two inches tall.

Lady Penrose's eyes flicked open and bored into her as she said, 'And then, of course, my own maid came in with my chocolate, full of the gossip that was raging below stairs about how you had been found, dead drunk, in Lord Ledbury's bed, following a night of torrid passion. Which was another story I could not credit, knowing the pair of you as I do. Besides there being no reason for it.'

A maid had seen her? 'Oh, no...' she moaned, burying her face in her hands. Gone was any hope of trying to persuade Lord Lavenham and Lady Penrose to keep the whole incident between themselves. 'I have been such a fool. And Lord Ledbury is going to have to pay the price....'

'Do not for one moment succumb to any sympathy for that young man! His behaviour has been disgraceful!'

Lady Jayne looked up, bewildered. 'But I thought you said you believed me...'

'I do believe you. And I therefore acquit Lord Ledbury of deliberately getting you drunk and seducing you. But do not forget the scene which met my eyes when I came in and found you together was very far from innocent. You were sprawled across his lap half-naked—both of you. And he was taking full advantage of your helpless condition. Had we not arrived when we did, I have no doubt he *would* have accomplished your seduction.'

'No. Not Lord Ledbury. He wouldn't...'

'Of course he would. He's a man. And they are all

governed by the basest of urges. No matter how cunningly they conceal the fact.'

She pulled herself up with what looked like a considerable effort.

'But that is all beside the point. You were caught in his room, half-naked, having clearly been there all night. You will have to marry him. And that is that.'

Defeat washed over her. *He* would have to marry *her.* That was what Lady Penrose meant. He was going to have to pay a terrible price for an incident that was entirely her fault.

'You will get dressed now, if you please, and we shall go downstairs for breakfast, where we shall announce your betrothal. You will *not* behave as though you have done anything to be ashamed of. And let anyone make any conjectures about what happened last night if they dare!'

Chapter Fourteen

It was too much to hope that even *one* of Lord Lavenham's house guests might be unaware of the gossip.

But they were all at the breakfast table when she went down. And all looking far more alert than she felt.

The shock of realising she had trapped Lord Ledbury into a betrothal he didn't want had dispersed the haziness left over from the brandy. But she still had a pounding headache. And her knee and shoulders hurt like the very devil. When she lowered herself into a place beside Lady Penrose at the table she did so gingerly, trying hard not to jar any of the myriad scrapes and bruises she had sustained from her barely controlled descent from the roof.

Lady Susan smirked and made a comment behind her hand to Miss Twining, who was sitting next to her, which made Miss Twining blush and stare very hard at her plate.

And Lady Jayne realied that to any onlooker the stiffness of her movements as she took her place at table must have made her look exactly like a young woman who had just spent the night being thoroughly ravished.

While she was still thinking about how close Lady Penrose considered she had come to that, the door opened and Richard walked in. There was a distinct air of expectancy around the breakfast table, rather like that in a theatre on the opening night of a new performance. Everyone was either looking at her, or at him, or from one to the other. And, in spite of Lady Penrose's warning not to look as though she'd done anything to be ashamed of, she felt her cheeks heat. It didn't help when Lord Lavenham stalked in, not two paces behind Richard, with a face like thunder. She couldn't believe how angry he still was. That he could have condemned Richard's behaviour without even giving him a fair hearing in the first place. Why, Lady Penrose, whom she had known for only a few months, had been willing to hear *her* side of the story—yes, and had believed her, no matter how unlikely it must all have sounded.

But Richard behaved as though he didn't care what anyone in the room might be thinking of him. With a breezy smile he walked straight to her, and wished her a cheery good morning.

She could not hold his gaze for more than a split second. One look at him was all it took to remind her that not two hours since he'd had his hands all over her. That smiling mouth had suckled at her breast. How could he just saunter in, looking all cool and collected, when she was so flustered she hardly knew what to do with herself?

When he took her hand and planted a kiss on her knuckles, like a practised lover, it struck her that this was the difference between them. He almost certainly *was* a practised lover. He'd likely had his hands all over lots of other women in his time.

The image that conjured up didn't help at all.

'May I get you some toast?'

'Toast?' She was almost dying with mortification, and he was talking about toast?

'Or eggs, perhaps?' He summoned a footman. 'Peters, why have you not poured Lady Jayne a cup of tea?'

'I was just about to my lord,' said the footman, hastening to fetch a teapot.

He had not let go of her hand. And he did not look as though he was the least bit cross with her. From the ease of his manner, anyone would think that marrying her was his fondest wish.

It was so...*decent* of him to shield her from public censure by putting on this show. He didn't seem to bear her any ill will at all now that he'd recovered from the initial shock of finding himself forcibly engaged to her. But then he knew she hadn't meant to bring all this down on his head. That she'd just been trying to help and, being the idiot she was, made a total hash of things.

She returned the pressure of his hand, finally finding the courage to look into his eyes. He smiled, pulled up the chair next to hers and sat down.

'I expect we should tell everyone our news. Though it looks as though they all suspect something anyway.'

He gave a devil-may-care grin that sent a pang straight to her heart. Perhaps he really didn't care. He had already accepted he was going to have to marry for duty. She could just imagine him shrugging fatalistically as he shaved and deciding that, after all, she was no worse than Lady Susan or Lucy Beresford.

'I have the privilege,' he said, looking round the table with a glint of challenge in his eyes, 'of being able to announce that Lady Jayne and I are to be married. Is that not so?' He gave her hand a squeeze. 'My love?'

It was her cue to back him up.

She opened her mouth to agree. But the power of speech seemed to have deserted her. She had never been at such a loss. Normally she had no trouble maintaining a cool facade. Where was it now that she so desperately needed it?

She looked at him and nodded. It was the best she could do. But it seemed enough for Richard, who smiled at her with all the tenderness anyone could expect from a newly engaged man.

She wanted to weep for him.

'Well, then, congratulations, I suppose,' said Berry, a little doubtfully.

Lucy stayed silent, but the spark of jealousy in her eyes said it all.

And Lord Lavenham made an angry sort of growling noise as he took his seat at the head of the table.

Lady Jayne bristled. She knew he had never liked her. And now he probably thought she was some kind of a drunken…slut, who could only get a proposal by creeping into a man's bed at night. And the glower on his face as Watkins hurried over to pour his coffee would only confirm everyone's suspicions about what had gone on the night before. And tell them that he thoroughly disapproved.

It was the outside of enough. If Richard did not care, then neither would she give a fig for what any of them thought. Anger gave her the strength to lift her chin and freeze them all out.

Richard watched her pulling on her public armour

with disappointment. He much preferred her all flustered and shy.

But he had seen pain flit across her face, too. She hated the thought of having to marry him. He only had to think of how many times she had protested when both her chaperone and his grandfather had insisted it was the only way out of the mess.

He might be getting his heart's desire, but it was coming at a very great cost to her.

Being discovered together like that had solved the problem of how he was going to get her to marry him. But he had wanted to win her heart, not force her compliance. He wanted her to be thrilled at the prospect of marrying him. Not looking haunted. Ashamed.

He glared at the other occupants of the breakfast table, who were adding to her distress with their mixture of avid curiosity and blatant disapproval.

For two pins he would throw the whole pack of them out of the house!

But there were another two days to go of this house party. And the matter between Berry and Miss Twining was not quite settled. Besides, if he turned them out in anger they would all go straight back to Town and start spreading the kind of malicious gossip about Lady Jayne that would taint their marriage for years to come. It would be better to carry on as normal.

'Do we have anything in particular planned for our guests' entertainment today?' he asked his grandfather.

Lord Lavenham glowered at him for a moment, before replying, 'With the weather being so unpredictable, I thought to have some targets set up on the lower lawn for some archery. Not too far for the ladies to run back to the house if it rains.'

Under cover of a muted chorus of approval, Richard leaned and whispered in Lady Jayne's ear.

'Since nobody else is likely to want to brave the weather, I think we should go out for a ride together. I need to talk to you privately. Will you meet me at the stables?'

It was so different from the way he'd ordered her to meet him clandestinely before. And her feelings about doing so had completely changed. She *needed* to speak to him. If they put their heads together, surely they could come up with some way to extricate themselves from this unholy mess.

'Of course,' she said.

If nothing else, she owed him an apology.

Several apologies.

'You look lovely,' he said, when she walked into the stable yard an hour later, wearing the same riding habit he'd admired so much before. The military style of it reminded him, again, that she would have made a wonderful soldier's wife. Though if he had still been a serving soldier—a pang shot through him—he might never have met her. He thanked God, for the first time, that he had been obliged to sell his commission. What would his life have been like had she never come into it? It didn't bear thinking about.

Lady Jayne was eyeing Ajax with a troubled expression as his groom led him to a mounting block.

'Is he safe for you to ride?' she asked, as the beast flung its head up and down, then skittered sideways on the cobbles in his delight at getting out of his stall.

'Oh, yes. He's just eager to get going. He will enjoy our gallop as much as we shall.'

'Gallop? Are you sure? Richard, last time we went out you were on that awful slug of a horse...'

'Last time *I* went out,' he corrected her, 'Ajax and I came to an understanding.' He clapped the horse on the neck. 'Didn't we, old boy?'

'You rode Ajax last night? When you went after...?'

Richard shot her a look, warning her not to discuss last night's events in front of the grooms. Then he swung himself up into the saddle with an athletic grace that almost made her gasp.

A groom helped her mount, and they had hardly passed out of the stable yard before Richard turned to her with a grin and said, 'Race you?'

'Do you mean it?' She had never had anyone willing to race with her before.

'Why not?'

'Well, because...' She nibbled at her lower lip. When she had gone to live with her grandfather he had decreed it was unlady-like to go careering all over the place astride her pony, and had set a groom to teach her the technique of riding side-saddle. It had been one of the worst restrictions he had enforced upon her behaviour.

But Richard wanted to race?

'Where to?'

'The Workings,' he said, and dug his heels into Ajax's flanks.

'That is not fair!' she cried as he set off.

And Mischief seemed to agree. For the next few minutes both she and her horse were equally determined to catch up with the males of the party. By the time she reined in at The Workings she was so exhilarated she scarcely felt any of the aches and pains that had so plagued her at breakfast.

'Oh, you beast!' she said, laughing down at Richard, who had already dismounted and was unlocking the door to the pavilion. 'You cheated.'

He came and helped her to dismount.

'You would surely not wish me to *let* you win a race, would you?' He took Mischief's reins and led her to the iron ring set in the wall to which he'd already tethered Ajax.

'No, but neither do I think you should take unfair advantage. I was riding side-saddle, you know, which is very far from easy.'

'But I have a wounded leg, which cancels out the disadvantage of your awkward saddle.' Having securely tethered both horses he turned and made his way back to her.

'But you still set off without giving me due warning,' she protested. 'And anyway, you said your leg was not that bad.'

'I do not think riding side-saddle is that bad, either. I have seen ladies riding side-saddle leading the hunting field. Looking quite magnificent.'

He ran his eyes over her figure in a way that made her acutely aware of the fact that he'd already seen most of it naked. She felt herself blushing with pleasure at his blatant appreciation. Not only had that statement indicated he didn't object to behaviour her grandfather decried as hoydenish, but Richard also seemed to have pleasant memories of that morning's interlude.

Pleasant enough that he was not dreading consummating their marriage, anyway.

'I think you are getting away from the whole purpose of coming out here,' she said, before his kindness went to her head and she started to entertain the misapprehension that he actually *wanted* to marry her.

'The purpose?'

The whole purpose of coming out here had been to get her alone and hopefully persuade her that marrying him was not such a bad idea. The way she'd run straight to him when she'd been so frantic about Milly proved she trusted him. And the fact that some of her concern was for his feelings also indicated that she cared for him to some extent. For a while there, last night, he had begun to hope she was beginning to feel physically attracted to him, too... But then, when she had looked so appalled at the prospect of marrying him, he had worked out what must really have been going on in her head. Alcohol often had the effect of making people feel amorous. And half-asleep, and probably waking from a dream about the man she *did* love...

The guilt he'd felt then had all but crushed him. How could he have taken advantage of her trusting nature? How could he have deceived himself into thinking she was truly responding to *him* when she had been so sleepy, so befuddled...?

'Is this a dream? Are you going to kiss me?'

He had only to recall the shock on her face when she'd fully woken—the number of times she had said *no!*

She had not really been aware of what she was doing. Or, more importantly, *with whom*.

'You must tell me what has become of Milly,' said Lady Jayne earnestly. There was a tension in the air between them she did not know how to deal with. A look on his face she wanted to dispel. 'She has not come back. And neither has Lord Halstead. Yet nobody seems to have got wind of the fact they ran away together.'

'Well, apart from the fact that they did not, they have far more juicy gossip to discuss today, do they not? Our supposed night of drunken debauchery.'

She hung her head. 'At least my foolish behaviour has resulted in some good, then. Everyone is so busy sniggering at me they have hardly noticed Milly is missing.'

'Well, nobody is ever very interested in the fate of a lady's companion. And Lord Halstead had the foresight to leave a message to the effect that he had been called away on urgent business. But they will never connect her disappearance with that of Lord Halstead anyway—not once she has married my valet.'

'Your valet? I don't understand. Why would she do something like that?' As if it wasn't bad enough for Milly to run off with another lord, now he was telling her she was marrying someone else entirely.

He glanced up at the sky. 'Shall we go inside? It looks as if it's going to rain any minute.'

He opened the door for her and she preceded him into the summer house built to take advantage of the view down into the valley and the canal that ran along its floor.

'Yes, thank you, Richard. But... Well... Though I can see that marriage was a better option for Milly than...' She trailed off uncomfortably and walked across to the window. 'But to your valet?'

'Don't you recall me telling you that the man came hotfoot from London when he thought Milly had disappeared? It turns out that the poor sap has been head over ears in love with her for months, but never dared speak up because he thought he had nothing to offer her. Which showed me that—'

'Wait a minute… That is the end of the tale, to be sure. How did you prise her away from Lord Halstead?'

'With remarkable ease. He took one look at my face, understood I meant what I said, and beat a hasty retreat.'

'I suppose the pistol you took with you had nothing to do with it?'

He grinned. 'I might have had it in my hand when I told him I took exception to his sneaking off in the middle of the night with one of my guests.'

She could just picture the scene. Richard could be downright intimidating when coming across couples meeting clandestinely—even without a pistol to back up his words.

'And then Milly decided she'd rather accept your valet's proposal?' She frowned in perplexity.

'Not quite. To start with I was just seeking a way to get Milly out of Courtlands. I was so angry with her. I decided to track Fred down and get him to take her back to Town. She didn't want to go, needless to say. She even tried to make me believe it would break her heart to be forced to leave my side,' he finished, with a distinct curl to his lip.

'You didn't believe her?'

'I have known for some time that she doesn't love me.'

'No!' She walked over to him and seized his hands, her eyes full of sympathy.

'Oh, yes. In fact I think she said it at first in a blind panic. You know—when I told her and Fred that because I'd come into the title I would have to remove to Lavenham House and find a suitable wife. I think she really thought I would just turn my back on the pair of them. And she employed the one weapon she knew I was powerless to resist.'

'Oh, yes,' she breathed. 'I know *just* what you mean. If someone says they love you, when nobody else ever has, it gives them a terrific hold over you...'

'Exactly so.' His voice gentled. He took her to the window seat and they sat down, still holding hands. 'She had got to know me well enough by then to understand the power of such a declaration. But even when she first made it I wasn't completely sure I believed her. I had always thought I was...well, her ticket out of a nasty situation. We were about to push into France. She'd seen how brutally the Portuguese and Spanish peasants treated the French soldiers and anyone associated with them. She was just starting to become a woman, and a target for men's lust. Her father wanted her safely out of the way in case the French populace gave a similar reception to English troops. I don't blame him for that. Or her for going along with his plans. I couldn't have asked for a better nurse, or a more cheerful companion through all the months I spent recovering. But she never wanted me for myself. Only what I could provide for her.'

'Cream horses and a box at the theatre,' put in Jayne. 'She was just the same over the red-satin dress. She'd seen one once, and promised herself if ever she had the means she'd get herself one just like it. Without once thinking about how inappropriate it was, or what she might have to do to earn it.'

'She came to her senses when she saw the state Fred had drunk himself into after he'd not been able to dissuade her from running off with Lord Halstead. That reached her in a way perhaps nothing else could have done. He absolutely worships the ground she walks on. And it turns out she needs a man to worship her more than cream horses or red-satin dresses. Though it helped when I promised to secure their future prosperity by buying them a tavern for a wedding present,' he added dryly.

'A tavern?'

'Yes. It is every soldier's dream to leave the army and own his own tavern. By the time I left Milly was full of plans for their new venture.'

'She will make a great success of it, I'm sure,' said Lady Jayne bleakly.

Milly was a competent person. Richard had told her once before that she was well able to look after herself. And she could just see Milly ordering supplies, bustling about and charming her customers.

'But I warn you,' he said sternly, 'I don't want you to go seeking her out and having any kind of association with her in future. She is capable of causing you no end of trouble.'

'I don't care about that!' She reined in her flash of temper, lest he think it was directed at him. 'I just don't think I will ever be able to forgive her for the way she used you and betrayed you.'

His heart swelled with love. Though he was not going to read too much into her reaction. She considered him her friend. He looked down at their linked hands. She would feel as outraged on behalf of anyone she considered her friend. It was the kind of person she was.

'I am so sorry, Richard, for the way it has turned out,' she said, looking at his downbent head. 'It is humiliating to discover that a person who has said they

love you has only been using you all along.' And then
to find himself compromised into marriage, while he
was still trying to recover from Milly's perfidy.

She wanted to put her arms round him and kiss away
his hurt. Milly had said all she would have to do would
be to offer him that sort of physical comfort and all
would be right with his world.

But then Milly hadn't really been in love. She didn't
understand that there was no substitute for the person
you loved. Besides, she didn't want to be a substitute
for anyone else. She didn't want Richard to be thinking
of Milly when he kissed her.

'We're trapped in such a terrible situation.' She let
go of his hand to rub at her forehead.

He looked up at her sharply.

'I only wish I could think of some way out.'

Panic chilled his gut into a block of ice. She was so
resourceful she would soon come up with dozens of
ways to wriggle out of this marriage—if he didn't put
a stop to it right now.

'There is none. So do not even bother trying to think
of escaping,' he said sternly. 'Your reputation would
never recover if I did not put a ring upon your finger
now. And mine would be irrevocably tarnished. People would think I was the kind of man who would turn
my back on a woman after seducing her. Do you think
I want that kind of notoriety?'

'N-no. Of course you don't. But it is so unfair! You
did not seduce me. And I do not want you to have to
pay the price for my own reckless…stupid… Oh!' She
leaped to her feet and began pacing up and down in
agitation. 'There must be *some* way out.'

'Well, there is not one. We have announced our

betrothal to our guests. In spite of his protests my grandfather will even now be sending the official announcement to the papers. It is too late to stop him.'

She stopped pacing and hugged herself round the middle, head bowed. He got to his feet, turned her round and laid his hands on her shoulders.

'Will it be such a terrible fate, Lady Jayne?' he asked her gently. 'Don't you think you could get used to being my wife? Could you not—' he squeezed her shoulders '—make the best of it?'

It would not be the least bit terrible being married to him—if only he did not think it was a situation *he* had to *get used to.* Her lower lip began to tremble. She caught it between her teeth.

He made a strangled sound in his throat, before grating, 'Now, now, don't cry.'

He put his arms right round her awkwardly and she sagged against him in despair. It was a pathetic parody of the kind of embrace a man ought to give the woman to whom he had just become betrothed.

'We have come to know each other pretty well over these past few weeks,' he said in such a reasonable tone it made her want to scream with frustration. 'I am sure we will be able to rub along tolerably well together, if only we put our minds to it.'

Rub along tolerably well? Oh, it hurt so much to hear his opinion of what their marriage would be like that it was actually growing hard to breathe.

She kept her face buried in the front of his waistcoat, since she could not bear to see the look of stoicism that must be on his face.

'I know you are a brave girl,' he said, running his hand up and down her spine in a soothing gesture. 'I know you have experienced a bitter disappointment quite recently, and that it is too soon to talk of anything more than friendship between us. But we have become quite *good* friends over the past few weeks, have we not? We have learned that we can trust one another. At least I trust you, Lady Jayne. I know that once we are married you will stay true to your vows. And I promise you I will be faithful to mine.'

It was no consolation at all to hear him declare that he intended to stay faithful to his vows. It was the kind of thing an honourable man did. Stuck to vows made in church.

But she wanted him to love her so much he would not *dream* of looking at another woman.

'We can make it work, this marriage of ours. I am sure we can. In fact, if you tell me what you want, I swear I will do all in my power to give it to you. What do you want from marriage?'

'Me?' She blinked up at him wide-eyed. Nobody had *ever* asked her what she wanted from marriage. Only insisted that it was her duty to marry well.

No wonder she couldn't help loving him.

'When Grandpapa sent me to Town to find a husband, I was so determined to thwart him that I never thought about what might actually tempt me into taking such a step. Though I have always known,' she said on a surge of certainty, 'what I don't want. And that is to end up living in a state of open warfare, like my parents did.'

He frowned. 'I have heard that your father was not the most pleasant of fellows.'

'He was perfectly beastly to Mama. He despised her for her inability to give him the heir he felt she owed him. She became dreadfully ill, with all the miscarriages she had. As long as I can remember she was practically an invalid. But she refused to lie down and die, and leave him free to marry again. I'm sure it was only her hatred of him that kept her going. For she did not outlive him by more than a few weeks.'

'That is appalling.' God, what she must have suffered as a child. 'I thought my own parents' marriage had been a disaster, but that...'

'Your parents' marriage was unhappy?'

'It was a pale imitation of your own parents', in some ways. My father was an incorrigible womanizer and my mother soon grew to despise him. And, then... Well, because he adored my older brother, his firstborn and heir, she despised him, too. But for some reason she took a shine to my baby brother. Which made my father, in his turn, despise Charlie. So it wasn't just the two of them involved in the battles, but the entire family.'

She noted he'd left himself out of the picture, and asked in a soft voice, 'Which of them either loved or despised you, Richard?'

'Me? Oh, neither of them bothered about me in the least,' he informed her, in a matter-of-fact tone that she could tell concealed a world of hurt.

For she remembered him saying that nobody had come to his aid when he'd been so ill—and the look on his face when he'd told her about all those letters that had gone unanswered while he lay hovering between life and death.

'They were quite wrong to treat you so,' she said indignantly.

'They were quite wrong to make my other brothers pawns in their ongoing war, as well. But never mind them. One thing I can certainly promise you. We won't end up like any of our parents. I...I like you too much to ever treat you with the disrespect my father showed my mother. In fact, I...' He took a deep breath.

Was now the time to tell her he loved her?

He hesitated. She'd said that having someone say the words gave them a kind of power over you. A kind of power she clearly didn't like.

And she'd already had one man tell her he loved her and prove false.

Dammit, if he'd only paved the way for such a declaration he might have stood some chance she would believe him. But as things stood... He would hate doing anything that might make her look upon him with suspicion, instead of the trust that was blazing from her eyes right now. Besides, every time he'd tried to start telling her how he felt he'd made a complete mull of it. Making plans and barking orders at troops were a far cry from uttering words of love. Especially when he was so unfamiliar with the emotion. When it made him never sure whether he was on his head or his heels.

He shook his head. He might have decided he was going to tell her how he felt today, but with everything that had happened since he'd made that decision he had a very strong suspicion that it might be counter-productive.

'I admire you very much,' he finished.

That was a start. She might not believe him if he blurted out some clumsy words that would, knowing him, be open to misinterpretation anyway. But if he demonstrated by the way he treated her, by the care he took of her, that she meant the world to him... After all, actions spoke louder than words. This building in which they stood was testimony to that. His grandfather had shown the wife his parents had chosen for him that he loved her by building this place just to keep the rain off her while she watched the progress of the canal being dug through the valley.

Since they were going to be married he had a lifetime to convince her of his utter sincerity by the way he pampered and cosseted her. His spirits lifted.

'Now, you say you had not thought about what you wanted from marriage. But—forgive me if you find this an insensitive question—you *would* have married Lieutenant Kendell if you had been able to. So what was it about him that made you willing to flout all the rules?'

She blushed and lowered her head. When she looked back on her behaviour with regard to Harry it made her cringe. She had not loved him at all! Nor wanted to marry him—not once he had kissed her. But it would be too humiliating to admit that.

Though she did want to be able to tell Richard the whole truth one day. Perhaps after they'd been married a few months, and she'd had a chance to prove she wasn't the silly girl she'd shown herself to be in all their dealings thus far.

'You have to understand what my life has been like.' For today, it would have to be enough to explain some of the steps that had led her into the tangle with Harry. 'When I was a little girl, you see, nobody much cared what I did as long as I stayed out of the way. So I ended up left in the care of a groom, mostly, haring about all over the estates. But then my parents died, and Grandpapa took me to Darvill Park. He was so shocked by my uncouth ways that he spent the next few years beating them all out of me.'

'He beat you?'

'No. Not physically. But I felt…trampled on. I was watched every moment of the day. And drilled relentlessly. And I was never allowed to mix with anyone he had not first approved. Eventually, after years and years of imprisonment on the estate, he thought he had succeeded in making me behave like a *proper* young lady, and allowed me to go to a few local assemblies. Well, he could hardly not! Not when other girls my age, from good families in the area, were going to them. It would have looked like failure. And Grandpapa never fails!

'Anyway, Harry came and asked me to dance without first getting approval from my chaperone. He asked *me* if I wanted to. He looked so dashing in his uniform. I felt so daring when I said yes without checking first. And when Grandpapa forbade me to see him again, I… dug my heels in. You see, no matter how hard I tried, I never managed to please him. So I decided to stop trying.'

Richard flinched. God, he knew exactly what that felt like! The letters he'd written home when he'd first gone away to school that nobody had ever replied to. The creeping realisation that nobody cared where he was so long as he wasn't underfoot.

'I just could not stand it any more. The confinement. The rules and restrictions. I just had to make a stand over Harry. Do you see?'

'Only too well.'

'And then when Harry followed me to London I was completely overwhelmed by what I thought was his devotion. Nobody had cared so much for me before. Not my parents. Not my grandfather, who disapproved of everything about me. And I had never had any friends that I had chosen myself. But there was Harry, telling me he would risk everything to be with me, and I...I lost my head.'

Her shoulders slumped. 'Of course, it turned out not to be me he wanted at all, but only my money. I do not know why I did not see that from the start.'

Richard hugged her. No wonder she had fallen prey so easily to a glib, personable fortune-hunter. Nobody else had ever shown her a scrap of affection. She had no means of telling the genuine from the counterfeit. He had almost made the same kind of mistake with Milly—although, having been an officer, he had a sight more experience of spotting a lie when it was told him.

'My poor darling,' he said.

He was glad now that he had not spoken words to her that had been used to deceive her in the past. It would be better to *show* her what real love was all about. Day by day, month by month, year by year, he would love her so wholeheartedly that it would wipe away all the years of hurt and neglect she had endured thus far. Seeing to her welfare, ensuring her happiness, would be his prime objective.

To his last dying breath.

Chapter Fifteen

When she got back to the house, Lady Jayne found a very tense-looking Lady Penrose waiting for her in her rooms. With some very surprising news.

'My dear, your grandfather has arrived.'

'How did he know that—?'

'Oh, he did not know anything about last night—how could he? No, he came because he was angry to find, when he returned to Darvill Park, that you were not in London, waiting for him as instructed. He was quite furious when he got here...'

Her heart sank. 'And now, of course, he must be even more angry...'

'No! Far from it.' Lady Penrose's lips twitched with wry amusement. 'The news that you are betrothed went a long way to appeasing him.'

'Oh. Of course.' For as long as he'd had control of her life he had been training her to become a fitting wife for a man of high station. Lord Ledbury was exactly the kind of man of whom he would approve. Catching him would atone for any number of other transgressions. 'Does he know...everything?'

'Unfortunately, yes. That buffoon Lord Lavenham gave him the scurrilous version of events.'

'And how did he take it?'

Lady Penrose sobered. 'You will find out for yourself when you see him. He is waiting for you in Lord Lavenham's study.'

Knowing that his temper would only increase the longer she kept him waiting, she hastily changed from her mud-spattered riding habit into a gown more becoming for a meeting with her formidable guardian.

Her heart was hammering as she made her way down the stairs, even though Lady Penrose was at her back, providing much welcome support.

She hesitated outside the door, making sure her emotional armour was in place before facing him. But when she went in the first person she saw was Richard. She did not know how he had managed to get there before her, but she was incredibly grateful that, for the first time in her life, she was not going to have to face her grandfather's wrath alone.

Part of her wanted to run straight to his side. But she detested revealing any form of weakness to her grandfather. So she stiffened her spine and turned towards the chair upon which Lord Caxton was sitting. She dipped a curtsy and then, when he motioned her to approach, bent to bestow a dutiful kiss, as though she had nothing whatsoever to fear.

At the last moment he raised his hand to his face, as if he was suddenly recalling something. And that was when she noticed he had three nasty-looking gashes on his face. It looked like something, perhaps a cat, had raked its claws across his skin.

He turned his other cheek for her to kiss, and then,

when she would have straightened up, grasped her hand in his. 'Do you *want* to marry this young man? Will he be able to make you happy?' he asked.

When she could not hide her astonishment that his first words were not a reproof, his expression turned wry.

'What? Has it never occurred to you that your happiness is of great importance to me? It is all I have ever wanted for you.' He grimaced. 'All I ever wanted for all my girls. I dare say you think I have treated you harshly in the past. But you were such a wild little creature when you came to me. I thought my primary duty was to tame you. For there is a streak of rebelliousness in you to which, alas, the Vickery women seem particularly prone.'

Tears sprang to his eyes as he said in a quavering voice, 'I was afraid that if I did not subdue it you would end up just like your aunt. And I could not have borne to lose you to some adventurer, as I lost her.'

She had never seen him looking so emotional. She had always thought him such a rigid disciplinarian. Yet all the time he had been concealing a deep abiding fear that she would turn out like her Aunt Aurora.

Her aunt's elopement and subsequent estrangement had clearly cut him much deeper than he had ever let anyone suspect. She had always thought he refused to let her name be spoken because he was angry with her. But that was not the case at all. It was because it hurt too much.

Suddenly she understood him as she had never done before. Because he was acting in exactly the way *she* would have behaved. People accused her of being cold, because she could fix her expression into a mask that concealed what she was feeling. The more she hurt, the colder she looked. They had said she got that trait from her father. But now she saw how absurd it was for them to say that. He had *never* bothered to conceal his feelings. Particularly not the contempt he'd felt for her, nor the hatred he had borne for her mother. His pride had been of the kind that made him impervious to what anyone thought of him.

Her pride was the pride of the Vickerys, which made it an absolute necessity never to let anyone suspect they might have wounded her. She was a Vickery through and through, she realized on a wave of relief. Not a Chilcott after all.

For the very first time she felt a real connection with this proud old aristocrat sitting before her. And the minute she understood that she was far more like her grandfather than she'd ever suspected, she saw what her refusal to welcome his long-lost granddaughter back into the family must have done to him.

'I am so sorry I did not obey your summons to meet my cousin, Lady Bowdon. I hope she was not offended.'

Or perhaps hurt. Oh, how ashamed she was of flouncing off in completely the opposite direction from where he'd ordered her, without considering what effect it would have on her poor cousin. She caught her lower lip between her teeth. She might at least have written to Lady Bowdon. But she'd been so angry it just hadn't occurred to her.

To her surprise, instead of following up her apology with a stinging rebuke, as was his wont, Lord Caxton smiled, a soft faraway look in his eyes.

'We can make all right with an invitation to your wedding now. I cannot begin to express my relief that you have found a man of substance to marry. A man who will be able to care for you when I am gone.'

She caught a quick, searching look in his eyes which prompted her to say, 'Yes, indeed he will.' For had not Richard promised as much? He would do his best, he had told her, to make sure they never became enemies—which, considering the way this betrothal had come about, was much more than she deserved.

Her eyes flew to Richard's. He was staring into a glass of what looked suspiciously like brandy with a wooden countenance.

'You will be married from Darvill Park, of course,' said Lord Caxton. 'Lady Bowdon and her husband will come to stay beforehand, which will give us all time to get to know one another before the ceremony.'

From that moment on he and Lady Penrose practically ignored her while they discussed arrangements.

At first Jayne was inclined to bridle at the way he had walked in and simply taken over. But she very soon realized that she had no real objections to any of the plans they were making on her behalf. She *would* be only too glad to get to know her cousin and her husband, and any friends of theirs, before her own wedding. It would just be less annoying if they at least pretended to consider her wishes.

Besides, she could see that Lord Caxton was really looking forward to hosting the wedding of the Season. He seemed to grow younger and more animated by the second. And letting him enjoy himself like this felt like a good way to atone for having so badly misjudged him all these years. She had been so used to unkindness from her parents that she hadn't understood he'd been trying to eradicate the effects of all those years of neglect and abuse.

It was Richard's grandfather who injected the only jarring note into the proceedings, by rather caustically pointing out that it might be better to get a special licence.

'You don't want to delay the ceremony for too long. Since they have already anticipated their vows.'

Her own grandfather looked at him down the length of his long, aristocratic nose, his nostrils pinched.

'I will not have my granddaughter married in some secretive, hasty fashion which will give others leave to suspect she has done something of which I disapprove,' he said in a withering tone. 'I intend to tell anyone who is vulgar enough to enquire—should they hear any of the gossip that is running rife through *your* household— that they are so much in love with each other they simply could not wait. And that I have decided to forgive their youthful impetuosity. If *you* are foolish enough to imply that this is anything other than a love match, all you will achieve is to drag the names of both our families through the mud.'

Lady Jayne could hardly believe it. For the first time in her life, her grandfather had spoken in her defence.

Lord Lavenham got to his feet and glared at Lord Caxton, his face suffused with purple. Lord Caxton lounged back in his chair, a slight sneer curling his lip. For a second or two the others all held their breath. It was rather like watching two stags preparing to lock horns.

The battle that might have ensued would no doubt have been of epic proportions had not Lady Penrose defused the situation by bringing them all back to practicalities.

'So we are agreed. Lady Jayne will leave here tomorrow and go to Darvill Park, so that the banns can be read at the parish church this Sunday. Three weeks should give us enough time to organize everything.'

Lord Ledbury's heart sank into his boots. He felt just as he had when his own cavalry had ridden over him at Orthez. Only this time he was not in physical pain. But in mental agony.

They were taking Lady Jayne away to Kent, to prepare for their wedding, just when he most needed to keep her at his side and convince her that marrying him was not such a terrible fate. He had begun to hope, that morning, that he had made some progress with her. She had agreed that they were already friends, at least. Nor had she objected to letting him hold her, for a few moments, in a comforting sort of way. But then for some reason she'd pulled away and dashed outside. He hadn't been too worried then. He'd thought he would have plenty of time to find out what had spooked her and soothe away whatever insecurities still plagued her.

But now he felt hope slipping through his fingers, leaving him grasping at air. Why couldn't anyone else see how suspicious it was that from the moment Lord Caxton had set foot in Courtlands she had turned back into that expressionless little porcelain doll, meekly agreeing with everything they decided? *Look at her!* he wanted to shout. Couldn't they see that the way she was sitting, with her hands folded neatly in her lap, that expression of polite acquiescence on her face, was a pose to hide what she was really thinking?

It was a trick he'd learned himself, when hauled up

before a commanding officer to answer for some misdemeanour. *All* soldiers perfected the knack of keeping a wooden countenance whilst internally cursing the pompous ass who was dressing them down.

God, what was she *really* thinking? What did she *feel* about the arrangements they were making on her behalf?

And, more importantly, what was she planning to do about it?

He should never have let it come to this. When she had come to him last night he should have escorted her straight back to her own room and let Milly go to the devil her own way. Except that Lady Jayne had been so upset at the thought of her friend's ruin. And he couldn't bear to think of her living with that distress for the rest of her life.

And what had happened to all those fine decisions he'd made on his way back? About how he was going to tell her everything, lay his heart bare before her, and then lay siege to her heart until she surrendered?

He'd seen Lady Jayne naked, that was what had happened, and it had all gone to hell in a handcart.

It was all he could do not to groan out loud. Nobody else was asking her what she wanted, but *he* had to know. He had to straighten things out between them or he was going to spend the next three weeks worrying that when he got to the altar his resourceful bride would be miles and miles away.

No doubt in the mistaken belief that it was for his own good.

Lady Jayne blew out her candle and flopped back onto her pillows. If she had been the kind of girl who got headaches she was sure she would have one now, even though her grandfather's timely arrival seemed to have nipped the threat of scandal in the bud.

She had been amazed, at dinner that night, how much the atmosphere had changed since breakfast. Even Lady Susan had remarked, albeit rather waspishly, that she had seen from the start that she and Richard had only ever had eyes for each other. Not that she believed that tale for a minute. The chaperones had probably counselled all the disappointed contenders for Richard's hand that it would be far wiser to stay on good terms with the scions of two such influential families than say anything to precipitate a complete breach.

She was sick of all the pretence. In some ways she would be glad to leave Courtlands in the morning. If only it did not mean that she would not be seeing Richard again for more than three weeks. He had tried so hard to make everyone believe he was perfectly content to be marrying her. But she hadn't been able to help noticing that he was looking more and more strained as the day wore on. After three more weeks of contemplating the marriage to which her thoughtless actions had condemned him he might well have built up quite a store of resentment.

If only she could—

What was that? It sounded as though something large and heavy had just landed on the roof of the *porte-cochère*.

She sat up and stared at the window, even though the darkness and the drawn curtains prevented her from seeing out.

Then there was a scraping noise…as though something metallic was sliding across the tiles.

She got out of bed just as something rattled down the roof and then smashed onto the gravel path beneath. One of the tiles, by the sound of it.

She had just put her hand to the curtains, to draw them back so she could look out, when there was a rasping sound, and then a click and then the casement creaked open.

Someone was breaking into her room!

She dashed back to the bed, looked wildly around for a weapon, and seized upon the candlestick.

She turned round, half crouched defensively, to see a man's booted leg, which he had clearly just been thrown over the windowsill, appear through the curtains.

Swiftly followed by...

'Richard!' She stood up straight. 'What on earth do you think you are doing?'

'Climbing up to your room, obviously,' he said, pushing the curtains aside so that he could get his other leg over the windowsill and stand up.

Immediately shafts of moonlight silvered the scene, taking her back to the time they had been alone in the library.

Her heart, which had been beating fast with trepidation just a moment previously, hesitated and then settled into a heavy rhythm which had nothing to do with fear at all. She was wearing only her nightdress. And he was dressed in a uniform which had clearly seen better days. There were patches, and holes with charred edges all over it. And as for his boots—they were the very antithesis of the highly polished Hessians he wore about Town. They were scuffed, and creased round the ankles, as though they were far too comfortable for him to throw away even though they looked so shabby.

It reminded her of how rakish and daring he had looked on the night of the masquerade. Only tonight he was not in costume.

This was the real man. The man he had told her about. The soldier who had marched across scorching plains and slept on frozen ground.

The man who climbed into a lady's window and... what?

'What do you want?' Her voice had gone breathy, and was barely more than a whisper as she asked, 'Why have you come?'

He stalked across to where she stood, his mouth curving into a grin. 'That's my Jayne,' he said approvingly. 'Straight to the point. No vapours or feeble feminine protests about impropriety.'

'Well, there would be little point, would there? Everyone already thinks I am ruined.'

He grimaced, coming to a halt only an inch or so from her.

She could feel the heat from his body through the flimsy material of her nightgown. He was breathing heavily from his exertions, and a faint sheen of sweat made his brow glisten. Was he going to ruin her properly tonight? Lady Penrose had said if he had not been interrupted he would have done so that morning. And at The Workings this morning he'd looked for a moment as though he'd been thinking about what they'd started.

Her tummy flipped with excitement.

Then from his cross belt he plucked out two roses that had been tucked there. A white one, and she thought a red one—though the moonlight had robbed it of its colour.

'You climbed up to my room...to bring me roses?'

It was a lovely, romantic gesture. But she couldn't understand why he should think that at this stage it was necessary. Unless… Perhaps he thought it would make it easier for her to become reconciled to this forced betrothal if he gave her some reassurance? Looking back over the day, she realized she'd done nothing but talk about finding ways out of it.

Yes, that was just the sort of thing he would do to ease her over what he thought she saw as a dreadful hurdle.

She laid the candlestick down and took them from him.

'And to tell you that to me,' he said with deliberation, as though he had rehearsed what he was about to say, 'you are as lovely as any rose. I know you can be a little unapproachable at times. I think you have deliberately cultivated a hedge of thorns about yourself, to stop anyone from getting too close to you and hurting you.'

'You…you think I am prickly?'

'You know very well you can be, my lady.' He stepped closer still, his voice low and urgent as he said, 'But it does not lessen my regard for you. A rose is a wonderful flower. Nothing can compare with its voluptuous, velvety petals.'

He reached out and twined one curl, which had escaped her plaits, round his forefinger. She caught her lower lip between her teeth.

'Or the heady perfume it gives off,' he grated. 'Lady Jayne, will you…? I came here to ask you…' He was staring at her mouth. 'Whatever it was has gone completely out of my head now,' he said irritably. 'All I can think about is how much I want to kiss you.'

'You want to kiss me?'

'God, yes,' he said, his voice throbbing with yearning.

Then, slowly, he began to lower his head towards hers. Giving her the chance, she realized, to refuse him. But she did not want to. So she tipped her head back, offering him her lips.

And he did kiss her.

Not swiftly, as he had done just before going out to chase after Milly. Or with that edge of desperation he had displayed when he'd come back. But slowly, as though he had all the time in the world and intended to savour every minute. He slid his arms round her waist and pulled her close. She clung to the facings of his jacket. The scent of roses filled the air as the flowers were crushed between their two heated bodies. Indeed, by the time he finished she felt as though she was melting.

But still a faint feeling of unease nagged at her.

'You don't need to do this. I don't want you to pretend something you don't feel for me, or—'

'Very well, then,' he said raggedly, stepping back. 'Listen to me, Lady Jayne. I am not pretending any more. I'm done with pretence. I have to tell you...'

'Yes?'

'That nightgown of yours is virtually transparent,' he groaned. 'Don't stand just there in the moonlight, please, or I won't be able to think of anything but how beautiful your breasts are. How much I want to see them again, taste them again...'

She went weak at the knees as her memory supplied the feel of his hands cupping her breasts. His tongue lapping. His teeth nipping.

The roses fell from her hands as they flew instinctively to her neckline.

He sucked in a short, sharp breath as she loosened the ribbons of her gown with trembling fingers.

'Maybe I don't want you to think about anything else,' she said, pushing the fine lawn from one shoulder, revealing the upper slope of her left breast. But then her courage ran out. He had not seemed to like it when he found her naked in his bed. Would he lose all respect for her if she fully exposed her breast to his gaze? Would he think she was wanton?

She was just about to cover herself up again when his hand shot out and stayed hers. Then, very gently, he stroked the fabric of her gown aside.

For a moment he just stood there, breathing heavily as he gazed at her. His hand hovered an inch above her flesh so that she could feel the heat of it, tantalizingly close. The tremors that ran through his body made it look as though he was exerting all his willpower to hold himself back.

So she stepped forward, pushing her breast into his outstretched hand. Her nipple beaded into his palm immediately.

And then it was as if whatever had been holding him back snapped. He tore open enough fastenings to expose both breasts. His mouth swooped to suckle feverishly on one while his hand caressed the other. The sensation was incredible. And it was not restricted to the area where he was touching her, but flooded the whole of her being with heat and yearning and wonder.

'I want you,' he said.

'Y-you do?' she gasped.

'More than anything. Oh, Jayne,' he murmured, running kisses along her collarbone and up the side of her neck. 'Jayne.' He sighed into her ear.

'Oh, yes, Richard, yes.'

'Yes? You mean that?'

'Mmm…'

She wanted to reach up and put her arms round his neck, to show him that she was a more than willing participant in whatever was going to happen. But her nightgown had slid down to her elbows, imprisoning them at her sides. And it suddenly felt much more satisfying to leave him entirely in charge. To know that whatever followed was all going to be exactly as *he* wanted. She did not want to feel any guilt, any shadow of doubt about who had seduced whom. Not tonight.

He walked her backwards to the bed, hastily undid the rest of her ribbons and slid her nightgown down over her hips. Then he picked her up and laid her gently down on the bed.

She felt very shy about being so exposed while he was still fully dressed. But he only stood looking down at her for a moment before joining her on the bed. He paid such sweet homage to her—with his hands, his lips, his tongue—that it was as though he was worshipping her body. He made her feel like a goddess as he bestowed reverent kisses upon every inch of her. He untied her plaits, sifted her hair through his fingers as though it was some rare treasure, then spread it out across the pillows. He stroked her flanks as though enchanted by the curve of her hips, the indentation of her waist. And whenever he encountered a bruise or a scrape he placed a particularly tender kiss there.

But eventually he began to restrict his attentions to the parts of her that were crying out for attention the most. Pretty soon the sensations he evoked were so intense she had no power left to think, only to feel.

And what she felt was beautiful. Men had told her before that she was beautiful. But she had dismissed their words as just that. Mere words. Only Richard could make her *feel* she really was beautiful. To him.

Yet though it was glorious it was not enough. She needed to touch him, too. Needed to kiss him.

'Richard, please,' she whimpered, reaching for him. 'Kiss me.'

At her pleading, he rolled her onto her side so they were face to face and did as she bade, kissing her long and languorously. Prising open her mouth with the insistent probing of his tongue and thrusting it inside when she opened to him.

It felt incredible, having his fully clothed body all along the length of her sensitized skin. The roughness of the material of what she was certain was the uniform in which he had served created such delicious friction.

She raised her leg, rubbing her foot along the supple leather of his boots, feeling the material of his breeches abrading the soft skin of her inner thigh.

He pushed her onto her back, reared up and pulled off his jacket.

'Buttons,' he muttered. 'Don't want to hurt you.'

And then he was back, kissing her with a feverishness that was even more glorious than anything that had gone before. For even in her inexperience she could tell his passion was raging almost beyond his control. The satisfying proof of that came when he fumbled open his breeches, pushing material out of the way, and nudged her legs apart.

And then suddenly he froze.

'I should not be doing this,' he said through gritted teeth. 'Lady Jayne, can you ever forgive me?'

When he made to roll off her she let out an indignant squeal and locked her hands behind his neck. 'I shall never forgive you if you stop now—and that is a promise!'

'It is wrong,' he insisted, though she noted with satisfaction that he wasn't trying all that hard to pull away from her. 'I did not come here for this.' He groaned. His whole body was shaking. 'I must not force myself on you like this....'

'You think you are forcing me?'

'Yes.' He lay down and pressed his face into the crook of her neck. 'You have to marry me, Jayne. I want you so much...too much,' he murmured.

His breath was hot on her ear. And the weight of him on top of her, with her legs spread like that, made it hard to concentrate on his words. She could only feel.

'Richard, please stop talking and just take me.'

'You are still that wild little creature your grandfather described this morning,' he said softly as she butted her hips up against his pelvis with a little whimper. 'You think right now that this is what you want because you are being ruled by your senses. But in the morning, when you think about it...'

'I shall be glad that you made me yours completely,' she declared. 'I shall ride back to Darvill Park in the carriage, hugging the knowledge that you saw something in me that made you climb up to my room and behave completely disgracefully, for once.'

And with that she spread her legs wider and hooked her ankles round the backs of his knees. The slight shift in position brought his member to the exact spot where she needed to feel it.

'Oh, God,' he groaned. 'I cannot fight you any more.'

He reached between her legs. Stroked along the slick folds of skin with his fingers. Then repeated the action with his rigid length. Sliding repeatedly towards the place where she felt an aching need to have him. The need increased as he continued to tease her until she was writhing beneath him, clawing at his back and panting, 'For God's sake, Richard, now. *Now!*'

And at last he pushed up, and in, and he was there, seated deep within her. Exactly where she needed him.

For a few glorious moments they both went wild. He plunged and she bucked. She clung and he grasped. He suckled on her neck. She sank her teeth into his shoulder. She flung her head back to cry out her ecstasy. He buried his face in her hair to groan out his, his fingers kneading into her buttocks so hard she knew she would still feel the imprint in her flesh the next day.

'You are mine now,' he panted. 'You will *have* to marry me.'

'And *you* will have to marry me.' She sighed with utter bliss. 'You are too much the gentleman to abandon a woman you have so thoroughly ravished.'

He winced. 'A real gentleman would never have done what I just did.'

'I don't think I will ever have much use for a real gentleman.' She sighed, running her hands up his shirt, which was stuck to his back with sweat. And then she giggled. 'I cannot believe you climbed up here and made love to me without so much as taking your boots off!'

In the silvered light that shimmered across her bed she saw a look of anguish flit across his face before he said, 'I wanted to show you who I really am. I came to you in my uniform because deep down I'm just a soldier, Jayne, not a lord. But I never intended to rob you of your innocence. I...I only meant to take you out for a moonlit picnic at The Workings. So I made a grappling hook to fix into the ridge tiles, and brought a rope ladder for you to climb down so you wouldn't graze your knees like last time. To demonstrate that if you need to climb out of a window for a little adventure I will be right there with you, making it better than anything you could have on your own. But the minute I saw you standing there bathed in moonlight,' he said huskily, 'I just couldn't resist you.'

He shook his head ruefully and rolled to one side, holding her tight, as though he was determined not to let her go even though they were no longer conjoined.

'No, it was before that. When you nibbled on your lower lip.' He sighed, tracing it with his thumb. 'That *always* has the effect of making me almost forget my own name. Though that's no excuse. I should have stuck to my plans tonight, our last night together for weeks, when it was so important that I bared my soul to you. Instead of which I was still...trying to protect myself.'

He shut his eyes, as though he was ashamed to meet her gaze.

'I have been a soldier most of my life, and soldiers get battered about. My leg, especially, is not a pretty sight,' he said sombrely. 'But then nor is a great deal of the rest of me. I made love to you with most of my clothes on because I didn't want you to see my scars. For you are so breathtakingly lovely. A vision.' He opened his eyes and tangled his fingers into her tousled curls. 'Far too beautiful to have to be tied to a wreck of a man like me.'

'Oh, Richard,' she said, 'what you look like has nothing to do with how I feel about you.'

'I know, I know,' he said swiftly. 'You are very far

from being vain or shallow, like most of your sex. But, even so, I am not quite what you wanted from a husband, am I?'

Before she could refute this allegation he had propped himself up on one elbow and was looking down into her face with such an earnest expression that she did not have the heart to argue with him. Whatever it was he was about to say was coming from some deep place in his heart, and she knew she needed to let him say it.

'Jayne, I love you. I love you so much that I won't ever try to repress any aspect of your nature. That is why I climbed up here tonight. I wanted to persuade you that we are made for each other. To tell you that I adore you exactly as you are. To show you that I don't want to *tame* you, like your grandfather has tried to do. Well,' he said ruefully, 'that is only half the tale. To be completely truthful I wanted to climb up after you through your bedroom window that first night we met.'

'You love me?' she gasped. 'You have wanted me since *that* night?'

'Yes. Even though I knew you were in love with Harry. I even started plotting ways to get rid of him. I grew so desperate. The only thing holding me back was knowing you would never forgive me....'

'Oh, how I wish you'd told me. Richard, I *never* loved Harry. I tried to explain to you this afternoon that he was just a rebellion against my grandfather's tyranny. I didn't realize that myself until he kissed me and it was so disgusting. After that, all I could think of was how to get rid of him, too.'

She checked at the look of astonishment on his face. And suddenly, from feeling like some kind of goddess, she shrank back to being just a child on the verge of a scold again.

'Does that make me a bad person?'

'No. Quite the reverse. You told me earlier, remember, that his declaration of love gave him a hold over you? And you are such a warm-hearted person that I can understand exactly how hard it must have been for you to find a way to break it off with him without hurting him. Even though it was all lies. But, Jayne, I am not lying to you. I really do love you.'

She looked at him doubtfully. 'How can you? Milly only ran away yesterday...'

'Ah, but I never loved Milly, either.'

'What? Never?'

'No. I admired her greatly for her courage and resourcefulness. I wanted to be sure she was going to be happy when we had to go our separate ways. But...'

'But she said...'

'I am sorry she misled you. But, Jayne, I had no idea you thought I was in love with her until you told me yesterday when we were out riding. I did try to explain, several times, but something always got in the way.' His eyes dropped to her mouth as she took in a great, shuddering breath.

'You didn't love Milly at all?'

'Not one bit.'

'All this time,' she said, 'I have been doing my utmost to make things work out for the pair of you. Because I thought if *I* could not have your heart, the least I could do was ensure you could marry the woman you did love, and not one of those dreadfully *accomplished* women.'

'Well, I *am* going to marry the woman I love, so...

Wait a minute—that sounded as though... What you said... Do you...?'

'Yes. I love you, Richard. I have been so miserable because I thought you could never love me.'

'How could you think that?' He closed his eyes and winced. 'No, I know only too well *exactly* why you felt unworthy of love. Your wretched childhood. And then Harry's lies on top of it all.'

'Richard,' she said in wonder. 'I don't think there is anyone in the whole world who would just *understand* me the way you do. And still...I...like me.'

He smiled tenderly. 'I more than like you. And the best of it is we have the rest of our lives to get to know each other even better.'

'Then would you mind explaining why you thought I would ever want to climb out of a window again when I have all I need right here?'

'Well, I didn't know you loved me then.'

'*Your* wretched childhood,' she said, quick as a flash, and hugged him hard.

'And as I've already said,' he murmured, burying his face in her curls, 'I couldn't let you leave without telling you how desperately I do want to be your husband. The moonlight picnic was supposed to give me the chance to lay my heart bare before you went away.' He pulled back abruptly. 'It's still there, laid out for us to enjoy. And there are two horses saddled and ready to go...'

'Richard,' she said tenderly, reaching up to stroke his scarred face, 'I don't really want to have to climb out of a window ever again.'

'You don't?'

'No. I've already told you. I have all I need right here. Except...'

'What? Tell me what you want. Anything, any-thing…'

'For what I have in mind you need to stop talking, Major Cathcart.'

She gave a sultry smile and settled back against the pillows.

'And take off your shirt.'

* * * * *

COMING NEXT MONTH from Harlequin® Historical
AVAILABLE JULY 24, 2012

MONTANA BRIDE
Jillian Hart
Left widowed, pregnant and penniless, Willa Conner's last hope is
the stranger who answers her ad for a husband. Austin Dermot, a
hardworking Montana blacksmith, doesn't know what to expect
from a mail-order bride. It certainly isn't the brave, beautiful, but
scarred young woman who cautiously steps off the train...
(Western)

OUTRAGEOUS CONFESSIONS OF LADY DEBORAH
Marguerite Kaye
I am the Dowager Countess of Kinsail, and I have enough secrets
to scandalize you for life. Only now I have a new secret, one that
I will risk my life to keep: I am accomplice to Elliot Marchmont,
gentleman, ex-soldier and notorious London thief. His touch
ignites a passion so intoxicating that surviving our blistering affair
unscathed will be near impossible....
(Regency)

A NOT SO RESPECTABLE GENTLEMAN?
Diane Gaston
Since returning to London, Leo Fitzmanning's kept his mind off
a certain raven-haired heiress. Until he discovers that Miss Mariel
Covendale is being forced into an unscrupulous marriage! Leo must
re-enter the society he detests to help her, but soon there's *nothing*
respectable about his reasons for stopping Mariel's marriage!
(Regency)

LADY WITH THE DEVIL'S SCAR
Sophia James
Badly disfigured Lady Isobel Dalceann has
fought fiercely to defend her keep, with little
thought for her safety—why, then, has she let
a stranger within her walls? His battered body
mirrors her own scars and tempts her to put
her faith in him. But what would she do if she
were ever to find out who Marc de Courtenay
really is?
(Medieval)

You can find more information on upcoming Harlequin®
titles, free excerpts and more at www.Harlequin.com.

HHCNM0712

REQUEST YOUR
FREE BOOKS!

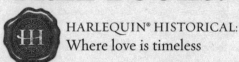

HARLEQUIN® HISTORICAL:
Where love is timeless

2 FREE NOVELS PLUS 2 FREE GIFTS!

YES! Please send me 2 FREE Harlequin® Historical novels and my 2 FREE gifts (gifts are worth about $10). After receiving them, if I don't wish to receive any more books, I can return the shipping statement marked "cancel." If I don't cancel, I will receive 6 brand-new novels every month and be billed just $5.19 per book in the U.S. or $5.74 per book in Canada. That's a savings of at least 17% off the cover price! It's quite a bargain! Shipping and handling is just 50¢ per book in the U.S. and 75¢ per book in Canada.* I understand that accepting the 2 free books and gifts places me under no obligation to buy anything. I can always return a shipment and cancel at any time. Even if I never buy another book, the two free books and gifts are mine to keep forever.

246/349 HDN FEQQ

Name	(PLEASE PRINT)	
Address		Apt. #
City	State/Prov.	Zip/Postal Code

Signature (if under 18, a parent or guardian must sign)

Mail to the **Reader Service:**
IN U.S.A.: P.O. Box 1867, Buffalo, NY 14240-1867
IN CANADA: P.O. Box 609, Fort Erie, Ontario L2A 5X3

Not valid for current subscribers to Harlequin Historical books.

Want to try two free books from another line?
Call 1-800-873-8635 or visit www.ReaderService.com.

* Terms and prices subject to change without notice. Prices do not include applicable taxes. Sales tax applicable in N.Y. Canadian residents will be charged applicable taxes. Offer not valid in Quebec. This offer is limited to one order per household. All orders subject to credit approval. Credit or debit balances in a customer's account(s) may be offset by any other outstanding balance owed by or to the customer. Please allow 4 to 6 weeks for delivery. Offer available while quantities last.

Your Privacy—The Reader Service is committed to protecting your privacy. Our Privacy Policy is available online at www.ReaderService.com or upon request from the Reader Service.

We make a portion of our mailing list available to reputable third parties that offer products we believe may interest you. If you prefer that we not exchange your name with third parties, or if you wish to clarify or modify your communication preferences, please visit us at www.ReaderService.com/consumerschoice or write to us at Reader Service Preference Service, P.O. Box 9062, Buffalo, NY 14269. Include your complete name and address.

HHI1B

HARLEQUIN® HISTORICAL:
Where love is timeless

Fan-favorite author
JILLIAN HART
brings you a timeless tale of faith and love in

Montana Bride

Willa Conner learned a long time ago that love is a fairy tale.
She's been left widowed, pregnant and penniless, and her last
hope is the stranger who answers her ad for a husband.

Austin Dermot, a hardworking Montana blacksmith, doesn't
know what to expect from a mail-order bride. It certainly
isn't the brave, beautiful, but scarred young woman who
cautiously steps off the train....

Trust won't come easily for Willa—it's hard for her to believe
she's worthy of true love. But she doesn't need to worry about
that, because this is just a marriage of convenience...isn't it?

Can two strangers be a match made in the West?

Find out this August!

www.Harlequin.com

HH29699

When Lady Deborah Napier blackmails notorious London thief Elliot Marchmont into becoming his accomplice, the thrill of adventure is *nothing* compared to the sudden rush of intoxicating passion that he incites within her….

"If I take you, it will be because I want to."

The words made Deborah shiver. Did he want her? Want *her?* No one had ever wanted her like that. "And do you—want me?"

Looking around swiftly to check they were quite alone, Elliot pulled her to him, a dark glint in his eyes. "You are playing a very dangerous game, Deborah Napier. I would advise you to have a care. For, if you dance with the devil, you are likely to get burnt. You may come with me, but only if you promise to do exactly as I say."

"You mean it!" *Oh God, he meant it!* She would be a housebreaker. A thief! "I'll do exactly as you say."

"Then prove it. Kiss me," Elliot said audaciously, not thinking for a moment that she would.

But she did. Without giving herself time to think, her heart hammering against her breast, Deborah stood on tiptoe, pulled his head down to hers and did as she was bid. Right there in Hyde Park, in the middle of the day, she kissed him.

She meant it as a kiss to seal their bargain, but as soon as her lips touched his, memories, real and imagined, made the taste of him headily familiar. His lips were warm on hers, every bit as sinfully delicious as she'd imagined, coaxing her mouth to flower open beneath his, teasing her lips into compliance, heating her gently, delicately, until his tongue touched hers.

It was a kiss like none she had ever tasted, heated by the

bargain it concluded, fired by the very illicitness of their kissing here in a public space, where at any moment they could be discovered. She could not have imagined, could not have dreamed that kissing, just kissing could rouse her in this way.

"Are you quite sure you want to do this?" he asked.

"Oh yes," she said, "I'm sure."

Elliot *always* gets what he wants. But will this most accomplished thief steal his greatest prize to date—Lady Deborah's heart?

Find out in
OUTRAGEOUS CONFESSIONS OF LADY DEBORAH
by Marguerite Kaye,
available from Harlequin® Historical in August 2012.

Copyright © 2012 by Marguerite Kaye

HHEXP0812

Harlequin Presents

Discover an enchanting duet filled with glitz,
glamour and passionate love from

Melanie Milburne

THE *Outrageous* SISTERS

The twin sisters everyone's talking about!

Separated by secrets…

Having grown up in different families, Gisele and Sienna live lives
that are worlds apart. Then a very public revelation
propels them into the world's eye….

Drawn together by scandal!

Now the sisters have found each other—but are they at risk of losing
their hearts to the two men who are determined to peel back
the layers of their glittering facades?

Find out in

DESERVING OF HIS DIAMONDS?

Available July 24

ENEMIES AT THE ALTAR

Available August 21

www.Harlequin.com

HP89062

SADDLE UP AND READ 'EM!

Look for this Stetson flash on all Western books this summer!

Pick up a cowboy book
by some of your favorite authors:

Vicki Lewis Thompson
B.J. Daniels
Patricia Thayer
Cathy McDavid
And many more...

Available wherever books are sold.

www.Harlequin.com/Western

ACFEM0612R